SUMMER
OF LOVE

Also by the Author:

Ricky Nelson: Idol for a Generation

Monterey Pop

JOEL SELVIN

SUMMER OF LOVE

*The Inside
Story of LSD,
Rock & Roll,
Free Love
and High Times
in the Wild West*

A DUTTON BOOK

DUTTON

Published by the Penguin Group
Penguin Books USA Inc., 375 Hudson Street, New York, New York 10014, U.S.A.
Penguin Books Ltd, 27 Wrights Lane, London W8 5TZ, England
Penguin Books Australia Ltd, Ringwood, Victoria, Australia
Penguin Books Canada Ltd, 10 Alcorn Avenue, Toronto, Ontario, Canada M4V 3B2
Penguin Books (N.Z.) Ltd, 182–190 Wairau Road, Auckland 10, New Zealand

Penguin Books Ltd, Registered Offices:
Harmondsworth, Middlesex, England

First published by Dutton, an imprint of Dutton Signet,
a division of Penguin Books USA Inc.
Distributed in Canada by McClelland & Stewart Inc.

First Printing, August, 1994
1   3   5   7   9   10   8   6   4   2

 REGISTERED TRADEMARK—MARCA REGISTRADA

LIBRARY OF CONGRESS CATALOGING IN PUBLICATION DATA:

Selvin, Joel.
    Summer of love : the inside story of LSD, rock & roll, free love, and high times in the wild
West / by Joel Selvin
        p.   cm.
    ISBN 0-525-93675-0
    1. Rock music—California—San Francisco—1961–1970—History and criticism. 2. Rock
music—California—San Francisco—1971–1980—History and criticism.   I. Title.
    ML3534.S45   1994
    781.66'09794'6109046—dc20   94–170
                                                                                         CIP
                                                                                         MN

Printed in the United States of America
Set in New Caledonia, Orpheus and Stone Informal

Designed by Steven N. Stathakis

To Dave and Sue,
who made all possible

INTRODUCTION

The Summer of Love never really happened. Invented by the fevered imaginations of writers for weekly news magazines, the phrase entered the public vocabulary with the impact of a sledgehammer, glibly encompassing a social movement sweeping the youth of the world, hitting the target with the pinpoint accuracy of a shotgun blast.

What happened in a small neighborhood in San Francisco among a relatively small circle of people was never fully understood even by the people involved. Events, once set in motion, overtook them. The public instantly romanticized what they thought was going on. From the moment that word of strange goings-on leaked out of the Haight-Ashbury, the truth and the fantasy became entangled.

A handful of rock musicians acted as electric *gamelons* for this bizarre new culture, both articulating the language, dress and style and spreading the infection. And, in doing so, they changed the way music was played and heard around the world.

In the beginning, they lived in the same neighborhood as the people who came to the dances. They ate in the same restaurants.

They shopped for clothes at the same second-hand stores. They took the same drugs.

At the ballrooms, there were no spotlights, only blankets of pulsing, throbbing designs of colored lights that covered the musicians and dancers alike. Stages were a foot or two above the floor and no Apollonian "Gateway to the Gods" separated the audience from the performers. These were tribal rites, often conducted under the influence of exotic and wonderful potions.

At the center of this new community was LSD, the mysterious agent that connected the musicians, the artists, the writers, the dancers. The drug opened a new window on the world for those who took it, and many were determined to follow the vision they saw.

By the time the San Francisco musicians took the stage at the Monterey Pop Festival in June 1967, popular mythology already enshrouded them. The record industry was scrambling to figure out a way to sell this potent new brew, able to intoxicate millions. The news magazines were pointing their fingers at the Haight-Ashbury and proclaiming the coming months the "Summer of Love." Thrust into the national limelight, these musicians, suddenly removed from the tiny utopian village that initially nurtured them, often didn't know what to do.

Many went on to fame and misery. Many were never heard of again outside the parochial confines of the San Francisco underground. This is the story of a community, a shared tale only parts of which have ever been told. It is, in many ways, a parable of their times, a brief era that wobbled from the days following the incursion of Britain's Beatles on American shores to a sputtering close many months after the end of the decade.

Hippies dancing barefoot in the park, huddled in the mud of Woodstock by the hundreds of thousands or marching in protest through the streets of Washington don't have a role to play in this account. This is the personal story of the San Francisco rock musicians. It begins with a band of intrepid souls not much known beyond the Golden Gate, and their journey to the foothills of Nevada, where, a century before, crazed miners dug for silver.

1965

May you live in
interesting times.
    —Ancient Chinese curse

SUMMER 1965

Dosed.

The Charlatans arrived in town to audition for the job as house band at the Red Dog Saloon. All the plans, all the long hours rehearsing, all the careful preparations and the owner walked up to the band a couple of hours before the audition, his hand extended, little pills in the palm.

The old Comstock House had been for sale, no takers, for years when Mark Unobski tumbled into Virginia City. A troublesome youth from a well-to-do Memphis family, Unobski grew up spirited from private schools to mental hospitals all over the East Coast by his parents, without their ever holding great hope for the boy assuming much responsibility for his life. Consequently, they were practically overjoyed to underwrite such an ambitious project as the restoration of an abandoned gambling hall in a former ghost town where Mark Twain once wrote for the *Territorial Enterprise*.

A ruddy Southern bad boy, Mark Unobski had spent the five thousand dollars his father lent him to renovate the renamed Red Dog

Saloon and, job completed, was laying out an epicurean feast before his staff, a private revel before he opened for business and summer tourists stalked the streets of this western town in the Sierra Nevadas. They had reason to celebrate. An antique mirror ran the entire length behind the dark hardwood bar. Gold trim and red-flocked wallpaper were complemented by velvet drapes and gold braids brought from the old Fox Theater in San Francisco. The gaslight fixtures were for show only, but the chandeliers worked. Framed pictures ringed the walls and slot machines stood in the corners.

Unobski, who could play a fair Robert Johnson on slide guitar and had a passion for gun collecting, had assembled a crew around him of similar disaffected reprobates and social misfits. But with their predilection for long hair, cowboy clothes and firearms, they fit comfortably into the frontier town ambience of Virginia City. He assembled quite a cast of characters.

Don Works, called Silver Don because of his premature gray hair, was a world-class house painter who swabbed down the exterior of the place fire engine red. Al Kelley came up from the Pine Street commune in San Francisco. He grew up on a dairy farm in Maine and escaped a life of painting pin-stripes on motorcycles in Connecticut to deal grass in San Francisco. Milan Melvin was a disk jockey in nearby Reno. His girlfriend, Zella Mortimer, had worked as a waitress at the Peppermint Tree, a North Beach nightclub in San Francisco. Short, blond and surly, she fell right into the Red Dog scene, dressed like a dancehall floozy, carrying a porcelain doorknob on her drink tray to advise order among the rowdier customers. She also kept a derringer tucked into her garter, just in case. Gourmet cook Jenna Nichols worked the kitchen and her lunches already attracted everybody from the entire town constabulary to Lucius Beebe, the eccentric dandy and entrepreneur who lived in a private railroad car and spearheaded the rebirth of the old silver city. Bookkeeper Lynne Hughes, in floor-length velvet gowns, played Miss Kitty to this version of the Longbranch Saloon.

It was the Wild West all over again with one additional element. LSD.

That was the brain food fueling all these fantasies, a cerebral prod to the Gary Cooper movie these longhairs had substituted for their beatnik ways. Acid had been blazing through subterranean bohemian circles that year and many of the misbegotten malcontents who labored on Unobski's edifice had been sampling its deranging delights all through the Nevada spring. The drug mixed irony into the delicious disorientation, a secret smile on the faces of these freaks disguised as cowboys.

The Charlatans showed up like somebody's dream of a rock band for the Red Dog, from their celluloid collars to Mike Ferguson's black onyx pinkie ring. Their women dressed like Victorian queens in lace-trimmed velvet. They had perfected their old-timey look through countless hours of rummaging in San Francisco's well-stocked thrift stores. The musicians took rooms on the hotel's second floor and, after several days of doing nothing, were informed the audition would be held that night after Unobski threw a dinner party for the staff. The audition by the Charlatans would be the post-dinner entertainment and, to ensure everybody's maximum enjoyment, Unobski handed out tablets of LSD to all. With mischief in mind, he made sure the band members took their medicine.

Bandleader George Hunter had taken acid once before. But he had never sung in public. He had scrupulously rehearsed his group for months in his apartment, seeing to the band's creation down to the finest detail, his own intense obsession for the entire past year. Hunter rehearsed the band, dressed the band, designed the old-fashioned lettering with which he spelled the band's name. He wheedled, worried, fussed about this rock band whose future he saw as clearly as the silvery clouds over the Sierra Nevada foothills.

But Hunter was not a musician. He couldn't play a thing, although he toyed with the autoharp. He didn't know one chord from another. His singing was brave but inept. He was a visionary, a former architect's model-builder, a boy wonder whose own designs for houses had actually been built before he was twenty years old. The Charlatans, in fact, began as a design on his drawing board and only took human shape when he met baby-faced Richard Olsen, a fellow S.F. State student, waiting at a bus stop for the 22 Fillmore headed back to the Haight.

Olsen, too, had taken LSD once before. He was more or less a real musician who had played clarinet since he was a boy. Benny Goodman was his idol. Hunter's girlfriend, Lucy Lewis, drafted Olsen to dance in one of the experimental programs she choreographed at S.F. State. Hunter made the taped collages that served as music for these artsy "happenings." But, before long, Hunter realized the real action was in rock and roll. He taped an album cover of the Rolling Stones to his wall and tapped Olsen to start his group.

The two began by dressing the part, showing up at parties looking like Hunter's impression of the Stones. A third member was recruited, someone Hunter knew from high school days in the San Fernando Valley, and this one, Mike Wilhelm, could actually play guitar. Mike Ferguson, the fourth Charlatan, ran a store called the Magic Theater for Madmen Only on Divisadero Street, at the edge of San Francisco's Haight-Ashbury district. Ferguson sold exquisite Victorian knick-knacks, along with cigarette papers, pipes and, under the counter, a little something to actually smoke. He brought not only his piano playing to the party, but his artful sense of Victoriana, which, mixed with Hunter's visions of the Old West, gave the Charlatans the band's highly developed sense of style.

At first, Hunter's upstairs neighbor played drums and, since the band never ventured out of Hunter's living room in the enormous flat further up the hill in the Haight-Ashbury, the question of his competence never really arose. But when a drummer with real musical experience showed up at the Downey Street flat looking to buy marijuana, he was pressed into service in place of the convenient neighbor. Unlike the other Charlatans, Dan Hicks actually worked as a musician, playing in jazz bands and dance orchestras around Santa Rosa where he lived.

Another S.F. State student, Hicks thought these guys were quite a bunch of characters with their vintage World War II sign bearing a star and the motto "My Son Is in the Service," which they hung in the apartment window as a coded message that the illicit goods were in stock. Hicks enjoyed the rehearsals, the smoke-filled afternoons and evenings where visitors came and went with no apparent purpose. But when Hunter first told him about the job in Virginia City, Hicks balked.

If the invitation to the Red Dog seemed heaven-sent, that may have been partly because it practically fell out of the sky. Olsen and Wilhelm had been wandering around the coffee houses and bars of North Beach one night, dressed in their regulation Charlatans gear, when Chandler Laughlin approached them. Laughlin told them he was one of the crew restoring the Red Dog Saloon in Virginia City, this 1860s boomtown of the Comstock Lode slowly undergoing a transformation from ghost town to tourist attraction, and he was in San

Francisco on a mission to find more antique fixtures and a house band for the silver-rush dancehall. He had mistaken the two Charlatans for members of the Byrds, a decidedly better known rock group who not only actually performed in public, but made popular records. He offered the Charlatans the job anyway.

But drummer Hicks had problems. He was facing a draft induction physical and his final exams at college loomed. He didn't really know how seriously he wanted to commit himself to this dubious enterprise. But when Hunter stuffed a hundred dollar bill in his pocket, the scales were tipped. He graduated from college, flunked the intelligence portion of his draft physical—a connection apparently not made by draft board officials—and left for Virginia City all in the same week.

The audition could scarcely have gone worse. As the tingling sensation of the LSD trickled down the sides of their heads, a mounting nervousness swept through the band. Wilhelm had neglected to bring his guitar and was forced to borrow one. Despite all the rehearsals in Hunter's front room, the band's repertoire was limited. The front doors were locked. A small banquet was consumed by the staff of almost thirty people, all ascending into the ether by the end of dinner. Everyone in the room was blasted, by no means least of all the Charlatans themselves.

Of course, the performance was a shambles. Arrangements were forgotten. Keys were diverse. The musicians were overcome with mirth. The piano kept moving just out of the reach of Ferguson's rubbery fingers. Band members traded instruments. At one point, Wilhelm simply sat down on stage and watched as the room pulsed with colored vibrations. The performance didn't stop so much as disintegrate and Hunter stumbled offstage, chagrined, to face Unobski.

"That was the funniest thing I have ever seen in my life," Unobski said once he stopped laughing. "You guys are hired."

His shoulder-length, ash-blond hair and dark, full beard lent Chet Helms an appearance not altogether dissimilar to popular conceptions of Jesus Christ. The lanky, bespectacled Texan first visited 1090 Page Street making his rounds. Helms supported himself through a variety of sundry tasks and trades—from Dumpster diving looking for salable antiques outside Victorians under restoration in the Western Addition to small-time retail sales of underground Mexican imports, which is what first brought him to the rambling rooming house in the heart of the Haight-Ashbury.

Light poured down on the foyer at the foot of the giant staircase that was open to all three stories of the grand building, bulging with bay windows and topped with gables. But it was the rosewood-paneled ballroom in the basement that interested Helms. With a proscenium stage, alcoves along the wall, hardwood floor and outside entrance, the room was perfect for parties and dances, a fact immediately obvious to Helms, a regular on the weekend party circuit.

Helms was guided by a strong inner vision. Raised by his strict, fundamentalist Baptist minister grandfather after his sugar-mill–worker father died when young Helms was nine years old, as a lonely youth living a Tom Sawyer life in the Ozarks, he often dreamed of serving as a missionary in faraway lands. Once he entered the University of Texas in Austin, however, away from his grandfather's steely command, he was soon seduced by left-wing politics and other subversive practices. But he never lost his missionary zeal.

After dropping out of college in 1961, he led an aimless, somewhat dissolute existence, wandering the bohemian highway between Austin, San Francisco and Mexico, sleeping on other people's living room floors and making his way as he could. He had, for all intents, settled in San Francisco by the time he took his first LSD trip early in 1965.

A heaven-and-hell vision of his own life worthy of Hieronymous Bosch, the acid experience convinced Helms that he would have to stop shooting speed. To help wean him off the pernicious drug, Helms was virtually held prisoner by the girlfriend of one of his closest dope-shooting buddies, an aggressive, powerful woman named Luria Castell. As a political demonstrator, she had been washed down the steps of City Hall by a firehose while protesting the House Un-American Activities Committee in 1960 and she did not hesitate to take extreme measures to rid these two miscreants of their evil habit. She kept Helms and her boyfriend sequestered inside her North Beach apartment for two weeks, while they undertook the cure.

Restored to health, Helms fell in love. He met doe-eyed Lori Hayman at a point in her life where she had dropped out of college but not told her wealthy parents. Living in a windowless room in another rooming house down the street from 1090 Page Street, she was severely depressed, crying for hours every day. Helms freely devoted his renewed energies to making her life happy. He moved her into a new room, spruced it up with paint and furnishings. He settled into a placid and euphoric domesticity, wondering what direction his renovated life would take him. The new rock music attracted him. Impressed by the Rolling Stones after attending a concert in May at the S.F. Civic Auditorium, he briefly tried to put together a band. But that short-lived enterprise had fallen apart after only a couple of fruitless rehearsals when he happened upon 1090 Page Street.

House manager Rodney Albin talked his uncle into letting him operate the massive Victorian at 1090 Page. His uncle and some partners had bought the huge run-down home, built in 1898, as a real estate investment and nobody objected to his nephew's bringing in a sum that would help underwrite the modest payments and taxes. The six-bedroom house had been converted into sleeping quarters for twenty-five as a boarding house for the many Irish-American workers that had gravitated to the neighborhood after the Second World War. With Albin charging as little as fifteen dollars a month—bigger rooms went for as much as thirty-five—he quickly developed an artsy clientele drawing largely from S.F. State, where both he and his brother Peter Albin also went to school. The two brothers had played together in mid-peninsula folk and bluegrass groups, Peter on guitar and Rodney on fiddle, before moving to San Francisco to attend college and run their uncle's boarding house. Music often poured out of the open windows of this giant, garish house on the sloping street corner.

Sam Andrew also lived in the neighborhood. Walking by 1090 Page one day, he heard guitar wafting out of one of the upper floors, went in and introduced himself to the guitar player, Peter Albin. Andrew was an Army brat who learned to play guitar and led his own rock and roll band in Okinawa while still in his teens. He soon began to frequent the rooming house. He worked up duets on recorder of Bach and Telemann with one tenant, a Hindu who also juggled and practiced acrobatics. Another fellow who lived at 1090 and played tenor guitar taught Andrew an intriguing descending line he used on the old Gershwin standard "Summertime," that Andrew never forgot. Sometimes he would go to the top of the stairs and recite Chaucer, full volume, just to hear the florid Middle English reverberate in the cavernous entrance hall.

Helms started jam sessions in the basement ballroom, revolving around Andrew and Peter Albin, who picked up the bass. An informal band began to form. For a while another young man named Paul Ferrez—who also went by the name Paul Beck—did his Dylan imitation, complete with corduroy cap and harmonica cage, in front of the rotating crew of musicians. Another young player, David Eskerson, held down the guitar chair, although as a teenager he was too young to work in nightclubs, when and if it came to that. Chuck Jones, who lived at 1090, played drums, but he, too, left something to be desired. Polio had rendered his leg too weak to strike a bass drum soundly and what his associates assumed was a speed habit often caused violent outbursts and screaming matches between him and his girlfriend clearly audible from behind closed doors.

Beck/Ferrez was intolerable as a lead vocalist, his wheezing vocals only slightly less unappealing than his bleating harmonica playing. But he came up with a name for the loose aggregation, Blue Yard Hill, that never stuck. When Helms wandered into this scene—his import sales trade brought him in contact with a number of the burgeoning hipster enclaves like 1090 Page—he instinctively understood that what was needed was some organization and direction, which he could supply.

Charging admission of fifty cents, Helms began that summer to host free-for-all jams using this basic group as the nucleus. It took little more than rumor to draw capacity crowds to the basement sessions. Luria Castell, now living at a Pine Street commune that was taking shape as another critical outpost in this amorphous new community, brought her friends. A chubby biker-type blues singer called Pigpen, who played with a band somewhere down the peninsula, hung back one night in the crowd, just watching. The crowds also included high school kids from out in the Avenues and curious black neighbors. These Wednesday night parties reeked of the atmosphere of a sub-rosa speakeasy. Helms, in fact, sometimes worried that all the joint smoking or the sizable contingent of underage patrons would attract the interest of the police. Other times, he took in the sprawling panoply he had set in motion with a sense of great wonder and smug contentment. The missionary in him was hearing a calling.

In the bathroom at 1090 hung a blackboard, a space for witticisms, profanities, whatever. On it, a tenant called Willie the Wizard first scrawled an aphorism after hearing Rodney Albin's wife say it, and Helms tucked it away in his brain when he read it: "May the Baby Jesus Shut Your Mouth and Open Your Mind."

• • •

Bill Graham thrived on confrontation. The lines of battle had been drawn on this sunny Saturday in August and Lafayette Park was filled with an air of anticipation. More than a thousand people, drawn largely by the publicity Graham had drummed up over the battle between the Parks Commission and the S.F. Mime Troupe, waited to see what would happen once the actors went ahead and staged their play in defiance of the Commission's ruling.

Graham didn't care about the politics of the Mime Troupe, a hand-to-mouth bunch of activists and theatrical guerillas. He had left the well-paid security of his job as regional office manager for Allis-Chalmers because he had never gotten over the allure of show business. A failed New York actor who wound up in San Francisco, Graham signed on with the Mime Troupe as business manager, but it wasn't long before he started adding a critical line of type atop all their posters and advertisements: "Bill Graham Presents."

From his desk in the Howard Street loft that served as combination office and rehearsal space, Graham pleaded, cajoled, inveigled and bullied on behalf of the perennially impoverished theater troupe. While director R. G. Davis attended to his leftist political agenda, Graham saw to what he thought of as the show business end, like making the stoned-out blackface minstrels in the civil rights satire snap their tambourines more smartly during their entrance. But the current battle with the Parks Commission was shaping up as a minor epic of a conflagration, a dispute with a clearly drawn battleground, just the sort of righteous fight Graham loved.

He came by his contentious nature honestly. He did not remember the years when his mother stowed him in a Berlin orphanage to escape the lengthening shadow of the Nazis. But he did remember the long march across France at age ten with sixty-three other children, living on oranges. Only eleven survived to land in New York; his sister was not one. Living with a foster family in the Bronx, he carefully eradicated his thick European accent. He changed his name from Grajonka to Graham by looking in the phone book for a similar but Americanized name. After serving in the Korean War, he bounced around in various jobs—Catskills waiter to cab driver. He once drove a brand-new Mercedes across the country for comedian Buddy Hackett and promised himself that one day he would drive one of his own.

All the time he nurtured ambitions to be an actor. He took classes and landed a few minor parts, as close to Broadway as Long Island. He moved to Los Angeles, where he again supported himself as a waiter. He was one of two finalists for a major role opposite James Whitmore in a new TV series, *The Law and Mr. Jones,* where he would play the young sidekick to the old pro. The other actor got the part, his agent told him, because Graham's physiognomy played too heavy. His face was too strong. Two days later he left Los Angeles.

Every summer during the previous four years, the Mime Troupe had specialized in performing for free in local parks. This summer the Parks Commission raised a finger of caution. "I don't want to be a prude or a censor," said Commission president Walter Haas, chairman of jeans manufacturer Levi-Strauss, "but your play caused us a lot of trouble last year. There is such a thing as good taste." The play in question, *Il Candelaio,* was written in 1582 by Giordano Bruno, although Mime Troupe adapter Peter Berg streamlined the language for modern audiences. At the same time, the Troupe was mounting in local theaters a more pointedly political statement, *A Minstrel Show or Civil Rights in a Cracker Barrel,* but the Italian *commedia dell'arte* concerning an aging candlemaker worried about his potency, bawdy but excised of foul language, was the production planned for the parks.

A stormy meeting of the Parks Commission was held following the first show. Parks Commissioner James Lang reported that the performance he attended contained four-letter words and one member of the troupe even pretended to relieve himself onstage at one point. "Far too much vulgarity," he said. Director Davis upbraided the park board. "We are being judged by a commission which could not distinguish between Jean Genet and James Bond," he said. Graham himself took the microphone to note that he had heard "the same objectionable word" one hundred forty-seven times during a recent evening of theater downtown. Davis left the meeting flinging down a gauntlet. "We'll see you in the parks and we'll see you in the courts," he told the commissioners.

With Graham orchestrating considerable newspaper coverage, even leading costumed members of the troupe on a noontime parade distributing leaflets through downtown and landing on the evening TV news, a crowd swarmed over the small park adjacent to the Russian embassy. "Mime Troupe, Sí! Park Commission, No!" read one sign. Luis Valdez, who customarily played Brighella, the first actor onstage, demurred, muttering something about a previous arrest record. Davis himself donned the gaudy costume and mask.

The police huddled with Graham, Davis and Commissioner Lang. A couple of Minstrel Show performers in full tails and blackface were hovering in the background, as were members of The Committee (the city's popular satirical improvisational theater group), poet Lawrence Ferlinghetti, novelist Herb Gold and, of course, a full complement of press. Lang talked quietly with Davis and Graham about the permit revocation. The Mime Troupe attorney arrived and he worked on the cops, while Ronny Davis turned to address the crowd.

Sergeant James Egan headed the police detail and tried cheerfully get everybody to quiet down and adjourn to the stationhouse to talk the situation over. Graham and Davis played to the crowd, trying to figure out what to do. If the actors stopped to try and erect a stage, the police would intercede immediately. A space was cleared and the cast began to warm up. Someone played a recorder. The actors sang and formed ranks, moving into the improvised performance area. Davis danced into the center.

"Signor, Signora, Signorini," he announced. "Madame, Monsieur, Mademoiselle, Ladieees and Gentleman, I Troupo di Mimo di San Francisco presents for your enjoyment this afternoon . . . AN AR-REST." With that Davis leapt in a pirouette, as the cops grabbed him midair. His feet never touched the ground.

As they escorted Davis to a waiting wagon, the police found themselves instantly surrounded by a roiling mob. Marvin Garson, a reporter for the underground *S.F. Express Times*, flicked a cop's hat off his head and was seized. Another bystander threw a handful of grass in an officer's face and he, too, was suddenly paddywagon-bound.

Once the police left the scene, Graham quickly organized an impromptu performance. Ferlinghetti, Gold, Alan Myerson of The Committee and a couple of other lefties on the premises took turns reading from the script without further event. Davis was released from jail later that afternoon on fifty-six dollars bail, after being charged with performing in a public park without a permit.

The drink and date crowd frequenting the Drinking Gourd that night paid little attention to the three songs Paul Kantner played. Although such cloddish inattention was always annoying, Kantner was not really pissed off. The collegiate scene at these hootenanny nights on Union

Street was further than a few miles away from the bohemian gardens of North Beach. They were parallel but separate universes. Still, decent folksingers could be heard any night at the Gourd, so Kantner was not surprised when someone emerged from the crowd clearly hip despite an obvious recent haircut. As Kantner packed up his banjo and twelve-string, the young man suggested they go somewhere and talk.

His name was Marty Balin and he had recently cut his hair to look for work as a lithographer. His father worked as a printer and he, too, knew the trade. But he had some specific ideas about where folk music was headed and serious plans for a folk group that incorporated some elements of rock. Kantner listened intently as he spilled them out.

Recently separated from his wife and child, Balin shared an apartment with an old high school friend, Bill Thompson, who worked as a copy boy at the *S.F. Chronicle*. For someone so young, he had already accumulated considerable experience in show business. He had danced in *West Side Story*. Johnny Mathis once heard him sing and encouraged him. He changed his name from Martyn Buchwald to Marty Balin and recorded a pair of teen-appeal singles for a Hollywood record label. But he also had a more artistic side; he painted, sculpted, wrote poetry and followed the folk movement. He once saw a young Bob Dylan sing at Gerde's Folk City in New York. Most recently, he belonged to a Kingston Trio-type folk group called the Town Criers.

The quartet had formed two years earlier in the back room of the Drinking Gourd, harmonizing over "Greenback Dollar" and some other conventional folk-era standards. The Town Criers wore matching suits and ties and were straight enough to play lounges in Reno. But Balin had experimented with acid and seen beyond all the "Michael Row the Boat Ashore" stuff. The Criers began to dissolve once one vocalist left after about a year. Not long after that, Balin talked to him about his idea for a new folk band. But he didn't see it.

Kantner did. He came from the South Bay folk scene, where he fell in love with the wife of a friend, helping spell an end to that marriage, and took pharmaceutical uppers to aid his work in a local cannery. He moved to Los Angeles where he lived in Venice with a similar group of Bay Area folksters—David Freiberg, Steve Schuster, David Crosby, Sherry Snow and Ginger Jackson, his old married girlfriend who had left him to follow another folksinger to Southern

California. They kept all their money together in a jar on the mantel and shared whatever they had. They dreamed of hitting the bigtime L.A. folk scene that surrounded the Troubador, but spent most of their time smoking dope on the beach. The stars of the scene were song-sters like Hoyt Axton, Barry McGuire and a friend of Crosby's named Dino Valente, who blew Kantner and Jackson away when they first heard him sing one night at a Sunset Strip nightclub. Freiberg watched another folkie hopeful named Jim McGuinn play Beatles songs on a twelve-string at a Troubador hoot night.

But Kantner came back to San Jose and started performing and hanging out at a local coffee house called the Off Stage, where there was also a small music store and a steady supply of pot. It was at the Off Stage that he first heard a young girl from Texas named Janis Joplin belting out Memphis Minnie songs, backed by a nimble-fingered folk-blues guitarist, Jerry Kaukonen. Acid was around. One musician flashed blue vials of liquid LSD to Kantner. He attended LSD-drenched parties at the La Honda headquarters of wildman Ken Kesey and his band of Merry Pranksters. "Goodnight Irene" and all that was getting further and further away for Kantner, too. One night somebody brought a Fender Vibralux amplifier by the Off Stage and plugged in a Gibson acoustic guitar, and the assembled folk musicians strummed in amazement, visions of Pops Staples in their heads. But when the club owner went to jail after getting caught smoking a joint, the Off Stage closed and Kantner moved to San Francisco. With eight people, including David Freiberg, Steve Schuster, Ginger Jackson and Sherry Snow from his Venice commune, Kantner shared the $100 monthly rent on a giant Victorian flat in the Fillmore district. The first night he packed up his banjo and twelve-string and headed out to hoot night at the Drinking Gourd, where he met Marty Balin.

Slowly, Kantner and Balin assembled a group around them. Re-hearsals were held at the Haight-Ashbury home of Jerry Peloquin, a drummer who had previously played with the New Tradition Singers. Bob Harvey was a friend of Balin's who owned an upright bass, in it-self enough to earn him an invitation to join. Kantner heard Signe Tole at the Drinking Gourd and he asked Balin to contact her. One of the other Town Criers found her phone number and Balin called her. She had only recently moved to San Francisco from Portland and had never sung professionally. But her sunny contralto blended like colors in a sunset with Balin's shadowy tenor. At first, a nylon-string guitarist completed the decidedly folkish sound of the band, but Balin wanted something a little stronger and Kantner remembered Jerry Kaukonen, who had reverted to using his given name, Jorma, from the Off Stage.

Kaukonen played in rock and roll bands as a teenager in Washington, D.C., even recording a 78 RPM record called "Magic Key" with his band, the Triumphs. He spent six months in New York while going to college—haunting Greenwich Village and drinking in the folk scene: Dylan at Folk City, guitar lessons from Reverend Gary Davis—before dropping out of school and rejoining his family in the Philippines, where his father was serving in the foreign diplomatic corps. He ended up enrolled in the University of Santa Clara, back in college to avoid the draft, because the credits he earned attending a Catholic university in the Philippines would only be honored by another Catholic university stateside.

He met his wife, Margaretta, on a boat the previous summer, taking a trip with his grandparents from Stockholm to Leningrad. The statuesque Nordic beauty spoke five languages and bowled over young Jorma with her poise and command. Once ensconced in Santa Clara, he began a passionate correspondence with this woman he had known for a week. Within a couple of months, she was living with him in Santa Clara and they were married.

A year later, he graduated from college and was planning to go to Europe and play with expatriate blues pianist Champion Jack Dupree when Kantner called. Dubious at first, Kaukonen went to San Francisco to check out the scene and found Ken Kesey, madcap Merry Pranksters honcho, toying with an electronic echo device. They plugged in Kaukonen's guitar and stayed up all night enraptured by the sounds. He began rehearsing with the still unnamed band—the nylon-string guitarist went off to join the Army. Kaukonen commuted back and forth from San Jose, where he was still teaching guitar lessons, while he and Margaretta lived in a thirteen-dollar-a-week North Beach fleabag.

One day he returned from San Jose to find his wife arrested. A police officer, mistaking her for a hooker, came on to the long-limbed Swede for a blowjob and she punched him out. Eventually the cop was fired and his wife fully exonerated, although only after his father persuaded the mayor and other highly placed friends to intercede. But the process dragged on long enough for Kaukonen to forget his plans to leave for Europe and to become fully ensnared in the Kantner and Balin enterprise.

The band hadn't played a single date, didn't have a name, but they were raising dust. Balin convinced a friend of his, Ted Saunders, to put together a partnership to buy a club in which the group would perform. Saunders and his two roommates, engineers who liked music and had some money, bought a former pizza parlor on Fillmore Street for $12,000. Saunders and his partners, operating as the U.S. Pizza Corp., signed a contract with Balin that called for them to give Balin $1300 for band instruments and a one-quarter interest in the corporation. In exchange, Balin agreed his band would play one hundred and five free performances for the new club over the next seven years. The other three Pizza Corp. partners would also split up twelve percent of the band's future earnings. Work commenced on turning the pizza spot into a revolutionary forum for this new sound in electric folk.

With his flat-brimmed Spanish hats and velvet-lined capes, Matthew Katz—he pronounced it "Cates"—certainly cut a dashing figure. His eyes bristled with intensity and the neatly trimmed goatee lent his appearance a vaguely Mephistophelean air, but he could be courtly and charming, eloquent as a Shakespearean actor. An imposing Jesuit-trained intellectual in his thirties who had been a ballet dancer and an Air Force chaplain, Katz had skirted the periphery of show business and talent management for years. At one point, he handled the affairs of author Fred Goerner, a San Francisco radio announcer who turned a personal obsession into a best-selling book, *The Search for Amelia Earhart*.

It was Peter Albin who mentioned to Marty Balin that Katz had some unreleased Dylan tunes. Anxious to acquire gems like that for his band's repertoire, Balin called Katz in Los Angeles. Katz, who had briefly managed a folk group called the Countrymen, remembered Balin from seeing the Town Criers at San Francisco's hungry i the previous year. He listened as Balin described the concept of his new band and, intrigued, he agreed to fly to San Francisco and bring the Dylan tunes within days. Katz scrambled to get Dylan's publisher to send him acetates and lead sheets and the prized package arrived at the last minute at the Press Club, where Katz was staying in San Francisco.

Katz was already dabbling in the new folk field, casually handling the affairs of one Stinson Beach folksinger and another voguish folk group. But the unnamed group Balin invited him to hear reeked of promise to Katz. He met with the band at Peloquin's, listened to some rehearsal and discussed the possibility of managing the new group. But Balin wanted the Dylan tunes, not a manager.

The band did work up a version of "Lay Down Your Weary Tune," originally an outtake from the sessions that produced "Another Side of Bob Dylan." The group's initial repertoire leaned heavily on the folk background of the musicians—Fred Neil's "The Other Side of This Life," Billy Edd Wheeler's "High Flyin' Bird"—although Wilson Pickett's "In the Midnight Hour" certainly represented song selection outside the folk fold. "Tobacco Road" Balin first heard sung by Lou Rawls. Balin also began writing songs, and his "It's No Secret" explored the untrammeled ground between folk and the Merseybeat rock and roll of the English groups.

Kantner's roommate Freiberg was arrested after he made a left turn the wrong way into a one-way street and the cop saw him tucking a Baggie of pot under his seat. He cut his hair, moved to Marin and decided to follow a relatively straight and narrow course. But within weeks Freiberg was nailed again, this time for accepting five dollars from a narc he gave some seeds and stems. It was a setup, but he was given thirty days in the Marin County jail, with the other charge still pending in San Francisco. Kantner came to visit him in jail and rather obviously passed him a joint through the little window in the visiting room. He told Freiberg the new band now probably had a name: Jefferson Airplane.

Balin and Kantner exhausted the list of potential names from the animal world—handles like the Byrds and the Turtles were the current fashion. Balin tried out the Establishment and Kantner lofted the Nest (he was a big fan of the Robert Heinlein sci-fi epic, *Stranger in a Strange Land*). Kaukonen kept kidding around about using his own facetious pseudonym for the band, Blind Thomas Jefferson Airplane, and with the opening of the Matrix, as the pizza-parlor-turned-nightclub had been titled, looming, the band finally resigned itself without great enthusiasm to the shortened version.

Balin and Kantner hammered, nailed, painted and wired the Matrix. Balin painted portraits of musicians and a large collage/mural that covered an entire wall. In the middle, he sailed a jaunty biplane with the members of the band arrayed along the wings and body. Kantner thought up the slogan "Jefferson Airplane Loves You" and Balin's father printed bumper stickers and buttons bearing the motto.

Matthew Katz returned to town a couple of weeks prior to the opening and pitched the band in another meeting at Peloquin's apartment. He told the musicians he would organize a fan club, which prompted a few chuckles. Nevertheless, Kantner called him the next day at the Press Club and told Katz the group wanted him as manager. Copy boy Bill Thompson, Balin's roommate, went about promoting an article at the *Chronicle*. When it came time for the opening, Friday the 13th of August, word had spread adequately for a capacity crowd to turn up.

Bluesman J. C. Burris, who played a set of rhythm bones and accompanied some numbers by simply slapping his legs and thighs in time, opened the show and Peloquin's girlfriend, Jacky Watts, worked as a waitress. Her roommate Janet Trice was a fairly straight nurse who was seeing Balin at the time. Thompson landed his article the following Sunday when John L. Wasserman, the junior drama critic at the *Chronicle*, wrote up an interview with Balin that suggested that this new sound might possibly be "the new direction of contemporary American pop music."

But the big fish Thompson wanted to land was Ralph J. Gleason, the *Chronicle*'s distinguished daily jazz columnist. A Columbia graduate and one-time editor of *Down Beat*, Gleason had won a nationwide reputation for his fierce love of jazz and dread of anything he perceived as chicanery, boldly proclaimed in *Chronicle* columns since the late forties. With his handlebar mustache and deerstalker hat, he often presented as colorful a figure as the musicians he covered, but his integrity was unquestioned. Before long, Gleason turned up at the Matrix.

He predicted great things for the new group in a column devoted entirely to his remarkably prescient review of the nascent Airplane. "It's not really a rock and roll group," he wrote. "Few are any longer. It's a contemporary-popular-music-folk-rock unit and we have no less cumbersome phrase so far. They sing everything from Bob Dylan to the blues, from Burl Ives to Miriam Makeba, from Lightnin' Hopkins and Jimmy Reed to 'Midnight Hour.' It's a shame there isn't dancing, but in San Francisco's archaic manner of handling this sort of thing, it's hard to get a dance permit. Someone would probably accuse them of operating a topless guitar. . . . I don't know who they will record for, but they will obviously record for someone."

The Charlatans quickly fell into the Wild West masquerade in Virginia City. They were living theater in their Edwardian coats and long mustaches. The local hardware store sold guns at the counter and soon every band member had at least one. Pianist Mike Ferguson kept a Baretta tucked in a holster under the back of his jacket. A shotgun leaned against the back of the stage when the band played. They outfitted their ladies with tiny handguns and everybody frequently adjourned to a canyon outside town to test ordnance. Wilhelm once surprised some sleeping campers he didn't see in the tall grass, but, amazingly, nobody ever got hurt.

With hotelier and gun collector Mark Unobski encouraging the firearms play, going so far as to subsidize their purchase and deduct appropriate sums from paychecks, band members traded in their guns on different, more exotic models every week or so. There were inevitable mishaps like the time a rifle was discharged on the ground floor, the bullet piercing two floors before coming to rest harmlessly in a chest of drawers. Bartender Don Works was known for firing off rounds at targets real or imagined as he grew increasingly drunk throughout the evenings and tired of acting the servile publican, filling the room with smoke from the black powder ammunition he always used. None of this gunplay bothered the Virginia City locals. Many of them routinely carried sidearms as part of their Old West costumes. They treated the Red Dog staff as welcome additions to the community and there was never trouble with the law. The nearest police officer was an old gunfighter who kept a pet bobcat on a leash and lived in a neighboring town anyway. "If you have any trouble," he advised Unobski, "just shoot 'em."

The town sheriff went along with the theater. Shortly after the saloon opened, he walked in and presented his piece to bartender Works. "Check my gun," he said. Works sighted the pistol, opened the chamber, spun the cylinder, closed it and squeezed off two rounds into the floor. "Works just fine, Sheriff," he said, and handed back the gun.

Lucy Lewis never liked the Victoriana, but she played her part gamely, wearing her hair in a bun, draping her wraithlike frame in floor-length velvet gowns. Acting the role could be fun, even if someone else was writing the script. She first met Hunter while she attended state college in the San Fernando Valley. He followed her north when she moved to San Francisco, another dancer drawn by the lure of the renowned Ann Halprin workshop. After she split with Halprin, Lewis led her own experimental dance company. Hunter helped make tapes for her performances. Their friend Richie Olsen, who formed the initial core of the band with Hunter, donned a costume and danced. But this was all before the Charlatans.

At first, Hunter envisioned the band as a unisex futuristic outfit called the Androids, but gave that up for a dark and druggy William Burroughs-inspired theme, the Mainliners. Ferguson introduced the Victorian element and he was off and running, building the Charlatans. Hunter saw the band as a reaction to an increasingly plastic society, a harkening back to more genuine American values. The clothes, the style, the lettering, the songs all were supposed to recall an imaginary era that spanned the Wild West to the First World War—horses and airplanes. He developed a repertoire of pieces of Americana: Jelly Roll Morton's "Alabama Bound," New Lost City Ramblers' "East Virginia," Roy Acuff's "Wabash Cannonball."

As Hunter grew immersed in the rock band, Lewis collapsed after her dance company dissolved in anger, troupe members scattering across the country. She repaired to Los Angeles to recuperate for a couple of months, returning in time to leave for Virginia City with Hunter. She dutifully played dancehall hostess, mingled with the crowd and prodded people into dancing.

Dan Hicks fell in love with a gorgeous seventeen-year-old who came down from Portland to investigate the scene, Candy Sterniolla. She showed up for a weekend and wound up spending the summer living with Hicks in his room upstairs, dolled up like a frontier harlot. All the Charlatans' women dressed for the costume party, as did the Red Dog staff.

Tuesdays the saloon closed and the staff all customarily dropped acid. Sometimes they would head out to Hobo Hot Springs, where warm mud bubbled up from the depths of the earth and they would wallow in the warm, primordial ooze before retiring to a casino breakfast in Carson City. One time everybody headed over to Carson City, whacked out of their brains, to make a public spectacle of themselves while they caught *Fantasia* at a local movie theater. Another time, band members and lady friends adjourned to Pyramid Lake, where Hunter shot a trippy home movie while they cavorted stoned on the mud flats. Lewis didn't particularly care for LSD and on one Tuesday run to San Francisco, when she, Hunter and Olsen all took acid to stay awake for the drive, she nearly flipped out and buried her head in the backseat, not looking up until the car pulled to a stop in North Beach.

After one Monday night show, the band took the train out of Reno for an audition in San Francisco the following day with Autumn Records, the small label owned by ex-Top Forty deejays Tom Donahue and Bob Mitchell that had struck gold earlier that year with a British-sounding group from San Francisco called the Beau Brummels. Stumbling into the studio, bleary-eyed after a sleepless night eating bennies and riding the train, the Charlatans met the producer of the session, a disk jockey from an Oakland soul station who called himself Sly Stone. Spieling at lightning speed, Stone explained to the band that he could play all the instruments himself, arrange the songs and produce the record. They weren't really necessary. The record company had prepared a list of songs for the band to record like Dylan's "Masters of War" and Gordon Lightfoot's "Early Morning Rain." "The Charlatans don't do songs about airports," he was informed. Instead, four songs from the Red Dog repertoire like "Jack of Diamonds" and "The Blues Ain't Nothing" were quickly recorded. The results impressed nobody.

But the Red Dog scene flourished. Gourmet chef Jenna Nichols attracted quite a following for extravagant fare like suckling pig and the governor of the state made a few visits during the summer, even staging a kickoff luncheon for his reelection campaign at the Red Dog. A magical light box attracted considerable interest. Built by Pine Street residents Bill Ham and Bob Cohen, the large box with the opaque, milky white glass front changed colors with the music. Certain records on the Red Dog jukebox became popular simply because of the appealing effect they had on the colors in the light box. Locals accepted the strange longhairs, although they never guessed at what true weirdness lay behind those sparkling eyes, and the summer passed with only minor episodes of tension, like the time some roughnecks left an old tombstone with the name "Charlatans" carved in it.

In August, Charlatans guitarist Mike Wilhelm joined Red Dog staffer Chan Laughlin, who found the band in the first place, on an overnight supply run to San Francisco. On the return trip in Laughlin's rusted-out wreck of a Nash, hood missing, the pair dropped LSD to stay awake and were smoking pot to make the journey more pleasant. The heap of a car began to overheat and they pulled off the freeway in Rodeo, a renowned speed trap in the far reaches of the East Bay. Laughlin was filling the radiator in a gas station when a county cop drove up. He spotted Laughlin's enormous pistol resting on the car's dashboard and pulled it out of the car, emptied the bullets. It didn't take much cop instinct to tell these two weirdos were up to something and he slowly turned up the heat under them. Laughlin began telling the cop his life story, a mile a minute, explaining how important it is to stay armed living in the frontier towns of Nevada. As he bent over the engine to replace the radiator cap, the cop caught a glimpse of a vial of pills stuck in his belt. The bust was on.

The cop found a Baggie of dozens of caps of acid stuck inside his shirt and shook down Wilhelm. A joint was found in one of his pockets. Martinez jail was their next stop.

The arrest went out on the wire and the idea that citizens of Virginia City were nabbed in a drug bust didn't sit well with the local powers-that-be. A raid on the Red Dog flushed out some contraband venison in the freezer—its presence previously unknown to the kitchen staff, who smelled a set-up—and Unobski was arrested for poaching. The honeymoon was over.

While Wilhelm was caught in his legal dilemma, guitarist John Cipollina turned up in Virginia City, asking if the Charlatans required the services of a replacement guitarist. They didn't. Wilhelm and Laughlin had been bailed out the following day by Laughlin's father and were back in Virginia City after one more day. But the young Marin County guitarist loved the Old West look, firearms and the entire Charlatans trip and clearly ached for a piece of the derangement.

The Charlatans packed up and cleared out of town, leaving in the proverbial cloud of dust of the western movie they had been living the past three and a half months. Virtually as soon as the band left by the back door, a converted bus painted in Day-Glo swirls with loudspeakers and other crazy contraptions attached to the outside pulled up out front. A sign on the front announced the destination— "Further"—and a sign on the back warned "Caution: Weird Load." Ken Kesey and his Merry Pranksters had arrived at the Red Dog.

1966

We're a San Francisco
band. We found the
five nearest musicians
and started playing.
                —Huey Lewis

WINTER 1965-66

John Cipollina climbed onstage at "A Tribute to Dr. Strange" just to look at the crowd. His eyes hurt as he scanned the cavernous concrete bunker of the Longshoremen's Hall. All these people that looked like him, hair over their collars, Army surplus and thrift store clothing, the whole hall full of them. He stepped down and walked back out in the crowd slightly dazed.

A roomful of freaks. More than a thousand strangely garbed, wild-eyed, like-minded malefactors who had crawled out of God knows what woodwork. Most wore on their faces the same shock of recognition that Cipollina experienced. Most, also, were blasted sky-high on LSD. A carnival of the willfully deranged. A subterranean community was meeting itself for the first time. These people had been holed up, growing their hair, getting dosed good and strange in the privacy of their own meager cells, without knowing that across the city, hundreds upon hundreds of others were doing the same under the cover of their rooms. This tribal rite brought them out. Some unseen hand, some unspoken voice bid them don joyous apparel and make their way to the Longshoremen's Hall, previously headquarters to "Teens and Twenties" dances that drew a regulation and often rough kind of suburban crowd. But those leftovers from rock and roll rudeness didn't make this scene. The mere title—"A Tribute to Dr. Strange"—coupled with the scrawled handbill with lettering that looked like drippings from a candle carried the message to the people it was intended to reach. Dr. Strange, indeed.

The dance was thrown October 16 by a group of people living in the Pine Street commune calling themselves the Family Dog who were looking for a safer, more legal way to make money. Al Kelley, Luria Castell, Ellen Harmon and Jack Towle had all spent time that summer in Virgina City and traveled in the hip circles that sensed changes in the cultural climate, tiny blips on the distant horizon, with the unerring instinct of birds sensing changes in the weather. In the band's first performance outside the Matrix, the Jefferson Airplane would be appearing with the Charlatans, back from the hills of Nevada for more than a month. Also appearing was a group from the East Bay called the Marbles, and a band making only its second public performance, the Great Society, that featured a female vocalist named Grace Slick, her husband Jerry Slick on drums and his brother Darby Slick on guitar. Serving as master of ceremonies was a late-night Top Forty disk jockey from KYA with a cult following based on his irreverent wit and on-the-air "bombing," complete with appropriate sound effects, of popular records, Russ (The Moose) Syracuse, an anomaly on the verge of extinction, although nobody knew that at the time. Richie Olsen of the Charlatans, high on acid, merely marveled at how Syracuse's pancake makeup was moving all over his face.

Chet Helms showed up in morning coat and blue jeans and experienced the same sodden flash as Cipollina. "They can't bust us all," he thought. Wanting to pitch in and help in some way with this gorgeous scene, Helms dashed over to the Tape Music Center on Divisadero and borrowed a strobe light to splatter dancers in flashing pools of light.

He watched Luria Castell break up a fistfight between two drunks, leftover "Teens and Twenties" types, by simply jumping in the middle and punching it to a stop herself. She was quite a powerful lady, hardly the fragile hippie squaw. A warm, aggressive earth mother sort whose political past included travels to Cuba in addition to assorted sit-ins, demonstrations and arrests, she had lived at an Ashbury

Street rooming house run by Danny Rifkin while attending S.F. State, before moving to the Pine Street Victorian known as Dog House because of the tenants' penchant for owning dogs, many of which were run over in the busy traffic in front of the house. During one late-night brainstorming session about what to do for money, her war council hit on the idea of separating the idle rich from some of their money with a pet cemetery and the name Family Dog was born, honoring both the morbid inspiration and Ellen Harmon's own recently deceased victim of the Pine Street rush hour.

Cipollina ran into Chris Brooks that night. She was a mother hen to musicians who was especially fond of Cipollina with his long black hair and frail, wan look. With her were two musicians from the Central Valley, currently sleeping in her basement room, drummer Greg Elmore and guitarist Gary Duncan. They had belonged to a band called the Brogues that once gigged at the Coffee Gallery and recorded a pair of singles for a small Hollywood record label, but broke up after one of the other musicians was drafted and another fell out with his wife. Duncan and Elmore gravitated toward North Beach and were looking for work in a Top Forty bar band when Brooks introduced them to Cipollina.

A couple of nights later, Cipollina was jamming at 1090 Page Street with his two new associates, playing a long version of an old Bo Diddley song, recently reprised by the Rolling Stones, "Mona."

Joe McDonald and Barry Melton shared similar backgrounds. Melton, who grew up next door to Woody Guthrie in Brooklyn, moved with his family at age eight to Van Nuys in the San Fernando Valley, his union organizer father chased out to the coast by red-hunting FBI agents. After a resign-or-be-fired ultimatum, McDonald's father quit a phone company job with eighteen years seniority after the FBI unmasked him as a card-carrier. Both of their mothers were Jewish women who married these militant working-class men from the Midwest.

Watching his father descend from the relative security and middle-class comfort of suburban Los Angeles life in El Monte to earning a subsistence-level living with a chicken and egg route through Watts made McDonald a serious young man who took every odd job he could find to help contribute to his family. Overcome with shame and anger, he stopped talking and fell into the world of music—

rhythm and blues, jazz, country and western. He learned trombone and picked up guitar at age sixteen. The next year, he joined the Navy.

He heard about beatniks while serving in Japan, but came home, entered L.A. State College and got married. Eventually tiring of student life, he moved to San Francisco to lead the life of a beatnik. In Berkeley, he fell in with the performers who sang folk and protest songs live every week on the local listener-supported radio station, KPFA, left his wife and started putting out a folk music magazine called *Rag Baby.*

Melton used to find his way as a teenager from the Valley into Hollywood to soak up the folkie bohemian atmosphere at the Ash Grove, a Melrose Avenue coffee house where that crowd convened. He moved north to attend S.F. State, but soon dropped out to be a musician. The two met at the Berkeley Folk Festival that summer, started jamming and hit it off.

When McDonald came up with the idea of a talking issue of *Rag Baby* in time for the Vietnam Teach-In, he asked Melton to play guitar with him on a couple of songs. In the Berkeley hills living room of Chris Strachwitz, who ran the folk-blues Arhoolie Records label, they recorded the songs, slapped on another pair of tunes by the Dylan of Berkeley, folksinger Peter Krug, and got Strachwitz to arrange to have the four-song record pressed. At the last minute, McDonald and Melton tagged their collaboration Country Joe and the Fish, an obscure reference to Mao Tse-tung's dictum that a true revolutionary must "swim among the people as a fish." *Songs of Opposition* was available in time for the massive antiwar protest, the same weekend "A Tribute to Dr. Strange" was taking place at Longshoremen's Hall across the bay.

The two-day event began at the UC-Berkeley campus with a series of speeches, including Ken Kesey taking a bizarre turn, mumbling about the similarities between the antiwar movement and the military and concluding by wheezing a garbled "Home on the Range" into the harmonica. The first night's march was, predictably, turned back at the border of Oakland by a phalanx of Oakland police. The second day, McDonald, Melton and some associates performing as the Instant Action Jug Band played from the back of a flatbed truck in the parade. This time, just as several thousand marchers reached the Oakland border and the long blue line, members of the Oakland chapter of the outlaw motorcycle gang Hell's Angels swooped down and took up battle, stomping the peaceniks. An all-out melee ensued with six Angels arrested and one cop taken to the hospital with a broken leg.

But all over Berkeley that day, protesters picked up their cue from armed forces veteran McDonald, singing his song:

And it's 1 ... 2 ... 3 ...
What are we fighting for?
Don't ask me, I don't give a damn
Next stop is Vietnam

After serving his thirty days in Marin County Jail, Freiberg returned to San Francisco to be sentenced to sixty days in San Bruno on the first drug charge. The night before he was due to go inside, he dropped copious amounts of LSD—with his old roommate Crosby and the Byrds singing "Turn Turn Turn" on the radio—and showed up the next morning still tripping his brains away. The elevator door stuck and kept sticking. As he watched it try to close again and again, he finally decided if the door sticks open one more time, it would be an omen he was not supposed to go to jail and he would walk away. The door closed.

With "Turn Turn Turn" ringing in his ears, the longtime folkie saw his future in rock music. He had performed for years as one-half of the duo David and Michaella and once toured Mexico in the trio Folksingers for Peace that was deported by the Mexican government as subversive. But now he decided he would learn bass as soon as he finished his little stretch. He knew Cipollina from hanging out together at the Sausalito folk club on an old scuttled ferryboat called the *Charles Van Dam*. Cipollina, who was sleeping in his '54 Plymouth parked on Mount Tamalpais, loaned him an old bass that had been banging around in his car trunk. Cipollina and his friend Jimmy Murray had been hired to form a rock band behind folksinger Dino Valente, a mesmerizing character who grew up in carnival midways and used to stalk the streets of Greenwich Village with methamphetamine ampules tucked in the leather wristband of his wristwatch. But Valente now appeared jail-bound himself, following a pot bust that took place before the newfound band had a chance to play a single note together. They were looking for a drummer and vocalist the night Cipollina ran into Elmore and Duncan at Longshoremen's Hall.

• • •

The second time Girl Dreyer and Martha Wax ran away, David Crosby, their old pal from Sausalito and now a big star with the Byrds in Los Angeles, stowed the two teenagers in the Tropicana Motel on Santa Monica Boulevard. Kantner and Balin, who knew the two girls well from San Francisco, were in town at the time and applauded their liberation. The runaways eventually made their way to Big Sur, where they heard Freiberg had been released from jail. Girl Dreyer headed back to the Bay Area, where she soon found herself in Juvenile Hall in San Francisco, on the verge of being declared an incorrigible runaway by the courts, and getting eyed daily by the black hookers—honeys—who called her "Future Honey." She faced three choices: go to jail, go back to school or get married.

Freiberg married Girl, a nickname she picked up as the only daughter in a six-child family, in a simple civil ceremony with her mother's wedding ring. Martha Wax was staying at Kantner's house when the newlyweds returned from City Hall. "Well, we're married—do we look any different?" Girl asked. The high-spirited honey-blond, voluptuous and petite, was hardly a candidate to keep the home fires burning, but marrying Freiberg kept her out of jail.

Gary Duncan, one of the other members of the nascent rock group, was also a newlywed. His sixteen-year-old bride met him three months earlier, when she saw him playing with the Brogues in Merced. Her family had moved to Los Angeles, where she cut school every day before running away to San Francisco and her nineteen-year-old boyfriend. She spent the weekend at the North Beach basement room Duncan and Elmore shared, but when she called her mother to ask for busfare back to Los Angeles, her mother was so appalled that she simply told her daughter to stay where she was. Duncan and Shelley Eidson were married in Reno a month after he met Cipollina.

Living in the North Beach basement, the band began to stitch together a repertoire, even playing a couple of dates at the Matrix, although without a name at this point. One gig was performed as Vulcan. Cosmic Crystal Set was briefly considered. Finally Murray and Freiberg came up with a name based on the astrological dominance of Mercury in the group—all five were Virgos and four of the musicians actually shared two birthdays. Thus, Quicksilver Messenger Service.

The now-named band's first job came from The Committee, the North Beach improvisational comedy troupe and local hip institution.

Committee member and North Beach bartender Howard Hesseman paid the group two hundred dollars and two ounces of grass to record a rock version of "The Star Spangled Banner" to replace the Kate Smith version the troupe used to open its shows. The results so pleased the improv group, they also hired the band to perform at their annual Christmas party at Muir Beach.

The band used this windfall to move into a house, little more than a shack really, on the mudflats of Larkspur in Marin County. The Freibergs' bedroom was nothing more than a space in the living room cordoned off by an old Indian bedspread. Leaks in the roof above the fireplace were cleverly rerouted by taping tinfoil conduits to the ceiling. Nobody had any money, food was scarce and when it grew cold enough for ice to cover the boardwalks leading to the house, they often resorted to ripping up the neighbors' walkways in the middle of the night to keep the fireplace stoked.

The Gleason review alerted the record industry to the Jefferson Airplane and, within weeks of the band's first engagement, artist and repertoire men from many labels took the trip north to check the band out at the Matrix. Producer Barry DeVorzon of Valiant Records, the man behind such fluffy pop confections as "I Wonder What She's Doing Tonight" by Barry and the Tamerlanes or "Rhythm of the Rain" by the Cascades, flew up, heard the band and made the first offer. Matthew Katz, acting as the band's manager, found the group didn't even want to hear about rinky-dink Valiant Records.

Phil Spector also saw the Gleason column. In September, the band went to Los Angeles and met with the reclusive millionaire producer in his Beverly Hills mansion. Surrounded by bodyguards obviously carrying guns, Spector did not impress the band, who found the scene uptight and quickly split, leaving Katz behind to talk with Spector. Oddly, it was Rod McKuen who brought Katz and the Airplane to RCA Victor. Katz met the poet in Los Angeles. McKuen had heard of the Airplane during a recent San Francisco run at the hungry i and wanted to give Katz some dubs of songs he thought the band might use. Katz dropped by a McKuen recording session at RCA Studios, where he was introduced to artist and repertoire director Neely Plumb.

Also while in Los Angeles looking for a record deal, three members of the band signed Katz's management contract after long arguments about the deal. Balin, in the spirit of communality, wanted Katz to take an equal share and Katz insisted on a twenty percent commission. He allegedly insinuated to band members that without signing his management contract, they couldn't sign the recording contract he had negotiated with RCA Victor, that the company would not accept the band unless he managed the group. Anyway, the band members understood him to say that this particular contract they would be signing didn't matter. A mere formality. He would take the document to a lawyer the next week and fix it up to their satisfaction. Balin, Kantner and Kaukonen signed.

But there were musical considerations pressing. Balin and Kantner obviously had a sound more securely fixed in the rock realm in mind. That spelled an end to upright bassist Bob Harvey, who found out about his pending dismissal by arriving one night at the Matrix to find the drawing of him on the airplane altered. Instead of standing on the wings, Harvey was now portrayed as hanging by his fingers from the tail. Balin made it official backstage.

Drummer Peloquin was another matter. A brusque, often obnoxious ex-Marine and former military drummer, he didn't fit in comfortably with the more relaxed members of the band all that well. But when Kaukonen found out that Peloquin used to work as a security guard, he exploded. "I won't work with a cop," he said. "It's him or me." The decision was easy. Kaukonen was a very gifted player. Peloquin, too, was out.

Balin happened by the Matrix one afternoon when the as-yet unnamed Quicksilver band was trying out a new guitarist, a tall, handsome fellow Cipollina and Murray knew from hanging around the Sausalito park, Skip Spence. Balin took one look at Spence, judged him teen appeal material. "You're our drummer," he announced to an astonished Spence. "Do you play drums?"

"No," he said, "I sing and play guitar."

"Why don't you get some sticks and work with them, you know? You'd be a great drummer. I can tell," Balin said.

"I don't play drums," said Spence.

"Play for a week and see what happens. If you can play in a week, you can play in our group," said Balin. So Spence became the Airplane's new drummer.

But Kaukonen appeared determined to take charge of recruiting the bassist. After first trying to get their father to allow his younger brother Peter, a Stanford student at the time, to take the chair, he turned instead to a childhood friend from Washington, D.C., Jack Casady. Jorma was initially friends with Jack's older brother, but as the younger Casady grew more proficient on guitar, he and the three-and-a-half-years-older Kaukonen became friends. Casady played lead guitar with Kaukonen in his teenage rock and roll band, the Triumphs. When Kaukonen went away to Antioch College in Ohio, Casady started playing bass in rhythm and blues bands and strip joints around the D.C. area. He kept in touch with Kaukonen and visited with him in New York on occasion, where they checked out blues shows in the Village together.

Casady knew nothing of the Jefferson Airplane when Kaukonen caught up with him by telephone, but the promise of fifty dollars a week guaranteed and a plane ticket provided ample inducement. Kaukonen, who had never heard Casady play bass, picked him up at the airport. "You better be able to play bass," he warned him sternly.

With the band's first major concert appearance booked three days later, October 30 at UC-Berkeley's Harmon Gym, Casady expected some hard-working, disciplined rehearsals. He didn't know quite what to make of these long-haired musicians. Nothing on the East Coast rhythm and blues circuit, where the musicians wore suits and ties and rehearsed diligently, prepared him for these San Francisco ways. The band members, on the other hand, didn't know exactly what to make of Casady with his collegiate mustache and corduroy jacket. Kantner, a big fan of Chris Hillman of the Byrds, was the biggest detractor. But the mustache was an even bigger problem. The band demanded he shave. He didn't want to. Instead, he shaved half of it off. "You can look at me this way and I won't have a mustache," he told them. Balin cracked up. Casady was in.

The Harmon Gym appearance was a bust. The anticipated crowd never showed. The band sounded horrendous. Everything was out of tune. Kantner stopped the band at one point, which horrified Balin. Casady merely sat down, pulled out a rag and started polishing his bass. Instead of the fifteen hundred dollars the band had expected to make, they took home the grand sum of fifty dollars.

The Lovin' Spoonful starred in the second Family Dog dance, "A Tribute to Sparkle Plenty," October 24 at the Longshoremen's again. Luria Castell caught the Spoonful before the band started breaking big at a Sunset Strip nightclub called The Trip and she was determined to bring the band to a Family Dog dance. The group's first single, "Do You Believe in Magic," lit up the radio that fall and the band looked poised to join the Byrds at the forefront of the new American rock movement. The Spoonful had just finished a week's engagement at the hungry i, but stars didn't impress the crazed community that came to dance with the Family Dog. John Sebastian and Zal Yanovsky of the Spoonful strolled across the ballroom floor to the Coke stand without drawing a second glance. Not on the bill this time, the Jefferson Airplane came just to dance, having spent the afternoon introducing the band's new drummer to the pleasures of LSD. Another band from Palo Alto that had been working for the past few months at pizza parlors and toilets like Big Al's Gas House up and down the peninsula also showed up after taking acid and enjoying the Marin County woods all afternoon. The lean, blond-haired bass player for the Warlocks took Ellen Harmon aside. "Lady, what this little séance needs is us," he confided.

Pine Streeters called him Weird Jim Gurley and he called himself the Archfiend of the Universe. Like many of the Pine Street communards, Gurley came from Detroit, where he used to work with his father, the stunt car driver, as the human battering ram. His father would strap Gurley to the hood of his car and drive him through a burning plywood wall. Even with a helmet, the impact would leave Gurley dazed, nearly unconscious, barely able to wave to the crowd. His hair was singed so often, he shaved his head and he arrived in San Francisco missing his front teeth.

He started out on guitar playing lots of Lightnin' Hopkins and typical folk-blues of the coffee houses in the late fifties, but after hearing John Coltrane at a Detroit nightclub one earth-shaking evening in the early sixties, Gurley saw his musical mission. He thereafter devoted his most intensive energies to transforming the ecstatic frenzy of Coltrane's saxophone to the acoustic guitar. He used to sit in a closet in Pine Street for hours, a stethoscope taped to the body of his guitar, finger-picking cascading notes into his own ears alone.

Chet Helms brought Gurley by 1090 Page Street to play with the band. He arrived dressed in all black with his pregnant girlfriend and their swaybacked German shepherd, Mishka, a pickup taped to his mahogany Martin guitar. Gurley proved to be the missing puzzle piece in this gaseous cloud condensing into a rock band. Masterminding the metamorphosis with the authority of a ringmaster was Helms, whose role was celebrated in the name the musicians finally selected, actually two names that stuck together when they were read aloud from a list, Big Brother and the Holding Company. Nobody ever doubted who Big Brother really was.

The band went public that December at the Open Theater in Berkeley, a dark, enclosed performance space with walls painted black, home of the notorious experimental theater where cast and audience frolicked together without their clothes. Helms dragged along some film and slide projectors—filmmaker Bruce Connor ran a bunch of choppy bits edited from stock footage at 1090 Page one night while the group jammed, creating an intriguing effect Helms thought should be expanded upon—and skewed the theater's modular staging around. With Gurley scraping metal-rending, glass-breaking cacophonies from his amplified Martin, the band roared and rolled through a largely instrumental, almost entirely improvised performance, Gurley spearheading the walloping sound like a victorious demolition derby driver.

The jury only took forty-five minutes to convict Ronny Davis of performing in a public park without a permit. The judge's instructions neatly sidestepped any of the Constitutional issues the Mime Troupe wanted to raise, so from that point forward, the guilty verdict became a foregone conclusion. Even without paying attorney Marvin Stender, costs mounted on the always strapped Mime Troupe and it was Bill Graham who suggested holding a benefit or "Appeal Party," as the handbills called the event. Graham knew nothing about the scene. The Jefferson Airplane sometimes rehearsed at the Mime Troupe loft, so he booked the rock band. Folk guitarist Sandy Bull and Greenwich Village poets-turned-rockers the Fugs were on the bill. Supporters of the Mime Troupe from The Committee to beat poet Lawrence Ferlinghetti were also advertised, but so was the Family Dog, which Graham supposed to be an animal act.

When members of the Mystery Trend pulled up the afternoon of November 6 in their '51 Chevy delivery truck to set up their equipment, they found a line already in front of the Howard Street loft. The band, centered around the S.F. Art Institute, had also agreed to let Graham borrow a Heathkit amplifier to run the sound system. The Mime Troupe owned some lighting. Graham scrawled the sliding scale admission policy on a piece of Sheetrock he placed at the top of the stairs—"If you earn $12 a week and live within the city, a dollar's okay" and so on, up to a fee of $48, which a couple of people actually paid. Graham drove back from dinner at David's Delicatessen on his '56 Lambretta motor scooter, wondering if anyone would show up.

He pulled up to see a line in front of the building running around the corner. By the time Ronny Davis arrived from a performance in Sausalito, he found Graham at the front door gleefully, almost hysterically, stuffing dollar bills in a green cloth bag, reaching over people, grabbing money out of their fingers. The crowd going up the stairs was so thick, the bag had to be hoisted to the loft by a rope to be emptied periodically. When the police burst on the scene, threatening to close the show down for overcrowding, Graham turned on all his unctuous charm, calling the sergeant "captain" and making up tales of expecting Rudy Vallee and Frank Sinatra from the airport any minute. He took the microphone and asked the people in the crowd who had been there awhile to leave and make more room. The police shuffled off in the night confused if not mollified. When it ended, with Allen Ginsberg chanting mantras at six in the morning, Graham stuffed more than four thousand dollars into an Army knapsack and drove away on his scooter, a changed man, to have breakfast at Mel's Drive-In on his way home.

Luria Castell and Al Kelley of the Family Dog had dropped by the Mime Troupe loft to talk with Graham about his intended fundraiser some time in advance of the show's taking place. The Dog had signed contracts obligating the producers to a third Longshoremen's Hall show the same night and they wanted to try and convince Graham to change his date. They offered to produce a benefit for the Mime Troupe on another date. They were concerned there was not enough audience to go around, but they did not find Graham cooperative. "I'm not interested in putting on rock and roll dances," he told them.

Seams were splitting at the Family Dog anyway. Kelley and Ellen Harmon were breaking up. Some guy Luria Castell met at George Hunter's apartment wanted her to go live in a cave beside Pyramid Lake with him and she found the idea appealing. A good-sized crowd attended the third Dog dance at Longshoremen's Hall, "A Tribute to Ming the Merciless," featuring another one of Castell's Sunset Strip connections, the Mothers, as well as the Charlatans, the Family Dog house band. This crowd was somewhat different from the previous two dances. A lot of Mission district toughs with razor cuts and hot rods checked out the scene. A plate-glass door was smashed. Fights started in the parking lot and the hall, while bandleader Frank Zappa improvised lyrics about the violence from the bandstand, as if it was just part of his sardonic act. Ellen Harmon hated the bad vibrations. She moved out of Dog House shortly thereafter. Luria Castell also packed up and found lodgings at Hemlock Street, where Richie Olsen was living with his girlfriend.

The first public Acid Test took place December 4 following the Rolling Stones concert at San Jose Civic. Ken Kesey, bull goose looney of his own asylum, wanted nothing to do with the Eastern-influenced gobbledygook slowly enveloping the LSD cult. None of those incense on the burner, lotus-position, flickering-eyeball retreats into the inner sanctum. He wanted collective anarchy, the full zap!, pow!, bang! of pooling the lunacy. After a dry run outside Santa Cruz, at the house occupied by Kesey's Merry Prankster lieutenant Ken Babbs, leaflets handed out to teens exiting the Stones concert directed them—"Can YOU Pass the Acid Test?"—to a private residence currently inhabited by one Big Nig, who loaned Kesey the use of his humble home unaware of the madness waiting to overtake him.

He stared goggle-eyed as the Pranksters brought a vast store of electronic equipment—speakers, tape recorders, instruments, film projectors—followed by a group of musicians, who loaded in equipment of their own: a variety of amplifiers, guitars and a Hammond electric organ. Having just recently changed the band's name from the Warlocks, this scraggly collection of obvious deviants was making its first appearance under the group's newly minted name—the Grateful Dead. Fresh from an assortment of horrible jobs over the past several months at dives up and down the El Camino Real, the Dead linked up with the Pranksters for the first time at this Acid Test, although Kesey remembered the band's lead guitarist, Jerry Garcia, as one of the younger kids who used to live at the Chateau, ramshackle bohemian quarters not far from Perry Lane, where he used to live in Palo Alto. Garcia and some of his pals would occasionally try to crash parties at Kesey's pad, but there was little interaction between the nascent Pranksters and these dirty-fingernail ex-bluegrass musicians.

Playing at beer-slurping pizza parlors, the Warlocks had stayed close to conventional rhythm and blues and rock songbooks—the Rolling Stones to Jimmy Reed—but with the whooshing roar of LSD blowing through their brains, these musicians began to loosen themselves from their moorings and drift far afield. It was both a sound and a concept perfectly suited to the atmosphere Kesey sought for his Acid Tests. The Grateful Dead played house band to the dawning of the psychedelic apocalypse.

The Fillmore Auditorium was a beige brick building on the corner of Fillmore and Geary streets in the heart of the heavy black Fillmore district. With storefronts on the street level, the ballroom was approached from a stairway. A long, ornate bar with a mirror behind it ran along one side of the dance floor and a balcony ringed the rear of the hall and one wall. It was a real theater, complete with a stage, tall ceilings and a large floor.

After the revelation of the Mime Troupe benefit, Bill Graham changed religions. He had truly experienced a vision and he was determined to follow where it led. No more nickel-and-dime tin cups. No more pointless political polemics. Suddenly he was very interested in putting on rock and roll dances. He could see his days with the Mime Troupe coming to an end. But Appeal II, meanwhile, was already in the works. Whether Graham remembered Kelley and Castell mentioning the Fillmore, or Ronny Davis wanting to stage "A Minstrel Show" there, or whether he picked up a suggestion by Ralph Gleason, he found his hall.

Owner Charles Sullivan, an imposing black businessman invariably dressed in suit and tie, had run rhythm and blues shows in the hall for years. He presented Ray Charles, James Brown, Bobby Bland, the Temptations and the whole laundry list of ghetto attractions. He owned a liquor store, operated cigarette and vending machines and often booked shows at various places up and down the coast. He and Graham arrived at an accommodating arrangement. This time there would be no poets or actors; strictly musicians. The Airplane and Mystery Trend returned, along with the Great Society, a soul band called Sam Thomas and the Gentlemen's Band and jazzman John Handy, who had appeared briefly at the first Appeal and was probably the sole performer on the bill with a national reputation. Mystery Trend, once again, loaned Graham the band's Heathkit amplifier.

Graham captured a prize publicity coup during a televised press conference held by Bob Dylan, who was in town with his electric rock shows, riding the high tide of "Like a Rolling Stone" and the sort of frenzied acclaim that makes pinnacle events out of mere concert appearances. The day before he opened a series of Bay Area concerts, he held forth for the members of the press assembled at the San Francisco public television station, playing cat-and-mouse with their questions. Toward the end of the press conference, Ralph Gleason asked Dylan what he had in his hand and Dylan held up a copy of the poster promoting "Appeal II" that Graham had pressed on him as he walked into the room. "Yeah, it's a poster somebody gave me," said Dylan. "It looks pretty good. I would like to go if I could, but unfortunately I won't be here." He read off the date, place and names of the acts.

Chet Helms went to the benefit with his friend John Carpenter, who was managing Great Society. They were standing by the bar where the sign read "No Booze" when Graham walked by. Carpenter introduced Graham to Helms and the three began to talk. Helms, who had wanted to participate in the Family Dog from the first night at Longshoremen's, had loaned Castell some money in anticipation of producing shows together at California Hall. He and Carpenter between them not only managed two bands, but arranged for a commitment from Matthew Katz to book the Airplane. Now that Graham was interested in putting on rock and roll dances, people such as Helms and Carpenter looked like they could be particularly helpful. They agreed to meet soon and talk further.

Signe Tole resisted signing the contract with Matthew Katz. Something about the flamboyant goateed entrepreneur in his black capes and white Jaguar disturbed her. He seemed so smooth, so charming, so richly intelligent at times, but some of his ideas reeked of someone who didn't get it. He tried to coin the word "fojazz"—a combination of *folk* and *jazz*—to describe the Airplane's music. He printed business cards for the Matrix that said "San Francisco's Fojazz Night Club." Katz envisioned a uniformed cadre of females from a fan club he wanted to call Jefferson Airplane Stewardesses calling out individual band members' names at concerts. He thought the band should back topless dancer Carol Doda. He wanted to include records on the inside of coffee can lids. His twin brother invented and manufactured the plastic lids and Katz thought that might be a terrific promotion.

But it wasn't just his ideas. Something more fundamental about Katz simply aroused her suspicions and she did not want to commit her signature to a document she would regret. "Matthew doesn't have dime one," she told the band.

She kept her job as a secretary at Trader Vic's restaurant. In September, she married the man she lived with, Jerry Anderson, a brutish fellow who worked the lights at the Matrix and used to run with the Pranksters. In December, following a dramatic phone call from Katz, she and Anderson flew to Los Angeles to meet with the rest of the band and Katz and solve the contract problem. A great heated argument ensued. Balin had strong words. Signe largely sat by quietly, as Anderson spoke out loudly on her behalf. He objected to Katz's percentage. He objected to a clause giving Katz control over what was called "artistic endeavors." An agreement for Katz to give back to the band twenty percent of the money he collected for publishing and production was drawn up. Katz left the musicians believing that if his management contract wasn't signed, the RCA Victor deal was at risk. Signe signed the contract, as her husband protested loudly. She immediately wanted to retract the action.

Kaukonen finally blew up at Anderson. "You asshole," he said, advancing on Anderson with a folded pocketknife in his hand. He pulled up next to Anderson, towering over him menacingly. Balin told Katz to tear up the contract. He hesitated, caught Balin glowering at him and ripped the paper into pieces he let flutter to the floor. The Andersons left to consult an attorney, who added a rider releasing Signe from any obligations if she should leave the group or be fired and, two days later, she added her signature to the rest of the band.

Although the original fliers placed the third public Acid Test December 18 at Stinson Beach, Kesey moved the location at the last minute to the lodge on the marshy crescent of Muir Beach, a few miles away in a remote corner of Marin County, accessible only by a treacherous, winding road over Mount Tamalpais. Either people would find their way there or not. The Dead knew of Augustus Owsley Stanley III— who in the LSD underground didn't know the famed acid chemist? He knew the Pranksters and had been supplying Kesey's crowd with his material for many months. But when he heard there were a bunch of musicians getting high and playing music, he wanted to see that for himself.

Not that many could have missed him that night in his hipster finery, but when he started screeching the chair across the floor, a terrible, grating, teeth-gnashing sound like fingernails on a blackboard, everybody noticed him. He was well gone on his own product and everytime someone asked him to stop, he would. For a few minutes. Then this noxious grinding would start all over again. The evening ended for him with a classic freak-out, a time-travel vision transporting him back to the seventeenth century. He left the log cabin screaming about survival and denouncing Kesey at the top of his lungs, dragging his expensive recording equipment behind him by the microphone. He crashed his car by the side of the road and stayed there, gunning his engine, until sanity returned with the dawn.

After Kesey and other Pranksters went to Oregon and held an Acid Test in Portland over Christmas, Kesey finally brought the Acid Test to San Francisco on January 8 at the Fillmore Auditorium. With a stack of Pranksters electronic madness piled high in the middle of the floor and the Dead's formidable gear onstage, the Fillmore looked infested with a jungle of gleaming metal, lights and wires. Several hundred freaks, zonked to their eyeballs, spilled into the hall, flailing and writhing, as the Dead raised a snaking cloud of sound. Kesey picked up one of the ubiquitous microphones and surveyed the scene. "All I know," he announced, "is that if I were a cop and I came here, I wouldn't know where to begin."

LSD was not illegal and one of the rent-a-cops smiled at the suggestion the crowd might be trouble. "Oh no," he assured, "they's in love." But the police finally did arrive around two in the morning and immediately moved to shut down the festivities just as the molten core of the scene was turning liquid. They started unplugging microphones and, as they did, Mountain Girl, the often impudent and always independent Prankster with whom Kesey was currently paired, would plug others back in. She darted into the balcony with microphones, taunting the cops. They couldn't find her, but she kept shouting instructions over the speakers to police and revelers alike. Finally the police ordered the Pranksters to close down the party and they did. All except Ken Babbs, who sat down in a chair in the center of the floor and refused to budge. The police threatened arrest and only the last-minute intervention by Kesey's attorneys stopped Babbs from getting hauled away in handcuffs.

●   ●   ●

Rock Scully and Danny Rifkin, Luria Castell's new partners, worried that Kesey's throwing his Fillmore Acid Test the same night as their Family Dog dance at California Hall would hurt attendance. So they worked out a deal with the Pranksters for tickets to either event to be good for admission at both places and they ran buses between the two halls.

Scully grew up bouncing between sylvan Carmel-by-the-Sea, a couple of hours down the coast from San Francisco, and European boarding schools. His stepfather, Milton Mayer, an eminent scholar, traveled all over the world serving on various university faculties, while Scully and his brother stayed in school, returning to Carmel for summers. He first tumbled onto psychedelics attending college in Switzerland and by the time he found himself in graduate school at S.F. State, hanging out on the lawn with Helms, Hunter and the others, he was fully immersed in the soup. Living in the Haight, he made friends with Danny Rifkin, taking the streetcar out to State together. Eventually, Scully moved into the Victorian at 710 Ashbury that Rifkin was managing from his basement apartment.

Scully finally convinced the reluctant Rifkin to join forces to produce dances at California Hall with Luria Castell, whom Rifkin knew from when she lived at 710 Ashbury before she moved to the Dog House. The large building two blocks from the Civic Center with its sizable ballroom was owned by the German-American Association and reportedly used for bund meetings prior to the war. Scully wanted to manage the Charlatans and Hunter helped design the poster that featured the Charlatans top-billed over the Jefferson Airplane. Enough people showed up to deplete the supply of Cokes before intermission and Scully had to pass word to the band to keep playing while Rifkin went to the store to replenish the stock. At last, a Family Dog dance was going to make some money, maybe as much as fifteen hundred dollars.

But somewhere along the way, Scully hopped on board the bus headed to the Fillmore. He had caught the Dead a month before at the Acid Test held at the Palo Alto nightclub called the Big Beat and came back raving about the band to Rifkin. This time, he walked into the Fillmore with the band raising a full war cry and was even more overwhelmed. He never made it back to his own show.

• • •

Graham knew he was going to keep on producing shows, but the next benefit, Appeal III, would be the final association with the Mime Troupe. Fed up with the radical politics of the Troupe, Graham stood up at a meeting and argued that the Troupe should join him in producing these benefits on a regular basis, that presenting plays as political statements was addressing words to the breeze. A work of art can't be a political statement, he said. A real social statement would be the creation of a venue for a new culture. Ronny Davis and Graham always disagreed. Graham would argue with him that the Mime Troupe should present more commercial plays. Davis was a dedicated radical, not interested in the business of theater. When the question of going into the benefit business with Graham was put to a vote, only Graham and one other voted for the benefits. Shortly thereafter, Graham negotiated a long-term lease with Charles Sullivan and took over the Fillmore.

He knew he could not keep asking musicians to play for free, so for the third benefit he offered minimal sums. He visited with John Handy at his home. They drank tea and Graham told Handy about his harrowing childhood escape from the Nazis. Handy felt like he was making a new friend. Graham offered Handy $250 to play the third benefit, but Handy already had a nightclub booking in Berkeley the same night. No problem, Graham told him, just come to the Fillmore and play after the nightclub job. Handy agreed.

Graham also held several meetings at Mel's Drive-In with Helms and Carpenter in those heady days immediately following the second Mime Troupe benefit. On a handshake, they decided to share the Fillmore on alternating weekends, with Graham bankrolling the operation, while Helms and Carpenter would help book and stage manage all the shows.

When Mystery Trend manager Mike Daly called Graham to say the band's guitarist no longer wanted to loan the Heathkit, Graham exploded. The band was not invited to participate. Drummer Bill Kreutzman phoned Graham about getting the Dead on the show, but Graham hated the band's new name. After a protracted argument, he advertised the group as "Formerly the Warlocks . . . the Grateful Dead." Grace Slick of the Great Society sat on the side of the stage that night and watched in amazement as the Dead performed. She had never seen a bunch of guys that ugly and unwashed. "We'll have to wipe the mikes off after they play," she told her friend.

John Handy could still hear the applause in the club as he darted out the back door of the Albatross in Berkeley and headed off in a hurry to make his late call at the Fillmore. He and his band arrived to find the line outside the door and down the block, choking the stairway to the ballroom. He signaled the band to wait at the bottom of the stairs as he fought his way through the crowd toward the stage. Crouched by the speakers was his new friend, Bill Graham. He smiled and extended his hand. Graham flashed a severe look and pointed at his watch. "Look at the fucking time," he screamed, his voice rising. "Look at the fucking time."

Handy turned and walked away. He made it down the stairway where his band was waiting, and told them they would be leaving when he heard Graham coming after him. He turned and saw this—there was no other word for it—madman. Face creased, livid and still screaming, Graham was raging to the verge of violence. Handy, a former amateur boxer, turned and squared off. Just then, Graham stumbled and disappeared in the crowd. Handy and his band split forthwith and never played the Fillmore again.

The Monday before the Trips Festival, Judge Louis DeMatteis of the San Mateo Superior Court sentenced Kesey to six months in county jail on a possession of marijuana charge. Seventeen sheriff's deputies, a Federal narcotics agent and one police dog had swooped down on the La Honda headquarters of the Pranksters the previous April and arrested thirteen people, including Kesey. Officers claimed they found Kesey and an associate flushing pot down the toilet and were only able to make them stop at gunpoint. Charges against all but Kesey, his friend and one other were dropped and the severe sentence came as a shock.

On Wednesday night, San Francisco police arrested Kesey and Mountain Girl on the North Beach rooftop of Trips Festival producer Stewart Brand. They attracted the attention of neighbors by tossing pebbles at the toilet their buddy Margot St. James used for a planter box outside her apartment in the adjacent building. They watched, amused, as a police car pulled up in the alley below, red light blinking in the night. Nothing could have been more surprising when the cops burst in on the pair, who were lying on a plastic mattress, and found a pouch with a small amount of pot belonging to Mountain Girl. Kesey and one of the cops struggled over the plastic bag, but not before

Kesey managed to throw it off the roof and add resisting arrest to the charges. The pouch and its contents were retrieved.

Kesey was breaking under the stress. The whole Prankster trip was his scene, his money, his high profile in the press and, now, in the courts. The joke was wearing thin. A second marijuana conviction could carry a five-year sentence and, at the very least, he stood to have probation revoked on the San Mateo charge and have to serve the entire three years on that conviction. He told Mountain Girl, seven months pregnant with his child at the time, he was going to take off running after the Trips Festival that weekend.

After pleading not guilty to the San Francisco charges Friday morning, Kesey and Mountain Girl joined the crew that pulled up in the Day-Glo school bus the Pranksters had made a public emblem during the past couple of years. They had changed costumes. Kesey now wore a striped workshirt, sky blue boots and white Levis with "Hot" spray-painted on one hip, "Cold" on the other, and "Tibet" across his ass. Mountain Girl wore an Indian headband, orange stretch pants and purple sequined vest. On a mission to drum up publicity for the two-day Trips Festival scheduled for Saturday and Sunday at Longshoremen's Hall, Kesey and company blew up and released weather balloons inscribed "Now." They brought along Ron Boise's thunder machine, a familiar prop from the Acid Tests, this freeform conglomeration of sheet metal, taut wires and long springs that Kesey and others strummed, thumped and plucked to the astonishment of lunchtime passersby.

Brand had hired Bill Graham to supervise this exercise in controlled—or, perhaps, not so controlled—madness. This screaming acidfest, advertised as an LSD trip without the LSD, was anything but. In Pranksteresque doublethink, this was just a ruse to bamboozle the straights. The clear message to initiates was exactly the opposite and thousands streamed through the doors whacked out of their gourds. Graham ran head-on into the acid thing and he was stunned. With his clipboard under his arm, he scurried around trying to rein in an event that was designed to run out of control. Acid was being handed out everywhere. People went through the crowd dispensing handfuls of pills. He had no idea what to make of the Pranksters themselves. Graham ran up to Ken Babbs at one point, grimly concerned that people were climbing in over the back fence and getting in *without paying.* "Don't worry, Bill," Babbs told him. "People have made enough money." Graham glared at him like he was crazy.

Graham never laid eyes on Kesey the entire first night, but about fifteen minutes before the doors were supposed to open the second night, Graham spied someone wearing a silver space suit, complete with helmet on top, letting Hell's Angels in free through a side door. Graham ran up to him. "Why are you letting these people in?" Graham demanded. "Are they working here?" The man in the space suit turned and regarded Graham without expression and turned back. He continued to let people through the doors. Graham lost his composure and started screaming. "Would you mind answering me—what the hell are you doing here?" Then something struck Graham. "Are you Ken?" he asked. "Do you mind telling me what the hell you think you are doing?"

Kesey turned again to face Graham, gave his head a quick nod and, plop, the visor on his helmet fell shut and he walked off without a word.

In the center of the room, the Pranksters had constructed scaffolding on which rested projectors, all kinds of lights, and sound equipment. Kesey would scribble away, writing in gels on an opaque projector, and then splash water on his writing and watch the words on the wall dissolve.

Big Brother and the Holding Company, fresh from the band's first public performances, followed a group of conga drummers onstage. Sam Andrew, who fell into a screaming match with Graham walking in the door that evening, was soaring on acid. He whipped back and forth between terror-stricken stage fright and intense joy. He marveled at women in the crowd dancing without their blouses. He spent the rest of the evening strolling the hall, basking in the wonderful dementia. Peter Albin, on the other hand, went home immediately after the band played so he could get to bed early.

Jerry Garcia saw the message flashed on the wall—"Jerry Garcia Plug In"—and meandered toward the stage. Lost in a haze, he picked up his guitar, under the vague impression the band was supposed to play now, and realized the neck was broken. Strings were sticking out. The body was swinging free in his grasp, attached only by the remaining strings, a hopeless wreck. It doesn't look like we'll be playing tonight, he thought, when a stranger in a cardigan sweater with a clipboard under his arm strode up. "It's broken," stammered Garcia.

The stranger fell to his knees, taking the guitar, and applied himself to its repair, trying to fit the irretrievably ruined piece back onto the body with all his might. Garcia felt the beneficence of the futile gesture and it warmed his first impressions of Graham. The Dead never did play that night.

Kesey met with the Pranksters at Ken Babbs's house outside Santa Cruz and told them his plans. Nobody wanted him to go, but he was determined. First, one last prank. A Prankster with a resemblance to Kesey was dispatched with the minibus bearing a suicide note Kesey and Mountain Girl composed amid great giggling—"Ocean, ocean, I'll beat you in the end"—and the bus was left abandoned near the coast beyond Eureka in the northernmost reaches of the state, while Kesey headed south to Mexico.

The Pranksters followed in the psychedelic school bus with "Further" as its destination, planning to hole up in Los Angeles and conduct a few Acid Tests. The Dead was already down there, living with Owsley, who had taken the band under his wing. The acid king first located his operations in Los Angeles the previous year, following a raid by Berkeley police on his East Bay laboratory. Charges were dismissed after the alleged methedrine police confiscated turned out to be a stage or two short of completion. Owsley successfully sued for the return of his lab equipment. He set up shop in Los Angeles and began producing still-legal LSD at an enormous rate, ordering $20,000 worth of chemicals from one supplier alone and paying in cash. With his girlfriend and lab partner, UC-Berkeley chemistry major Melissa Cargill, he wanted to flood the world with the mind-altering drug.

He hired electronics whiz Tim Scully to build sound equipment for the Dead. Owsley held strong, usually unconventional opinions on almost everything, always willingly expressed in detail. The price of his patronage was to be subjected to his peculiar regimen. At the Los Angeles home he shared with the Dead, only meat and dairy products were allowed in the refrigerator. He believed in a strictly carnivorous diet and kept huge slabs of beef, gallons of milk and flats of eggs. There was no furniture, only mattresses on the floor, so the band fed themselves by slicing off hunks of steak and eating them, standing up, straight out of the frying pan.

Owsley brought Rock Scully down to manage the band. He and Rifkin completed one more successful California Hall show with the

Charlatans the same night Luria Castell split for Mexico to hook up with Ellen Harmon and Jack Towle. Scully found Owsley and the band ensconced in a three-story pink house off Western Avenue in South Central Los Angeles. The band's rehearsing downstairs covered up the noise from the pill-tabbing machine upstairs. Owsley sank great sums of money into equipment, expensive microphones, fine tape decks, cumbersome but excellent Voice of the Theater speakers. He devised a way for the band to play in stereo. But Owsley also harbored some deep paranoid delusions about Kesey, how he was trying to wire Owsley's brain and steal his thoughts. "He's doing it again, he's doing it again," he whispered to Scully.

"Who? What?" Scully said.

"Ken. Ken is. He's doing it again—watch out. He'll get into your head," said Owsley.

The Pranksters without Kesey were having problems of their own. Ken Babbs placed himself in charge as soon as Kesey departed and he proved to be a more dictatorial leader, giving orders, making sarcastic remarks. They put on several Acid Tests at various locations around Los Anegeles, but the spirited unity of the group was disintegrating. Alliances were shifting all throughout the group, a pattern that infected the Dead, too. Garcia and his wife, Sarah, spent much of one Acid Test evening engaged in serious dialogue over their future, the LSD they had taken serving as a catalyst to major changes in their lives on the spot. They were parents of a small daughter, Heather, and once sang folk music together in Palo Alto coffee houses. But Garcia was treading a new path, one that he saw heading in a direction far different than husband and father. And his wife had met someone else who, for the moment at least, seemed somewhat more promising. They came to the conclusion that they would split up and that Sarah would raise their daughter on her own, without interference, influence or even contact from her father.

At the Watts Acid Test, held in the Youth Opportunities Center, a warehouse in Compton on the fringe of the city's racially tense ghetto that had exploded in flames and riots only five months earlier, the frayed fabric began to unravel. Pranksters wheeled out a pair of garbage cans filled with Kool-Aid. Hugh Romney, a local comic whose hip credentials spanned all the way back to the beatnik era, signed on to help the Pranksters on this Los Angeles visit and he did everything he could to make the presence of LSD in one of the two cans clear to everyone present. "The one on the right is for the little kids," he said. "The one on the left is for the big kids. The one on the left is for the kittens and the one on the right is for the tigers." The brew was strong, stronger than usual, and, with the weather hot and dusty, people drank more than usual.

"Who cares?"

A shriek piped through the sound system. "Who cares?" Someone in the throes of an old-fashioned general freak-out in the other room was screaming into a microphone held by Babbs. With some effects added, the cry sounded truly terrifying, echoing through the crowd like a shiver. Romney got on the mike and asked for volunteers to try and talk down the freak-out case, all the while "Who cares?" boomed through the hall. With the Dead uncomfortable with the kind of invasion of privacy in which the Pranksters specialized, this incident drove a great wedge between the band and the Pranksters.

The epic madness of the event swirled into wisps by dawn. Police spent the evening traipsing in and out of the lobby, wondering what was going on. Strange. No booze, just a wild party that lasted all night. As Julius Karpen of the Pranksters took out the barrels of Kool-Aid and dumped them down the storm drain, a policeman casually watching perked up. Whatever was washing away down the drain was the key, he just knew it, and there wasn't a thing he could do. Inside the hall, Mountain Girl and Garcia swept the floor together, laughing and noticing a fresh connection taking place between them. When they were done, she piled into a Volkswagen bus with nine other people and drove slowly through the night to make a court date the following morning from the rooftop bust in San Francisco.

SPRING 1966

Ron Polte shot and killed his best friend accidentally. They were planning to scare some tough guy who had been harassing employees at the diner Polte ran in Chicago and Polte made blank ammunition by pulling the bullets out of the cartridges with a pair of pliers. One of the bullets broke off in the casing and he didn't know it. When his friend dropped by the restaurant and asked if he fixed up the gun and the ammo, Polte pulled out the pistol and cranked off a round, pointing it at his friend as a joke. His friend crumpled as the sheared-off slug smashed into his chest. Polte was aghast.

The incident culminated a life on the seamy side for the onetime hood. At age seventeen, he had drawn five-to-life for sticking up savings and loans. On his release, he opened a locksmith's shop that was not particularly discriminating about its clientele. The basement of his diner, dubbed the Fallout Shelter, often served as a folk club, but also doubled as an impromptu market for wayward shipments that never quite made it to their intended destinations.

Out in California, Polte's old friend Nick Gravenites, who grew up in Chicago but had been spending a lot of time in San Francisco, heard about the incident and drove straight to Chicago to get Polte out of jail after he was arrested for murder. Gravenites then went looking for the fellow Polte meant to scare in the first place with every intention of killing him. The cops ran across Gravenites before he caught up with his quarry and arrested him and his accomplice, Paul Butterfield, on concealed weapons and drug charges.

The coroner's jury cleared Polte of any responsibility in the shooting death of his friend. Some of his friends didn't. Fearing for reprisals, Polte lit out to California, where his brother was working on a guest ranch in the Gold Rush country. He turned his back forever on his sordid ways. In California, he discovered LSD. Having closed the door on his past life, it was like a door opened in front of him and he stepped through it into a new life.

Living in the Mission district with his wife and their young son, nearly every day Polte would drop acid and hike up Market Street a mile or so, where he would sit on the sidewalk with a toolbox and repair cars people dropped off, a freelance mechanic without a garage. One day in March 1966, one of his buddies dropped by and said something about how Polte's old Chicago pal would be playing the Fillmore that weekend with his group, the Paul Butterfield Blues Band. Polte thought back to the smart-aleck harmonica player that used to come by the Fallout Shelter with Gravenites and figured there was no way it was the same person. But he went by to see anyway. On the way up the stairs, he heard David Freiberg of Quicksilver Messenger Service singing the old Buffy Sainte-Marie folk song, "Codine."

The Butterfield appearance qualified as a major event for the coalescing scene. While the San Francisco bands were composed largely of former folk musicians fumbling their way into the arena of electric music, each member of the Butterfield band was a certified monster. The rhythm section used to back Chicago blues great, Howlin' Wolf. Guitarist Mike Bloomfield was already annointed by no less than Dylan himself, who cast the guitarist in a featured role on his breakthrough record, "Like a Rolling Stone." The band had backed Dylan at the historic performance the previous July at the Newport Folk Festival, where the crowd jeered Dylan for his folk-rock heresy.

Helms and Carpenter had presented two previous shows with Graham at the Fillmore. With Luria Castell and the rest of her original associates long gone and far away, Helms adopted the name Family Dog for their enterprise. They delivered the Jefferson Airplane with Big Brother for the first show, titled "A Tribal Stomp," and double-billed their respective charges, Great Society and Big Brother, for the second show, "King Kong Memorial Dance." But the three-night Butterfield booking, March 25–27, was their crowning coup, a hip triumph of savvy and taste. The band came to San Francisco and slept on Helms's floor.

Graham initially balked at the stiff $2500 price tag for Butterfield. But Carpenter and Helms prevailed. Almost two thousand people jammed into the hall the first night alone. The performances simply astounded the Fillmore audiences. Although the recording wouldn't be released until much later in the year, the band was already playing the epic "East-West," a raga-inspired piece Bloomfield anchored around a Nick Gravenites tune after listening to Ravi Shankar while under the influence of LSD one night in Boston. The extended piece contained four sweeping crescendos that developed slowly. The final section was a caterwauling free-for-all that sent the acid-soaked Fillmore audience into other realms.

As Helms and Graham counted money and stacked the bills in empty apple boxes at the end of the third night, they agreed the band should be brought back soon. Graham went home, set his alarm clock for six in the morning and called New York to speak with Butterfield's manager, Albert Grossman, about a return engagement. He sealed the deal with Grossman before Helms was out of bed. When Helms straggled into the Fillmore that afternoon, feeling hurt and betrayed, Graham simply snapped a piece of advice at his long-haired counterpart. "You want to stay in this business," he told Helms, "get up early."

Graham opened his Fillmore operations the weekend following the Trips Festival, presenting the Airplane in a show advertised as "Sights and Sounds of the Trips Festival." Graham took his secretary and girlfriend, Bonnie MacLean, and the one Mime Troupe associate who voted with him on the benefits issue, Jim Haynie, to run the Fillmore. Graham met MacLean when he worked for Allis Chalmers; she applied for a job and he turned her down. When she called up to complain, he relented and gave her the job. Before long, they were dating. When he went over to the Mime Troupe, she went along as secretary. By then, they lived together in a small apartment in the Sunset district.

Plastic sheets covered the dancehall walls and liquid projection light shows bathed the hall in pulsing, squirting colors. Black lights hung in the rear and an apple barrel greeted every patron at the top of the stairs with the sign "Take One Or Two." Graham did everything from move equipment to sweep up at night. A compulsive worker, he always seemed to be in a hurry, bustling from one chore to the next.

When Graham went down to City Hall to apply for his own dancehall permit, a process he assumed would be simple rubber stamping, objections were raised by both a police lieutenant and the rabbi from the synagogue next door to the Fillmore. His permit was denied. Graham went ahead and presented that weekend's "Batman Dance and Film Festival" using Sullivan's permit. The three-night event featured several bands including Big Brother, Quicksilver, Great Society, Mystery Trend, screenings of a forties Batman serial and a door prize of a mynah bird, which spent the weekend hanging in a cage on the stage. Unfortunately, three nights of loud rock rendered the poor bird deaf.

Graham contacted big-wheel attorney Bill Coblentz and went after the permit again. While he was able to turn around Rabbi Burstein and many of the other neighborhood shopkeepers who originally objected to his dances, he ran head-first into the antipathy of Captain John Cassidy of the Northern Station. "We don't want your element around here," Cassidy told Graham. For the second time, the Board of Permit Appeals denied Graham's application. Graham announced he would seek a re-hearing and continue to hold dances at the Fillmore until the new appeal was decided. The editorial page of the *S.F. Chronicle* joined the fray, chiding the board for "misdirected and highly unfair malevolence" toward the Fillmore. The next night the cops struck back. On April 22, police carrying copies of the editorial swept through the hall, arresting fourteen youths for violating Section 558 of the Municipal Code, a 1909 ordinance which made it illegal for a minor under eighteen years of age to visit a public dancehall or for a proprietor of a dancehall to admit such minors. Graham was arrested along with the teens. A month later, all charges were dropped. On June 7, Graham won his dancehall permit, having marshaled the rabbi, a neighborhood mother who attended the dances with her daughter and *Chronicle* columnist Ralph J. Gleason as witnesses. Although police had yet to make one arrest since Graham began operating the hall in February, outside the Section 558 violations, police still objected to granting the permit. This time, the board overruled their objections.

Helms and Carpenter threw one more dance at the Fillmore after the Butterfield brouhaha. Carpenter and Graham were openly antagonistic. They butted heads over the issue of pot smoking, Graham adamant that it would not be allowed in his hall and Carpenter scornful of Graham's edict. Helms, the gentle soul, tried to mediate, but Graham always looked at him as a hapless hippie, a loopy pothead who lacked the drive and determination to be a success. Anyway, they were no longer necessary to Graham, so the Family Dog partners were out shopping for a new hall. To their last Fillmore show they brought John Whooley, proprietor of the Avalon Ballroom, an old swing ballroom upstairs in a building built in 1911 on the corner of Sutter and Van Ness called the Puckett Academy of Dance. The Avalon was smaller than the Fillmore, but was a gem on its own. The ceiling was covered with acoustic drapes. An L-shaped balcony surrounded the sprung wooden dancefloor that bounced back at dancers' feet. There were lots of mirrors, columns, red-flocked wallpaper and gilded booths. The stage was close to the floor and tucked away in the corner. Whooley ran Irish dances at the Avalon, but for the not insubstantial sum of eight hundred dollars a month, he was persuaded to lease the hall to Helms. Helms opened on April 22–23 with the Blues Project and the Great Society. Willie the Wizard's graffiti from the bathroom at 1090 Page supplied a motto for the new enterprise: "May the Baby Jesus Shut Your Mouth and Open Your Mind."

When Ambrose Hollingworth, manager of Quicksilver Messenger Service, crippled himself in an auto accident going to a party, Nick Gravenites suggested he ask Ron Polte to take over for him. Gravenites had been instrumental in getting Hollingsworth to come to San Francisco from Chicago in the first place. Hollingsworth, a mystic who did astrology and whose wife read Tarot cards, first heard the band at the Christmas party by The Committee. He bought an amplifier for the band and moved the group out of the mudflats shack into a home on Creek Lane, smack in the middle of downtown Mill Valley. It was while the band lived at Creek Lane that drummer Greg Elmore stopped talking. During an acid trip on Muir Beach, Elmore separated from the rest of the band and their wives and girlfriends. Eventually the others worried about him and went off looking for him, without success. When he finally showed up back at the house, he obviously had undergone some sort of traumatic experience. But nothing he said anything about. In fact, he said virtually nothing at all from that day forward. Maybe a word or two, but that was his limit. He and his girlfriend from Merced, a high school friend of Shelley Duncan's who ran away from home to live with the band in North Beach, decided to get married and did, on her eighteenth birthday. Her parents showed up at the house with the police, but wouldn't come in, just stayed at the door yelling for her to come out.

The house, in fact, became something of a haven for runaway girls. Police made a practice of checking the Quicksilver house for the latest errant teens. In the sleepy little community, such a situation would not have been tolerated at all were it not for John Cipollina's father. As a contractor and kingpin real estate salesman, Gino Cipollina was the unofficial mayor of Mill Valley and cops put up with a lot on his account. But the first job for Polte as the band's new manager was to find a new place for the group to live. He located a deserted dairy farm outside Olema, a quiet hamlet on the far reaches of western Marin.

Life looked pretty sweet at this point. With rent mere a eighty-five dollars a month for the ranch and the band gigging somewhere in San Francisco practically every weekend, getting paid as much as a thousand dollars for three nights at the Fillmore, not to mention having all the drugs they could smoke, swallow or otherwise ingest handed to them, the Quicksilver fellows were living in hippie heaven. Polte outfitted everybody with used Dodge Darts, second-hand state government cars he picked up at auctions for fifty dollars or so apiece. Cipollina bought a Mackenzie timber wolf cub, a cute little pup who could shred an arm playfully. The band began to think in terms of a recording contract and went so far as to hold some experimental sessions late at night in a small jingle studio in the City.

Once Dino Valente was released from jail, he moved onto the ranch. If he had any notions that he should be greeted as a full working member of this band that was supposed to have been formed around him, he didn't voice them. He simply sauntered around the grounds as if he owned the land. The first time he laid eyes on Ron Polte, whose hair was still trimmed short, Polte was shoveling manure. "What's your job here?" Valente said.

"I manage these guys," said Polte.

"You don't even look like a manager," sniffed Valente. "Look at your hair."

Polte didn't mind. He certainly had seen tough-guy acts before.

• • •

Recording surely occurred to the Charlatans as the next step. Luria Castell, the band's tireless booster, ran across producer Erik Jacobsen during one of his visits to San Francisco and pressed a tape and a photograph of the band on him. Jacobsen, tall, blond and Nordic, produced the Lovin' Spoonful, currently the hottest American rock band. He looked at the picture of the Charlatans and couldn't take his eyes off it. Jacobsen had fancied himself an old-timey stylist of some repute back in New York, where he, John Sebastian of the Spoonful and Fritz Richmond of the Jim Kweskin Jug Band were developing reputations in circles for their antique fashion sense: watch fobs in their vest pockets, wire-rim glasses. But the Charlatans made them look like effete dilettantes.

Jacobsen flew out to San Francisco in the fall to meet the band. Hunter met him at the airport gate and escorted him out to the parking lot, where the band's 1941 Langendorf Bread van was waiting. Hunter opened the rear doors and a cloud of smoke wafted out. Inside, the van had been arranged like someone's living room, couch, chairs, lamp, coffee table. Jacobsen jumped in and the van careened into San Francisco to Hunter's place on Pine Street. Jacobsen kept looking at Wilhelm, whose unnaturally black hair was bent, no, creased, and askew like thin, dark straw. When Hunter finally told Jacobsen that Wilhelm was wearing a wig because of the recent Rodeo pot bust and pending court date, Jacobsen was relieved. Nevertheless, Hunter, running the conversation at a manic clip, seemed to Jacobsen like the only one in the group who was marginally sane.

But once in the recording studio, Hunter was no help. His flailing at autoharp and tambourine bashing amounted to nothing under the scientific scrutiny of the microphones and the Charlatans were left to their devices as musicians, which were limited. Jacobsen came and went and the album progressed slowly in this piecemeal fashion. The band took a job as house band working five nights a week at a topless bar off Broadway called the Roaring Twenties that featured a nude girl on a swing. The straight businessmen who frequented the place didn't always appreciate a loud, long-haired rock band with their tits and ass. When an ashtray thrown from the audience hit Dan Hicks in the head and broke, he picked up the biggest piece and threw it back. But the steady work gave the band a chance to get good and tight in the process. The band's instrumental work, however, wasn't the problem for

Jacobsen, although he never could quite settle on which of the two drummers to use, Dan Hicks or Mike Ferguson. To Jacobsen, the problem was vocalists. Between Hicks, Wilhelm and Olsen, the Charlatans never developed a cogent lead vocalist.

At Coast Recorders on Bush Street, the three-track sessions moved slowly. Jacobsen found it difficult to communicate with the band. Wilhelm often seemed to be out in some zone of his own. He thought Hicks was unnecessarily sarcastic. The record company insisted the band cover the old Coasters number, "The Shadow Knows." Lynne Hughes from the Red Dog came in and sang on a couple of numbers. By and large, the experience simply left Jacobsen frustrated.

In many ways, the crowd was a little fast for the lanky Midwesterner. Hunter took him to visit Owsley one afternoon and handed him a pipe loaded with DMT, a powerful psychedelic known as "workingman's acid" because the ensuing trip was compressed into about forty-five minutes—long enough to last a lunch hour. Jacobsen took a small hit, felt his head spinning, grew disoriented and insisted on leaving. Hunter wanted to stay, but Jacobsen made enough of a scene, irritating everyone else around, that Hunter took him home, where he came down soon enough.

The days of Chuck Jones as drummer for Big Brother and the Holding Company were numbered. Besides the band's suspicion that he was shooting speed behind closed doors at 1090 Page Street, which would help account for the erratic behavior that made his personality so unbearable, he really wasn't a very gifted instrumentalist. They tried Fritz Kasten, the jazz drummer also living at 1090 Page. He could give the band that cross-rhythm, that float they were looking for, but he just wasn't loud enough. Kasten played a week's worth of dates with the band at the Matrix. Norman Mayall also tried his hand at the job. Finally, Peter Albin found David Getz.

Albin heard drumming from a loft in the Mission district while he was eating lunch at a diner downstairs and walked upstairs to investigate. Getz, an ex-New Yorker who was an accomplished painter, had earned a master's degree in art and studied under a Fulbright grant in Poland and was teaching beginning painting at the S.F. Art Institute. But he had also played drums since he was a teenager and once toured Europe as part of a Dixieland band. At the Art Institute, his colleagues in the Studio 13 Jazz Band called him Baby Dave. He joined Big Brother already in full stride, one rehearsal before his first date.

The band was developing a decided style of its own. Jim Gurley adapted his unique finger-picking approach to electric guitar, bombarding the strings with furious flurries, visions of Ornette Coleman and Coltrane dancing in his head. He discovered that Standell amplifiers contained a spring reverb system that made for a particularly explosive sound if the amplifier was dropped on the floor. So he began a practice of picking up the amp, feedback screeching painfully, and throwing it down on the stage to give this satisfying, resonating thud that could provide fitting climaxes to the band's more epic instrumental onslaughts, like the rock transformation the band performed on Grieg's "Hall of the Mountain King."

As much as the band was working, Gurley still needed welfare to support himself and his new family. He had been living with his girlfriend for six years, since before leaving Detroit for San Francisco, and she had recently given birth to their son, Hongo Ishi, named in honor of Gurley's transcendent experience eating mushrooms with Indians in the mountains of Mexico. The name translated means "mushroom man." He told the welfare bureau that he and Nancy had already been married in a church in Mexico. To his surprise, they checked the church records. So James and Nancy, the infant in her arms, went to City Hall and made it official. Peter Albin was already married. He and his pregnant girlfriend made the altar trip the same day that Chet Helms married his longtime girlfriend, Lori Hayman, the previous December.

Nancy Gurley met her future husband when he was still in high school and she was working as a waitress at an all-night coffee house called the Cup of Socrates, an establishment that catered to the beatnik element, such as it was, of Wayne State University. In distinct contrast to his demolition derby driver father, her father was a doctor with season tickets to the opera, symphony and ballet. Although she was only a year and a half older than James, Nancy Gurley completed her master's degree before she was twenty-one years old and eagerly fed his ravenous intellectual appetite. After the baby was born, they moved out of the Pine Street house and settled in a small apartment of their own on Oak Street near the Haight.

The band rehearsed every day in a former firehouse on Henry Street where poster artists Stanley Mouse from Detroit and Alton

Kelley—the founding member of the Family Dog now turned his creative energies to intricate and imaginative psychedelic poster designs—kept their studio. At first, Getz was surprised to watch the band learn songs by playing them over and over the same way. He later came to appreciate the usefulness of this kind of drill as Big Brother was called upon to perform under most adverse conditions, usually self-induced.

With Andrew and Albin trading off lead vocals, the group could get by on the few vocal numbers now included in the sets, either old songs reworked from folk days like "I Know You Rider" or daffy originals like Albin's "Caterpillar." With Signe Anderson of the Airplane and Grace Slick of Great Society in mind, the group toyed with the idea of adding a female vocalist. They tried out Lynne Hughes, the sultry folksinger from the Red Dog who played occasionally with the Charlatans. Mary Ellen Simpson of the all-girl rock band Ace of Cups was also auditioned. With her big crop of blond hair and wild, untrained voice, Simpson certainly could cut an impressive figure. But neither suited the raucous sound of Big Brother.

Peter Kraemer watched the guitarist at the Cedar Alley Coffee House pick up a wine bottle and sing the label copy. The impromptu performance left Kraemer fairly impressed. Although he personally couldn't play an instrument, he thought he could do a fair Mose Allison impression. Kraemer grew up in an artistic household in Virginia City, but moved to the City to attend S.F. State and missed the whole Red Dog Saloon episode. His mother's best friend was Caresse Crosby, famed Paris bohemian of the twenties whose husband ran Black Sun Press and published early works by Henry Miller and Ernest Hemingway. Salvador Dalí once was a house guest and journalist A. J. Liebling was married in their backyard. Kraemer had only recently moved from a Haight-Ashbury Victorian, where Chet Helms and Lori Hayman had also lived, and was working for an independent film distributor, contemplating taking the civil service exam and getting a job at the post office. Like many people his age, he was quite taken with rock and roll after seeing the Beatles in *A Hard Day's Night*. He attended the Rolling Stones concert the previous May at the S.F. Civic Auditorium and couldn't help but notice the Edwardian cowboys taking seats not far from his who turned out to be the Charlatans.

He left the coffee house for a nearby bookstore owned by a friend, who was working behind the counter. "I think I could write some songs instead of taking the civil service exam," he told his friend, "if I could find someone to play guitar."

"I play guitar," said Terry MacNeil, stepping around a bookcase. MacNeil, a student at the S.F. Art Institute, and Kraemer left the bookstore together for someplace around the corner from where MacNeil lived. They began by drinking a bottle of wine and singing the label. Then they wrote "Hello Hello."

The pair spent many late nights until four in the morning sitting in Bob's All Nite Diner on Polk Street working on songs together. After putting together more than a dozen acceptable numbers, they went looking for other musicians. Helms sent them to see Rodney Albin at 1090 Page Street. Albin took out his violin—he and his brother Peter had started out playing together in mid-peninsula bluegrass bands like the Liberty Hill Aristocrats—and he introduced them to Fritz Kasten, the jazz drummer currently living in the rooming house. They made peculiar-sounding, all-acoustic music, a kind of Arabian Nights feel to go with Kraemer's surrealistic compositions like "Anthropomorphic Misidentification Blues." They called the band Sopwith Camel after the World War I fighter plane, also prominent in the "Peanuts" cartoon strip, and recorded a two-track version of a campy Kraemer tribute to Batman in anticipation of the upcoming TV show. But Kraemer and MacNeil wanted to head more in the direction of rock and roll.

Kraemer met Norman Mayall, who was running around with a movie camera at the Trips Festival. Mayall, who had belonged to one of the early incarnations of the Paul Butterfield Blues Band, could supply the big beat Kraemer sought. Mayall brought along his pal, Willie Sievers, a guitarist and songwriter. Bassist Martin Beard, a trained musician they found through a newspaper ad, completed the lineup. Bobby Collins played bass briefly with the band and sent a tape of three tunes—including "Hello Hello"—to Erik Jacobsen, whom Collins knew vaguely through associations in the folk scene. The first time he heard the song, Jacobsen knew it would be a hit and wanted to make the record. The parallels with the Spoonful were obvious and Jacobsen flew out to meet the band.

Collins picked him up at the airport in a hearse and drove him to a parking lot outside Corte Madera in Marin to wait for the band. Collins lived in an old duck-hunting house suspended on stilts above a muddy marsh and reached only over a precarious walkway, perhaps a hundred and fifty yards long, made of boards balanced on a frame hammered into the mud. The band, who had played a party for a hoity-toity private girls school that night, pulled up and emerged from the car, all dressed in evening clothes, top hats and tails down to the ebony walking sticks. "Thank you for coming," said Kraemer. "Come with us please," leading Jacobsen, Collins, the band and their manager—the owner of the bookstore where Kraemer and MacNeil met—across the bog to this otherworldly house, decorated in animal skins, dinosaur bones and other unusual clutter. Collins slept on a pallet surrounded by prisms and windchimes.

The band needed a real manager, Jacobsen insisted. If the Camel signed with him, the band would also have to sign with his management associate. Sievers, a relatively accomplished musician, once belonged to a band in Dallas that had scored a modest regional hit and he was adamant that the Camel make hit records. The band had only recently started playing around local clubs like the Matrix and, although Kraemer did not see himself as a terribly valuable vocalist, the band was received as having an almost professional look. But the prevailing sentiment on the burgeoning San Francisco rock scene was to be suspicious of the established industry, to not sell out and, especially, to not go to New York. After lengthy consideration, the Camel decided what to do. Sell out and go to New York.

Joe McDonald took his first acid trip that autumn, walking through the streets of Berkeley, watching the leaves changing colors, bending, twisting and melting in front of him. He was sleeping on the living room floor of Ed Denson, his partner in producing *Rag Baby* magazine, having left his wife and any semblance of the straight life inalterably behind. He and Barry Melton were joined by a younger friend of Melton's from high school in Van Nuys, Bruce Barthol, another product of a progressive family whose father was a psychology professor and encouraged his interest in politics.

The three of them took an apartment behind the Jabberwock, the Berkeley folk club down Telegraph Avenue less than a mile from the campus. McDonald and Melton did a short tour of Pacific Northwest campuses in the wake of the *Songs of Opposition* record the previous fall. Barthol dropped out of UC-Berkeley at the beginning of the spring semester. They lived on peanut butter, powdered milk and white bread. With tambourine player Paul Armstrong, they played as an acoustic band at the Jabberwock. But with drummer John Francis Gunning, the band started to dabble in electric music. Barthol rented a Mosrite bass with screw-in pickups that routinely worked themselves loose. Ed Denson signed on as manager, a laissez-faire associate, hardly a hustler, barely a businessman.

McDonald, whose writing veered sharply toward impressionistic and away from the political once he started taking acid, had composed an ethereal ode to pot smoking called "Bass Strings." For the public debut of the piece, the band all ate peyote and went to perform at another Berkeley folk club called the Cabal. McDonald experienced deep pangs of paranoia, thinking the cops would burst in at any moment and drag them off the stage for singing this song about grass. But when it was over, the band all knew some new realm had been breached, some new plateau realized. With this breathless gestalt, they were wed to rock.

Politics was never far away from the band. Barthol worried about the draft, having applied for a conscientious objector's deferment and being subjected to all the attendant humiliations. Paul Armstrong had already won his CO deferment and at one point worked with the Navy, where he unloaded bodies shipped home from Vietnam, a horrifying and shattering experience for him. He was currently spending his CO time volunteering for Goodwill Industries, a much more acceptable alternative service.

The band began to make twice-weekly appearances to packed houses at the Jabberwock. After hating the appellation at first, McDonald was even getting used to his stage name, Country Joe. He answered the phone one afternoon at the Jabberwock and heard a cheerful voice on the other end. "Hi, this is Dynamite Annie." McDonald knew her well, Annie Johnston of the Cleanliness and Godliness Skiffle Band. "Hello, Dynamite Annie," McDonald laughed. "This is Country Joe."

Before ever setting foot on the stage of the Fillmore, the band was a full-fledged Berkeley phenomenon just across the bay. The next "issue" of *Rag Baby* was another record—this one a 33⅓, seven-inch disk featuring a Melton rocker, "Thing Called Love," McDonald's "Bass Strings" and a minor masterpiece of acid rock, basely loosely on Grieg's "Hall of the Mountain King," which McDonald recalled from his days as a symphony trombonist and performed on harmonica, titled "Section 43." The cover pictured the band leaning against a Goodwill truck, a farewell gesture for Armstrong, who left the group shortly thereafter. With the record on sale only at the counter of Moe's Books in Berkeley, copies nevertheless sold faster than Ed Denson could keep them in print.

Matthew Katz may not have become more imperious and inaccessible once the members of the Airplane executed their contract with him, but it certainly seemed that way to the musicians. When Bill Graham wanted to book the band for his opening weekend at the Fillmore in February, Katz put him through one of those prolonged circuitous dissertations in which he sometimes seemed to specialize. Graham called on Katz in his California Street digs, where Katz was laid up in bed, but meeting with an insurance salesman anyway. For several hours, Graham listened to Katz discourse on subjects as far-flung as theology and as near at hand as how to run the Fillmore. When Graham finally made his offer, Katz acted offended. "You've got a lot of gall," he told Graham. "Don't you know you're talking about the greatest group in America?"

"I didn't realize I was touching gold," Graham said. And so it went. When Graham finally departed, he had sealed a deal for the Airplane to play the three nights for fifteen hundred dollars, exactly the price he went into negotiations planning to pay.

Katz didn't have much luck booking the Airplane. He arranged for a pair of dates in British Columbia in January. The band slept on floors and lost money. In March, the group was added to a bill at the San Jose Civic Auditorium starring jazz pianist Ramsey Lewis, although Lewis strongly objected to the band's performing that night. In April, the Airplane played three weekends at the Fillmore (including supporting the triumphant return of the Paul Butterfield Blues Band). During the first weekend that month, Katz left town, with the group under the impression he went to New York on business. Actually, he took a vacation in the Bahamas, but what pissed off Balin was that Katz made a gift to his girlfriend of Balin's only guitar, a really fine forty-year-old Martin that Kaukonen helped him buy. Balin had lent it to Katz at his request and was astonished when he asked for its return to have Katz casually allow that he had given it away.

Balin also collected the two-thousand-dollar fee from Graham that weekend and disbursed most of the money among the members of the group, scrupulously noting the payments and the amounts, with receipts for everything. Balin, already voicing dissatisfaction with the way Katz kept records, handed the package over to the manager when he returned the next week. "Here," he told Katz. "This is how you keep a record." None of the musicians had seen any of the twenty-thousand-dollar RCA Victor advance. Kaukonen was borrowing money from his parents and grandparents.

Katz served as co-producer of the album sessions taking place during the spring at RCA Victor Studios in Hollywood, along with Tommy Oliver, a friend of Katz's since Air Force days together in the early fifties and a square, old-fashioned record producer. The Airplane insisted on getting engineer Dave Hassinger, who had recorded the Rolling Stones doing "Satisfaction" in the very same room the previous year, but Katz and Oliver kept having bright ideas, like the glockenspiel part they added to the middle of Balin's tender "Come Up the Years." Flying on acid, Casady looked at Katz one night in his red-satin-lined black robe, wide-brimmed Spanish hat and neatly trimmed Van Dyke beard and thought he was looking at the devil.

Meanwhile, drummer Skip Spence wanted to take a leave of absence from the band. He was hanging out at the Russian River one weekend when the idea of a trip to Mexico came up. Spence, Martha Wax and another couple took off in a van on the spur of the moment, stopping in Los Angeles, where Spence duly informed Katz he would be out of town a while and Wax picked up a phony ID. Wax had known Spence for a couple of years, since she introduced herself to him in the park in Sausalito. In those days, he was a happy spirit with bright eyes and a light, airy attitude. Wax didn't think he was handling the drug scene very well. He was often spacey and somewhat scary. They stayed in Mexico a week or so, then Spence went back to San Francisco, leaving his sixteen-year-old friend stranded penniless.

When he returned, Spence found Balin furious. Spence was fired—as soon as a replacement could be found. Balin talked to a couple of drummers around town, but it was Katz who contacted Earl Palmer, top Hollywood studio drummer, who suggested Spencer Dryden. A former jazz drummer making a living playing behind strippers and giving rim-shots to comics at a Sunset Strip club called the Interlude, Dryden would take his breaks downstairs at another club called the Trip, where he was introduced to the new rock sound of groups like the Byrds, the Mothers of Invention, Lovin' Spoonful. He saw the future and started growing his hair.

When Katz called, he wouldn't tell Dryden the name of the band, but he did play an indecipherable snippet of a record over the phone. Finally, Katz broke down. "They're from San Francisco and they're going to be the next big thing," he told Dryden. "They're called Jefferson Airplane." Oddly enough, Dryden had heard of the band. Katz and Dryden flew up to San Francisco.

Dryden listened to the band rehearse at Balin's Haight-Ashbury apartment, while kids danced in the street outside. He was captivated. He watched in amazement as Kantner walked down the street smoking a joint. They all talked at Lynell's Coffee Shop on Haight, where the band frequently held business meetings, and Dryden was asked if he would move to San Francisco. The following night, the deal was cemented over espressos at Enrico's and Dryden headed back to Los Angeles to settle his affairs and move north. Spence, on his way back to Mexico, shared the plane ride down to Los Angeles with the Airplane's new drummer. "Are you sure you want to do this?" Dryden asked Spence.

"Man, this stuff is happening up here," Spence said. "I'm a guitar player. I'll be back."

In Katz's absence, Balin also accepted an offer from the Berkeley Folk Festival to be the first rock group to appear at the established event. Katz disapproved. He had already scheduled dates in Seattle that would conflict with the Fourth of July festival appearance. He didn't like Balin's assuming his responsibilities, although he was able to rearrange the Seattle dates. Balin was frustrated and angry with Katz. Tension had been mounting between band and manager for several months, although Katz was still able to command enough loyalty in May for the band to sign a publishing contract with him. But until Balin collected the money for the Fillmore weekend, Katz had been the only person who could write a check on the Airplane bank account. After that, accounts were opened for every band member. Katz never showed the band any books or bank records, no matter how often he was asked. Balin decided to have it out with the band's manager. The two met at Katz's Washington Street office, where the Airplane also kept the group's equipment and sometimes rehearsed.

Balin told Katz he was disgusted with the poor job he thought Katz was doing. Katz was not living up to his promises, Balin said.

People didn't want to talk with him, didn't want to do business with him. Balin heard bad words about him everywhere he went. He asked, once again, to see the books. Katz blew up.

He wiped his hand across his desk. Papers and folders went flying. He told Balin he didn't have to tell him anything. Balin was nothing, Katz said. *He* was the Jefferson Airplane, he told Balin, his face growing purple with rage. Katz stood up and looked straight at Balin. "You're fired," he said.

That was too much for Balin to take—Katz thinking he could fire him from his own band. He walked out of the office without another word. When he told the band about the episode, a good laugh was had by all.

James Gurley remembered Janis Joplin from hearing her sing the blues at the Coffee Gallery in North Beach a couple of years before. Peter Albin recalled sitting next to her about the same time at the KPFA folk circle, this unattractive woman with the acne-pitted face, belting out white-hot blues and strumming a guitar, while he stole glances down her unbuttoned shirt front at her braless breasts. She originally came to San Francisco with Chet Helms in January 1963 on a whirlwind fifty-hour hitchhike out of Austin, where Helms first met her when she was attending the University of Texas and singing "Silver Threads and Golden Needles" in local folk clubs. But life in San Francisco turned into a living hell for her and Joplin had grabbed a bus back home the previous June, an eighty-eight-pound desperate wretch ravaged from shooting speed.

Her North Beach days had not been happy. Supporting herself with a series of odd jobs and occasionally dealing speed, she made the rounds of the folk clubs—Coffee and Confusion, Coffee Gallery, Fox and the Hounds—blazing out blues with a husky, wrenching voice far removed from the birdlike contraltos common to female singers of the day. Bessie Smith was her idol and Billie Holiday her role model. *Lady Sings the Blues*, the autobiography of the tragic jazz vocalist, was her bedside reader. A month after she first arrived, she was arrested in Berkeley for shoplifting. Her love life was a blur of different men and women. She tried hooking, without success—she was too ugly for guys to fuck and pay for it, she joked. She moved to New York for a summer, but returned and grew even more deeply under the spell of methedrine. She fell in love with another speed freak, who ended up

68

in a mental hospital, unhinged by his drug use. Joplin herself tried to gain admittance to the psychiatric wing of S.F. General, but was refused by hospital officials leery of drug addict scams. She ultimately scurried home to Port Arthur, beaten into submission by her hopeless life.

Back home, she reverted to cashmere sweaters and pleated skirts, her hair worn up in a prim bun, as if making over her appearance could serve as antidote to the grubby, poisonous existence she fled. Seeking the conformity of the small-town life she had previously scorned may have seemed like a balm to heal some deep wounds, but it wasn't long before she was back in Austin, singing in clubs, contemplating hooking up with the 13th Floor Elevators, the first psychedelic Texas rock band.

Helms, no longer devoted exclusively to managing Big Brother, was too busy running his new enterprise, the Avalon Ballroom, so he dispatched another former Texan, Travis Rivers, who knew her from her hometown of Port Arthur, to bring Joplin back to join Big Brother. She allowed Rivers to sexually suborn her. It made a good story and she had been without a lover of any kind for a long, dry spell since coming back to Texas. But she was also clearly impressed by the important new role Helms had carved out for himself in San Francisco. She had never sung with a band before, but she was anxious to try this new rock and roll thing. She believed Helms's assurances that San Francisco had changed, although a residual fear nagged her that she could, once again, fall in with bad company.

Big Brother went to Virginia City in May to play the Red Dog Saloon. Peter Albin rushed home between gigs, a mad five-hour dash back to the Bay Area, to witness the birth of his daughter and return to play the next night. Lacking the Charlatans' sense of living theater, Big Brother didn't fit in the same way. To owner Unobski, the musicians were savages, reckless drug fiends with little else to recommend them. In the intervening year, San Francisco had opened up and Virginia City changed barely at all. When Sam Andrew casually lit up a pipeful of pot in the barroom at the Red Dog, the bartendress turned apoplectic. "Put that out, quick," she hissed under her tongue. "That's the sheriff over there."

David Getz had dreamed about the new chick singer from Texas, that she would be beautiful and they would have a mad affair. He wasn't the only one in the band surprised when this rather plain, almost homely girl with bad skin in shorts, a thin sleeveless cotton blouse with her hair piled in a bun showed up at the Henry Street rehearsal hall that afternoon early in June. She sang a couple of songs. She was nervous and her voice sounded thin and frantic. That weekend at the Avalon, Big Brother started out with the band's typical car-crash avalanche, Gurley hurtling sonics onto a rumbling heap of crashing drums and runaway rhythms. With no particular fanfare, Janis Joplin was introduced. She sang a couple of numbers without making a big impression on anybody either way. The other band members talked about whether or not to keep her. They kept her.

SUMMER 1966

David Getz never came any closer to his dream about having an affair with the new singer than a fumbling encounter in a backseat that never went anywhere. But Janis Joplin nevertheless could shock him when they were off shooting pool together at the Anxious Asp, a noted North Beach hangout, early in her days with Big Brother. Getz still worked his day job at the Old Spaghetti Factory and Janis was living at Pine Street with Travis Rivers, shortly after first arriving in town. An attractive young black woman, obviously someone Joplin knew, kept hanging around. When Getz and Joplin left, she let out a low moan. "Oooh-wee, does she turn me on," Joplin said.

The admission startled Getz. "Oh yeah," Joplin told him, "we had a thing going." She certainly didn't seem embarrassed to Getz, who didn't want to talk about it. He couldn't believe that she was a lesbian, bisexual or whatever she was, and put the thought out of his mind.

It was James Gurley, not Getz anyway, who first initiated a full-fledged affair with the band's new singer, a circumstance over which Nancy Gurley expressed profound displeasure. In fact, she threw

Gurley out of their apartment and he went to live with Joplin for a couple of weeks before going back home to his wife and their infant son. That didn't keep Nancy Gurley and Janis Joplin from striking up a deep friendship when the band moved in July to live together in a woodsy, former hunting lodge said to have been visited by Teddy Roosevelt outside a tiny town called Lagunitas in the hills of Marin.

Nancy Gurley combined the literate intellect of someone with a master's degree in English and the funky warmth of a hippie earth mother. Like a gypsy queen, she swathed herself in colorful scarves, layers of clothing and wore slips as dresses, her arms covered in bracelets. She quickly became an important role model for the malleable Joplin. She showed Joplin how to use different essential oils on each finger and sniff the scents when stoned. She lent Joplin a sense of style at this critical juncture in her development. Perhaps more significantly, she also reintroduced Joplin to her old nemesis—speed.

Janis settled upstairs in a large sunny room of the main house, next door to Peter and Cindy Albin and their infant daughter, Lisa. Also living in the main house were David Getz and James and Nancy Gurley with Hongo Ishi. In the small cabin in the back was Sam Andrew and his short, dark ladyfriend, Rita Bergman, whose nickname was Speedfreak Rita. The other band members could hear them late into the night, raising hell in their cottage. While neither Cindy nor Peter Albin did drugs, the other three women often stayed up all night talking, stringing beads and shooting speed. They covered an entire wall with beads and Nancy Gurley made a practice of draping herself in strands of antique glass beads.

"Wanna shot?" Rita would ask. "C'mon, let me shoot you up." She liked to handle the injections, a habit Joplin soon enough picked up. All three of them fought over who would fix David Getz, the first night he joined the ladies. Nancy won.

Nancy Gurley insisted on living on her own terms. Peter and Cindy Albin tried in vain to establish more or less conventional hours for the household, so they could put their infant daughter to bed. They clashed with Nancy and Rita over housekeeping, a bourgeois affectation Nancy Gurley spurned. As far as she was concerned, if Cindy Albin wanted the dishes done, she could do them. Mishka, the Gurleys' hyperactive German Shepherd, chewed furniture or whatever she wanted without discipline. When she gave birth to a litter of puppies, Nancy Gurley showed no interest in getting the dogs vaccinated.

They all developed distemper. James Gurley and David Getz accepted the nasty chore of killing them. After first finding it impossible trying to dispatch the stricken puppies by bashing their heads with a beer bottle, they finished the job by strangling the dogs with their bare hands.

The band auditioned for Bobby Shad of Mainstream Records, a practiced shyster who rummaged the peripheries of jazz and blues, making cheap records and paying the artists as little as he could. Somehow Shad caught wind of this pastoral parochial rock scene growing in San Francisco and came to check it out. In a studio housed in the old Spreckels mansion on Buena Vista Park in the Haight, Shad paraded through the room Big Brother, Wildflower, Final Solution, Harbinger Complex, along with a couple of other even lesser lights. While Big Brother went through its paces in the other room, Shad gleefully told Helms in the control booth how easy it would be to screw the band out of publishing money and sales royalties, attempting to enlist the group's manager in a rather typical record industry ripoff. But Shad misjudged the ethics of the circumstance. Helms stopped the band mid-song and indignantly marched the group out of the audition.

Janis Joplin and Pigpen's getting together was an inevitability recognized by everyone who knew them. Both were hard-drinking blues singers, uncomfortable in the psychedelic realm in which they found themselves. Both shielded their insecurity and sensitivity with tough-talking exteriors. When the Dead moved to the vacant Girl Scout camp, Camp Lagunitas, down the road from Teddy Roosevelt's hunting lodge, she used to make her way down to Pigpen's cabin at night, where he kept a beat-up piano and a healthy supply of booze. The rest of his band could hear their singing, laughing and moaning through the still night air long past midnight.

The Dead returned from Los Angeles in April to accept what seemed like a lucrative date at Longshoremen's Hall, headlining a three-night event advertised as "Trips 196?", a transparent effort to capitalize on the original Trips Festival. Rifkin wanted to take over the Ashbury Street rooming house he managed and install the Dead as tenants. He started by giving Pigpen the room off the kitchen. By May, however, the band had made summer headquarters out of Rancho Olompali, a home for mentally retarded children empty during the summer. Built on the site of California's only Indian battle, Olompali was a rambling ranch house with swimming pool and barn, a comfortable, wide-open space nestled in the rolling hills of Novato in northern Marin County. Under the hot summer sun, acid-soaked bacchanals took place with great regularity.

Writers, dealers, local teenagers, motorcycle gangs, scenesters of every description mingled with the musicians. Quicksilver lived only miles away on the dairy ranch. Big Brother was just down the road. The musical community was small and not elite. Little-known bands like Clover or the Ph Factor Jug Band were as welcome as members of the Charlatans, who would show up, as was their custom, armed with antique rifles and sidearms. One afternoon, Hunter, looped beyond comprehension on acid, cranked off a few rounds into the hillside with his Winchester carbine, only to have a naked couple jump up out of the tall grass, terror-stricken, and run away. Garcia wandered out to talk to Hunter, who was raving, unsure whether or not he had shot someone, a distinction somewhat too fine to get across in his state of agitation. The chemicals didn't help and Garcia had ingested his share as well. All that the Grateful Dead guitarist understood was Hunter's wild gestures and the cocked gun he was waving around. Garcia flipped, unsure if Hunter intended to shoot him or not, and quickly made his way back to the house. Richie Olsen and his girlfriend drove Hunter home, reassuring him all the way that he had not shot anyone.

The Dead would set up the band's equipment on the lawn between the house and the pool and long, free-for-all jam sessions ensued. A good percentage of the crowd ran around naked. These frolicsome events fostered a sense of community and camaraderie among those who attended. Sometimes the weekend-long revels ended with the Dead's packing up the group's instruments and amplifiers and heading down to San Francisco for an impromptu concert in Golden Gate Park on Sunday afternoon.

The band alternated between weekends at the Fillmore and at the Avalon through the summer, sharing bills with the Airplane, Quicksilver, Big Brother, Country Joe and the Fish and Sopwith Camel, among others. Joan Baez and her sister Mimi Farina, along with a few members of the Airplane, joined the band one night at the Fillmore for the Pigpen specialty, a workout of "In the Midnight Hour" lasting nearly a half-hour.

The band drew a repertoire from old folk-blues like Jesse Fuller's "Beat It On Down the Line," a few Dylan tunes, a handful of originals and several brilliantly transformed pieces—"Viola Lee Blues," an old country blues, or "Dancing in the Street," the Motown anthem—reshaped and extended into creations far removed from their origins. Pigpen handled salacious blues numbers like "Good Morning Little Schoolgirl" or "The Same Thing."

The band moved to Camp Lagunitas late in the summer after the lease expired at Olompali. One night the fellows headed down to the Quicksilver ranch without calling ahead. Dressed as Indians in feathers and war paint, they crept up on the main house, surrounded the building and surprised Quicksilver peering in their windows, blowing off firecrackers and smoke bombs. They spied a pipeful of pot and finished the Indian "raid" by smoking the peace pipe. Quicksilver laid plans for comeuppance.

Having arranged an elaborate conspiracy with Bill Graham, Quicksilver intended to stage the return raid on the Dead at the Fillmore during a performance. Dressed as cowboys, they figured to tie the Dead to their amps, dance around and sing "Kaw-liga," the Hank Williams song the band set about learning specifically for this event.

Unfortunately, when the raiding party arrived at the Fillmore on the designated night, the show was running late, so they waited outside. Jimmy Murray, Gary Duncan, David and Girl Freiberg went back to the 1950 Dodge panel truck the band had borrowed for the assault to smoke a joint. Someone saw the band members climb in carrying rifles and called the cops. Racial violence had been flaring all night in the black neighborhood around the Fillmore, with fresh memories of the Watts riots from the previous summer. Consequently, an otherwise innocent sight like a bunch of white guys dressed as cowboys carrying rifles around a black neighborhood struck a raw nerve. When the back door to the panel truck opened a crack and a pistol pointed in at the band members, everybody laughed. When the policeman attached to the pistol appeared, the smiles disappeared. Murray tossed a film can of pot under the seat and everybody went to jail on drugs and weapons charges.

With all the action in the streets of the Fillmore, it was not a good night to be thrown in jail. Angry blacks gave amiable Freiberg a beating, although six-foot, three-inch Murray escaped a similar fate.

Girl Freiberg, still underage, spent the night in familiar surroundings, juvenile hall. Cipollina and Dino Valente, now out of jail and living at the Quicksilver ranch, had gone around the corner for a cup of coffee and missed all the fun. Attorneys Brian Rohan and Mike Stepanian, fearless legal defenders to the San Francisco underground, went to bat, pointing out the drugs were only found on the truck and the truck didn't belong to the band. Charges against the band members were dropped, but their friend's truck was impounded. When they bought it back at auction, the drive shaft had fallen out and had been thrown unceremoniously in the back.

After appearing at the UC-Berkeley Greek Theater in May, guitarist Zal Yanovsky and bassist Steve Boone drove their rental car to the Pacific Heights home of Bill Love, manager of The Committee introduced to the pair by Larry Hankin, one of the stars of the improv troupe and a musical associate of the Spoonful. They wanted to score some pot and Love obliged, selling them a couple of lids. Not far from Love's house, the rock musicians executed an illegal, high-speed U-turn that drew the attention of the police. The pot was found and Yanovsky and Boone were arrested.

Yanovsky, a Canadian citizen already having visa problems, felt especially vulnerable. Red-hot off four consecutive Top Ten singles, the Spoonful stood to lose a lot if half of the band took a drug bust—especially if the lead guitarist was sent home to Canada never to return. They agreed to turn in their source. Some time later, these two, along with their manager and an undercover officer, once again visited Love looking for grass. He didn't have any to sell, but he smoked a couple of joints with the visitors.

Love, who worked during the day at a medical laboratory, wasn't home when the police showed up with warrants. They arrested his girlfriend, who left her baby with the downstairs neighbor on her way to jail. Eventually they came for Love at the lab and led him off in handcuffs. Charges against Boone and Yanovsky were dropped.

The Spoonful never came to his aid. His girlfriend was released, but Love was charged with sale of marijuana. He started a leaflet campaign that the underground press picked up, asking people not to buy Spoonful records or go to their concerts, asking disk jockeys not to play their records, and asking groupies not to ball them. Word of the musicians' deed flashed through the hip underground, promptly branding the favored rock band a traitorous pariah. No less powerful a personage than Bob Dylan manager Albert Grossman attempted to intercede.

Grossman contacted Ron Polte and arranged to fly Polte, Love and his girlfriend to New York, where they attended meetings with a powerful entertainment attorney representing the Spoonful and the group's management. Polte and Love flew home expecting Boone and Yanovsky to appear to testify on Love's behalf, but that never happened. They did submit affidavits, but in their absence and the face of the police officer's testimony, Love was convicted. He did not receive any jail time, but the episode finished the Spoonful in underground circles.

The Tivoli Ballroom engagement in Seattle didn't work out all that well for the Airplane. Katz booked the dates with a promoter who also happened to be an important disk jockey in the market. But the scheduled week-long run ended up cut in half after the unknown band failed to draw a crowd. Signe Anderson had to battle a private security guard before he would allow her baby into the club with her. Club management also tried to enforce a rule allowing only five musicians onstage at a time, expecting the band to perform without the female vocalist. The band left town on the heels of rumors that the Seattle police were looking to arrest the musicians for smoking pot.

After the band played one weekend in July for Chet Helms at the Avalon, Graham raised such an angry stink about the group's working for his competition that the Airplane never appeared again at the Avalon. The group had practically become the house band at the Fillmore, playing at least one headline weekend a month for Graham through the summer. Katz and Graham did not get along, but business was business. Katz so strenuously objected to the band's playing a benefit at the Fillmore, however, that he took off his shoe and threatened to bash it through the amplifier speakers and drum heads if the band tried to take the equipment to the Fillmore. Graham loaned the Airplane the equipment necessary.

The appearance at the Berkeley Folk Festival qualified as a success. Not only did the band make a well-received appearance at the traditional day-long "Jubilee Concert" at the UC-Berkeley Greek Theater that featured all the festival performers, but they played a "Dance Happening" the night before at the Pauley Ballroom on campus with Country Joe and the Fish. Katz approached the Berkeley band about managing the group, promising the musicians weekly stipends, places to live, the works. McDonald called Balin to ask his opinion and Balin told him the Airplane was having its own problems with Katz.

The band appeared on a bill at the Cow Palace with national hitmakers like the Beach Boys, Lovin' Spoonful, the Byrds, Percy Sledge and the Sir Douglas Quintet on June 24 without incident, but the group watched in horror as Katz threw one of his dramatic tantrums in the face of Tom Rounds, program director of San Francisco's chief Top Forty station, who was promoting the July 26 concert at the Cow Palace starring the Rolling Stones in which the Airplane was also to appear. Katz had originally cut a deal with Rounds calling for the Airplane to appear immediately prior to the Stones. He arrived at the concert to have Rounds inform him that the Airplane would instead have to close the first half of the concert. The Stones carried a one-hit, East Coast-based garage band called the Standells ("Dirty Water") as an opening act of their own and the stars of the show were in no mood to be sandbagged by some local favorites.

Katz threatened to sue the Stones, storming after Rounds, making a scene everyone in the backstage area witnessed. He told the band that a lawsuit against the Stones would be good publicity, but the group talked it over with Ralph Gleason, no fan of Katz, who assured the band it would be better if they went ahead and performed anyway. They did.

The following week, the Airplane worked a San Jose club called Loser's North, where they met Jackie DeShannon. Although best known for her hit from the previous year of the Hal David–Burt Bacharach song "What the World Needs Now," she was a savvy veteran of the music business, a songwriter herself and wise to the industry in ways the Airplane didn't yet understand. She talked to the band backstage about managers and bookkeeping. If the band starts to make real money, she told the group, you'll really get screwed if the manager doesn't keep proper, complete financial records. The books Katz never showed the band already were a sore point. The group decided to take action. As soon as the San Jose engagement was over, they found an attorney and had a letter drafted that fired Katz. The next month RCA Victor released *Jefferson Airplane Takes Off.*

Graham tentatively began to develop a gift for showmanship. In April, beat poet Lawrence Ferlinghetti of City Lights Books convinced him to present Soviet poet Andrei Voznesensky, whom Graham double-billed with the Airplane. In June, he booked comedian Lenny Bruce along with the Mothers of Invention. Bruce showed up for his performance two hours late, whacked out of his brain on speed, and proceeded to put on a pathetic performance. He was a defeated soul, obsessed with his martyrdom at the hands of a repressive society. He was no longer funny, only sad. He died six weeks later. His Fillmore show turned out to be the last performance of his life.

When Sopwith Camel was scheduled to appear with Allen Ginsberg at a benefit at the Fillmore, Ginsberg thought it might be a good idea to have the band accompany him as he chanted a few mantras. He visited the group at the huge upper flat the band occupied in a Victorian not far from the Fillmore. Peter Kraemer had taken some especially potent blue acid and Ginsberg found him blissfully walking from room to room, humming to himself. Ginsberg changed his mind about having the band back him. The show went fine. The Camel played an endless jam and Ginsberg recited his mantras by himself. Kraemer also met a beautiful nineteen-year-old ballerina that night who was dancing with Ginsberg, and the meeting proved to be the beginning of a luminous love affair.

Graham also dabbled with theater at the Fillmore. In July, he staged one night of the controversial Michael McClure play, "The Beard," controversial because at the climax of the two-character production Billy the Kid goes down on Jean Harlow. In September, he brought two one-act plays by LeRoi Jones, who came out from New York to direct the production, and piggybacked the one-acts with the Byrds, to ensure an audience.

He ran the hall a minimum of three nights a week and could easily pack twenty-five hundred people in a room with a legal capacity of less than a thousand. At the end of the evening, he and Bonnie would stuff a duffel bag full of cash and head off to their apartment on the Lambretta with as much as five thousand dollars in singles, fives and tens on their back. Once home, they would pour the money on their bed and laugh, before sorting the bills and counting the take on their kitchen table. On Mondays, Graham would tuck a pistol into his coat and take the deposit to the bank.

Over at the Avalon, Helms bought out his partner John Carpenter. His sound man, Bob Cohen, and his light show artist, Bill Ham, and a third member of the Avalon staff became his new partners. For three weekends in a row in July and August, Helms packed the Avalon for Bo Diddley, the pioneer rock and roller, who drew more than two thousand people into a hall even smaller than the Fillmore.

Both ballrooms advertised their shows with elaborate psychedelic posters drawn by a new breed of artists. While Graham favored the relatively more legible handiwork of Wes Wilson, Helms sponsored some of the most inspired and outlandish designs produced by Stanley Mouse and Alton Kelley. The LSD-inspired imagery began making its way into commercial artwork beyond the simple rock concert handbills and people were grabbing the posters themselves off walls and store windows as fast as Graham and Helms could post them.

Crowds jammed both halls every weekend, no matter who played. The bands happily took home a thousand dollars. The small staffs necessary to run the operations worked for their roles in the exciting scene. Business was good. Very good.

Paul Rothchild stepped backstage to talk to Big Brother the last weekend of the Bo Diddley gigs. The Elektra Records artist and repertoire director was riding high through his association with the Paul Butterfield Blues Band, really the first breakthrough on this new underground rock scene, whose second album, *East-West,* produced by Rothchild, had just been released. He was effusive in his compliments. In the cramped dressing room, there was not room for private conversations. "I want to talk to you about doing some recording," he said. "If I could meet you tomorrow, Janis, we can talk about the details."

"Why don't I bring James?" she said.

"Why don't you just come yourself," Rothchild said. "I've got some other people I want you to talk to."

What Rothchild had in mind was contriving a group around a set of hand-picked musicians that would play blues, which he saw as the coming thing on the music scene. He had already contacted guitarists Ry Cooder, Stefan Grossman and Taj Mahal. Taj Mahal was no stranger to prefab groups, having once belonged to a band called the Seven Wonders of the World where each member took his name from a different wonder, and he had kept his name. Rothchild told Joplin she would have a house in Hollywood and a car.

When she told Big Brother about the meeting, tempers flared. The band was scheduled to leave the following week for their first major out-of-town booking, a four-week engagement at Mother Blues in

Chicago for a thousand dollars a week, a run the Airplane had just finished. Peter Albin turned testy with her. "Listen, Janis," he said, "you're going to have to decide right now. Either you're with this band or you're not. Because we're going to Chicago and if you're not, we're getting a new singer."

Janis broke down and cried. "All my life I've been a nobody," she sobbed, "a nobody from Texas everybody looked down on. He's going to give me a house and a car. He wants to make me a star. How can I turn this down?"

When nobody in the band expressed any great sympathy with her plight, she turned indignant. "Don't bandy words with me," she snapped at Sam Andrew like a haughty schoolmarm. She agreed to postpone any decision and make the Chicago trip with Big Brother.

The event shook the band. Having a singer had imposed structure on the band's music and the growth was evident even in the short time Janis had been with Big Brother. Living together lent the enterprise an almost familial bond and her sudden display of self-interest interrupted that particular reverie. Chet Helms allowed that he thought the band could go on just fine without her, but he was spending all his time running the Avalon and his days as manager of Big Brother were coming to an end, his influence on the wane. The band members had come to see their future with Joplin in ways contemplating her departure only made clear.

The band arrived in Chicago having officially severed ties with Helms as manager. He made no hotel reservations for the band and they found themselves pushing amplifiers and equipment up and down the street, systematically rejected by every hotel they approached. Finally, the group descended on Peter Albin's uncle and aunt in suburban Glenview, devout Christians who believed they should open their home to the needy. Of course, suburban Chicago, downtown Chicago for that matter, had seen nothing like the looks of this crew. Joplin dressed in an old bedspread, her hair an uncombed bird's nest, chicken bones for a necklace, patchouli oil for perfume. Beyond the watchful eye of his wife, James Gurley and Joplin resumed their affair. Albin's uncle and aunt were quickly alienated, but his cousins prevailed on their parents to take an unplanned vacation to Florida for the duration of the engagement, leaving the band the run of the house. Sam Andrew and Rita Bergman preferred to find lodging near the club in Old Town, where they could drink in the burly big-city bustle, catching blues giants like Howlin' Wolf in their native habitat.

The booking was nothing short of a disaster. With authentic blues by titans of the field like Muddy Waters or Buddy Guy playing at clubs just up the street, these hippies from San Francisco with their untamed, untailored sound hardly amounted to more than freaks in a sideshow. Nick Gravenites was back in Chicago at the moment and caught up with the band. He thought Janis screeched like a wounded owl. But worst of all, nobody came and club management refused to pay the band halfway through the run. He offered to let them work for the door, but with less than a dozen customers a night, that added up to lunch money and little more. The band went to the local office of the Musicians' Union, old-fashioned Italian fellows who provided sympathetic ears and offered to close the club down, but couldn't think of any way to make the management pay the money. So now Big Brother was stranded in Chicago without any money.

With playwright's timing, in walked Bobby Shad, like Mephistopheles, with a record contract. He offered the band the money necessary to get home in exchange for signing with his Mainstream Records the deal the band had rejected only a few months earlier. Peter Albin thought, money aside, the Mainstream contract might be a way to bind Joplin to the band. The band took the contract to a lawyer Shad recommended, who told the musicians essentially that this was the kind of contract Shad customarily offered and he wouldn't offer anything better. The lawyer knew the Shad operation well since he represented Shad, too.

Anxious to record anyway, the band signed the deal and Shad whisked them into a Chicago studio for a marathon nine-hour session that netted almost half an album. The band played crisply and efficiently, tight from five sets a night at Mother Blues, and Joplin enthusiastically double-tracked her vocals. The other musicians couldn't make the engineer record their instruments with anything approaching the band's customary volume. He had no experience or understanding of this new rock music and insisted on keeping levels far below distortion, which was a standard part of the Big Brother sound.

Ultimately, Shad explained to the band that he never gave advances, so the group resorted to picking up a driveaway car, a 1965 Pontiac Grand Prix, and stuffing all the band's equipment, luggage and five riders in the car and a small trailer. Albin's uncle and aunt gave him airfare home, so Joplin, Andrew, Gurley and Getz headed out across the plains states for the West Coast.

In Nebraska, the wayfarers pulled over to the side of the road in jubilation. Everywhere they looked marijuana was growing. The government first planted the pot during the Second World War to grow hemp for rope, but the weed just took off and spread beyond control. The Big Brother folks quickly yanked up enough to stuff Getz's bass drum full. In Nevada, the party wound up in the courtroom of some small town speed trap, where the judge gave them hell for nothing more than having long hair. Joplin went mad and Getz quietly clamped his hand over her mouth, stifling the profane insults that could have caused some genuine trouble. Back home, they tried the Nebraska bounty, only to discover it useless, all impotent male plants that wouldn't get anyone high no matter how much was smoked.

1967

*It really is much
better than it sounds.*
  —Mark Twain, on first
    hearing the music of
      Richard Wagner

WINTER 1966-67

Jerry Anderson grew to be quite a problem. He went wherever the Airplane did because, in addition to being married to Signe, he worked as the lighting director. But he saw his most important role as sticking up for what he perceived as slights against his wife, making demands on her behalf and generally interfering in what the other musicians saw as matters strictly not his business.

He drank a lot. At the Monterey Jazz Festival, where the Airplane became the first rock band to perform at the prestigious annual event through the influence of Ralph Gleason, a tipsy Anderson stuck a "Jefferson Airplane Loves You" pin on an RCA Victor executive—right through the poor man's shirt into his flesh. Casady, who stayed with the Andersons when he first came to town, suspected him of using heroin, a dark, unwelcome drug in the giddy, psychedelic Airplane camp.

In August, when the band preceded Big Brother into Mother Blues in Chicago on the Airplane's first significant road trip, Signe herself surfaced as the problem. When the band first arrived at the unsavory hotel where they were registered, while equipment was still being unpacked and details sorted out, she realized the luggage carrying the things for her three-month-old daughter was lost. She imperiously dispatched road manager Bill Thompson for diapers, although he thought there were probably more important matters at hand.

After the show that night, Thompson and some of the band members went out to Big John's, a blues club where they hung out hours past midnight. As Thompson crawled into bed around three in the morning, his phone rang. Signe, hysterical, had been trying to reach him for hours. She was quitting, she told him. For an hour and a half, she repeated that it was impossible for her to tour and have a family, while Thompson tried to calm her down.

Balin and Thompson called Bill Graham in San Francisco the next morning and he spoke with her. Eventually, the band conceded several special privileges and higher pay to keep her with the group, and she accepted. That evening, she showed up for the job with her baby and Thompson baby-sat through the performance. When he returned to San Francisco, he talked over the situation with Gleason. "Every band with a female singer has had problems," Gleason told Thompson.

Both Kantner and Balin thought Grace Slick could be the answer. The Airplane and the Great Society had shared many bills over the previous months, so everybody in the band had had a chance to witness her way with an audience. Kantner and Casady in particular were fans and Kantner put Casady up to asking her if she might consider joining the Airplane. He caught up with her at a Great Society performance at the Avalon early in September.

After more than a year ensnared in a nowhere record contract with Autumn Records, the San Francisco label run by ex-Top Forty deejays Tom Donahue and Bobby Mitchell, the Great Society appeared to be on the verge of landing a major record deal. Autumn producer Sly Stone put the band through exacting, practically humiliating paces in the studio, extracting a flimsy version of the Darby Slick song, "Somebody to Love," written in a depressive fog around dawn one morning, coming down on LSD after spending the evening waiting for his girlfriend to come home. The label had pressed up some copies the previous March, but had never really released the record. Mitchell was dying from a brain tumor and Donahue was taking too much acid to show great interest in his business as it crashed against the shoals. Having deposed hippie scenemaker John Carpenter as manager in favor of a Los Angeles-based music industry professional named Howard Wolf, the band held hopes of joining the ranks of the Airplane inside the recording industry.

But guitarist Darby Slick was exploring his growing interest in Indian classical music. He and Society bassist Peter Vandergelder took classes from master sarodist Ali Akbar Khan and talked about going to India to study. Darby Slick was also using heroin at the time. He and his brother, Jerry Slick, filmmaker and Great Society drummer, were raised in the elite enclave of Palo Alto next door to Grace Wing, the privileged daughter of the investment banker who went to all the best schools and grew up to marry the boy next door, Jerry Slick, and thus become Grace Slick.

At posh Finch College, she hobnobbed with the young, rich and beautiful. Smart and literate, she opted for a bohemian life in San Francisco with her S.F. State film student husband. They turned on to psychedelics, started sleeping around on one another and grew bored in a listless marriage. Inspired by their friends in the Charlatans and the early performances of the Airplane itself, the three Slicks banded together with a couple of other associates as the Great Society in fall 1965. The second performance the band gave was at the first Family Dog show at Longshoremen's Hall. After the Great Society appeared with the Blues Project, the accomplished new rock band from New York, at the opening of the Avalon the previous April, Grace Slick started to look more and more critically at her little homegrown band. Although Darby Slick possessed a certain skill on guitar, the band really began and ended with Grace Slick, singing, playing keyboards or simply fronting the group. She wanted to play with better musicians.

So Casady's entreaty couldn't have come at a more propitious intersection of lifelines. She was receptive, but didn't commit. The following night, Great Society topped a bill also featuring both the Airplane and the Dead at the Fillmore, a benefit for the Divisadero Street jazz club, Both/And. A friend of Darby Slick's joined the band for one of the most thrilling performances Darby remembered the band's giving, with Grace filling the hall with the ringing finale of her song "White Rabbit" to close the show: "Feed your head . . . feed your head."

While the band was packing up equipment, getting ready to leave, Jerry Slick called bassist Vandergelder and his brother together. "The Airplane has asked Grace to join them," he said, "and I've advised her to accept."

The Great Society never performed again. The following week the record contract Howard Wolf negotiated with Columbia Records arrived in the mail. Darby Slick, angry and feeling betrayed, did go off to India to study music. Bill Thompson bought Grace Slick's contract from Wolf for $750, although Wolf kept the publishing rights to the three songs she brought to the Airplane: "Father Bruce" (her ode to Lenny Bruce), "Somebody to Love" and "White Rabbit."

A voluptuous brunette who once contemplated a modeling career, Grace Slick was also a confident, mouthy wiseass who strong drink only made more so, ready to hold her own even among the formidable company of the Airplane gentlemen. It only remained to inform Signe. To handle that odious chore the band appointed Thompson, acting as temporary manager since the firing of Katz ("We want you to talk to the straights," Kantner told him).

Thompson found her at home playing with the baby. He told her nobody in the band wanted to play anymore with her, her husband and the baby. She took the news stoically at first, until she heard who was replacing her. Devastated, she kept repeating that the real reason was that the band preferred Grace to her. Thompson finally blurted out the truth. It isn't you, he told Signe, it's your husband nobody can stand. He left, having calmed her down somewhat with the offer of six thousand dollars severance pay the band had voted, and drove back to his apartment, where the band waited. Thompson delivered a detailed account of the conversation. She was the fourth member jettisoned in the first year of the band's existence, but the group still decided to send her a big bouquet of flowers for the Fillmore stage that weekend.

Grace Slick rehearsed in the solitude of her own apartment, studying the band's album over and over. She finally got a chance to rehearse with the band when Signe had to take her baby to the doctor one afternoon. The disorganized, nutty rehearsal astonished her. Kantner discussed a song with Kaukonen they had played three weeks earlier. Kaukonen allowed he didn't remember it. Conversations ran everywhere. All suggestions were considered and chaos ruled. When Grace left after two hours, she hadn't sung one song all the way through.

It was decided that she should watch the band from backstage at the next show to learn the repertoire and, for that purpose, she showed up that weekend in October at the Fillmore. Kantner rushed up to her. Signe wasn't there. "Do you think you can do it?" he asked. Without time to agonize over clothing, makeup or any part of ordinary stage fright, Grace Slick stepped onto stage with the Jefferson Airplane and sang, ready or not. Scared shitless, she discovered the Airplane to be about ten times as loud as the Great Society. She couldn't hear herself. She didn't know the songs. What she did know, she couldn't remember. Somehow she made it through the set.

Kesey crossed the border at Brownsville, Texas, with alcohol on his breath, riding a horse and wearing bright red boots and a cowboy hat. When border officials asked him his name he told them "Singing Jimmy." When they asked him how long he'd been in Mexico, he said he didn't know. He'd been drunk the whole damn time. They let him back into the country without question.

The Pranksters that traveled south after the Watts acid test found Kesey in Mazatlan posing as a mild-mannered ornithologist in a tweed jacket and horn-rimmed glasses. The arrival of the Day-Glo bus and encampment of crazies blew that disguise. But the only people who didn't know Kesey was in Mexico by this time were the FBI. The bus moved on to Manzanillo and the group took a pair of houses on the beach. Mountain Girl delivered her baby in May and named her Sunshine.

Ron Polte wrote his old Chicago friend, Julius Karpen, while Karpen was in Mexico with the Pranksters to tell him that he was now managing Quicksilver Messenger Service and that Karpen should come back to San Francisco and help out. Thinking it was strange for Polte to be working in the communication business, he nevertheless packed up, his leg still in a cast from a near-fatal car crash, and took the bus back to Tijuana. He walked across the border, wrote a bad check to Western Airlines and headed back to the City.

Kesey himself made his way back to Palo Alto, and couldn't resist a public appearance of sorts. He turned up October 1 at the S.F. State Trips Festival, a three-day affair featuring, among other performers, his old pals, the Grateful Dead. Somebody dosed Pigpen, who, despite living in the thick of the Dead, had never taken acid before. Scully took him back to the rooming house at 710 Ashbury, where the band had settled after leaving Camp Lagunitas, Rifkin having managed to clear the place out for the band. He whiplashed back and forth between anger and fear, crying and not being able to move his feet. "I can't move my neck," he moaned. Scully sat up with him until his girlfriend, Veronica, showed up. She trained her anger at Scully. "You're the manager and you let this happen," she said.

Veronica Barnard had moved in with Pigpen only a few weeks earlier. She quit her job as a bank teller and became his full-time lady. A buoyant black woman who grew up going to Seventh Day Adventist schools around her hometown of Vallejo, she loved acid herself, but thought it criminal to rabbit-punch Pigpen, who, despite a gruff exterior, was a teddy bear of a man who wouldn't dream of hurting anybody. "It's a sin," she snapped at Scully.

But around four in the morning, holed up in the campus radio station with Hell's Angels guarding the door, Kesey, the LSD fugitive, made his return by electronics, broadcasting to the whacked-out assemblage in the school cafeteria, strumming a guitar and rapping his delirious nonsense from the bowels of a nearby building: "You who stand, sit and crawl around and about the floor about you and above you on the ceiling that madness that's running in color is your brain."

Now the game was afoot. A few days later, he dropped by an English class at Stanford taught by a friend of his and eluded the cops, who missed his impromptu lecture by a mere ten minutes. Next he gave an interview to a reporter from the *S.F. Chronicle* where he taunted the FBI. "I intend to stay in this country as a fugitive and as salt in J. Edgar Hoover's wounds," he said. Kesey also announced he planned to throw a giant "Acid Test Graduation Ceremony" for users of psychedelic drugs somewhere in San Francisco on Halloween. "They'll wear costumes so I can be in a costume without being noticed," he said.

The bus was parked plainly in sight during the Love Pageant Rally in Golden Gate Park panhandle on October 6, the day the California legislation making LSD illegal went into effect. Kesey in a cowboy suit popped up in the middle of the madcap festivities—a parade through the Haight-Ashbury, acidheads in comical costumes, music by the Dead and Big Brother—and disappeared again. Bolder and bolder, Kesey even gave an interview to television news and was still laughing about it less than an hour after it was broadcast when a carful of FBI agents pulled over the bright red truck in which he was riding on the freeway. It was a chance sighting, an unhappy piece of serendipity, but Kesey surrendered after a brief dash over the freeway fence and through a children's baseball game, agents in full pursuit.

His intrepid attorneys devised a novel plan to gain his freedom on bail, pleading that Kesey was one of the few people in society with the credibility to talk teenagers out of using the dread LSD. Kesey described his graduation ceremony as an "uncompleted mission" and both judges in his two pending cases were convinced. Kesey was freed on bail.

In the six months since Kesey skipped town, the scene had changed drastically. Turf had been staked out. Bill Graham, the man with the clipboard who tried to keep Kesey from letting Angels in the side door at the Trips Festival, now bossed the Fillmore. Chet Helms conducted his fiefdom at the Avalon. The Grateful Dead were no longer the scraggly little band that played Prankster parties. Quicksilver Messenger Service, as Julius Karpen discovered on ending his Prankster exile, was not a communications business. Many individual entrepreneurs had set up shop, hoping to snag some little corner of the growing community to call their own. But Kesey still held some sway. He signed an agreement with Graham to produce this LSD graduation at Winterland, an old ice rink with a capacity of more than five thousand two blocks from the Fillmore. He talked another group of producers, the Calliope Company, into releasing the Grateful Dead from the band's scheduled gig Halloween at California Hall.

Kesey announced he wanted the psychedelic community to take the next step beyond acid. He said he didn't know all of what that meant, but he knew some. "Leary's supposed to be coming out and he's supposed to know pieces of it," he told reporters. "And Jerry Garcia with his music knows pieces of it."

Word filtered back to Graham that Kesey and Owsley were planning to tap the water system at Winterland and zap everybody out of their gourds, that they were going to smear LSD on doorknobs, railings, walls, chairs, that the whole scheme was one big shuck, one giant prank. In a panic, Graham scrambled for advice. He went so far as to call Chet Helms and ask what Helms knew. The night before the event was scheduled, Graham pulled out. With him went Winterland. Kesey and the Pranksters held a private graduation at the Calliope Company warehouse and the Anonymous Artists of America played.

Joe Smith and his wife were dining at Ernie's, the elegant San Francisco eatery where film director Alfred Hitchcock kept and regularly visited his wine collection. Smith, vice-president of Warner Brothers Records and a former disk jockey who always looked like the man who walked off the top of the wedding cake, wore a dark blue suit. His wife was in basic black and pearls. Tom Donahue reached him by phone at dinner. "The Dead want to talk with you now," Donahue told Smith. "They're at the Avalon."

"We're dressed up," Smith said.

"No one will notice," said Donahue.

The four-hundred-fifty-pound former Top Forty deejay whose nightly radio opening line was "I'm here to clean up your face and mess up your mind" had assumed a statesman-like role in the burgeoning scene after folding his Autumn Records label. He, in fact, sold his artist roster to Smith and Warner Brothers. Donahue and his partner, Bobby Mitchell, had also operated the city's first psychedelic nightclub, Mother's, on Broadway the previous year, where the Byrds and the Lovin' Spoonful, among others, appeared before that enterprise ran out of steam (and money). Now Donahue took a lot of acid and lunched daily at an outdoor table at Enrico's on Broadway and never, never picked up his own check.

When Smith and his wife climbed those stairs on Sutter Street leading to the ballroom, they might as well have been stepping into another world. At Warner's, Smith had built a successful record label on hits by acts like comedian Allan Sherman, sanitary folksingers Peter, Paul and Mary and chirpy pop vocalists like Petula Clark. The company forayed into current rock no more daringly than Dino, Desi and Billy, two teenage sons bearing the names of their famous Hollywood star fathers and a friend of theirs. What on earth could have prepared him for the sights and sounds of the Grateful Dead on the rampage and the Avalon Ballroom swimming in a tureen of colored, pulsing lights? The excitement made him tremble. Even the group's name bespoke some kind of new, slightly intimidating realm Smith had never imagined.

"Tom, I don't think Jack Warner will ever understand this," he told Donahue. "I don't know if I understand it myself, but I really feel like they're good."

Smith left his wife outside the dressing room and proceeded cautiously with Donahue, who introduced Smith to the Dead and the band's management. Smith recognized Rifkin and Scully as streetwise schemers. Garcia appeared the obvious leader but scrupulously refused to speak for the group. Phil Lesh was openly hostile. Pigpen barely acknowledged his presence. Smith was dazzled.

The Dead appointed attorney Brian Rohan to negotiate the contract for the band, for no reason other than they knew him from handling various criminal cases for Kesey. Rohan, who had no experience in such matters, found a local colleague who once represented jazz pianist Dave Brubeck. Other companies expressed interest in the group—Jerry Wexler of Atlantic Records came to see the band— but Smith made his case for Warner Brothers and it only remained to work out the details.

Rohan went to Burbank to begin contract talks and, on hearing what Warner's had to say, he simply got up and walked out of the office. The Warner's executives stood up and followed him. He shook his head and walked out of the bungalow, the Warner's people trailing, changing their tune as they went. By the time Rohan was done, the Grateful Dead had an unprecedented contract that allowed the band such historic concessions as unlimited studio time and a royalty rate calculated on the amount of time per album side, and not the number of cuts, since the Dead didn't plan on filling up albums with two-minute tracks like Ricky Nelson or somebody. The group also retained complete control of song publishing, rare at the time.

Still that wasn't quite enough for Rifkin and Scully. When Joe Smith came up for the signing and met the two Dead managers at Donahue's apartment, they confided in Donahue there was one more thing they wanted. They wanted Joe Smith to drop acid. How could he really understand the band's music otherwise, they said. Smith made it clear he wouldn't be dropping any LSD and they signed the deal anyway.

Most of the band was now firmly ensconced in 710 Ashbury. When Garcia and Mountain Girl reconnected in December—Kesey left everybody behind, devoting his energies to quelling the legal maelstrom in which he was enmeshed—she moved into his upstairs room with him. She thought smoking the fragrant joints from the kilo of Acapulco gold kept in the kitchen pantry put golden halos around everywhere she looked. She would spend hours in the afternoon sitting on the front steps talking and carrying on until the chill of the evening fog drove everybody back inside.

Three band couples lived at the sprawling three-story Victorian two blocks up the hill from Haight Street—Scully and his ladyfriend, Tangerine, Garcia and Mountain Girl, Pigpen and Veronica. Rifkin maintained the basement apartment that had been his original toehold on the building. Laird Grant, who handled equipment, and Bob Matthews, who worked on sound, lived there, as did guitarist Bob Weir and Lady the Dog, a large black labrador. Jim and Annie Courson lived downstairs and ran the place. Bassist Phil Lesh lived around the corner on Belvedere Street with drummer Bill Kreutzman, still calling himself Bill Sommers, who had left a wife and young child living on the peninsula.

These were not idle times. The band practiced daily at the Sausalito Heliport. Most nights, everybody at 710 Ashbury was in bed by midnight except for Pigpen. He would often stay up drinking and softly singing blues. But Garcia customarily rose around six in the morning to begin his day by practicing guitar in his room. He played so much the calluses on his fingers were as hard as thumbtacks.

That Thanksgiving, after playing the night before at Bill Graham's Thanksgiving Eve party with Quicksilver, the band hosted a Thanksgiving dinner. All the sliding doors were pushed open and tables were placed end-to-end through the whole downstairs. The entire extended family, members of the Airplane, old Pranksters, broke bread and made merry. At one point, Lesh stood and offered a toast. "These *are* the good old days," he said. All nodded in agreement.

When the time came to actually record the Warner's album, the band traveled south in January and went to RCA Victor Studio A in Hollywood to work with producer Dave Hassinger, the same engineer the Airplane chose for *Jefferson Airplane Takes Off* because of his work with the Stones. The album went down in a three-day Dexamyl blitz that left the tempos eternally rushed and minor fixes forever unrepaired in the wake of the amphetamine tide. Essentially a distillation of the band's ballroom songbook, the recording repertoire concentrated on shorter pieces because that was as much of a studio mentality as the Dead could supply. At the Avalon or the Fillmore, the Dead would play songs as long as they felt good, as long as they made people dance, and when most of the audience is high on something, that can be a long time. The idea of reducing these numbers to three minutes simply provided the band another reason to approach the endeavor with a certain degree of disdain.

Matthew Katz had no intention of letting what happened to him with the Airplane ever happen to him again. He planned to build a band from the ground floor, starting with the former Airplane drummer, Skip Spence, now back from Mexico and back to playing guitar and writing songs. Marty Balin wanted to record one of his songs, "My Best Friend," on the new Airplane album. Katz heard Peter Lewis playing in a Los Angeles club and pitched his idea. The guitarist didn't like Katz, but Lewis, bassist Bob Mosley and their drummer went to San Francisco.

Lewis had never heard of the Jefferson Airplane, but Katz told him that he had managed the group. On their first night in San Francisco, Katz took Lewis and company to the Fillmore to see the Airplane. After an initial scene where Bill Graham confronted Katz at the entrance to the ballroom and threatened to throw him down the stairs, they saw the band and Lewis was impressed. They met Spence and began to jam together. Mosley decided the drummer wasn't good enough and Lewis drove the unhappy trapsman, a friend of his, back to Los Angeles, while the search was on in San Francisco for a lead guitarist and drummer.

Katz drove a Jaguar and seemed flush with funds. He rented an apartment for Mosley and Spence. Lewis, son of TV star Loretta Young, was using a $10,000 gift from his grandparents for his living expenses, so Katz didn't need to float him. But Katz already imbued the fledgling enterprise with the atmosphere of impending success.

Guitarist Jerry Miller and drummer Don Stevenson had come down to San Francisco from the Pacific Northwest to play Righteous Brothers medleys in matching suits and razor cuts with a band called the Frantics. The group worked at a popular Chinatown discotheque called the Dragon a Go Go, only a few blocks from North Beach where something less retrograde was stirring on the music scene. But the Frantics broke up and Miller and Stevenson were living with their wives in suburban San Carlos trying to figure out what to do when they hooked up with their old associate Bob Mosley.

Spence, Lewis and Mosley had been trying out various sets of musicians at the Washington Street church basement Katz rented when Miller and Stevenson came by. Within a half-hour, everybody in the room knew this was the band. Spence practiced a crude but chugging rhythm guitar against which Lewis fit his finger-picking folk style, leaving Miller to fill in the holes and glue it all together. Their voices blended like a little choir. Katz arranged an engagement at the Ark, a nightclub in the scuttled ferryboat *Charles Van Dam* that had played such a key role in the Sausalito folk scene only a couple of years earlier. Jerry Miller came up with a name from a joke popular at the

time: What's purple and lives at the bottom of the sea? Moby Grape.
Things started to happen fast.

Big Brother and the Holding Company dropped by the Ark and
told Chet Helms he should book the band. Stephen Stills and Neil
Young of Buffalo Springfield stopped in looking for Spence and the
band knocked them out. The Springfield, too, was dealing with a
three-guitar lineup and Stills went so far as to plug in and play along
with the Grape from the audience. Young, in fact, sat in a chair strumming a guitar one night in October in the upstairs office at the Ark as
Katz harangued the band over an addendum to the management contract the band had signed the month before. Katz got his way. They
signed the addendum too. The two-paragraph paper was brief but
sweeping. It gave Katz the power to hire, fire, add or subtract musicians at will from the group. It gave him complete ownership of the
name Moby Grape and the right to revoke the use of that name. What
happened to him with the Airplane would not happen again.

Paul Rothchild of Elektra Records took the band into the studio
for some demo recordings. Ahmet Ertegun of Atlantic Records
weighed in with serious offers. The band played the Avalon in November and Helms hired the group to play on New Year's Eve. Graham
booked the band in December at the Fillmore. Columbia Records
staff producer David Rubinson, in town to check out a Los Angeles-
based group called the Sparrow at the Ark, saw the Grape opening the
shows and forgot all about the headline band. While Ertegun dealt
with Katz, Rubinson and his label's local promotion man went straight
to the musicians, underwriting a lot of their expenses on American Express cards, courting them and bringing them along.

Already the band was beginning to sour on Katz. He tried producing a dance with the Grape on his own at California Hall that bombed
miserably and failed to land several jobs for the band simply because
there were so many people who refused to deal with him. Lewis began
to quietly arrange bookings at places like the Matrix and the Fillmore
where Katz had burned his bridges. But other things unsettled the
group even more. He seemed so paranoid, so tightly wound, so obsessed with keeping a firm rein on the band. He was a jealous, angry
overlord. The band began to ask record companies if they could get rid
of Katz. The Elektra people were so interested, they assured the group
Katz would go—until they saw the addendum to his personal manager
contract. While the group thought the label's ardor cooled substantially

after that tawdry revelation, on the sly Elektra offered Rubinson, who increasingly appeared to have the inside track with the group, a job as staff producer if he could bring the Grape with him.

The people running Kama Sutra Records flipped when they saw the advertisement George Hunter drew for the first Charlatans single from the Erik Jacobsen sessions, "Codine." With the band's picture and the title of the record drawn like a label on the middle of a bottle, the headline read "Remedy for a Drugged Market." Kama Sutra had already watched the label's million-selling star act, the Lovin' Spoonful, go down in flames around a drug bust and its devastating aftermath. The Spoonful's hit records still sailed into the Top Ten, but the band had been seriously damaged by the bad vibes resonating through the underground after they turned their dealer over to the cops.

Jacobsen saw a general disintegration taking place at the label. The partners were at each other's throats. Although Artie Ripp liked the Charlatans, his partners were not similarly disposed. The company quickly dumped the act off on Kapp Records, who decided to release "The Shadow Knows," a song the band didn't want to record in the first place, with Ferguson's vocal speeded up to make him sound younger. Even the Coasters' original version wasn't a hit and the Charlatans' long-awaited debut single sank without a trace when it was finally released in October.

Tension riffled through the band. Hunter's constant nagging and manipulating finally sent Hicks packing. He pinned a note saying "Fuck Off" to Hunter's pillow and drove to Los Angeles. He got as far as San Jose before he turned around and came back. Ferguson complained about everything. Hunter and Lucy Lewis were going through another stormy stage of their relationship. She felt like she was living in a stage set amidst the accumulated Victoriana in the Downey Street flat. It was a strange period. Nobody was thinking about the music.

Artie Ripp pulled up after midnight in front of Downey Street, his limousine filling the narrow lane. He arrived at Hunter's apartment to meet with the band after an Avalon show and, as he smoked the ceremonial bowl of pot, he felt his head swell as if it were going to burst. The Charlatans had salted the grass with DMT and Ripp was off on a trip, a whirring, arching blast out of reality into the white-hot netherworld of the mindscape beyond psychedelia. When his brain finally alighted like a bird on a perch, he heard the unmistakable sound of ammunition being cranked through a carbine chamber. Hunter was holding his Winchester and pumping cartridges into the magazine, mumbling obscure but dire suggestions. Vintage jazz hummed and hissed in the background, 78s spinning on the wind-up Victrola in the apartment. "What is that stuff?" asked Ripp.

The musicians showed him a release they had drawn up, freeing the group from the management-production-recording contract to which Kama Sutra originally signed the Charlatans. They wanted out. Now. Ripp tried to talk the band out of it, but Hunter kept running cartridges ominously through the antique rifle and the other band members wore grim expressions, unmoved by his arguments. He signed the paper and went back to his limo and driver.

In a basement at a deserted building on the UC-Berkeley campus over Thanksgiving, Steve Miller spent three days putting together his new band, the Steve Miller Blues Band. For the highly directed Texan, the San Francisco rock scene seemed a promise of opportunity, not a panacea of drugs or a utopian life. On a previous scouting trip to the Bay Area, Miller played a blues gig at the Berkeley folk club, Jabberwock, and sat in with his old Chicago pal, Paul Butterfield, at the Fillmore. Back home in Houston, tired of his nowhere job in the recording studio, he threw his belongings in the back of a VW microbus and answered the clarion call.

His father was a doctor with a hobby of tape-recording music. Growing up, Miller heard concerts in his living room by the likes of Les Paul, Charlie Mingus and T-Bone Walker. He formed his first band while still attending the elite private school for boys, St. Marks, in Dallas. Another member of the Marksmen, as the group was called, followed him to the University of Wisconsin a year later, Boz Scaggs. By that time, Miller had already started another band, the Ardells, and Scaggs signed up. When Scaggs went off to spend a year or more hitchhiking through Europe, Miller headed for Chicago. Another band, the Goldberg-Miller Band, with organist Barry Goldberg, led to a record contract, but soon enough Miller was back in the Chicago clubs playing rhythm guitar with bluesman Buddy Guy, before moving back to Texas, dispirited.

Now in San Francisco, he called Tim Davis, drummer for a rival band in college, who brought guitarist Curley Cooke and came out. Miller had run across bassist Lonnie Turner during his previous San

Francisco visit and he called them all together that Thanksgiving weekend in the concrete halls of academia while the students were away. He sold his tape recorder and an amplifier for living expenses, sleeping in his bus, but landed an audition in a short time, where Chet Helms caught the band. He hired the Steve Miller Blues Band for a December date at the Avalon and paid the group enough money to last a couple of months, five hundred dollars.

Ginger Jackson, who was now living with Jack Casady, and Jerry Slick were standing in the airport after watching their respective mates depart for Los Angeles to record the next Jefferson Airplane album. Jerry Slick turned to Jackson. "Your place or mine?" he asked.

Tears stung her eyes, but she knew what was going to happen down south. She had heard Grace talking about how independent she was and could tell her marriage to Jerry Slick was disintegrating. She knew Casady thought the band's new singer was fabulous. Turnabout seemed the only answer.

At the Tropicana on Santa Monica Boulevard, each band member installed in his own twelve-dollar-a-night room with kitchenette, Grace Slick returned from a grocery shopping trip at Ralph's, filled up her icebox, picked up a bottle of wine and went to knock on Casady's door to borrow a corkscrew. Sessions began the following night at RCA Victor Studio A and assigned to produce was Rick Jarrard, a young but straight-laced company man who went through the roof the first time he saw band members fire up joints in the studio. Pot smoking was confined to closets after that.

Acting as a kind of unofficial liaison between the band and the production staff, Jerry Garcia showed up the second night. San Francisco bands shared a fear of making records with a "Hollywood sound" and one glockenspiel overdub on a Jefferson Airplane record was enough. Garcia was brought in not only to add occasional guitar parts, but to bring a sense of the San Francisco sound—whatever that was—to the control room. The Airplane knocked out six songs over the course of four nights, October 31 through November 3, and then took a break to prepare the rest of the album. When the band came back to the studio ten days later, Skip Spence, as well as Garcia, added guitars to a pair of songs and the next night, with the recording of Kaukonen's solo guitar piece, "Embryonic Journey," the album was complete. The record cost a paltry eight thousand dollars to produce and when Garcia described the songs on the record to Balin as "surrealistic as a pillow," the album got a title.

The band capped the Los Angeles tour with a week-long run at the Whiskey a Go Go on Sunset Strip—highlighted by Balin's falling off the high stage while, looped on acid one night, his gaze was riveted on a particularly noteworthy pair of breasts he spied in the audience—and Casady's arrest for the collection of hookahs and hashish he kept in his hotel room.

"Wow, you must really like acid," someone said, watching Janis Joplin chug down swallow after swallow of cold duck straight from the bottle. They were sitting around the California Street apartment of David Getz's ladyfriend, who happened to serve as a distributor for one of the Haight's more noted purveyors, where a bottle of the cheap purplish champagne had been generously spiked with many, many doses of acid. Joplin, who abhorred psychedelics with a near pathological hatred, did not know the secret of the bottle being passed around. She thought it was regulation booze—her kind of drink—when she snatched the magnum and started gulping away.

"ACID!" she screeched, and headed for the bathroom to vomit. Too little, too late. The acid was coursing through her blood, next stop cerebellum.

Actually, she had taken the drug once during her North Beach days. "Blow my mind to see a bunch of wiggly lines," she said. "Not this girl." She wasn't alone in the band with that sentiment. Gurley, who took some of the first LSD to hit the streets of San Francisco, ate so many mushrooms with the Indians in Mexico that he never wanted to get psychedelic again. And he didn't. Peter Albin, the Ward Cleaver of San Francisco rock, was dosed once, but didn't care for the experience. Getz and Andrew liked it fine, but alcohol and speed were really the favored mood enhancers of Big Brother. Joplin coined the term "alkydelic" for the band.

She went that night to see Otis Redding at the Fillmore, a prophetic propinquity. The stocky black soul singer from Macon, Georgia, was not well known outside the urban ghettos of America. His earthy music dwelled on soul stations, not the Top Forty radio where Motown and even James Brown could be heard. But something about Redding was so essentially black, so indigenously soulful, that white

America had not discovered him, even though the band that backed him on his peerless Memphis soul sessions was half white.

Bill Graham knew nothing about black music. His earliest education came from Paul Butterfield, who sat Graham down and talked to him about Redding, the Staple Singers, Bobby Bland, James Brown, Chuck Berry. To Graham, these were just empty names. To Butterfield and thousands like him, these were the apostles of the blues, the keepers of the keys to the kingdom. Every time Graham asked musicians who *they* wanted to see—Butterfield, Bloomfield, Garcia—they all mentioned the same name: Otis Redding.

Graham needed to convince Redding to play for the hippies in San Francisco. He didn't routinely perform for white audiences outside the South and the stories wafting out of San Francisco made the scene sound a little strange to a cornpone soul man like Redding, voodoo rites and black magic, for all he knew.

Joplin arranged to be let into the hall early. So she was standing front and center, exactly where she wanted to be, when the twelve-piece band, sassy and brassy, hit it. Redding did not draw a full house and many who did come were blacks more common to his performances than Fillmore shows, even if they lived in the ballroom's neighborhood.

Redding blew the place apart. Strutting, smiling, gasping for breath between lyrics, he was sex incarnate. Prowling the stage like a predator, he found one gorgeous young black woman in a low-cut blouse enraptured, leaning on the front of the stage. So everybody in the room could see, he leaned down and looked her right in the face. "I'm gonna s-s-s-sock it to ya, baby," he said. "One, two, hunh." The Fillmore exploded. He just laughed.

Joplin, her mind dissolving and reassembling the picture like she was watching it through a kaleidoscope, soaked up every breath, every flinch, every eyebrow wag. He was tearing away at the cocoon that still surrounded her. No longer the homely blues singer, Joplin was transforming herself into a rock queen. Pieces of the vision she picked up wherever she could find them. Nancy Gurley helped her gain a sense of style, swaddling her in gauzy fabrics, colors and textures, a hippie gypsy in cheap costume jewelry and gaudy castoffs. Her hair now framed her face in soft curls.

Redding showed her what high energy could do, how blood-pumping fervor could induce ecstatic states in an audience. None of this was lost on the conscientiously evolving Joplin, who was making him part of her before he even left the stage. She was not alone among the San Francisco musicians in her reaction. Marty Balin of the Airplane was awestruck by the soul man at the Fillmore, remade as vocalist by the experience.

Jabbering and gesticulating, Joplin always seemed to be in a hurry. Whether she was rushing toward or running away from, nobody could tell. But when she called on friends, she always seemed to be stopping by on her way somewhere else. Above everything, Janis Joplin was a young lady with a destination, wherever it was. Since stepping on the Avalon stage less than six months before, she had found, if not herself, at least a direction to move in. Every step of the way, crucial tools could be added. And within the safety of the band, finally a family that approved of what she did, Joplin could accomplish remarkable feats.

Only the month before, one weekend in November, she, Andrew and Gurley had gone to the Both/And on Divisadero to see Big Mama Thornton, a blues singer Joplin greatly admired. Thornton, who recorded the original "Hound Dog" when Elvis Presley was still a shy, awkward teen in Humes High, wore a rumpled hat, played drums and kept her harmonica nearby in a glass of water. She liked it wet. She was a tough, grizzled blues bitch, quite capable of kicking the woebegone ass of one of her musicians if she didn't like the way he parted his hair.

In her set she played a song, a shuffle, that she recorded for a tiny Oakland-based record label called Baytone Records in the early sixties. Although the label never saw fit to release the record, the company did copyright the song. Gurley heard something in the number. He thought it could be slowed down, shifted into a minor key, and have a lot more angst wrenched out of it. He and Joplin went backstage to talk to Big Mama after the show to ask her permission to use the song. She readily agreed and painstakingly even wrote down the lyrics of the song she wrote and undoubtedly lived, "(Love Is Like a) Ball and Chain."

The timberwolf that belonged to John Cipollina found a willing partner in destruction with Mando, the Great Dane that Dino Valente brought to the Quicksilver ranch. The two animals would race after horses, nipping at their hooves until they dropped. Although Cipollina could command a modicum of discipline out of the animal, others approached the wolf at their own peril.

Polte raced back to the ranch from his apartment in San

Francisco one afternoon, after fielding an angry phone call from the mother of a fourteen-year-old daughter on the verge of calling the police on Quicksilver. The band's strict rule was that no underage females could be kept longer than twenty-four hours and Polte wanted to head off any potential problem. He discovered the house empty and, disbelieving, he walked from room to room calling out names. As he turned to leave Cipollina's room, he stopped. In the doorway, growling and baring his teeth was the wolf and Polte could do nothing but wait until the animal decided to let him pass.

The wolf and the Great Dane tore up garbage, chased cows and generally grew from amusement to nuisance. When nearby farmers began to complain that sheep were being killed, the problems really started. Locals refused to pick up garbage at the ranch, wouldn't serve the band members at the gas station or wait on them at the store. But the breaking point occurred when a vigilante committee turned up armed and serious at the ranch. They warned the band that if there were any more problems, they would come out shooting. The time had clearly come to move back to San Francisco.

With the band working virtually every weekend, the return made sense for other reasons. Shelley Duncan and Geri Elmore were both pregnant. Polte located adjacent apartments in Diamond Heights and the Duncans and the Freibergs shared one, with the Elmores and the equipment manager living next door. Cipollina and Murray moved into a Victorian a few blocks down the street. Keeping an unhouse-trained wolf as a pet hardly qualified Cipollina as an ideal tenant and he didn't know what to do. His mother suggested he call Anton La Vey, the noted Satanist who kept tigers and other exotic animals. He told Cipollina to try 1090 Page Street because they would take anyone. He ended up leaving the wolf with a friend in Olema and the wolf, deprived of the constant attention of the master who had raised it from a cub, soon ran away.

Jimmy Murray disappeared himself for a couple of days when it came time to move. Somebody else packed up his stuff and carted it over to San Francisco. He didn't like to work. Cipollina wasn't much help. He was always sickly and chronically late. He never directed traffic, he just went with it. Lazy and slow, what a pair they were.

Gary Duncan thought nothing of sending his pregnant wife down the dozens of stairs to the store on the corner for his cigarettes and sending her right back out again for something she forgot. Shelley

Duncan didn't mind. She was glad to be off the ranch, to have a semblance of privacy, a relative degree of peace and quiet, some sanity restored. Girl Freiberg thought Duncan abused his wife, all the yelling and running around behind her back. Even David Freiberg felt sympathetic toward the eighteen-year-old mother-to-be. "Someday, Shelley," he told her, "you're going to see the light." She never understood what he meant.

Onstage, the band was developing a fierce, highly personal style, based around the piston-like rhythms of guitarist Duncan, whose youthful experience in Reno lounge soul bands paid dividends of discipline and craftsmanship. At first, he only sang and played tambourine, until Polte heard him strumming a guitar one day and told him he should play with the band. Murray was not a strong player and Cipollina practiced the same solos over and over, never improvising, but honing his parts to unerring precision, a fluttering touch on the whammy bar and piercing drive. But Duncan became the band's musical high-dive artist. He would take the plunge, sometimes coming up empty-handed and sometimes galloping away on a rip-snorting ride. With Freiberg, the band could marshal a three-part vocal sound that drenched choruses in rich harmony. For material, the group delved into folkish numbers like "Pride of Man," "Dino's Song" or "Codine," giving them a gleaming hard edge, and specialized in extended workouts of Bo Diddley songs. Occasionally, Quicksilver would dedicate tongue-in-cheek "to all our young friends in the Haight-Ashbury" the Del Shannon oldie, "Runaway."

On January 14, the young advocates came together in the Polo Fields of Golden Gate Park, more than anyone imagined, tens of thousands. A Gathering, it was called, of the Tribes. A Pow-Wow. The Human Be-In. Poet Gary Snyder opened the unseasonably sunny afternoon with a blast on a conch shell and a procession of poets and rock bands traipsed across the stage into the late afternoon. A Zen Buddhist meditated onstage throughout it all. For once, the Haight-Ashbury community included the Berkeley radicals in the plans—politico Jerry Rubin attended fresh from jail—and the event drew a large contingent from the East Bay, many of whom had heard, but not yet seen or personally experienced this blossoming utopia just across the Bay Bridge. Country Joe McDonald took some acid, painted his face and went.

LSD was readily available. Handfuls of Owsley Stanley's latest pressing, called White Lightning, were passed around. Dino Valente danced around the crowd tootling his wooden pipes playing Pan in the woods. Allen Ginsberg led the crowd in chanting a Buddhist mantra. Lenore Kandel read from her "The Love Book," a work cited as obscene only a couple of months earlier when the cops busted the Psychedelic Shop on Haight Street for carrying the book. Acid guru Tim Leary recited his "tune in, turn on, drop out" routine. A parachutist descended on the crowd during the performance by the Dead. Freeforming jazz flautist Charles Lloyd joined the band on an extended version of the Pigpen specialty, "Good Morning Little Schoolgirl."

When the electric lines were broken during Quicksilver's set, the Hell's Angels volunteered to stand guard and current flowed without interruption for the remainder of the afternoon, as Big Brother, the Airplane, Sir Douglas Quintet, Loading Zone and the others came and went. In fact, the Angels also took care of lost children. Freewheelin' Frank, a noted member of the motorcycle gang who spent most of the afternoon sitting on a bus banging a tambourine on his leg, wept when his brethren reverted to form for one brief incident and beat up a passerby who messed with their Harleys. But with the San Francisco police keeping a watchful but distant eye on the affair mounted on horseback, it was the Angels that afternoon who served as the peace officers.

As fingers of fog trickled through the trees and Gary Snyder blew the event to a close on his conch shell, the crowd drifted away. They picked up all their garbage. Later in the evening, a small group flowed over the sidewalks into Haight Street, obstructing traffic, and the cops moved in and arrested almost fifty people. It was the most trouble they could find.

In Diamond Heights, Shelley Duncan, seven months pregnant, waited for her husband to come home. If she didn't know exactly where he was, she knew what he was doing. She just didn't want to admit that to herself. When he finally came home the next morning, she didn't ask any questions.

In January, Chet Helms decided to travel to England, swinging mod London, where he thought a second Family Dog enterprise just might be welcome. He had heard rumblings that Graham planned to open a hall in New York, and Helms wanted to take the high ground and establish himself in the heart of the rock and roll world, the land of the Beatles and the Rolling Stones. He planned to find a location, hire a staff and open the operation in three weeks. But after spending a couple of days exploring some World War II bomb shelters as possible dancehalls, he quickly abandoned the idea of trying to run another business eight thousand miles from his home base. He still needed a holiday and London happily hosted the Haight-Ashbury ambassador, the first key player from the San Francisco scene to hit those shores.

He found underground London agreeably comparable, if a little more stiff, less spontaneous, not as "street." He hooked up with the crowd that published *IT,* or *International Times,* the London underground newspaper, and ran UFO, the Avalon Ballroom's British counterpart, where Pink Floyd served as the house band in much the same way Big Brother and the Holding Company did at the Avalon. Joe Boyd, manager of Floyd and the UFO, called Helms with his waist-length hair and chest-length beard "the Sunshine Superman from Sunshine Superland."

The British underground was just finding itself, at this point blindly mirroring what they supposed to be taking place in San Francisco. The drug trade flourished and the psychedelic influence was being felt in music, fashion and other quarters of the always transitional English popular culture. Helms found the light show that appeared with Pink Floyd to be most rudimentary compared to the relatively sophisticated versions that had been up and running virtually every weekend for more than a year back home.

Helms also ran across a lady Fleet Streeter named Anne Sharpley, whom he quite liked despite her being past thirty years old, and she joined him for a three-week kaleidoscope of parties across London, a swirling panorama of the burgeoning London psychedelia. The climatic event was an *IT*-sponsored fundraiser at the Roundhouse, a "happening" that included such features as fifty-five gallons of Jell-O dumped at the feet of the partygoers, a naked painter who dragged his torso through his paint and then across a strip of paper. Paul McCartney and John Lennon attended, stoned out of their brains on acid.

When his journalist friend splashed a condescending, telescoped version of the events they attended together under the headline "My Lost Psychedelic Weekend," Helms sheepishly slipped out of town, feeling betrayed and embarrassed. By the time he returned to San Francisco, Helms thought he could forget the entire episode, but one of the press services had picked up her story and dozens of newspapers across the country ran the account, complete with the Helms rejoinder she saved for the punch line to her story: "If you think this is wild, you ought to see what we do back home."

Joe McDonald had worried about money for food and clothing since he was twelve years old and his father lost his job with the phone company. In the Navy, he knew he could walk into the kitchen and get something to eat twenty-four hours a day. Living in Berkeley, a political, pot-smoking, acid-dropping hippie rock musician, allowed him to put a gauzy filter over his fears and indulge in the pleasures that abundant drugs and sex offered. He still believed in the communist ethos of work together, share together with which he had grown up and, to that end, he assigned equal shares of his copyrights to band members Melton, Cohen, Barthol and manager Denson when the band signed with Vanguard Records. Producer Sam Charters talked to McDonald about the idealistic gesture. "You're stupid," he told McDonald. "This is nuts. What are you doing this for?"

But McDonald was grooving his way through life, like so many of his peers, without asking questions like that. Tomorrow was a long way away and such egalitarianism gave him the comfortable feeling that he was contributing to a new way of living, far removed and more evolved than the one his parents' generation knew. Already the band was earning more money than he ever imagined possible simply playing the Jabberwock and occasional East Bay dances and even more occasional dates at the San Francisco ballrooms. While the band really staked out the Berkeley area as home turf, the Fish began to make tentative inroads on the bustling San Francisco arena. In August, the group arrived to load equipment before opening the show at their first booking at the Fillmore, a last-minute substitute. Bill Graham greeted the musicians on the ballroom floor, while Sopwith Camel conducted a sound check onstage.

"Hey, how are you," he said, extending a hand. "Good to see you." He swiveled to the stage, dropping the smile and, at the top of his voice, screamed at the Camel. "Get the fuck off the stage," he shouted. "The show starts in ten minutes. Where do you think you are, Longshoremen's Hall?" Turning back to McDonald and his fellow musicians, Graham beamed broadly again. "Nice to have you here," he allowed genially, and sauntered off.

Although Country Joe and the Fish began to share bills at the Fillmore almost every month—including supporting the Yardbirds in October—and the Avalon, where the Fish rose in short order to headline the New Year's Eve show, Berkeley continued to serve as head-quarters to Fish fortunes, where the band easily commanded as much as five hundred dollars a night. In February, McDonald arrived soaring on acid to perform a concert at the Golden Sheaf Bakery, a short-lived enterprise on the edge of the Oakland-Berkeley border. Quiet, almost sullen, he exchanged few words with the brassy female vocalist burning it up with the other band on the bill, Big Brother and the Holding Company. But something about Janis Joplin stayed with him.

The first order of business when Julius Karpen took over as manager of Big Brother in January was to move the band back to San Francisco. Polte took his friend Karpen to see the band at the Matrix, where Karpen was astonished at the power and conviction of the performance. After the show, Polte asked him how he would like to manage the group. Big Brother had approached Polte, who felt his hands were full with Quicksilver, but immediately thought of Karpen, who had been sitting around Polte's office smoking pot and helping out as he could since leaving the Pranksters in Mexico.

Karpen bought a '57 Cadillac hearse to serve as the official Big Brother transport and found apartments scattered around the Haight-Ashbury. There were other logistical problems to solve. Joplin faced jail or stiff fines from her collection of overdue parking tickets. Karpen wanted to pay the fines and be done with the situation. Joplin preferred to take the jail time. The thought of having his vocalist unavailable for booking Karpen found untenable, so the two launched an argument. The more he battled, the more stubborn she became. Karpen finally capitulated. "You're one tough broad, Janis," he said.

"Well, I don't just sing that way, y'know," she said.

He found Joplin a sunny apartment overlooking Golden Gate Park on Lyon Street with a curving balcony on the front room, a small kitchen off the long hallway leading to the dark bedroom she decorated in velvet, lace and photographs of herself. Away from the communal living of Lagunitas, she stopped shooting speed. The next time Joe McDonald ran across this young lady he had found so bright, funny and, in her own way, pretty was at an Avalon Ballroom gig. Before long, he was sharing that bedroom in Lyon Street with her.

SPRING 1967

RCA Victor staged a sumptuous coming-out party for *Surrealistic Pillow* in New York. In the ornate marble and gilt surroundings of Webster Hall in Greenwich Village, the Airplane were introduced to the New York press, retail and other industry acolytes, who were not necessarily all that prepared for what they were about to experience. Presented with a smorgasbord of olives, celery, carrots, pastrami and potato salad beneath a giant ice sculpture that spelled out "RCA," the invited guests were attended by bartenders wearing buttons reading "Jefferson Airplane Loves You." While a film of an airplane in silhouette coming in for a landing played to the accompaniment of the onrushing roar of jet engines, the musicians straggled onstage and proceeded to pound the select audience numb with two hour-long servings of the sights and sounds of the Fillmore, a throbbing, pulsing, multihued light show imported for the event, culminated by an extended jam with members of the Butterfield Blues Band, plucked out of the audience for the occasion. The crowd drifted off. The musicians kept playing. The ice sculpture melted.

The promotion tour went next to Chicago, where band members piled on a chartered bus heading for Cleveland. Somewhere midway on the ride, Spencer Dryden looked back on this big, empty bus and saw Grace Slick sitting halfway back the aisle by herself. He walked back. "Pardon me, ma'am," he said. "Is that seat taken?"

Bill Thompson turned around sometime later to ask Slick something and was jolted by the sight of her and Dryden locked in a steamy embrace. When the bus pulled over for a brief rest stop, Thompson took Dryden aside. "She's married," he said. Of course, so was Dryden. "We've got a good thing going. Don't ruin it for all of us."

For the remainder of the ride to Cleveland, the two backseat lovers nuzzled and cuddled their way down the highway. When an RCA promotion representative asked if they were married, Grace spoke right up. "Yes," she said, "but not to each other." Dryden thought he could hear desks rattling all the way back to Los Angeles and New York. Potential Top Forty stars did not behave in this manner.

Although Dryden wore his wedding ring during the photo session for the album cover, he was asked to take it off for public appearances. Certainly nobody wanted to know he lived with one girlfriend in San Francisco, kept a wife and small child in Los Angeles and was conducting a hot and heavy affair with the married vocalist of the band. Not reaching Cleveland until six in the morning, with a performance scheduled for two in the afternoon, the budding romance was not consummated until the following evening in New York, after they checked into separate rooms at the hotel.

The band returned to San Francisco for a week-long engagement with trumpeter Dizzy Gillespie at Basin Street West, where Darby Slick, freshly returned from India, winced at the awkward attempts by Airplane musicians to jam with the jazz great at the end of his set. After the brief pit stop at home, the Airplane took off again for the East Coast for a handful of club and college engagements before returning to headline the Fillmore the first weekend of February. The new year was starting off fast for the band.

When the Airplane first jettisoned Matthew Katz, road manager Bill Thompson received a field promotion. Hovering in the background all along, however, was Bill Graham, a forceful father figure the band turned to for advice and assistance even before firing Katz. With the release of the second album holding such auspicious promise, the Airplane moved to galvanize his position and asked him to act as the band's official manager. No contracts were signed or even proffered. Katz had rendered the musicians gun shy. He had sought legal relief almost as soon as the Airplane dispatched him and the band had sued him in return. Katz had already won the first skirmish, but a long battle loomed. Graham agreed to accept an equal share with the musicians and asked nothing more than a handshake to seal the deal.

Graham expanded his staff beyond Jim Haynie and his girlfriend, Bonnie MacLean, although he was still capable of jumping on his Lambretta and stapling up his own posters. Marushka Greene, whose husband was the photographer who took the cover photo of the Airplane for *Surrealistic Pillow,* came to work as his secretary and her first job every Monday was to bank the weekend's proceeds, piles of cash usually stacked in an empty apple box. Graham used to admonish her about muggers: "If someone stops you and says, 'Your money or your life'—think about it."

Out of the already cramped office at the Fillmore, Graham began to handle the affairs of the Airplane. He represented to the musicians the successful businessman who could bridge the straight world and the underground. His efficiency and attention to detail were known to all who came in contact with him and he seemed perfectly positioned to steer the Airplane beyond the confines of the provincial scene the band already ruled. Stirrings could be detected on the horizon. *Surrealistic Pillow* hit the charts in March. Winds of change carried the seeds of San Francisco psychedelia far and wide and the Airplane served as avatars of this new wave of consciousness rippling through youth—figuratively and literally. When Owsley produced a fresh pressing he called Orange Sunshine, Kantner and Balin took bags of the LSD onstage and threw the tablets into the audience by the handfuls, sowing their outlook in fertile brains like so many psychedelic Johnny Appleseeds.

In England, where Chet Helms had been welcomed like a frontier scout returned from Indian country, no sooner had the Beatles finished that band's own acid-rock experiment, *Sergeant Pepper's Lonely Hearts Club Band,* than Paul McCartney left for America, where he borrowed Frank Sinatra's Learjet and swooped down in San Francisco to quietly investigate the phenomenon first-hand in April. He showed up unannounced at an Airplane rehearsal at the Fillmore.

McCartney repaired to the Oak Street apartment shared by Marty Balin, Jack Casady and Bill Thompson. Casady burst into

Thompson's room and told him to get his lunch box, which is where Thompson kept the apartment drug stash. They all toked up some DMT, a mind-crunching psychedelic mixed with pot, and smoked. McCartney played a dub of "A Day in the Life" from the forthcoming Beatles album and talked about a guitarist in England nobody knew in the States named Jimi Hendrix. Attempts at jamming were hampered by left-handed McCartney's difficulty in playing Casady's right-handed bass upside-down. But some kind of rapport was struck between the two bassists and Casady took the Beatle back to his hotel and continued the cross-cultural summit meeting long into the night.

Going to New York and selling out did not earn Sopwith Camel any respect among the San Francisco musicians. Having a hit record may have even made matters worse. To come back with a little mud dripping out of the corners of their mouths and the humility of failure might have lent the band at least the atmosphere of integrity. But, no, Sopwith Camel, that lightweight group that flitted around the edges of the ballroom scene and disappeared to New York without the good taste to have never been heard from again, actually turned back up on the radio, long before many of the more established bands around town had even recorded.

"Hello Hello," the song Kraemer started to write that first night he met Terry MacNeil, caught fire and burned, in some markets reaching into the Top Ten. The ricky-ticky, good-timey sound of the Erik Jacobsen-produced single broke onto the charts in December and proceeded to move upward through the shank of winter. The song captured the sharing mood of youth with its "Would you like some of my tangerine?" catchline, although the sexual entendre of the phrase also undoubtedly contributed to the tune's whimsical appeal. In any case, the first hit single lofted by one of the new San Francisco bands could not have been less representative of the sound of the ballrooms. "Hello Hello" was probably closer to "Winchester Cathedral" than anything out of any other San Francisco band's repertoire.

But with the lucky Top Forty strike, the Camel headed out on the road with Kama Sutra Records labelmates the Lovin' Spoonful, playing for screaming teens in hockey rinks and basketball arenas. When the band could finally schedule a homecoming in the wake of "Hello Hello," the Camel was booked to top the bill in April at an antiwar concert also featuring Country Joe and the Fish, Quicksilver, Big

Brother and the Dead at Longshoremen's Hall. The Dead had spent the entire day playing, starting in an apartment building in the Haight and moving into the open air of the Golden Gate Park panhandle and, once onstage, the musicians didn't feel like stopping just because the hall's one a.m. curfew meant the Camel wouldn't get to play. The Dead just rolled on until mere minutes ahead of the witching hour. Union stagehands turned off the power in the middle of the first number by Sopwith Camel.

Dissension and internal tensions gnawed away at the band even without such external aggravations. Later that month at the Hollywood Bowl, where the Camel was scheduled to appear with Eric Burdon and the Animals and an assortment of other bands with records on the radio, Willie Sievers walked into the dressing room just before the band was supposed to take the stage and announced he was quitting. His songs were not as popular as Kraemer's and he wanted to start a solo career. Jacobsen, for some reason, had encouraged him and agreed to produce his album. Kraemer was astonished, but Sopwith Camel had clearly thudded to a sudden end. Three days later, as planned, Kraemer married the teenage ballerina he met while she was dancing with Allen Ginsberg at the Fillmore, but it was not quite the happy occasion originally envisioned.

David Rubinson didn't like Matthew Katz. He distrusted the way the Moby Grape manager would look away when talking to him. He could never get Katz to look him in the eye. Rubinson caught up with the group backstage at a gig in Los Angeles, while the band was in town, fooling around with Stephen Stills and meeting with other record company representatives like Gary Usher, a onetime songwriting collaborator with Brian Wilson of the Beach Boys. But Rubinson impressed Peter Lewis with his trim beard and New York overcoat. To the band, Rubinson appeared both serious and sympathetic, someone who could understand what they were doing.

Only Skip Spence even vaguely qualified as a hippie. They hadn't lived together since the first few weeks and only Spence ever took acid. Down-home Jerry Miller, who grew up in the Pacific Northwest but moved to Texas to start his career, and Don Stevenson, his friend and colleague from Seattle, were both married. Peter Lewis was raised in show business; his father, Thomas Lewis, produced the television show starring his mother, Loretta Young, until she ended both their personal and professional relationships when Peter was eleven years old. He hadn't talked for several years to his mother, who was appalled that he was a rock musician. Spence, too, was married, although he didn't necessarily act it. Only Bob Mosley didn't have a wife and family. Nevertheless, Mosley, Lewis and Miller spent a lot of time together off the bandstand just hanging out.

Spence could be quite aggressive with the other band members, cocky to the point of arrogance. But he could also be a quick study. When the band first formed, he favored ethereal, folky numbers. But once he gauged the picture, he adapted his guitar style to a somewhat awkward but fierce strumming approach. He could exhibit spaciness at times, as well as some genuine cunning, although he was basically a guileless, innocent young man.

Rubinson took the Grape into Columbia Studios in Los Angeles, where union rules prevailed, to cut some demos. The scheduled two-hour session started late, since the musicians didn't show up on time, and, with three songs to record, the proceedings assumed a somewhat rushed atmosphere. When drummer Stevenson bobbled a part on a couple of successive takes, Spence grabbed the sticks. "Fuck this," said the former Jefferson Airplane novice drummer. "I'll play it."

The results left the New York executives of the label anxious to sign the band. Rubinson won the loyalty of the band members and Katz completed negotiating a deal for the band with Columbia Records. He insisted a clause be inserted reiterating his legal claim to the group name. Rubinson and the group arranged for Katz to be excluded from any involvement in the recording. The band received quite a bit of consideration from the label for signing, including the label's buying the band some equipment, in addition to advance money. Katz not only retained all publishing rights to the Grape songs, but he made Columbia include his own logo on the album cover.

The band rehearsed every day for weeks in Los Angeles, preparing to record the album. Because of union rules, Rubinson was forced to deal with strict session hours, no touching of the console by anyone but the engineer and no overdubbing, all of which he found highly frustrating. Nevertheless, on the primitive four-track equipment, he slowly etched out an album that cost an astronomical $18,000 to produce.

But he caught the brilliant balance of personalities and talents in the band, voices melting together on taut songs coming from the group's three writers. The material on *Moby Grape* ranged from the wistful acoustic "8:05" to the driving, three-guitar sound of "Hey Grandma" or "Fall On You"—straight from the band's Avalon repertoire, with the extended instrumental tails cut off. The album brimmed with a palpable excitement, a rich, charged sound and an abundance of potent songs. The label loved the record.

In fact, the uniform excellence of the tracks caused one of the Columbia executives to challenge Rubinson to name the potential single from the lot. "Single?" said Rubinson. "There's five singles." The executive took him at his word and ordered the simultaneous release of five singles, a display of confidence soon to be mistaken as a wanton publicity stunt. In fact, Columbia earmarked $100,000 for promotion, including the printing of the special Moby Grape emblem on thousands of buttons, a velvet-covered press kit and a lavish send-off for the album at the Avalon Ballroom, attended by loads of Columbia officers, jetted in from Los Angeles and New York especially for the event.

Rubinson strolled through the Haight that afternoon in May prior to the Avalon event with one of the label's top executives. "Sign anyone you want," he told the young producer, flushed with this imminent Moby Grape coup. That evening floated blissfully along on the sweet cloud of success billowing up underneath the enterprise. The perfume of orchids flown in from Hawaii filled the Avalon. Moby Grape wine was served. Square-jawed, flat-topped record retailers from Los Angeles mingled with the long-haired teens invited by Top Forty radio sponsors, KYA. Peter Lewis's father flew up for the occasion. The buoyant air was practically contagious. The band delivered a splendid performance. Janis Joplin sang on a couple of numbers, "The Letter" and "Murder in My Heart for the Judge," swapping lines with Mosley. A glowing David Rubinson took a midnight flight back to New York.

Peter Lewis was already home getting ready for bed when Spence rang his doorbell later that same night. He was slightly surprised, since Spence didn't spend much time socializing with the band. But the triumphant evening wasn't ready to end yet, so he took off with Spence to the Ark, where they caught up with Jerry Miller, who was riding around in a bright red borrowed T-Bird. Three seventeen-year-old girls from San Mateo joined them and, before long, the party moved to the dead end of a fire trail in the hills above Marin City, a secluded stretch often favored by local teens. When the cops pulled up, they found Spence without his pants and the entire scene in some disarray. A partially smoked joint turned up in Miller's pocket, so he was booked on an additional felony count of possession of marijuana, along with the same contributing to the delinquency of a minor charge that the other two musicians were also arrested on. The three young ladies were taken to juvenile hall.

The next morning, Peter Lewis's father bailed them out, as newspapers splashed news of the bust in large headlines. Their wives were not especially understanding.

The Haight had changed greatly since Big Brother moved to Lagunitas the previous summer. No longer a quiet, sunny confluence of long-haired acidheads from S.F. State living in the neighborhood's old Victorians, it was now a knotted mass of dreamers and schemers, artists and con artists, the devout and the jive, and growing daily. A carnival seemed to be taking place on every block. Clowns wearing costumes were everywhere. An explosion of color and character had taken place. Teenage runaways mingled with dealers. Hell's Angels were a ubiquitous part of the streetscape, esteemed colleagues of many of the musicians. The salty Mediterranean air that hung over the district hummed with electricity. As many as 100,000 people were expected to descend on the little mecca the coming summer.

To this burbling cauldron returned Big Brother. Rodney Albin no longer lived at 1090 Page Street. He could still maintain order among the unruly tenants by taking his shotgun into the hall closet and discharging a shell or two into the floor. That got their attention. But eventually he gave up, tired of contending with a nest of scraggly, ill-tempered speed freaks, which was what the rooming house had become, and took lodgings of his own elsewhere. But in these final innocent moments of the scene, before the Gray Line buses started ferrying tourists up and down Haight Street, some sweet capitulations to this appealing hippie outlook could be encountered. In May, sharing the bill at an event at the University of California Medical Center in the hills just beyond the Haight, Sam Andrew noted wryly the transformation of Steve Miller, careerist from Chicago. The hardened white blues boy played raga-like inventions on guitar while seated cross-legged on the stage, wearing an Eastern Indian outfit.

Tooling around in her Sunbeam convertible with the band's

God's-eye symbol painted on the door or walking her new dog, George, in the Panhandle, Joplin cut a glorious figure in this new community, perhaps not the kind of star a young girl growing up in East Texas dreamed of becoming, but a star nonetheless. A photographer shot her nude and draped in beads, her bare breast evident but discreet, and produced a poster that sold crisply around town. She was now the first hippie pin-up girl.

But she remained serious about her singing. The band rented a run-down warehouse on Van Ness Avenue for a rehearsal hall and worked every weekend through the spring, sometimes more, appearing five weekends at the Avalon, where Big Brother headlined, and two weekends at the Fillmore, where the band worked as supporting act. She readily agreed when Julius Karpen arranged for her to study with voice teacher Judy Davis, a stern regimentalist who had earned a heavy reputation for coaching Barbra Streisand. Joplin came back from the first meeting reduced to tears, crying in front of the band at rehearsal that Davis told her she had the worst voice she had ever heard. Her brassy veneer could still crack to reveal the scared little girl underneath.

The band landed a small part in the film *Petulia*, which director Richard Lester was shooting in San Francisco. The scene was filmed in the opulent lobby of the Fairmont Hotel, all sparkling cut-glass chandeliers and plush, blood-red carpeting, with Big Brother playing for a society benefit before an audience in formal gowns and tuxedos. Some cast members like Julie Christie and Richard Chamberlain were friendly, but it was an extra who would have the most lasting effect on the band. Sharrie Gomez, a long-legged, elegant model, came from a wealthy, socially prominent family and carried herself with the grace of her upbringing. She not only started dating Sam Andrew, but befriended Joplin, introduced her to the first fashion photographer to shoot her and indoctrinated her in the use of makeup.

The Country Joe McDonald idyll didn't last long. He stayed in her San Francisco apartment and the couple strolled Haight Street arm-in-arm, smiling, hugging. But McDonald liked psychedelics and she didn't. Drinking was taking ever more of her time and energies. He also was devoted to certain political ideals at odds with her own personal philosophy. She thought his sharing songwriting royalties with his band idiotic. Her approach was to take care of herself, not to trust other people to help. Get what you can, while you can. She was suspicious of politics and they argued about their differences.

She was also increasingly infatuated with her blossoming career. Just the small amount of adulation she had earned around San Francisco whetted her appetite. Country Joe and the Fish was also working a lot. In fact, Big Brother shared the bill at the Fillmore with Country Joe and the Fish for the band's record release party in May. Fish guitarist Barry Melton personally rolled a kilo into joints for the occasion. But more often McDonald and Joplin were only tired musicians passing in the night. Before bitterness intruded, McDonald agreed he should move out. She asked him to write a song for her and, with great tenderness and affection, he scratched out a gentle ballad on her behalf, "Janis."

Not that she stayed without male companionship long. Mark Braunstein was a handsome, dark-haired young man barely twenty years old who worked in the Psychedelic Shop on Haight Street, a kind of hippie general store where she liked to shop for candles and such, and they joked around together when she visited the store. They started going to movies and sleeping together. She wanted to have an old man, almost like one of the trappings, the just rewards of her newfound stature, and Braunstein's being four years her junior also appealed to her. Joplin took him with her that weekend in June when the band went to perform at the Monterey International Pop Festival.

ABOVE: *The Charlatans. (left to right) George Hunter, Richard Olsen, Mike Wilhelm, Dan Hicks, Michael Ferguson, 1966.* PHOTO BY HERB GREENE. LEFT: *Cover of the never-released album by the Charlatans.* COURTESY OF DAN HICKS.

TOP: *Bill Graham negotiates with the police at La-fayette Park prior to Mime Troupe bust, 1965.* PHOTO BY ERIK WEBER. ABOVE: *Bonnie and Bill Graham at their wedding party, 1967.* PHOTO BY JIM MARSHALL.

TOP, LEFT: *Bob Weir greets the crowd, as the police bust the Grateful Dead house at 710 Ashbury, 1967.* SAN FRANCISCO CHRONICLE. TOP, RIGHT: *Pigpen of the Grateful Dead watches the action from stageside at the Human Be-In, 1967.* PHOTO BY JIM MARSHALL. ABOVE: *Bob Weir and Phil Lesh of the Grateful Dead take the stage at the Trips Festival, 1966.* PHOTO BY JIM MARSHALL.

LEFT: *The Dead Family in custody at the Hall of Justice. (left to right) Bob Weir, Bob Matthews, Rock Scully, Sue Swanson, Pigpen, Veronica Grant, Antoinette Kaufman, Dan Rifkin, 1967.* SAN FRANCISCO CHRONICLE.

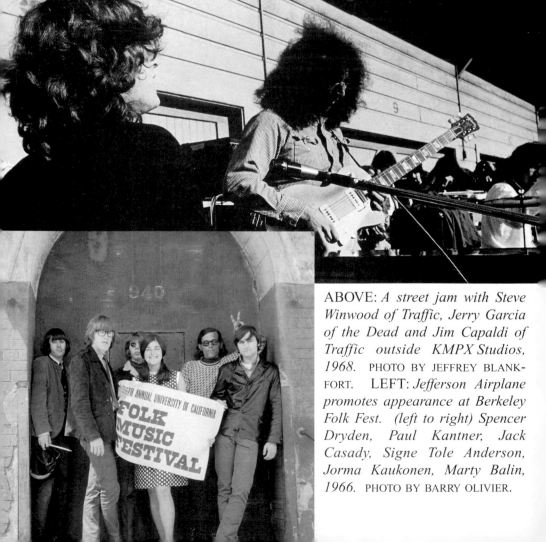

ABOVE: *A street jam with Steve Winwood of Traffic, Jerry Garcia of the Dead and Jim Capaldi of Traffic outside KMPX Studios, 1968.* PHOTO BY JEFFREY BLANK-FORT. LEFT: *Jefferson Airplane promotes appearance at Berkeley Folk Fest. (left to right) Spencer Dryden, Paul Kantner, Jack Casady, Signe Tole Anderson, Jorma Kaukonen, Marty Balin, 1966.* PHOTO BY BARRY OLIVIER.

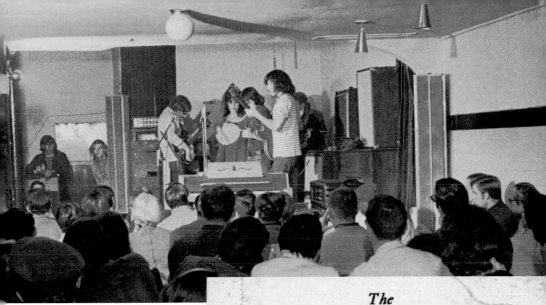

ABOVE: *Jefferson Airplane at the Matrix, 1966.* PHOTO BY JIM MARSHALL. RIGHT: *Jefferson Airplane manager Matthew Katz's business card, including his coined term "fojazz" for "folk-jazz."*

The

MATRIX

San-Francisco's Fojazz Night Club

GOOD ENTERTAINMENT IN A PLEASANT ATMOSPHERE

Fine Wines & Brews

3138 FILLMORE (in the Marina)   SAN FRANCISCO

jefferson airplane loves you

POLICE DEPT
BERKELEY CALIF
19433
2 21 63

Janis Joplin under arrest for shoplifting, 1963.
COURTESY OF MICHAEL REESE, II.

TOP: *Drawing by Sam Andrew of the Oak Street apartment of James Gurley, 1966.* COURTESY OF PETER ALBIN. CENTER: *Quicksilver Messenger Service. (left to right) David Freiberg, Greg Elmore, Gary Duncan, John Cipollina, recording first album at Capitol Studios, Hollywood, 1968.* PHOTO BY TODD CAZAUX. BOTTOM: *Quicksilver and families at first birthday party of Jason Elmore: Girl, David, and Jessica Freiberg; Gary, Shelley, and Heather Duncan; Geri, Greg, and Jason Elmore; John Cipollina seated in front, 1968.* PHOTO BY JIM MARSHALL.

RIGHT: *Dino Valente and Gary Duncan, 1968.* PHOTO BY JIM MARSHALL. BELOW, LEFT: *Moby Grape recording first album in Hollywood. (left to right) Skip Spence, Don Stevenson, Rob Mosley, 1967.* COURTESY OF COLUMBIA RECORDS/SONY MUSIC. BELOW, RIGHT: *Santana in transition. (left to right) Original drummer "Doc" Livingston, David Brown, Carlos Santana, Michael Carabello, Gregg Rolie, 1969.* COURTESY OF COLUMBIA RECORDS/SONY MUSIC. BOTTOM: *Moby Grape posed for cover to second album, although the shot was never used, 1968.* COURTESY OF COLUMBIA RECORDS/SONY MUSIC.

Wild West concerts that never happened, scheduled to take place the week after Wood-stock, 1969.

Cover of the self-released EP by Country Joe and the Fish, 1966. (Left to Right) Paul Armstrong, John Francis Gunning, Bruce Barthol, Joe Mc-Donald, David Cohen, Barry Melton. © 1966, COUNTRY JOE AND THE FISH. USED BY PERMISSION.

FALL 1967

The so-called Summer of Love left San Francisco a mess, the Haight overrun, and the Jefferson Airplane with two smash hits on, of all places, Top Forty radio, "Somebody to Love" and "White Rabbit." That it was Grace Slick, not Marty Balin, who sang his band onto the best-selling charts didn't bother the band's founder. It was just coincidence that he started to become more sullen and withdrawn around that time.

Of course, Jack Casady and Jorma Kaukonen didn't help matters. The two speed-crazed hard cases, enamored of the no-frills bluesmanship of the English rock trio, Cream, began to berate and belittle Balin over what they considered his wimpy love songs. The two grew so avid about the supersonic new British group that the Airplane rented a pair of private planes to whisk the band away from a concert in Bakersfield, about an hour's flight from San Francisco, in order to catch the first Fillmore appearance by Eric Clapton, Jack Bruce and Ginger Baker.

That night Paul Kantner chose to engage in one of his trademark

Teutonic tussles with the forces of law and order from his rarefied perch on the podium. The charter pilot had put Kantner in a foul mood on the way down by complaining about his cigarette smoking and turning apoplectic, threatening to file a police report, when Kantner opened the plane door during the flight and tossed out the offending butt.

At the concert, Kantner started off fairly harmlessly, suggesting the crowd push the folding chairs away and dance, merely direct defiance of the auditorium rules. Then, however, the hall manager complained about the band's volume to road manager Bill Laudner, who did not suffer fools. One of Kesey's band of merry men and a Santa Cruz colleague of Kantner's—Laudner was married to Ginger Jackson when she and Kantner started having their affair—he had carried equipment around for the group since volunteering during the early Matrix days and earned his stripes under fire. Laudner told the hall manager, clearly and plainly, that at their shows, they would play as loud as they wanted. "No, you have to turn down or I'm going to unplug this stuff," he told Laudner. "It's too loud."

Laudner warned him that he could damage equipment if he did. "I'll do what I want—I'm the manager of this building," the hapless functionary told Laudner.

True to his word, the arena manager leaped onstage as the band started the next number and started pulling plugs. Laudner, wearing a Superman T-shirt, quickly grabbed the man and threw him off the stage, which is where the police entered the picture. While Bakersfield's finest started holding earnest talks with Laudner, troublemaker Kantner caught an eyeful and took his case directly to the crowd. "You don't have to put up with this crap," Kantner exhorted the crowd. "There's more of you than there are of them."

The band barely escaped to the planes. But back at the Fillmore to hear Cream that same evening, Casady stood pasted against the rear of the hall reeling under the effects of a double dose of Owsley's notorious Purple Haze, his most potent fabrication yet, especially brewed for the Monterey Pop Festival, where Jimi Hendrix ingested enormous quantities just prior to his epic, historic performance. Under this expanded reality, Casady marveled at the British rockers pushing improvisation beyond the boundaries, and he returned the next night to see if they could wreak the same destruction on his brain without the psychedelics. They could.

Casady and Kaukonen had formed a hardened coalition, an alliance first forged in their childhood, where Casady looked up to his older brother's friend. They carried these roles into the band, where Kaukonen, once again, paved the way for his admiring colleague. They lived in adjacent flats in the same building, Kaukonen with his wife, Margaretta, and Casady with his new lady love, Melissa Cargill. He had come home to Ginger Jackson one day and explained he had fallen in love with Cargill, who not only lived as part of a ménage à trois with acid king Owsley Stanley, but was a chemist herself widely presumed to be a key player in the Owsley underground laboratory.

Kaukonen and Casady also shared many of the same musical fascinations, such as Chicago blues guitarist Buddy Guy, an idol they shared with Clapton and Bruce. The Cream cornerstones, in fact, rushed out of their Fillmore gig that weekend across the bridge to catch Guy at Berkeley's New Orleans House. The respectful British rock musicians ended up sitting in with the intense black guitarist, who represented a second generation of Chicago blues musicians coming up behind Muddy Waters.

This gritty sound from the urban blacks swept underground rock circles—B.B. King, Otis Rush, Freddie King, Junior Wells and Guy—not only because of the fluid, searing guitar playing in the music, but the sedate cool exuded by these seasoned, older ghetto attractions, as if they intuitively understood unspoken ideals these young rock players could only admire and hope to obtain.

So Kaukonen and Casady heaped scorn on Balin's wistful ballads with the gentle folky melodies and the tender romantic sensibilities. They spared no feelings, were often cruel and cutting. But Balin never complained or fought back. He took the blows silently, slinking away from ugly confrontations and growing more private. He had been an autistic child who learned to speak slowly and he refused to engage in battles with these brow-beaters pumped up on Eskatrol, a prescription upper Kaukonen and Casady gulped down in abundance, supplied by a friendly doctor. With Grace Slick absorbing all the public attention and the Kaukonen/Casady faction making the internecine warfare unbearable, Balin slipped into the background of his own band.

Earlier in the summer, the group began recording the follow-up to the smash *Surrealistic Pillow* a couple of weeks after appearing on the Saturday night program at the Monterey Pop Festival, easily the most anticipated performance of the three-day event. Produced by

John Phillips of the Mamas and Papas and his manager Lou Adler, a pair of Hollywood hipsters out to galvanize their standing in the emerging rock underworld, Monterey Pop practically backfired in their faces. Before the final chord of the closing performance by Phillips's own group, on a roll from six consecutive Top Ten singles, the bands from San Francisco and London had so clearly carried the shows that Adler and his associates were lost in the backdraft of suddenly ascendant acts like Jimi Hendrix, Big Brother and the Holding Company, The Who and the Airplane.

With the wild success the Airplane suddenly experienced, things could begin to get good and truly weird in the group's camp. Ready to begin work on a new album, the band left the Monterey Pop Festival—"Somebody to Love" slowly sinking from the Top Ten, "White Rabbit" rising—played a week of nights at the Fillmore with guitarist Jimi Hendrix as opening act, and moved into a five-thousand-dollar-a-month pink mansion in the Hollywood hills whose previous occupants included the Beatles. The musicians were determined to exercise their newfound clout on behalf of creative freedom, which meant forcing the record company to accommodate their derangement.

Drugs were no longer confined to LSD and grass. A dealer from Texas who hung around some with the Dead introduced Kantner to cocaine at Monterey Pop and the insidious white powder made an immediate splash on the band's scene. Casady spent a little spell in jail later that summer in Monterey after testing out Owsley's latest creation, an immensely potent hand-crafted psychedelic he called STP. The first batch turned out to be a mite strong and cops found Casady naked, baying at the moon in a mud puddle. Grace Slick and Spencer Dryden worked on perfecting their drinking habits, polishing off bottle after bottle of sticky sweet Southern Comfort, a drink of choice Slick was introduced to by Janis Joplin. Dryden often stayed up all night, powering through with the aid of speed. He carried a doctor's bag stocked with vials of uppers, downers and anything else he deemed suitable mood alteration.

The Airplane rejected the return of *Surrealistic Pillow* producer Rick Jarrard and opted instead for Al Schmidt, a savvy seasoned hand more accustomed to the sedate atmosphere of Henry Mancini sessions. When he encountered Bill Graham for the first time, Graham was throwing chairs around the Fillmore in a fit of pique. With *Pillow* passing the million mark in sales, however, Schmidt—and RCA—patiently put up with the nitrous oxide tank, Jorma Kaukonen's riding his motorcycles in the studio, the delays caused by band members' routinely commuting by commercial airlines from San Francisco to the sessions, the all-night schedule and general dementia that attended the enterprise. After the group accumulated an unheard of number of takes, several dozen, of an individual song, Spencer Dryden would show up at the studio around midnight and demand that Schmidt play him every one.

With one eye fastened on *Sergeant Pepper's*, the musicians were nothing less than certain that what they were producing would ultimately prove to be rock's greatest masterpiece yet. When they weren't indulging in extravagant wastes of studio time and album budget, band members were carousing at their rented mansion, swimming naked in the pool—generously endowed "security guard" Jim Haynie, Graham's old Mime Troupe colleague, never seemed to wear clothes anywhere around the mansion—or just generally running amok, cultivating a full-fledged entourage in the process. Kaukonen and his strong-willed Swedish wife, Margaretta, battled frequently and the guitarist blew up in anger at some people swimming in the pool at one point, pulling out a gun and peppering the water with bullets.

Progress, what there was of it, was continually interrupted by forays around the country to perform. With the Airplane album lodged inside the Top Five throughout the summer and into the fall, Graham could book the group for formidable fees with ease and he took as many dates as he could, routing the band to any concerts airline schedules would allow. Tension developed between the group and the manager. During one meeting in a hotel room, Graham told the band he was adding dates to the current sequence and they would be staying out on the road awhile longer. Dryden exploded.

"Bill, your brain is made of money," he told Graham sharply. Graham leveled a narrow stare at the drummer. "I'll never forget what you just said, mister," Graham said evenly.

Dryden kept up the attack and even Balin lent his voice, suggesting that he didn't want to worry about how long it took to finish the next album. He wanted to get off the road so the musicians could find something other than the road to write songs about.

In between two shows at Hunter College in New York, Graham thundered into the dressing room, furious that the band refused a third encore call. He screamed at Slick, who told him to fuck off. She hated encores. "Sinatra doesn't do encores," she informed Graham. He cracked.

"You people," he roared. "You fucking people. Who do you think you are?"

As Slick and Graham fell into a shouting match, the Airplane vocalist growing hysterical, Thompson finally grabbed Graham and pushed him physically out of the room. "Bill, don't you think you could have waited until after the show?" asked Thompson.

"I wait for nobody," said Graham.

But the slow rift developing between Graham and the group was not the only fissure beginning to show. The entire band was forming into factions. With Grace Slick and Spencer Dryden having formed an alliance, both personal and professional, they wielded considerable power in the group's politics, with her fresh starpower giving Dryden the wherewithal to throw his weight around. Kaukonen and Casady drove the band's instrumental sound and represented yet another firm division in the ranks. Kantner appeared to actually prosper under these adversarial circumstances, relishing the conflict and growing more domineering in his own role. He ended up writing more than half the songs on the new album.

On the other hand, Balin practically melted into the horizon. He couldn't find any other band member willing to collaborate on songwriting and, without the able assistance of a more competent instrumentalist, Balin was lost trying to come up with material. Harassed by Kaukonen and Casady, resentful toward Slick for her untrained, improvisatory vocal style, Balin became the odd man out in his own band. Dryden mocked his trendy clothing and relatively tame personal habits, sarcastically dubbing him "Bucky Mod." Balin retreated into silence.

The sessions ground on through the fall, finishing up on Halloween night when Dryden dragged a boxful of rented percussion equipment and motion picture sound effects into the studio. He fashioned a cacophonous epiphany, an almost random collection of rattles and crashes, while road managers Gary Blackman and Bill Thompson free-associated over the top. Blackman recited John Donne: "No man is an island."

"He's a peninsula," shouted Thompson.

After recording *Surrealistic Pillow* in around two weeks for a cost of eight thousand dollars, the new Airplane album took almost five months and cost something like $60,000, an unprecedented sum. The meandering pastiche of improvisation and fragmented song structure, including "Martha," a Paul Kantner song about his runaway friend, Martha Wax, and a loose adaptation of James Joyce by Slick called "rejoyce," represented a distinct departure from the carefully crafted folk-pop of the million-selling predecessor. Nothing on the new album could remotely be considered Top Forty fodder. The title, *After Bathing at Baxter's*, was taken from a line of Gray Blackman's poetry. Graham hated the album. "There's nothing on it you can hum," he said.

Graham took the Airplane and the Dead to Toronto for six nights at the O'Keefe Center the first week of August. Outside of a few isolated dates in the Pacific Northwest and a week at the Cafe au Go Go in New York just prior to appearing at the Monterey Pop Festival, the Dead had never really left San Francisco and played outside the provincial ballroom scene. At the Cafe au Go Go, New Yorkers received a healthy dose of the band's show business razzmatazz right at the top of the performance. With the disembodied voice of the club's emcee introducing the band to a totally darkened club—"Ladies and gentlemen, the Cafe au Go Go is proud to present the Grateful Dead"—the lights came up to reveal the band still tuning and fooling with their instruments. Jerry Garcia looked up and leaned into the microphone. "That's right," he smiled, turning back to his tuning.

At the Monterey Pop Festival, the band did not distinguish itself with a performance sandwiched between the pyrotechnics of the Who and Jimi Hendrix on the closing night, although Phil Lesh did tangle words with Peter Tork of the Monkees, who was dispatched by festival producer Lou Adler to interrupt the Dead's set to quell rumors about a Beatles appearance. Lesh looked at the phony hippie from the TV series and saw everything he hated about Hollywood. He sneered the teenybopper hero into humiliation and wound up by inviting the huge crowd standing behind a chain link fence at the perimeter of the concert site to come in. Ushers stood aside as the mob filled the aisles and Tork headed back to the wings chastised.

But for the band's first real road trip, the musicians packed everything. They brought trunks of belongings. On arriving in Toronto, the group redecorated all their rooms at the Royal York, hanging madras bedspreads on the walls, Persian carpets on the floors, lighting giant candles, burning incense and smoking hookahs. The two bands took all the rooms on one floor and with doorways connecting the rooms, a freewheeling, communal party convened. After the O'Keefe shows, both groups piled onto a bus and rolled to Montreal, where the two bands shared a postage stamp-sized stage in the Place Ville Marie in the morning and the Youth Pavilion at Expo '67 later the same day.

When the Airplane headed back to Toronto for a Canadian television show, the Dead were deposited unceremoniously on a street corner in old downtown Montreal, trunks and equipment simply stacked on the sidewalk. Fortunately, one of the entourage had a credit card, so rental cars were arranged and the group headed off for a kind of summit meeting at Millbrook, the upstate New York headquarters of Tim Leary, before moving on to Manhattan and playing on the roof of the Chelsea Hotel for the Diggers. The Dead then flew to Detroit, where they played two nights at the nascent ballroom scene developing around the Grande Ballroom, as well as a free show the following afternoon in Ann Arbor, before heading home to San Francisco.

Winding his own way toward San Francisco at the exact same time was Robert Hunter, who packed his few possessions and hit the road from Santa Fe almost as soon as he picked up the letter from his old Palo Alto pal, Jerry Garcia. Back in the days when Garcia fancied himself a bluegrass banjo player, fresh out of the Army, the two young bohemians lived next door to each other in adjacent parked cars. Hunter volunteered as a subject for psychological studies at a hospital where researchers gave him LSD, mescaline and other assorted mindbenders for three weeks and he reported the results back to the Chateau, where he and Garcia were living by then.

While Garcia, Pigpen, Lesh and the other habitués of the Palo Alto circle wandered off down the pathway that led to the Grateful Dead, Hunter drifted away in his own direction, pursuing ambitions as a novelist and writing anguished poetry and fragmented folk songs he considered somewhat Joycean. He caught the Dead every so often and was impressed with the enterprise his buddies had launched, but methedrine drove him out of town to the relative serenity of the pastoral skyscapes of the New Mexico high desert.

He was exhibiting his pencil drawings in a local gallery, recovering from hepatitis and generally cooling off when the letter arrived from Garcia, who wrote to let Hunter know that he had adapted the lyrics Hunter sent him and the band was performing the resulting songs, "Alligator" and "St. Stephen." Garcia suggested Hunter come back to San Francisco and work as the band's lyricist. Hunter was so eager he left Santa Fe the wrong way and literally wore out his boots getting to Taos before he realized his mistake and reversed direction.

He caught a lift to Denver from a truck driver for a carnival, but lost the connection during the stay overnight, after downing a providential bottle of tokay found in his motel room, and discovered himself stranded in Denver. For two weeks, he slept on living room floors and bummed around the local folk scene, before running across the Dead's first album in a supermarket rack one day and remembering his original mission.

In San Francisco, he asked Rifkin for an advance of two hundred dollars on royalties for "Alligator," which the band was recording for the new album, and bought an old Studebaker. He started working up lyrics for an unfinished piece of music emerging from band jams called "Dark Star" and less than a month after hitting town, he made the run to Rio Nido, a resort town on the Russian River about an hour north of the city, where he rapturously heard the Dead play his songs for the first time.

Everybody in the Dead knew Hunter from Palo Alto, but Mickey Hart, the final piece in the band's puzzle, practically fell out the sky as if destined to find this particular group of musicians. Drums were not just an instrument to dark, wiry Hart; they were a calling. His parents were prize-winning rudimentary drummers, although his father had vanished by the time he was born.

He grew up in Brooklyn and Long Island drum mad, haunted by a ghost of a father he never knew but who left behind a drum pad and a pair of rosewood sticks. Hart had enlisted in the Air Force when he ran across a yellowed pamphlet picturing his father, drum champion Lenny Hart, endorsing a brand of drums. While stationed in southern California, the young drum and bugle corpsman finally met his father, who was working at the time as a savings and loan executive. They spent a transcendent afternoon together, striking two pairs of sticks on anything they could find in Lenny Hart's office—telephone books, chairs, ashtrays—but his subsequent letters to his father were all returned marked "addressee unknown."

He mustered out of the corps in 1965 and had set about establishing himself as a professional union drummer in New York when, out of nowhere one day, a letter arrived from his father inviting him to join him in a business he had just started. Hart packed his suitcases and moved to the Bay Area, where his father had opened a music store in suburban San Carlos, thirty miles south of San Francisco. His son's passion for drums reignited the flame in Lenny Hart and within weeks the store had been renamed Hart Drum City.

Through drum clinics they held at the store, Mickey Hart came to know Sonny Payne, drummer with Count Basie. At the Fillmore to catch Payne and the Basie band during one of Graham's infrequent jazz bookings, he was introduced to another drummer, Billy Kreutzman of the Grateful Dead. He showed Kreutzman a few flashy rudimentary moves and Kreutzman invited Hart to go with him to a club named the Matrix where some friends were playing in a band called Big Brother and the Holding Company. Hart, intrigued, went along. Payne agreed to meet them there later.

When Hart and Kreutzman walked into the tiny club with the little stage in the corner, James Gurley had his arms wrapped around his amplifier, squeezing out an eruption of distortion and feedback before throwing it back on the floor for that resounding crash of the reverb coil. Janis Joplin was wailing away and, by the time Sonny Payne showed up, Hart was entranced. Payne made a face and leaned into Hart's ear.

"This stuff is awful," he said. "I'm getting a headache."

Payne started to leave, but Hart didn't budge.

"I'm gonna stay awhile longer," he told Payne. "I think this stuff is amazing."

Kreutzman and Hart became drum brothers after that night, cruising around the Haight in Kreutzman's Mustang, banging on things together. Kreutzman invited Hart to rehearsals by his band, but he could never find the practice hall. Finally, on September 29, about a month after the night at the Matrix, Hart turned up at a Dead show at the Straight Theater, a Haight Street dancehall opened by a crew of zealots and loons only a few blocks from the Dead house at 710 Ashbury.

He watched the first set enthralled. Pigpen looked like a misplaced Hell's Angel to Hart, yet he intuitively understood the ebb and flow of the tempos that distinguished these from any old blues. The sweaty ambience of the Haight Street crowd, the pervasive odor of pot smoking, the pulsating lights, and especially the big, loud, exciting noise the band made—it all transported Hart. When Kreutzman found him at intermission and suggested finding a second set of drums, Hart jumped at the moment. They raced out of the theater, borrowed a drum kit and had it set up before the band returned from the break and stumbled into the piece the Dead had been fooling around with using Robert Hunter's lyrics, "Alligator."

"Alligator creeping round my door-r-r-r," growled the Hell's Angel lookalike, while seemingly endless cascades of notes flew effortlessly out of guitarist Garcia, a benevolent grin crossing his lips as the music poured through his brain and out his fingers. Hart fell into the big whooshing sound like he had stepped into a jetstream. Two hours later, the song ended. The show was over. Kreutzman took him back to the apartment on Belvedere Street a couple of blocks up the street and showed him a closet. Mickey Hart moved in.

On Monday afternoon, after two nights at the Straight and a benefit on Sunday at the Greek Theater in Berkeley, Jerry Garcia and Mountain Girl left to go shopping in Sausalito. Two cars full of narcotics agents pulled up outside 710 Ashbury and, without a search warrant, bullied their way into the house, trailing a handful of press and television reporters. Pigpen was literally pulled off the toilet. Rosie McGee, who lived around the corner on Belvedere with her boyfriend Phil Lesh, gobbled down a lump of hash as the cops swept through the thirteen room Victorian, rounding up eleven people who happened to be there at the time, including managers Danny Rifkin and Rock Scully, who were grabbed walking up to the porch as the bust was going down. In the kitchen was the damning evidence: a bowl of weed being run through a collander to separate the seeds and stems. All eleven were placed under arrest. "That's what you get for dealing with the killer weed," snickered one of the narcs.

A crowd gathered outside. Garcia and Mountain Girl walked up the street toward the house, when the neighbors across the street hailed them. "Hey, come over here," they said. Garcia and Mountain Girl waved noncommittally and the neighbors grew insistent. "You've got to come over here, right now." They picked up the hint and wandered across the street and avoided arrest.

The cops confiscated the pot from the kitchen table—oblivious to the main stash, an opened kilo that remained undiscovered on a pantry shelf—along with various files, phone books and records belonging to both the band and the Haight-Ashbury Legal Organization, a legal aid group whose offices were in the front room. The perpetrators were handcuffed in pairs and led down the front stairs, as the crowd on the sidewalk jeered the cops. Ironically, the two band members caught in the raid, Bob Weir and Pigpen, were not dope-smokers, the only ones in the band who weren't. Pigpen, a committed juicer, eschewed all forms of drugs and Weir was following a macrobiotic diet regimen at the time that left him with a terrible flatulence problem but kept him off the weed. He nevertheless waved triumphantly as he was led down the front stairs cuffed to Rosie McGee.

Attorney Michael Stepanian, a boisterous young rugby player who maintained the HALO office in the Dead house, showed up at the Hall of Justice as soon as he could and was able to bail everybody out inside several hours. Stepanian took the offense with the newspapers. "The Dead live in the Haight-Ashbury," he told reporters. "If they lived on Russian Hill, they wouldn't be busted. If they lived in Pacific Heights, no officer would go near the house." Newspapers splashed the bust across the front page the following morning, including a very surly shot of Pigpen in custody at the Hall of Justice. To add to the situation, police served Scully with an additional arrest warrant when everybody returned to plead not guilty the next day, charging him with maintaining a house where drugs were used. "Well, you did it again," wisecracked Stepanian as officers led him away.

The Dead convened the press at 710 Ashbury on Friday morning. Danny Rifkin read a carefully prepared statement. "The arrests were made under a law that classifies marijuana along with murder, rape and armed robbery as a felony. Yet almost everyone who has ever studied marijuana seriously and objectively has agreed that marijuana is the least harmful chemical used for pleasure and life-enhancement. The law encourages an even greater evil. It encourages the most outrageously discriminatory type of law enforcement. If the lawyers, the doctors and political officeholders who use marijuana were arrested today, the law might well be off the books before Thanksgiving."

He criticized a system that sends pot-users to jail and slaps small fines on corporate executives whose decisions can cause death and injuries to thousands. He blamed the mass media for creating "the so-called hippie scene" and criticized police for responding to a manufactured popular image.

"Behind all the myths is the reality," Rifkin continued. "The Grateful Dead are people engaged in constructive, creative effort in the musical field and this house is where we work as well as our residence. Because the police fear and misinterpreted us, our effort is now interrupted and we deal with the consequences of a harassing arrest."

The press did not exactly match the high tone Rifkin took in his statement. Rifkin and the Dead were just hippies to these suit-and-tie types and, as such, not to be taken too seriously. "How long did it take to grow your hair that long, Danny?" asked one reporter.

"We always figured that if we ever held a press conference," smiled Rifkin, "the first reporter to ask a stupid question would get a cream pie in the face, and you're him."

The reporter cringed sheepishly as a huge bowl of whipped cream was ritually produced from the kitchen. But instead of pelting the poor man, the Dead served refreshments—coffee, cookies and cake. When it was all over and the reporters drifted away, the band brought out some of Pigpen's antique firearms and mugged for photographs on the front steps with a photographer from a new magazine with its first edition due to be published in a week or so called *Rolling Stone*.

The Monterey Pop Festival vaulted Big Brother into the forefront of the scene, so explosive, so incendiary had Janis Joplin's performance been. In fact, after manager Julius Karpen refused to let the festival producers film the band's officially scheduled performance on Saturday afternoon for a planned TV special and Janis blew a hole in the place, a second slot was made available to the band on Sunday night if the musicians could convince Karpen to relent and allow the group to be filmed. Janis besieged him, alternately screaming and crying. The other band members made their displeasure known and eventually Karpen caved in. But behind the scenes was the powerful talent broker Albert Grossman, who hovered around the backstage area that weekend like a fox stalking a chicken coop.

The cunning, some say unscrupulous manager of Bob Dylan, Grossman also managed the Butterfield Blues Band and handled that band's former guitarist Mike Bloomfield, whose new group, Electric Flag, was making a much anticipated public debut at Monterey. He offered Columbia Records president Clive Davis a package deal involving the Steve Miller Blues Band, Quicksilver Messenger Service and the Flag for a weighty $100,000 advance. Davis would have taken the deal, too, if Grossman had been able to deliver the acts. But he managed only the Flag and ultimately accepted a $50,000 contract from Davis for that band alone. But negotiating record contracts with bands he didn't represent wasn't alone among the questionable deeds in which Grossman engaged backstage at Monterey. He immediately recognized the potential in Janis Joplin and took his first tentative steps to intercept control of her career.

Janis sought out Grossman and asked his advice about the TV special. He suggested the film could help her career—while he held out for large sums of money for the groups he already managed, effectively barring his bands from participating in the very project he recommended to Joplin. Who was he kidding? If he was attempting to undermine Karpen's standing with his charges, he couldn't have done a better job. "Julius Karpen doesn't know it yet, but he just lost Big Brother and the Holding Company," Joplin told her date, Mark Braunstein, that weekend.

Big Brother returned to San Francisco from Monterey to find their world a different place. Even before waves from the festival lapped up on the shore—attention from national press like *Time* and *Esquire,* major labels bidding for the band's services—Bill Graham started booking the band at the Fillmore. Big Brother had played the Fillmore early the previous year, shortly after Graham began running the hall, but after that, Graham associated the group with his arch rival, Chet Helms, and his establishment, the Avalon, and rarely used the band. He even withdrew his typical courtesy of letting them in the Fillmore free, throwing a fit one night when Janis and a couple of the others showed up at his dancehall after he read a piddling comment Joplin made in a mimeographed fan magazine called *Mojo Navigator.* She told the interviewer the Avalon was the place for music; the Fillmore was where sailors went to get laid. Graham took offense. He met them at the top of the stairs and turned them away. Joplin, speed coursing through her bloodstream, started a shouting match, profane and loud, but Graham had the last word. Peter Albin called him a few days later, trying to smooth things over, but Graham was having none of it.

After the Monterey triumph, however, Graham sang a different tune. The very next weekend, he hired Big Brother to substitute for Jefferson Airplane on a bill that featured another one of the stars of Monterey, Jimi Hendrix. Joplin initiated an affair with Hendrix and helped convince the flamboyant guitarist to play one of the weekly free concerts in the Panhandle presented by her ex-boyfriend, Mark Braunstein of the Psychedelic Shop. Graham booked Big Brother back two weeks later on a double-bill with Bo Diddley, a program redolent of the Avalon shows that were so successful the previous summer.

Joplin enjoyed the new status. She found a new roommate in Linda Gravenites, a sensual earth-mother type who was house-sitting at the Dead house while the musicians were on the road and their womenfolk scouted New Mexico for possible living sites, a short-lived plan that came to naught. Joplin noticed a shirt Sam Andrews was wearing and he recommended Gravenites to Joplin as a seamstress. She went to work on Joplin, who was still wearing the peasant blouses and Madras skirts in which Nancy Gurley had dressed her. Gravenites, the ex-wife of Nick Gravenites who sewed costumes for local theatrical companies, cast Janis as a raunchy pirate chick and started to put some sex into her look, making tight-fitting dresses of sensual velvet with low-cut necklines that showed plenty of bosom. They started by planning an outfit for the September performance at the annual Monterey Jazz Festival and, when the Dead returned from the East Coast, Gravenites simply moved into Joplin's Lyon Street apartment, sleeping on the couch in the front room, and stayed.

Another close friend of Joplin's at the time was a long-legged, half-Indian woman called Sunshine, whom Janis first met during her North Beach days when Sunshine worked as a waitress at the Coffee Gallery. With tiny Suzy Perry, girlfriend of poster artist Stanley Mouse, these four Capricorn ladies cut quite a figure striding down Haight Street together, carrying bottles of booze in large purses and getting blind drunk on nighttime rampages around town when Big Brother wasn't working.

Joplin still enjoyed male companionship and her romantic—or at least sexual—liaisons spanned a wide range, from the Hell's Angel known as Freewheelin' Frank to part-time bartender and comic sparkplug of improv troupe The Committee, Howard Hesseman. She started up a long-running on-again, off-again relationship with Milan Melvin, a dark, handsome man often seen wearing a purple cape and carrying a violin case for a briefcase as he called on North Beach businesses soliciting advertisements for KMPX, the FM radio station where Tom Donahue was inventing "underground radio." One night Joplin entertained Jim Morrison of the Doors and his girlfriend,

Pamela Courson, at her Lyon Street place, along with Sam Andrew and Big Brother road manager Dave Richards.

Both Richards and Andrew recognized the signs and weren't surprised when Janis invited Morrison down the hall to her lace and velvet decorated bedroom, shutting the door behind them. With both men eyeing Morrison's girlfriend, they told her they didn't think anybody would be coming back down the hall until morning. At first, she didn't believe them. Then, in a tight little fury, she asked them to call a cab. When Dave Richards ushered her to the street and opened the taxi door, intending to climb in beside her and head off into the night, Andrew whisked past Richards into the back seat and closed the door.

The Joplin family—Janis's mother, father, younger brother and younger sister—came to visit in August, a strained meeting with the errant daughter still struggling for her parents' acceptance and the emotionally reserved Joplins withholding approval. She arranged for Big Brother to play a special performance at the Avalon, making an unannounced appearance to play a few numbers specifically for the benefit of her visitors, but the sound, the lights, the bizarre people were all somewhat overwhelming to the pointedly austere Joplins. At least, her parents never mentioned going back to college again to her.

In September, the Monterey Jazz Festival proved to be another sensational event for Joplin, who stomped and shrieked her way through a bravura performance that, if anything, might even have exceeded the scene-stealing show she gave three months earlier on the same stage at the Monterey Pop Festival. Once again, Karpen ruled out the performance's being filmed, this time for a documentary being made by *S.F. Chronicle* columnist Ralph Gleason.

They also had a blow-out with their hard-headed, often idealistic manager over a Hollywood Bowl concert Graham wanted to present with the Airplane, the Dead and Big Brother. Karpen objected to the group's serving as a mere opening act, didn't like the money being offered and generally feuded with Graham anyway. Graham took his case directly to the musicians, calling them behind Karpen's back and telling them their manager was ruining their career. The band members told Karpen they wanted to play the show. Karpen wouldn't allow it. Graham kept the pressure up. Back and forth they went. The band ultimately did not play the show, although Graham printed posters that included Big Brother on the bill.

But the final straw came when the group insisted Karpen show the musicians the books. They knew money was finally coming in, although they were still each drawing a meager $125 a week. Peter Albin's uncle, the same one who owned the Page Street Victorian where Big Brother originally came together, was derisive when the band sought his counsel. "You deserve to be robbed blind," he snorted.

To Karpen, it wasn't a question of hiding anything from the band, save perhaps his own incompetence when it came to record-keeping. It was an issue of trust. The request itself represented a breach of faith. Karpen was an LSD evangelist, a reformed alcoholic who smoked copious amounts of pot and, like his comrade Polte of Quicksilver, saw himself as a pilgrim pursuing a vision of a new world, not simply somebody's business manager. He certainly wasn't a thief, although he lost some of the band's money in an abortive investment with Polte in a San Jose nightclub. In November, the band decided to get rid of Karpen.

Talking among themselves, the musicians came up with the idea of contacting Grossman. He was a powerful figure in the music business and the members of Big Brother were duly impressed. Ironically, they asked Karpen's pal Polte, who knew Grossman from Chicago, to make the call. Grossman flew out to meet with the band.

He looked like a cross between Ben Franklin with his wire-rim spectacles and the man from the Quaker Oats box. Low-key in manner and speech, Grossman carried himself with enormous authority. He joined the band at Janis's Lyon Street apartment and laid out his program. He would take twenty percent off the top, plus his expenses. In exchange, he would do what the group wanted. Did they want to work enough to get by and spend the rest of their time hanging out? Did they want to be rich and famous? What did they want? Grossman wanted to know.

David Getz knew the band had made $25,000 that year. He picked a figure three times that amount—$75,000—and told Grossman the group wanted to make that sum in the coming year. Grossman calmly told the band he would guarantee $75,000. If he didn't earn that much for the group, he would cancel the contract and they wouldn't owe him anything. If the sum didn't seem like a great deal of money to Grossman, he never let on. The musicians took his offer as a sign of largesse, because $75,000 certainly seemed like a substantial amount of money to them. They were flattered to have the attention of someone so important as Grossman and somewhat dazzled by the prospects he represented. They eagerly assented.

"One thing," intoned Grossman seriously. "No schmeeze."

Nobody in the band had ever heard the Yiddish term for junk before, but everybody knew exactly what he meant and nodded their agreement. Three people were already lying.

Moby Grape finally fired Matthew Katz. Following the blissful launch of the debut album and the immediately subsequent debacle of arrest and public humiliation, the Grape bounced along a bumpy road. The band appeared two weeks later at the Monterey Pop Festival, but the opening slot at the Saturday evening concert hardly represented prime exposure. The sun was still out and people were taking their seats throughout the band's first set. Peter Lewis did relent later that evening and took his first acid trip with Skip Spence.

From Monterey, the band set out to tour with the festival's headliners and organizers, the Mamas and Papas, only to be thrown off the trip after a few dates. Musically incompatible with the svelte Hollywood folk-rock sound of the star attraction, the Grape didn't help matters by showing up late for concerts, brandishing bad attitudes and a manager who made everybody—even his own band—uptight.

Spence grew more troublesome. Unbeknownst to the group, he started experimenting with volatile psychedelic cocktails of speed and LSD, hoping to bring out greater personal magnetism, influenced by the English rock star decadence of Brian Jones of the Rolling Stones, whom Spence watched parade around backstage at Monterey, dressed like royalty gone to seed and absolutely stoned off the face of the earth.

Booked at the last minute into a ramshackle series of shows that had the band playing high school auditoriums, county fairs, anywhere the group could find a stage, the Grape chased around the country like an unraveling ball of string. After the publicity surrounding the arrest in Marin, the cops gave the musicians close scrutiny everywhere they went. Katz was no help. In one scrape, the band was thrown out of a Philadelphia hotel for fighting, while Katz stood by in the hallway. The band stripped naked onstage during one show in Seattle.

At a Catholic school in Milwaukee, Spence caused a scene. Mosley got a shock from the school's faulty microphone and threw it on the stage in anger. Spence, not to be left out, threw his down, too.

One of the school fathers, fearing the band would destroy the equipment, turned off the power. In the resulting fracas, Spence smashed his guitar on the stage, threw it into the audience, dropped his pants and mooned a nun. The police were summoned, only to arrive as Katz and the band were pulling away. When the officer thrust his arm inside the vehicle, Mosley rolled up the window and Spence stepped on the gas, with the helpless cop stumbling alongside while the group laughed. After dragging him a few dozen harrowing yards, they rolled the window back down, let him go and sped off into the night.

By August, Katz had negotiated a deal for the group to appear in a 20th Century Fox film called *The Sweet Ride,* a kind of thinking man's surf movie which counted chief among its attractions a topless scene featuring a young British actress named Jacqueline Bisset. The group settled into lodgings in the beachside colony of Malibu, not far from pal Stephen Stills, and set about recording material with producer David Rubinson for a second album. Four songs were laid down, but not finished. Katz arranged for the musicians to be paid ten thousand dollars for their services in the film and the rights to use the music on a soundtrack recording—although the band understood the deal to exclude soundtrack rights. Katz apologized for not getting a greater sum from the film's producers, but when the members never received any money at all anyway, his fate was sealed.

Without telling anyone, Mike Ferguson of the Charlatans went out for some barbecue, spilled sauce on his all-white suit and went home to change. The scrupulous Ferguson could not possibly appear onstage with a stain marring his carefully cultivated sartorial image. With a full house at Winterland for a benefit raising funds for legalization of marijuana, the city's first rock group may have slipped to the bottom of a bill featuring the full front line of the San Francisco bands—Jefferson Airplane, Grateful Dead, Big Brother and Quicksilver. But even opening such a show represented an increasingly rare opportunity for the fellows who started the ball in the first place a scant two years earlier, and his bandmates were mystified when it appeared that Ferguson had disappeared.

When it came time to play, he was still nowhere to be found and Bill Graham went on one of his trademark tears, screaming, berating, threatening, as Ferguson's helpless colleagues stood by. Graham himself began shoving the group's equipment to the back of the stage, the

appointed time to perform having come and gone. By the time
Ferguson actually returned to the scene, the Charlatans had been long
scotched from the program.

Since the failure of the group's foray into the recording industry
the year before, the fabric of the band had grown as frayed as the collars of their Edwardian coats. With groups around them left and right
landing record contracts and moving up the bills at the Fillmore and
Avalon, the members of the Charlatans all felt the frustration of the
band's apparent stagnation. A pair of Los Angeles-based music business types expressed interest in managing the band and brought the
group south to meet with Leon Russell, an arranger and session musician with considerable experience, but nothing came of that expedi-
tion. Some promising tapes were cut at Golden State Studios,
including a George Hunter original titled "A Girl Like You" that
showed signs of his finally finding a songwriting approach to match his
designer's eye for his band.

Drummer Dan Hicks began to assume a more prominent role in
the Charlatans. His own vocals on numbers like "How Can I Miss You
When You Won't Go Away?" or "We're Not on the Same Trip" featured his dry delivery and parched wit, while he took center stage and
Ferguson assumed the drummer's chair.

Smoldering resentment flared between the two during one afternoon sound check at the Avalon when Ferguson threw the drumsticks
at Hicks and Hicks chased Ferguson around the room, although no
punches were thrown. Ferguson also smashed a large ashtray in a display of anger after the band didn't get paid in full following one Avalon Show. His nerves were beginning to show.

He also clashed with Hunter, who still maintained his hold on the
group's reins. Although he could play hell out of bluesy, honky-tonk piano in certain keys, Ferguson was an instrumentalist of limited abilities, an artist first, a musician second. He was a diabetic who never
bothered to take care of himself or watch his diet, although somehow
his physique, almost miraculously, stayed in fine condition. Ferguson
had little patience with the obtuse character of a bandleader like
Hunter or the sarcastic jibes of an associate like Hicks. And Hunter
was no diplomat, and often handled communication through confrontation. Rehearsals began to unravel in fights. Ferguson started skipping them altogether.

At the next rehearsal following the abortive Winterland show,

Hunter stopped Ferguson on the front steps of his Oak Street flat. He informed Ferguson he was dismissed from the group he helped form. With Hunter, Ferguson had shaped the look, the style, the resonant image that was the essence of the band, but the innocence of those heady days was drying up and blowing away like so many fallen leaves. Crushed, Ferguson trudged back down the steps and, before long, was working at the post office, a common haven for hard-up hippies who refused to cut their hair to get a job.

Hicks had already heard Patrick Gogerty playing ragtime in a Los Angeles pizza parlor and identified the mustachioed pianist as a kindred spirit with garters on his shirtsleeves. Drummer Terry Wilson was also added to the lineup, freeing Hicks to play rhythm guitar and sing.

At first, Chet Helms didn't think opening a dancehall in Denver was such a good idea, even if his partner, Bob Cohen, had already signed a lease on a building. It wasn't for lack of capital. The Avalon was flourishing so much that when Cohen's landlady asked if he wanted to buy the house in which he rented an apartment and the one next door for fifty thousand dollars, he looked in his checking account and found he had enough money to write a check for the full amount. But with his rent a mere seventy-five dollars a month, he didn't see the need to own the houses.

Cohen convinced Helms to visit Denver and check out the scene. The fledgling hippie underworld of the mountain city approached Helms at his every stop, asking him to please bring the Family Dog to Denver. He was seduced. Helms pledged to expand the business by opening new temples of music, starting with Denver.

The building Cohen secured was a giant former factory, essentially a vacant rectangle surrounded by four walls. Helms and Cohen funneled some $100,000 from the Avalon operation into refurbishing the hall, the glistening centerpiece of which was the dance floor, with the Family Dog insignia painted in the center, surrounded by the twelve signs of the Zodiac. Thick coats of acrylic covered the floor, a glossy, experimental finish that took forever to get right. When it was done, the reflection in the floor made the support pillars appear to disappear down into infinity. Helms brought a crew of people from the San Francisco operation to run the Denver Dog. A full house of more than three thousand attended the August 8 opening weekend with Big Brother and the Holding Company playing the band's first out-of-town engagement since the Monterey Pop Festival. Opening the show was Blue Cheer, the high-decibel San Francisco rock trio.

Helms went back to San Francisco happy with the christening. The next four successive weekends in Denver, he brought Quicksilver and the Charlatans, the Dead, the Doors and Buffalo Springfield. While bands like Quicksilver and the Charlatans that didn't have records out failed to draw large crowds, the prospects looked quite favorable.

The Denver police had been keeping a watchful eye on the establishment from the start. During the summer, workers noticed patrol cars parked outside. But, the Denver Dog had apparently been targeted by one crusading cop on a mission to run all the hippies out of Denver. Detective John Gray, extolled as the leading enemy of hippies in an official police department press handout, fought a single-handed battle to bring the business to its knees. He accosted teenaged patrons in the parking lot. "Do your parents know where you are?" he asked. "Don't ever let me see you here again."

Dog management retaliated by printing parental permission slips in the local underground newspaper. Helms's hand-picked manager, Tony Guillory, did little to pour oil on the troubled waters. A black man with an earring given to wearing knee-high fur boots and spouting poetry, his very appearance gave offense to the cowtown mentality of the Denver powers-that-be.

Denver police routinely stopped longhairs, carded them and kept the records on file. Hitchhikers spent the night in jail. An archaic curfew law was used against Family Dog patrons. The police maintained not dozens, but hundreds of teenage informants, Denver attorneys charged, and paid them off with drugs. Detective Gray even went to court that fall and testified he arrested one young man after being invited to drop into his home anytime, doing so and finding pot. The young man denied Gray's story.

But Detective Gray did not count on the Dog's landlord, attorney Francis Salazar, amateur hypnotist, opera singer, the 1938 Mr. Universe and winner of the largest award ever won in court from the Internal Revenue Service, who presented, in the process, the longest brief in U.S. jurisprudence. Not a man to be trifled with, Salazar took Helms to meet with District Judge John Brooks, Jr., who found an obscure and ancient precedent and issued a restraining order barring Gray from entering the Dog premises, after Salazar filed a suit against

Gray, the police and the city on behalf of the Family Dog. That night, two other police detectives turned up at the Dog and issued citations charging Helms and his partners with operating without proper permits.

The next night, Gray himself arrested five members of Canned Heat in their rooms at the Rancho Manor Motel after the band performed at the Dog. Gray claimed to have entered the first motel room with a search warrant, found a handful of joints and, after searching other rooms, located a small quantity of hashish and a half-pound of marijuana hidden in a pair of men's shoes.

When Gray arrested a part-time Dog employee on charges of marijuana possession, robbery and curfew violation the next month, the alleged perpetrator turned around and smacked Gray and the force with a thirty-thousand-dollar false arrest suit. But Gray wasn't backing down. In an interview with the *Denver Post*, he called hippies "Communist dupes."

Ten years earlier, the Denver police department had been riddled with a scandal involving a burglary ring operating within the department. Salazar even represented some of the officers arrested when the rampant corruption was finally uncovered. The city remained sensitive to police abuse of power. When the American Civil Liberties Union announced the organization was collecting affidavits concerning the apparent crackdown on hippies, contemplating a class action suit, the community began to quietly stir.

When the restraining order on Gray and Helms's original suit came to trial, the courtroom was packed with rock fans. The judge ruled blue jeans inappropriate dress for court and ordered the bailiff to usher out any spectator so attired. The bailiff cracked he couldn't tell the gals from the fellows. For two days, witnesses paraded across the stand with tales of police harassment. But Judge Brooks ultimately ruled in favor of the department, lifting the ban on Gray at the Dog and ruling that if Salazar had asked for damages along with asking to bar Gray from the premises, he could have more properly continued the injunction. Three weeks later, Salazar filed a new suit in Federal Court, charging police harassment and asking for more than $125,000 in damages. Two weeks after that, the mayor fired the police chief and refused to offer any explanation.

It didn't matter. Gray had already intimidated young Denver into staying away from shows at the Dog. Winter and snowfall also settled in on the enterprise. Smaller and smaller crowds attended the concerts. Helms was rupturing money in Denver at a pace that even the fountainhead of the Avalon couldn't continually replenish. Gray and his associates kept their eagle eyes trained on the Denver Dog. The light show artist spotted the detective in the crowd at one show, flashed a warning on the screen and trained a spotlight on him, as a conga line formed behind him and snaked its way through the crowd at his tail.

In February, police arrested manager Guillory for writing a bad check. He was released and the charges were dropped. But expenses mounted on the Denver Dog and Helms dropped the lawsuit. While Salazar was on vacation, Helms was served with an eviction notice and the Family Dog trundled out of town, tail between its legs.

Paul Baratta came to work for Bill Graham only after a half dozen or more deli lunch meetings around the corner from the Fillmore Auditorium, while Graham tried to assess this other ex-actor from New York. Baratta was recommended to Graham by Marty Balin, who was still dating Janet Trice, the nurse he was seeing two years earlier when he built the Matrix, who also happened to be Baratta's cousin.

He knew even less about the music than Graham. His cousin took him to the Fillmore to watch the Airplane and he found the experience disorienting, like visiting a strange planet hidden away up those stairs from Geary Street. Baratta was a straight, with children and a Puerto Rican wife, but he and Graham found some common ground. Graham, knowing the exploding career of the Airplane would be drawing him away from the Fillmore, took Baratta onboard to help run the mother store.

He came to work the weekend of the Monterey Pop Festival, with the Who smashing guitars onstage as the finale. The Sunday before, he attended the small, private ceremony at which Graham and Bonnie MacLean were finally married. Their relationship had gone through some white water, practically foundered. But Graham proposed in Boston during a Jefferson Airplane road trip, hoping to stabilize their personal lives. They were married by a Unitarian minister at their Sacramento Street home, a definite step upscale from the apartment they first shared in the Sunset District, but hardly the opulent digs of a budding millionaire. In fact, shortly thereafter, they moved to considerably more comfortable quarters on the edge of fashionable Pacific Heights, a Washington Street address next door to a duplex occupied by two of his charges from the Airplane, the Kaukonens upstairs and Grace Slick and Spencer Dryden, who had moved in together, downstairs. But the wedding was a low-key affair, attended by some family, a handful of employees, a select few musicians and the few friends outside of his business circle Graham enjoyed. They did not take a honeymoon, although the next weekend, the newlyweds attended the Monterey Pop Festival.

The following week Graham opened the Fillmore for six nights a week, beginning with a run starring the Airplane, jazz guitarist Gabor Szabo and opening act Jimi Hendrix, who was paid the grand sum of seven hundred and fifty dollars for his entire week's work. Graham didn't even understand that the flamboyant black guitarist who had been the star of Monterey Pop was responsible for drawing the capacity-and-beyond crowds—he thought the Airplane was doing the business—until Baratta pointed out that the hall half emptied after Hendrix's second set each night.

Baratta and Graham booked the Fillmore by the seats of their pants, staying at the hall until four in the morning to call England and returning to work by ten the next morning. Neither were rock fans, but they learned to detect attractions practically by osmosis. They didn't even listen to KMPX, the new full-time "underground radio" that started broadcasting on the FM band in San Francisco that June under Tom Donahue's supervision. Graham booked the British heavy rock trio Cream for two weeks in August without having heard the band's music, just having heard people talk about the group. He paid Cream five hundred dollars a night. The first Saturday night of the engagement, he jammed more than thirty-five hundred bodies into the nine hundred-capacity hall. He grossed more than eighty thousand dollars during the run. The concession stands did more than sixty thousand dollars in business.

Nobody but Graham knew what happened to all this cash. No accurate count was available because of Graham's habit of not tearing tickets at the door and reselling the untorn tickets at the box office. Many people suspected him of depositing large amounts of cash in Swiss bank accounts. His secretary, Marushka Greene, would come to work on Mondays and take the empty apple cartons filled every weekend with small-denomination bills to the bank across the street. Graham himself kept a small pistol in his desk as a security measure in dealing with the bags full of money he collected.

When Graham worked as office manager for Allis-Chalmers before joining the Mime Troupe, he consolidated two offices into one and reduced the staff from forty-seven to twenty-one employees, so he knew the value of cutting costs and limiting overhead. He ran the Fillmore with a minimum of staff and there was no detail too small for Graham himself to attend to. He tested his operation outside Winterland, producing the Airplane and Dead in Toronto in August and at the Hollywood Bowl in September. He booked the enormous Cow Palace in San Francisco that September to throw a concert by Donovan, but was so embarrassed by the horrid sound and cold, sterile atmosphere, he whisked the popular British folk-rock troubador back to the Fillmore and Winterland for three grossly oversold shows in November.

He could be contentious and argumentative, a bully if he wanted to be. This rancorous side of his personality was rapidly becoming a trademark and, at times, he could flash his genial smile after bellowing some poor character into submission over the phone to let intimates present on his end of the conversation know it was just another acting exercise. Rage was just another tool to help him get what he wanted. After an indolent, cursory performance by the Byrds at the Fillmore in September, he swore at the top of his voice he would never book the group again. In December, the band returned, all his dire imprecations aside.

Managing the Airplane entailed Graham's using many of the same attitudes, dominating a situation by sheer force of personality. With the Airplane, however, there were other forceful personalities with which to be reckoned. And there came times when his wearing both hats—manager and concert producer—caused band members to mutter among themselves, like when he booked the group for New Year's Eve at Winterland for a price far less than what, as manager, he would have charged another promoter.

1968

*To one who doesn't
hear the music,
hear the music,
the dancers look crazy.*
          Sufi proverb

WINTER 1967-68

Graham wanted the Airplane to sign a management contract with him. Tired of the handshake deal, he wanted more leverage with the band. He knew that Albert Grossman had signed a strict contract with Big Brother, and Grossman was a man Graham admired. Nobody in the Airplane saw any advantage in signing any contracts, but that didn't stop Graham from campaigning for the idea.

At the Landmark Motel in Hollywood, he convened a band meeting to press the issue. He had a stack of contracts prepared for signature and was determined to resolve the matter. With the management contract the band signed with Katz under litigation, freezing all royalties from the band's first album, and attorneys' fees already mounting on the case, the musicians didn't think much of management contracts. Kaukonen finally stood up and walked out, announcing he was hungry and was going to get something to eat. One by one, the rest of the band trailed along, leaving Graham alone with a stack of unsigned papers.

Spencer Dryden led the opposition to Graham within the band.

Graham blew up at Dryden's insistence that Graham supply a bottle of Southern Comfort backstage at every concert. To Dryden, who stayed blasted on some combination of booze, pills and dope, it was difficult enough to get out of bed in the morning, let alone work the kind of demanding schedule Graham wanted. He and Grace Slick were not signed with RCA Victor personally and they made friends with David Anderle of Elektra Records, who made suggestions about a record deal of their own. With his paramour Slick not only the vocalist on the group's two hit records, but also the obvious star of the band, Dryden carried considerable weight.

Kaukonen and Casady exploded when they found out that Graham let the band rehearse at the former synagogue he bought next door to the Fillmore, but charged the group rent. Graham pressured the Airplane to play more concerts—Slick and Dryden especially didn't like the hectic pace the band was already keeping—and to write and record more commercial songs, haranguing the musicians over the relative failure of *After Bathing at Baxter's*, which sold a mere 350,000, as opposed to the more than 1.5 million-selling success of *Surrealistic Pillow*. Graham eroded any support he had inside the band. Only Kantner still liked Graham, but Kantner loved contention.

It all came to a head in January 1968 during a rehearsal at the Geary Temple next door to the Fillmore. Dryden told the band he and Slick had offers to do other records. He made it clear he was sick of Graham and delivered an ultimatum with Slick's blessing—him or us. The band saw little choice. Thompson was dispatched to make a round of calls to RCA executives and Airplane attorneys and sound them out about losing Graham. Graham was summoned from next door and told he was to be replaced as manager by Thompson. He turned livid.

"A copy boy," he practically screamed. "A fucking copy boy. How can you do this? You can't send a boy to do a man's job."

As successful as he was, Graham was regarded with a certain skepticism and wariness by the San Francisco bands. The Airplane and the Dead, in fact, so dreaded working for him, the two groups joined forces to open a third ballroom in San Francisco. The El Patio Ballroom, which had presented all the well-known big bands during its heyday, was owned by an Irish ballroom operator named Bill Fuller, who had similar properties in Chicago, New York, Boston, London, Manchester and throughout Ireland.

Spearheading the operation was a former Wall Street prodigy named Ron Rakow, who met Dead managers Scully and Rifkin through mutual friends at a period in his life when he had taken a year off from work to pursue a newfound hobby of archery. Rakow, who put Scully and Rifkin to work shortly after meeting them supplying phony signatures for one scheme of his, was a brilliant scoundrel, a visionary con artist who fit right into the anti-establishment mood of the Dead camp.

His first venture with the band was the All Our Own Car Co., a dummy company formed to purchase a small fleet of fourteen new Ford Cortinas that had been gathering dust on the lot of a local dealership. Rakow worked with one of the partners in the car company to finance the enterprise and, so anxious was the gentleman to move these unappealing compacts, he arranged with Rakow for the dealership itself to supply most of the down payment. The Dead made few further payments and, in about six months, the bank began calling around to repossess. Pigpen was heartbroken. He loved his car, the first new car he had ever owned. Actually, the Cortinas were the first new cars that any of the band members and crew had owned, but Pig kept his in pristine condition with special pride. Rakow hated his and donated the car to the Black Panther Party. When the bank called, he told them exactly where they could go to get the car.

Rakow and attorney Brian Rohan entered into negotiations with Fuller for a lease to the ballroom and, without a down payment, paid a premium rent and gave up a sizable percentage of the revenues. Saddled with an albatross contract and with wild-eyed maniacs running the venture, including one partner who belonged to the Hell's Angels, the enterprise was probably doomed from the start. But the psychedelic rock community clasped the renamed Carousel Ballroom to its bosom from the first moment as a happy alternative to the iron-fisted capitalism of the Fillmore or the pixilated clannishness of the Avalon.

With a capacity more than twice the size of the Fillmore, the Carousel, above the rug showroom on the landmark street corner of Van Ness Avenue and Market Street, had a parquet floor and velour curtain that draped over the ceiling and down along the walls. The entrance was a stairway off Market Street that led to the second floor of the building and opened up to a broad open space with a dancefloor surrounded by pillars. On January 17, Ben Franklin's birthday, the

Dead and Quicksilver played the first concert at the Carousel. The poster for the event featured a Ben Franklin portrait taken from a hundred dollar bill. At $2.50, the Carousel was a half-dollar cheaper than the Fillmore. The battle was on.

The next day, the two bands left for a tour of the Pacific Northwest booked, oddly enough, by attorney Rohan, dubbed "The Quick and the Dead." This incursion into the hinterlands took the San Francisco ballroom scene, complete with Jerry Abrams's light show, into foreign territory. Police dogged the caravan's every step. In a Keystone Kops scenario, Oregon police raided one hotel an hour and a half before the troupe checked in.

In Portland, Quicksilver guitarist John Cipollina bought guns and hundreds of blank cartridges at a pawn shop, all the better to continue the cowboys and Indians game the two bands had played since the Olema Indian raid. According to the rules, once a participant was shot—even if the pistol in questions was nothing more than a thumb and forefinger—the victim was required to stay dead for at least a couple of minutes. Cipollina spotted Pigpen, Rifkin and Scully driving down the street. He stepped out in the auto's path, shrieking some demented war cry and blazing away with the blanks. The car screeched to a halt, the doors flew open and the passengers fell out into the snow on the ground. A horrified bystander quickly and quietly called the police. But, by the time police patrol cars arrived on the scene, sirens wailing, the victims had long since moved along, nowhere to be found. Cipollina wound up the tour with calluses on his fingers from gunplay.

The bands took an early flight home from the final date in Medford, Oregon, and, once again, the police showed up too late to serve their search warrant. Only the equipment crew and trucks remained and the warrant didn't cover that. By the time this oversight was corrected, the trucks were rolling down the highway, where they were stopped by the cops. Every piece of equipment was unloaded by the side of the road—and the Dead and Quicksilver carried lots of equipment, not to mention the light show—and searched. The police could never manage to fit all the equipment back into the trucks and, after several hours, they let the crew go, having found no trace of incriminating contraband.

Quicksilver had made their debut as a quartet on New Year's Eve at Winterland, three months after Jimmy Murray left. Once the band began rehearsing regularly, the enterprise became simply too serious and rigorous for the unambitious Murray. Although the group held reservations about venturing into the recording business, Vanguard Records had earlier expressed interest. Demos were recorded and a label representative came out to talk to the band, only to find the always sickly Cipollina ill in bed, swathed in furs, attended by young girls in a room full of God's eyes and incense.

But in November Polte had landed an extraordinary contract with Capitol Records, who, fearful of being left out of the new gold rush, signed both the Steve Miller Band—no longer the Steve Miller *Blues* Band—and Quicksilver to astronomical deals. The Quicksilver pact, a four-year agreement, included a $40,000 advance against royalties, a $10,000 signing bonus and $100,000 options for each of the last two years. The group retained publishing rights and certain guarantees of artistic control.

To produce the album, Polte turned to his old Chicago friend Nick Gravenites, who had gone from sleeping on Cipollina's couch to putting together and singing with guitar hero Mike Bloomfield's first post-Paul Butterfield Blues Band group. Polte had given the band its name, Electric Flag. Gravenites and Flag bassist Harvey Brooks put Quicksilver through the paces at a couple of different sessions at Capitol Studios in Hollywood around Thanksgiving without much to show for it.

The band members were all living in San Francisco, with the group's three married couples having each produced a baby during the previous year. When Shelley Duncan went into labor, her husband simply dropped her and a girlfriend off at the hospital and told her to call if it was a boy. She phoned anyway after having a baby girl. "Are you disappointed?" she asked. "Yes," he said.

Ten days after returning from the tour with Quicksilver, the Dead presided over the official opening of the Carousel Ballroom, along with Country Joe and the Fish, who had released their second album three months earlier, featuring a re-recording of the agit-prop jug band number from the Vietnam Teach-In that started it all for McDonald and Melton, "I Feel Like I'm Fixin' to Die Rag."

To mark the event community-wide, the concert was broadcast live on KMPX-FM. The station had grown in stature and impact on the Bay Area scene so much since the inception of 'round-the-clock broadcasting the previous June—before then, the underground rock shared time with various foreign language programs on the same station—that not only had this one station made full-fledged stars out of acts like Cream, Traffic and Hendrix, but Tom Donahue now ran an identical station in Los Angeles, holding forth himself on a nightly airshift in both cities through the magic of tape recording. Even the pimple cream vendors of the AM dial like Top Forty kingpin KYA were struggling to keep up, adding tracks such as the full thirteen-minute version of "East-West" by the Butterfield Blues Band to night-time playlists. The live broadcast of the Dead performance not only announced the very existence of the Carousel in a wholly unusual and unexpected manner, but earmarked the operation as boldly innovative. The Dead show ran several hours: it was well past midnight when the band wrapped up the gala evening with a rousing "In the Midnight Hour."

Since the previous September, the Dead had been trying to record a second album. What the Dead had in mind was nothing like the restrictive format employed on their first outing, but rather an expanded, experimental approach to recording more akin to the extrapolations found in the band's stagework. Beginning at RCA Studio A again in Hollywood, the band confounded producer Dave Hassinger at every opportunity. STP, Owsley's extra potent variation on acid, did not help. Abrasive Phil Lesh constantly rode Hassinger about fine-point detail of the bass sound. At one point, Bob Weir asked Hassinger if he could re-create the sound of "heavy air." Hassinger just stared back blankly, although Weir was quite serious. Discussions were held about moving the band and equipment into the desert to record in a more purified atmosphere.

In October, the sessions had moved to American Studios in North Hollywood, where the band brought in enough equipment from Studio Instrument Rentals to fill half the studio. Two nights at Los Angeles's Shrine Auditorium were recorded in November. In December, the project traveled across the country to Century Sound in New York, where the Dead and Hassinger finally parted ways after the producer got into a fight with the band and walked out in the middle of a session.

After all that time, all Hassinger managed to accomplish was little more than two complete instrumental tracks with no vocals. He wanted the group to add gang vocals, since no individual vocalist in the band could match the power of the instrumental sound. But, by the time he stormed out of the studio in New York, all that was in the can was the beginning of a number called "That's It for the Other One" and instrumental tracks to "New Potato Caboose" and "Born Cross-Eyed."

Joe Smith at Warner Brothers, losing patience, fired off an angry letter to manager Danny Rifkin of the Dead. "Your group has many problems, it would appear," he wrote, "and I would believe that Hassinger has no further interest or desire to work with them under conditions similar to the last fiasco. It's apparent that nobody in your organization has enough influence over Phil Lesh to evoke anything resembling normal behavior. You are now branded as an undesirable group in almost every recording studio in Los Angeles. I haven't got all the New York reports in as yet, but the guys ran through engineers like a steamroller."

Recruited to add some prepared piano and electronic music to the album was Tom Constanten, an old roommate and experimental music colleague of Phil Lesh. He arrived from Las Vegas, where he was serving his hitch in the Air Force, having wangled the time off courtesy of a three-day pass he won as Airman of the Month. After adding some additional parts months later at the basement room called Columbus Recorders underneath Zim's Hamburgers in North Beach, Garcia turned to Constanten on the sidewalk after they were leaving the sessions together, the keyboardist on his way back to the Air Force base. "I think we can use you," Garcia told him.

Mickey Hart had slept in that closet at Kreutzman and Lesh's place on Belvedere Street for months. He drenched himself in psychedelics. Having only sampled a small dose prior to joining the Dead that night at the Straight Theater, he made up for lost time. He had experimented with self-hypnosis and began hypnotizing Kreutzman before they played together. They would take each other's pulses before playing, synchronizing their rhythms right down to their heartbeats.

Hart absorbed the new music, a dry sponge mopping up everything around him. He spilled candlewax on records, holding the flame close to the disks while he was high, trying to read the labels. Lesh gave him an album called *The Music of East India* and Hart, who had been fooling idly with a tabla, put the record on and began tapping the Indian hand drum. He stopped soon enough. The rich polyrhythms swimming in and out of the current of time in the music transfixed him. He couldn't believe one man could do all this by himself. He read the jacket over, disbelieving. Alla Rakha was the man's name.

While the band played over Christmas at the Village Theater in New York, Hart learned that Alla Rakha was appearing in Long Island, part of a troupe of Indian classical musicians that also included sitarist Ravi Shankar. Introduced to Hart as a fellow drummer backstage, Rakha invited the rock musician to his hotel room. Hart brought his sticks and pad and a peculiar device known as a trinome, a metronome that tracks three different rhythmic cycles simultaneously.

Rakha enjoyed the trinome and showed Hart, the eager disciple, a rhythm game where Rakha laid down a ten-count beat and called out various numbers—like twelve—for Hart to beat out on top of his steady ten counts. As Hart played nines, elevens, thirteens over Rakha's ten-count beat, a rhythmic universe opened up in the lifelong drummer's brain. His axioms exploded, as Rakha showed Hart rhythm was only time and he could carve up time anyway he wanted. Armed with this apocalyptic vision, Hart brought the knowledge back with him to the band.

The Dead rehearsed every day, seven or eight hours at a crack, at an abandoned theater on Potrero Hill, and it was at these sessions that Hart and Kreutzman began to map out the band's new floorplan. "The Eleven" throbbed to an eleven-count measure, a time signature heretofore unexplored in the realms of rock. But the Dead were pushing the parameters again, in this case, the boundaries of time itself. The band spent hours every day simply trying to play in groups of eleven. Once the musicians grew accustomed to that odd time, the group dove further into the unconventional, laying sevens over fives, elevens over nines, living out the little game Rakha played with Hart.

Hart's contagious enthusiasm spread easily to Garcia, always a willing participant in anything deliciously strange, and Lesh, who had dabbled extensively in experimental electronic music long before joining the Dead. Old-fashioned bluesman Pigpen and Bobby Weir, who sometimes struggled on his instrument to master even simple parts, were left behind as the group charged ahead into unfurrowed fields.

Dan Healy, a neighbor of a couple of the Quicksilver guys from the early days, had hooked up with the Dead at one of those early Fillmore shows and moved into 710 Ashbury not long after the pot bust. Healy had worked as an engineer recording jingles and did a few rock sessions—like the Quicksilver demos—in the after-hours. He had revamped the Dead's sound system and then left the commercial business and started handling the band's concert sound, so he went along with the band to attend the recording sessions. After the New York sessions ended abruptly, Healy and the Dead hit on the idea of recording the band in performance.

Owsley wired together two stereo tape recorders and Healy recorded almost every stop on the Pacific Northwest tour, as well as the Valentine's Day show at the Carousel. Another machine entirely captured three nights at Lake Tahoe. Five shows during the end of March at the Carousel completed the rough material and Healy repaired to the North Beach basement to assemble the album.

Some shows were recorded on two different machines running at different speeds. Some were recorded on half-inch tape and some on quarter-inch. Healy found himself varying the tape speed by applying his thumb to the capstan as it spun around, as he dubbed everything down to an eight-track machine. He spliced every few inches of tape. The final version contained hundreds, if not thousands, of edits. This ordeal lasted weeks, although the Dead's contract with Warner's specified unlimited studio time, so the label endured the growing expense.

The Dead had stationed themselves at the frontiers. The second album, eventually titled *Anthem of the Sun,* could be no less conventional, no less revolutionary than the band itself. Healy, Garcia and Lesh scrupulously stitched together a sound collage, a suite of songs built on rambling improvisations that blended one into the other, one long composition for each side of the album, not remotely like anything ever recorded before by a rock band.

But the Haight itself was growing hard. There had been a rape on the street. Speed freaks and other human flotsam and jetsam littered the sidewalks. The Dead didn't really belong in the neighborhood any longer. Hart was the first to leave. He wanted more space than Kreutzman's closet afforded anyway and, picturing himself as a cowboy, he found a ranch with a three-bedroom house on thirty-two acres renting for three hundred dollars a month outside Novato, about forty minutes north of San Francisco. After Veronica almost died from a brain aneurysm, just keeled over in the Belvedere Street digs where she and Pigpen lived across the street from Lesh and Kreutzman, they moved to Hart's new ranch and lived upstairs for a while, while she began the painfully slow process of learning how to speak again. One by one, the rest of the band began to follow Hart's lead and relocate to the pastoral serenity of deep Marin County. Hart's barn offered a perfect rehearsal space and, to complete his cowboy fantasy, he immediately got himself a horse.

As a kind of farewell gesture to the Haight, the Dead planned a guerilla maneuver. Scully conned the city into stopping the traffic on Haight Street for a Sunday afternoon street fair, without letting on what the nature of the event would actually be. Two flatbed trucks loaded with equipment backed up across Haight Street, adjacent to the Straight Theater, blocking the street. Extension cords were strung from the Straight to the trucks, so there would be no generator for the police to close down. The band sauntered down the hill and threw one final impromptu concert for the Haight. The crowd filled the street for several blocks as the band rummaged through the blues bag, chugging through "Smokestack Lightning," Pigpen growling out "Turn on Your Lovelight," the group driving "Viola Lee Blues" to the end-of-the-world crescendo.

The musicians and the people around them saw themselves as psychedelic settlers living on the frontier of a new wild west. Although they needed to leave the Haight behind, the Dead were pressing forward into the unknown. They remained advocates of a new worldwide movement, a role they treated with relish and whimsy. When the members of the British rock group Traffic arrived in San Francisco to play the band's first U.S. performances over two weekends at the Fillmore, an emissary from the Dead met the band at the airport bearing innocent-enough-looking capsules.

Later that night, at three in the morning, as they had been promising over the air all day, the entire staff of KMPX walked out of the station on strike. Several hundred listeners cheered the strikers on their exit like a victorious football team and a spur-of-the-moment street party was underway. A short time later, a flatbed truck pulled up and the Grateful Dead plugged in and wailed away. Before long, Steve Winwood and Jim Capaldi of Traffic, their minds still reeling under the psychedelic barrage Owsley laid down at the airport earlier that afternoon, were on the truck, joining the tumult on organ and drums respectively. One day in San Francisco and already the visiting dignitaries were hanging on for all their lives at the rim of Western civilization.

Skip Spence had been consuming Owsley's latest, a batch he called Blue Cheer, at a rate that alarmed the other band members. Moby

Grape had spent the entire month of November in New York working on the second record and Spence couldn't finish a single song. When the band returned to New York in January, he managed to cut a couple of insignificant pieces, "Motorcycle Irene" and "Funky-Tunk," as well as create the gimmick track of the album.

Wearing his most outgoing, smiling face, Spence waltzed into the CBS Radio studios across the hall from where the band was recording and hailed Arthur Godfrey, the aged broadcaster still doing his daily show on the CBS radio network. Somehow Spence cajoled Godfrey into bringing his banjo and trademark ukulele into the Grape sessions and appearing on a campy track Spence wrote titled "Just Like Gene Autry: A Foxtrot." Featuring the pure schmaltz of a bar mitzvah dance band hired for the track, this one cut was mastered on the album to be played at 78 RPM.

Peter Lewis had problems of his own. His wife was involved in an affair with another musician back in Mill Valley. A couple of months earlier, he confronted her about his suspicions during an acid trip and, after tears and angry recriminations, thought he had brought the situation under control. But in New York recording the album, his wife back home in Marin County, doubts and fears depressed Lewis. His work on the album mostly complete, he left the seedy Albert Hotel in Greenwich Village for a surprise visit to the Upper East Side apartment maintained by his mother, actress Loretta Young.

He hadn't seen or otherwise communicated with his mother in several years, but she welcomed him. When he found it difficult to fall asleep in the strange bed, she even accommodatingly offered him one of her sleeping pills, which he gladly accepted. But the pill, instead of putting him out, unlocked a Pandora's box of emotions and traumas. He came apart, crying, shaking uncontrollably. He left the next day for San Francisco without telling anybody in the band. Finding his wife still enmeshed in her relationship with the other musician, he continued on to Los Angeles, where he took refuge with a girlfriend of his own. His wife knew where he was. His marriage was rapidly disintegrating.

Lewis missed the final recordings for the album, a series of jam sessions featuring guests Al Kooper and Mike Bloomfield that would be included with the actual album on a separate disk titled *Grape Jam*. These loose, unstructured free-for-alls paved the way for Kooper to collaborate later that year with Bloomfield on a similar project which resulted in a million-selling album called *Super Session*.

At the Albert, a noted hangout for junkies and assorted low-lifes at the time, Spence fell in with unsavory companionship. He attached himself to one strange female in particular who made all the other band members uncomfortable. He just disappeared one night with her and didn't come back for several days. When he did turn up again, he looked like he had shaved with a rusty ax. No shirt, eyes blazing, Spence appeared like he was in the grip of a drastic episode. He threatened a Columbia Records graphic artist with a pair of scissors and guitarist Jerry Miller didn't wait long enough to find out what happened. He just split.

Miller took his time going back to the Albert, but when he arrived at his room, he was shocked to see the door splintered and hacked apart. Spence had arrived at the hotel ahead of Miller, grabbed a fireax off the wall and chopped open Miller's door, apparently intent on mayhem. Not finding Miller, Spence and his ladyfriend took the ax, grabbed a taxi and headed for CBS Studios, where Rubinson was putting some finishing touches on the album. Miller phoned the producer and warned him that Spence might be headed his way. Rubinson locked the studio doors and called the cops, who told him they couldn't do anything until Spence either attacked someone or destroyed some property. Until then, no crime had been committed and the police wouldn't interfere with his Constitutional right to carry a fireax through the streets of New York.

Terrified, Rubinson nevertheless tried to calm Spence down. He approached him. "Hi'ya, man," he said. "You must be freezing. It's cold out here. Now come on, give me the ax."

Spence started laughing. His laughter soon turned to sobs and Rubinson cautiously removed the ax from his grasp. With Spence disarmed, the police stepped in, strapped him in a straitjacket and took him away in a paddy wagon. Rubinson followed to the station and swore out a complaint. Spence wound up in the prison ward of Bellevue Mental Hospital.

Patrons packing the aisle parted like the Red Sea for Moses, silverware-tinkling and chatter came to a halt and all faces turned their way as the members of Big Brother and the Holding Company made their way through Max's Kansas City toward the big round table in the back. Over the sound system came the Joe McDonald song "Janis" from the new Country Joe and the Fish album, written at her request to commemorate their relationship.

The band arrived in New York in February with enough Haight-Ashbury egalitarianism intact for road crew David Richards and Mark Braunstein, the date Janis Joplin took to the Monterey Pop Festival, to take a suite at the Chelsea Hotel when the band checked in, while the musicians were consigned to relatively cramped single quarters. The reason they took the suite was because they arrived at the hotel first. They offered their room as a site for band meetings and Joplin went to survey their sumptuous lodgings, two bedrooms, sitting room and kitchen.

"You motherfuckers," she exclaimed. "You're the equipment men. What is this?" She was only partly kidding.

"You're right, Janis," said David Richards. "We're just the equipment men and we don't deserve all this. You're right. You take it."

"Oh, fuck you," she snapped, and turned on her heel.

The trip to New York was a journey of destiny, a turning point from which there would be no return. Grossman had brought the band out not only for a New York debut on February 17 at the Anderson Theater, but to sign recording contracts with Columbia Records. For the next two months, Big Brother would live in New York while playing concerts around the East Coast and starting work on the all-important new album, to make good, a half-year later, on the promise of Monterey.

Grossman kept an imposing office on East Fifty-fifth Street and an elegant apartment overlooking Gramercy Park further downtown. The first night the band arrived, he took everybody to Max's Kansas City, the favored hangout at the time for Manhattan's pop literati. Nevertheless, for almost every person in the restaurant that night, it was the first time they had actually seen San Francisco hippies. Soon the musicians were regulars who ran tabs at the place and, the surest imprimatur of their standing, took waitresses back to their hotel rooms after work ended. One tall, black and especially attractive Max's waitress who became attached to David Richards later confided to him her first impression when she saw the band walk into Max's that night. "I thought," she told him, "you looked like the happiest people I ever saw in my life."

The band gathered at the office for an introductory meeting with

Grossman and his staff. Seated in a circle in the somber, austere surroundings of Grossman's inner sanctum, one of his associates opened the meeting by putting everyone in the band immediately ill at ease. "How do you want us to promote you?" she asked. Band members exchanged nervous glances and said nothing, but she was undaunted and almost seemed to address her next question directly to Joplin, who was seated next to Grossman.

"I mean," she said, "what kind of image do you want?"

The band rehearsed for the Anderson show in a loft in the East Village and everything was an adventure to them—the snow, the coats and hats, the cab rides. When they weren't going somewhere or on their way back, the band cloistered themselves in the bar of the Spanish restaurant downstairs at the Chelsea, Joplin having the bartender line up six shots of tequila at a time and downing them by herself.

The Anderson was an old Yiddish theater on Second Avenue where a few rock shows had been staged in recent months, including a performance by Country Joe and the Fish. Although Big Brother was essentially an unknown entity outside of a whispered reputation—and, in fact, the hall did not sell out—as soon as the band ripped into the opening number, "Catch Me Daddy," fans leaped out of the reserved seats and rushed the stage. The catacylsmic performance blazed through the Avalon songbook, Joplin wrenching "Summertime," belting "Piece of My Heart," leading inexorably to the erotic ecstasy and agony of "Ball and Chain."

The audience came unglued. *New York Times* reviewer Robert Shelton, the man who wrote the first and most famous review of Bob Dylan, grabbed Grossman's press agent, Myra Friedman, in the lobby and demanded a picture of Joplin. Friedman, unprepared, snatched a group shot off the theater wall. Backstage, other members of the press clamored with willing female fans for the attention of the musicians. Sam Andrew went back to his hotel with the voluptuous photographer Linda Eastman. Joplin wandered off to a nearby Bowery bar, angry at the rest of the band for canceling a planned rehearsal scheduled to take place after the triumphant concert. When Shelton's review appeared Monday as the lead story on the *Times* culture page, the group photo had been carefully cropped down to a mug shot of Joplin only.

That afternoon, the musicians attended the ceremonial signing of the band's contract with Columbia Records at the conference room in the CBS skyscraper on Fifty-second Street invariably called "Black

Rock." The Mainstream Records contract was being bought out for a stiff $250,000, with Columbia only covering the cost after the first $100,000, which the band paid. Record label president Clive Davis, who had wanted to sign the band since first hearing Joplin at Monterey the previous summer, tried to put the group at ease by stressing the musicians should not be put off by the monolithic corporate headquarters and all the pin-stripe suits and ties. One of the band members noticed the time and, realizing they were about to be late for a press conference being held in their honor, took Davis at his word and simply started to take off his clothes to change into the fresh laundry he had brought with him.

The press function was held at a bustling Greek restaurant called Piraeus, My Love. Joplin, in a black minidress, was the center of attention, surrounded by admiring guests at all times. Correspondents from *Life* rubbed elbows with the rock writers from the *Village Voice*. Big Brother and the Holding Company had arrived with a splash in New York City. Joplin tore herself away from the press to momentarily look flustered at Myra Friedman. "I don't know what this is about," she said. "I'm no star."

Initially, Bill Graham felt reluctant to open a hall in New York. A cautious man, Graham spent all his time running the Fillmore in San Francisco, now that he was no longer managing the Airplane, and made what he thought was plenty of money. But when Cream played the Village Theater down the street from the Anderson Theater, Graham began to become more interested. He, too, attended the Big Brother show at the Anderson. During the intermission, he stood up on the stage and looked out over the house, making a quick calculation of two thousand customers.

The sixty-year-old Village Theater needed repair and the asking price was $400,000. Graham inveigled an $80,000 investment from Albert Grossman and managed to put together the rest of the down payment himself. Flying back and forth between San Francisco and New York to oversee the renovations and still run the Fillmore, Graham, more than ever, managed his staffs through sheer force of personality—yelling, coaxing, mulish insistence, whatever it took to get what he wanted. When it came time to open the theater—the name was changed at the last minute to Fillmore East—Graham chose as his starring attraction the latest talk of the town, Big Brother and the Holding Company.

Big Brother was still adjusting to the band's newfound status. James Gurley, who found himself intimidated by the rocketing pace of the sudden blastoff, was drinking heavily. He also found New York heroin particularly delectable, but this was not a new problem.

Grossman pegged Gurley as trouble. The previous November, he had attended a performance at the Golden Bear in Huntington Beach outside Los Angeles where Gurley, drunk and stoned on downers, made a spectacle of himself during a show. Not only did he play badly, he almost fell off the stage. Grossman was appalled. After the show, he sent an associate backstage to tell the band he wanted to speak with everybody without Gurley present.

Grossman did not mince words. He suggested the band give Gurley a lump sum, say ten thousand dollars, and let him go—"Give him some time away from the band," Grossman said. He even allowed that freelance guitarist Harvey Mandel would make a perfectly acceptable replacement. Letting Gurley go was not a conceivable notion to this group of people. The bond between the musicians did not grow out of professional aspirations, but rather the other way around. These people lived together, fought together, loved together and also played music together. Whatever was special about the character of the music they made came from the depth of that rapport, an intangible difficult to assay by someone as purely professional as Grossman, which the band also understood. Nobody thought any less of their new manager for his making the suggestion.

New York had turned out to be a nonstop party for Big Brother. All the band members enjoyed the ready availability of members of the opposite sex their new station afforded them. Even relatively straight-laced Peter Albin entertained company at the Chelsea. David Getz and his longtime love, Nancy Parker, had split up just before the New York trip anyway, but none of the wives or lovers came along. Joplin processed a procession of pretty young things, some little more than jive punks, others colleagues from the world of rock. She woke up in bed one morning unable to recall if the person sleeping next to her was the same Chambers Brother with whom she had gone to bed the night before. On another morning, she asked sullen Frank Zappa if he had been any good the night before. Offended, he split in a huff.

They were toasted wherever they went. In Boston, where Big

Brother appeared in February at the Psychedelic Supermarket, road manager John Cooke hosted a party for the group at an iron lung factory in Cambridge owned by his uncle. Cooke maintained an apartment tucked away on the third floor of J. H. Emerson and Co. and guests had to make their way through a bizarre maze of hospital equipment, surgical appliances and artificial limbs to find his front door. Peter Albin managed to get locked in one of the iron lungs and Gurley was forced to fend off the nearly aberrant advances of a buxom young co-ed from Providence in Cooke's living room.

Grossman had hired Cooke, son of British broadcaster Alistair Cooke, to ride herd on his new charges almost as soon as he signed Big Brother the previous November. A Harvard graduate with a major in Spanish, Cooke had belonged to the bluegrass group Charles River Valley Boys—he added the Beatles song, "Yes It Is," to the repertoire—and often relaxed by strumming his acoustic guitar and singing old cowboy songs for hours. Cooke introduced Joplin to his schoolchum Bobby Neuwirth, a ubiquitous presence on the Greenwich Village folk scene and a regular at Max's Kansas City, who, along with elfin actor Michael J. Pollard, became great running buddies with the girl from Port Arthur.

The original plan for the Columbia album called for the band to be recorded live and a remote truck was on hand to capture the performance March 1 at Detroit's Grande Ballroom. Producer John Simon had met the group earlier in San Francisco, conducting a pre-production session at Golden State Recorders, and the musicians were impressed with his savvy. He quickly straightened out some wrinkles in the arrangement of "Summertime" and coached the band into obviously improved performances in the short meet.

But Simon was probably not the best suited candidate to supervise the project. A classically trained composer and former staff producer for Columbia Records, Simon was fresh from working on the first album by The Band, extraordinarily seasoned musicians Grossman also represented, and Simon couldn't understand the lack of discipline in Big Brother. He was accustomed to working with much more technically proficient musicians and saw no special creative benefit in the personal rapport of the band members.

Not only did the band play horribly the night of the live recording in Detroit, but during a midnight meal at a coffee shop following the gig, one of the members accidentally dropped a small packet of heroin, an incident reported to Grossman. He summoned the musicians to his home in Woodstock for a stern discussion. He expressed his distress over involvement with drugs. Grossman also listened to the tapes from the Grande Ballroom and pronounced them a disaster. He suggested hiring studio musicians to overdub the entire rhythm section or, at least, the drummer.

The night of the Fillmore East opening, March 8, qualified as a certified event on the New York music scene. An additional five hundred people were squeezed in above the twenty-three hundred capacity. The people surging through the lobby practically crushed Judy Collins and Elektra Records president Jac Holzman against the wall. Tim Buckley and Albert King were the opening acts. Both the early show and late show were sold out.

One year before, when David Getz's father died and he went home to New York for the funeral, his mother was ashamed of his long hair. She worried out loud about what he was doing. He was throwing away his education, his fellowship, on what? But now he was back. His family all read the review of the Anderson show in the *Times*. He visited his mother and gave her five hundred dollars for new carpets. For the Fillmore East opening, he arranged for tickets for his mother, his Aunt Betty and other family members at the early show. They all knew the theater for its days as a Yiddish theater and were suitably impressed. Getz had redeemed himself in their eyes.

Joplin paused before launching the second song, darting a quick, mischievous glance back at the drummer. "This one's for Aunt Betty," she announced.

SPRING 1968

Peggy Caserta flew to New York to stay with Sam Andrew at the Chelsea. Owner of one of the first hip Haight Street boutiques, she mooned over handsome, long-haired Andrew—at the same time living with her female lover—and invited herself to come to New York for the visit. An aggressive, smartly dressed former Delta Airlines stewardess with the figure of a Playboy Playmate, Caserta knew the members of Big Brother from attending shows at the Matrix. Joplin sometimes shopped at her store. Joplin seemed surprised to stumble on the shopkeeper in Andrew's hotel room early one morning on her way to a recording session for the Columbia album.

Producer Simon abandoned the program of recording the band in concert after the Grande Ballroom fiasco and adjourned the sessions to Columbia Studios, but progress was anything but smooth. The first song the band started to record was "Combination of the Two." With the union engineer counting everything, false starts and all, as a take, the numbers quickly mounted up. Before the band noticed, the engineer's voice was booming out in the studio, "Okay, Big Brother and the Holding Company, Combination of the Two, take forty-three."

Simon suggested the band take a break or try something else, but the musicians demurred, plunging on. Every so often, he would bring them into the control booth for a playback. He would point out a wrong note on the bass or places where the rhythm slowed down. The effect was to make the musicians even more self-conscious, more tense. The unspoken antipathy between the band and producer only grew. Before long, the group was laughing and joking together in one part of the studio, while Simon waited in a corner, running his fingers through his hair. For Joplin, the natural response to this kind of stress was to drink.

She invited Caserta to the studio one night. Andrew paid her no attention, but Joplin fussed over her guest. She sent Caserta out to buy a bottle of Southern Comfort and proceeded to get good and gone. At one point, Grossman quietly asked Caserta to take the blotto vocalist back to her hotel. Joplin vomited outside the cab door and nearly passed out on the ride, but Caserta managed to take her back to her room, get her undressed and put her in bed. The next night she moved into Joplin's room for the remainder of her stay.

Simon discovered that Joplin would learn a vocal phrase a certain way and, to his chagrin, having once learned it, would repeat the phrase identically on every subsequent vocal performance. To Simon, such technique reeked of contrivance, not the true spontaneity of the blues singer. But it wasn't her vocals causing the delays and retakes. Instrumental mistakes made Joplin sing some songs over and over again, and she grew increasingly frustrated. She confided to Andrew that she wanted to leave the band and put something more soulful together, with a horn section perhaps, although he didn't treat her comment seriously. Once, she stomped out of the studio in a rage at the band. "I'm never going to sing with you motherfuckers again," she screamed.

Before leaving for Los Angeles to continue work on the album, having completed just two tracks in New York, the band played a week-long engagement with bluesman B.B. King, who had also opened the band's New York debut at the Anderson two months previous, at a new club called the Generation. Martin Luther King, Jr. was assassinated on April 4, the night the Generation was slated to open, and B.B. King moved the members of Big Brother with his thoughtful comments backstage before the show. Guest musicians dropped by virtually every night to play with the blues guitar great. Buddy Guy stopped in one night and Jimi Hendrix, Elvin Bishop, Paul Butterfield, Al Kooper and a few others joined King another night.

Sam Andrew went home that particular evening with a young lady who stirred him awake suddenly in the middle of the night. "Quick," she said. "My boyfriend's coming home." Sam slipped into the bedroom next door, only to discover, as he climbed in between the sheets, the bed already occupied by her roommate. They made love in the dark. In the light of the morning, Andrew rolled over to discover this woman was not only sexy but gorgeous. It was the beginning of a beautiful friendship.

Mickey Hart would come home to his Novato ranch from gigs that spring at the Carousel, where the Dead served as something like the house band, and head out to the corral. He would feed his Arabian horse, Snorter, a dose of acid adjusted for his body weight, do the same thing for his black dog, Glups, saddle up and the three of them would ride through the dawn in the misty morning of the Marin County forests. With his horse's awareness heightened, the ride was silken, each hoofstep carefully and deliberately placed, as Snorter glided through his paces over the hills and through the brush until the sun was high in the morning sky.

The rest of the Dead followed Hart's lead into the wilds of Marin. Garcia, Mountain Girl and Sunshine rented a small house in Larkspur and drove around in a beat-up Plymouth station wagon. Robert Hunter and his lady joined them. Phil Lesh found a place in Fairfax. Weir relocated to Nicasio. Rock Scully was living with Martha Wax at Dan Healy's house in Sausalito, indulging a newfound fondness for cocaine and not getting very much sleep. Little enclaves of Dead musicians, crew and family members cropped up around Marin, abandoning the urban communal life that had nurtured the group from the beginning.

As long as the Dead or the Airplane was on the bill, the Carousel could count on a full house. In fact, one weekend of joint appearances by the Airplane and the Dead managed easily to pack the hall, despite being announced a mere forty-eight hours before showtime. Other shows were not so successful. Rakow gave away tickets up and down Haight Street to one particularly slow-moving show and, when the crowd arrived, handed out ice cream and Cokes. He held open community meetings where anybody could contribute. Many musicians attended. They were encouraged to feel the Carousel was their place. Janis Joplin showed up at one carrying a string bag out of which she produced a bottle, a sausage and a loaf of bread. "Well, what is it?" she demanded. "Music or money?"

Rakow booked a show the first weekend in May that featured jazz great Thelonious Monk, the voodoo jive of Dr. John the Night Tripper and the Charlatans. Dr. John, whose first album was a major hit on the new underground station in town opened by the old KMPX staff, brought a full rhythm and blues style revue, complete with a pair of stunning black background vocalists. Rakow bade them strip to their panties, asked poster artist Stanley Mouse to decorate them in Day-Glo paint and bathed them in black light for the performance.

Hard as it proved to be just to get paying customers to click the turnstiles, the Carousel also began to raise problems with the authorities. Rakow handled police relations with judiciously distributed hundred-dollar bills—one afternoon he tucked the banknote in the breast pocket of an officer's uniform. He watched incredulously another afternoon while a police officer joined Rakow and a pair of Hell's Angels in a drinking marathon in the Carousel office. But the Free City Convention proved a little difficult to ignore.

A meeting of the minds between the Angels and the Diggers, the hard-core hippies and anarchists who handed out free food in the park every afternoon, the event turned into a free-wheeling bacchanal. Admission was gained through the regular box office entrance—one patron paid for his ticket in barter, handing over a bloody leg of lamb, which was duly placed in the cash box—or through a back entrance that required only throwing some money on a bonfire in the doorway.

Starting in the afternoon and lasting well into the next morning, the revelry ran unrestrained. Couples openly made love everywhere. A street preacher brought his portable public address system and went up to the stage. Another gentleman stood behind the preacher and began to disrobe without the preacher's noticing. When he finally caught a glimpse out of the corner of his eye, he left, still speaking, dragging his gear by the microphone. The audience liberated the concession stand storeroom and ate jars of mayonnaise and mustard. When someone set a fire in a giant seashell on the dance floor, Rakow took issue. The fire was doused by people standing around pissing on it.

Sometime during the night, some jokester crawled out to the marquee and changed the lettering to read "Free City Cuntvention." Not satisfied, he went back out and changed it again to read "Free Cunt." Countless thousands of downtown commuters saw this sign on their way to work in the morning and the police department was flooded with calls.

Short on the heels of the Free City Convention was the "Free Dirty Tom" benefit in May to raise funds for a recidivist Hell's Angel back under lock and key. Admission was one dollar and included free beer and music by Big Brother and the Holding Company. So much beer was spilled, the carpet squished under people's feet. The beer leaked through the floor into the electrical fixtures on the ceiling of the rug dealer downstairs and shorted out his lighting. One club member showed up carrying a bag full of capsules of a drug called Hog, an animal tranquilizer capable of transforming raging steers into docile pets. The room was so jammed, the crowd spilled out onto the Market Street sidewalk and into the actual street, which is where the police entered the picture.

The very notion of hundreds of Hell's Angels milling about the streets in the center of downtown San Francisco, cups of beer in their hands, sent a shiver of contempt through the core of the police department, who dispatched to contain and quell this threat to the safety and sanctity of the city highly trained specialists, the notorious Tactical Squad. This heavily armed, Gestapo-like wing of the corps deployed itself in full riot gear along a side street a half block from the Carousel, while combat-ready officers were sent to pow-wow with the ballroom operators. Rakow, himself reeling under a dose of Hog, his vision blurred, his depth perception askew, took matters in hand.

"There is no problem," he assured the officer. "I am following normal show business procedure."

He toured the policeman through the carnage that passed for a concert. "I am following normal show business procedure," he explained.

Outside, the cop reported to his commanding officer, who told him just to get the crowd off the street. Rakow had a plan. He summoned Sonny Barger, president of the Oakland chapter of the Hell's Angels and the single most publicly reviled member of the outlaw motorcycle gang. Rakow asked the police commander if he could borrow a police car with a loudspeaker and have Barger address the club members in the street. The officer agreed, but when Barger opened the car door and slipped into the seat, the policeman behind the wheel would have none of driving this cretinous knee-breaker and gang-raper around. No problem. Barger simply drafted one of his own gang to operate the official San Francisco police motor vehicle and the two drove up and down the block along Market Street, Barger working the loud speaker atop the cop car.

"This is Sonny Barger," he barked. "Get the fuck off the street."

While Rakow averted any major confrontation at the scene, he could not prevent being called before the permits board to explain why they shouldn't take his permit away. "You'll have to take away something else," he said. "I don't have any permits."

After the Martin Luther King assassination, Bill Graham grew increasingly convinced he would have to move out of the Fillmore Auditorium. Although there was no open rioting in San Francisco, racial violence flared in sporadic incidents and the Fillmore lay right in the middle of one of the city's toughest black neighborhoods. Not only was he getting reports of more robbings, beatings, purse snatchings and the like among his customers, but Graham even witnessed one episode of random violence on the street in front of the hall where a black man walked up to one of Graham's white customers and, out of nowhere, smashed him in the face.

Business was down everywhere—at the Avalon and Carousel, too—but people were especially afraid to venture into the neighborhood where Graham threw shows. He agonized over the mere existence of the Carousel. He took it as a personal slap in the face by the bands involved in establishing the operation—which, in many ways, it was. He engaged Rakow in bidding wars, driving prices of some acts well beyond their market value, glad to either pay the premium to keep the act away from the Carousel or make it impossible for the Carousel to turn a profit on a show if they did manage to outbid Graham for an act.

But with the Fillmore East also buying talent, Graham pulled a lot more weight with booking agents than Rakow, and he used that influence to keep hot acts out of the Carousel. Rakow finally realized the futility of bidding wars when, after he won a signed contract to present the Chambers Brothers in June at the Carousel, Graham threatened the agent until he got the act for the Fillmore anyway, signed contract or not. Rakow began negotiations with Graham to turn over the lease.

Graham always claimed he flew to Ireland to meet personally with ballroom owner Fuller, but Baratta never saw him leave town. Graham agreed to pay Rakow a settlement fee and allow Rakow to throw shows at the hall on off-nights until he recouped his own lost investment. Graham also cut a far more favorable deal with Fuller than the Carousel had been able to negotiate. The last show at the Fillmore Auditorium took place on July 4 and featured Creedence Clearwater Revival, a new band out of the East Bay that burst on the scene with a tape of an eight-and-a-half-minute version of the rock and roll oldie, "Suzie Q," that KSAN, the new underground station, couldn't stop playing. The next night Graham assumed control of the Carousel, now renamed Fillmore West. The bill included Paul Butterfield Blues Band, Ten Years After and Fleetwood Mac. Checking out the scene from backstage were former Butterfield guitarists Mike Bloomfield and Elvin Bishop, Dead guitarist Jerry Garcia, Airplane guitarist Jorma Kaukonen and blues harp virtuoso Charlie Musselwhite.

George Hunter walked up to Terré on the street. Wearing a Prince Albert coat and top hat, a watch chain across a brocade vest, Terré would naturally have attracted Hunter's attention, but something else was on his mind, too. He asked Terré to become the band's manager on the spot and took him to meet the rest of the Charlatans. "Yeah, you're right," Wilhelm said. "He does look like him."

Almost like a perverse Hunter joke, the new Charlatans manager landed the job not only because he clearly pursued the old-timey look with the same kind of single-mindedness as the group, but he also bore more than a passing resemblance to Matthew Katz, by now a vilified figure on the local music scene. Terré possessed no other qualifications for the job. Nor did he need to.

A vagabond who had landed in the Haight a year before all the craziness began, Terré dealt antiques, drew occasional posters for the Straight Theater, never used acid or smoked pot, but concentrated on taking nude photos of women with an antique bellows camera, then seducing them. His collection numbered in the hundreds and he told people his goal was to reach a thousand. He lived in back of a storefront next to a coffee house called the Blue Unicorn on Hayes Street and his quarters were Deco down to the lightbulbs. He was perfect for the role—except for the part about his expertise—and the resemblance to Katz was close enough to get him barred one night from entering the Fillmore.

But the Charlatans were unraveling anyway. Dan Hicks launched a sideline group of his own, Dan Hicks and his Hot Licks, and unveiled the folkish quintet featuring two female background vocalists, bassist Jaime Leopold and violinist David LaFlamme as the opening act for a Charlatans engagement at the Matrix. Toothsome Candy Sterniolla, his Red Dog girlfriend, helped fuel ambitions Hicks himself didn't entirely come by naturally. At another early Hot Licks engagement in April at the New Committee Theater, Ralph Gleason caught the show and gave Hicks a positively glowing review.

While the rest of the band's frustration not only with the lack of professional progress but with bandleader Hunter himself ballooned, Hunter dug in his heels. He was enormously enamored of a current crop of tunes the band was recording, including a bizarre Dixieland instrumental called "Banjorino" taken from a record by New Orleans clarinetist Johnny Dodds off an album titled *Jugs, Washboards and Kazoos* Hunter borrowed from Janis Joplin. Olsen and Wilhelm, who had seen it all before, were rapidly tiring of Hunter's mania. Both were relatively competent musicians who had been dealing for three years with this domineering lunatic who couldn't even keep time on a tambourine.

In April, the band took a rare trip out of town to play dates in Seattle and Vancouver, where Canadian immigration officials turned Olsen away because of the pot arrest outside a San Jose bowling alley during a Charlatans set break the previous May. He returned to Seattle and drove across the border to play the shows. Hunter smuggled an envelope of pot through customs by carrying it in his hand. One of the two shows was a concert in the park while it poured. Actually, the skies rained on the band through the whole trip.

Hunter and Gogerty butted heads frequently. Gogerty had an Irish temper and Hunter easily got on his nerves. But when Hunter discovered some peculiar tapes of Gogerty's on which the band's new keyboard player made private and graphic admissions of homosexuality and recorded raw details of his sex life, Hunter took an almost cruel delight in passing the tape around to the other band members. They began smirking about Gogerty behind his back, subtly ostracizing him.

He finally erupted in Seattle, kicking in the door of a rental car in a fury.

Hunter's turn to explode came later, when the attractive young blonde who had been making overtures to Hunter slipped off to the hotel with Terré instead. Hunter enlisted Hicks and the two went and battered away at the hotel room door, leery of the derringer Terré invariably carried, although Hunter did manage to wrest the blonde away—alas, to no avail. When the performances in Seattle concluded, Hunter tried to convince the other musicians to stay behind and enjoy the city for a few days, so infrequent were their travels beyond the Bay Area. But the band went home disgruntled, leaving Hunter behind in Seattle by himself, shopping for antiques.

When he returned, Gogerty had gone back to Los Angeles and Olsen and Wilhelm informed Hunter the band was no more. Hicks already planned to go off and do Dan Hicks and his Hot Licks, but Hunter didn't want to let go. He and Lucy Lewis spent the better part of an afternoon at Olsen's Hemlock Street apartment, trying to convince Olsen and Wilhelm to press forward. But they were having none of it. A meeting in the office of attorney Michael Stepanian finalized the dissolution. The few existing dates on the books would be completed and then the Charlatans were finished. Or so they told Hunter.

FALL 1968

Bill Graham and Paul Baratta stood onstage when Graham pointed her out, dancing under the strobe light. Baratta was mildly surprised because Graham had never mentioned women to him. But she was hard to ignore, limber enough to bend over backward so that she could sweep her long hair on the floor behind her. Graham couldn't keep his eyes off her.

Sixteen-year-old Diane LaChambre came to the Fillmore West that night with a friend. The PCP she took made her feel loose-jointed and rubbery, so her dancing may have been a little more uninhibited than usual, but she was no innocent Lolita. The half-Tahitian beauty was a flower child who belonged very much to the love generation. Her parents ran a Mission district bar and she paid little attention to school. At the Fillmore that night, one of her friends, speaking in an impressed hush, told her that Bill Graham was watching her dance. She didn't really know who he was, but suddenly this man was standing by her side.

"My name is Bill Graham," he said, "and I just want you to know that you add color to the place. It is my pleasure to have you here."

The next night, she dressed up in tight black hip-huggers slit up one side that she had made herself and headed back to the Fillmore West again. This time, the staff wouldn't take money from her, not at the box office or the concession stand, so she got the message. Three days later, she and Graham got together for the first time.

Four weeks later, on September 19, Bonnie Graham went into the hospital to give birth to their son, David. Her husband was in New York, ostensibly supervising the Fillmore East. His staff arranged to have pictures of the newborn air-freighted to New York. The light show threw the photos into the opaque projector and Graham was ushered from backstage to see his son for the first time on the Fillmore East screen. To celebrate, he went back to his apartment with Diane LaChambre, who had accompanied him on the trip.

She found him surprisingly unschooled in the art of lovemaking, awkward and even shy. But as they met in parks, secret hiding places, fooled around under blankets in the first-class cabin of airliners, made love in the backseats of limousines, Graham quickly became ensnared in the steamy affair. He called her his Ava Gardner. "It's like you've been eating broccoli all your life," he told Paul Baratta, "and somebody gives you a peach."

Around the Fillmore West, the relationship was common knowledge. Graham's nephew, who worked at the hamburger stand and was protective of his Aunt Bonnie, warned the young enchantress to stay away from her uncle. When someone finally told Bonnie about the affair, she called her husband's secretary, Marushka Greene. "I think this is something you should talk to Bill about," said a flustered Greene.

With both the Fillmore East and Fillmore West in full swing, Graham easily qualified as the country's top promoter of the new rock music. He drove himself fiercely, twelve- to eighteen-hour days, an absolute devotion to his work that precluded not only enjoying the fruits of his dedication, but any semblance of a normal personal life. The money no longer mattered. Some deep compulsion burned within. He had his name read into the *Congressional Record* in July, a deferential, pipe-dream portrait of the Fillmore impresario as a savior of misguided youth, a veritable Albert Schweitzer of hippies.

He opened his own booking agency, the Millard Agency, and signed up a handful of the top San Francisco bands, including the

Dead. He entered negotiations with various major record companies to finance his own entrance into the record business with a label of his own. He formed a management company he called with no small irony, Shady Management. He was building a horizontal empire.

His wife, since their marriage, had become increasingly less involved in the operation of his business, where she had once been his closest partner and confidante. She used her new spare time to learn painting. The baby would, of course, tie her even more closely to the home. Running into the teenage sexpot was like stepping on a landmine for Graham. But, at first, he didn't realize the threat to his equanimity the liaison posed. In his old-fashioned, European manner, he saw a sexy, young mistress as a natural prize for the rich, powerful man he had become.

Bonnie Graham thought differently. She was devastated. She confronted her husband. At first, he denied everything. Then he admitted the affair. Graham misjudged his wife, thinking she would stay for the money, the home, the clothes, the child. He finally promised her he would end the relationship, something that would prove harder than he imagined.

Country Joe and the Fish signed off every concert that year by shouting "See you in Chicago." Yippies organizers Abbie Hoffman and Jerry Rubin had met with Joe McDonald and bassist Bruce Barthol earlier in the year at the Chelsea Hotel. The band agreed to take part in the Festival of Life, a street scene the Yippies planned to coincide with the Democratic convention in Chicago. The Yippies hoped to ride a subversive groundswell into an antiwar tidal wave set to crash on the beach in Grant Park in August while the entire country watched on television.

The band balanced a flourishing popularity and a commitment to subversion, an apparent contradiction the group struggled with virtually on a daily basis. But the band's music caromed all over the ballpark, from the delicate experimentalism of "Grace" to the jug band humor of "Fixin' to Die Rag," so encompassing diversity served as one of the hallmarks of Country Joe and the Fish.

"Fixin' to Die Rag," the song written for the Vietnam Day march, had been left off the first album, considered too radical by the record producer. By the time Joe and the Fish entered Vanguard Studios in New York down the block from the Chelsea Hotel to cut the second album, they had developed a reputation for being a comic band. Mc-Donald suggested sticking a little pep rally cheer, where they spelled out the group's name like a high school football team, in front of the song so nobody could miss their tongues protruding into their cheeks.

These spokesmen for the youth revolution were also young men with wives and mortgages. Guitarist Barry Melton owned a home high in the Berkeley hills with a swimming pool in the backyard and a garage he converted into a studio. McDonald married actress Robin Mencken when they discovered she was pregnant and their daughter, Seven, was born earlier in the year. Although McDonald continued his lifelong anxiety about money, his wife suffered no similar problem. Only Barthol was alarmed at the evident drift away from the values on which the band was originally established.

A product of Berkeley political action by way of LSD evangelism, Country Joe and the Fish embodied certain ideas floating around the edges of the radical left at the time. By harnessing the power of rock to folk music's commitment to social change, the band began life as an instrument to carry the message to large numbers of people. The members were all attuned to common goals—McDonald and Melton both grew up red diaper babies, with fathers who both paid heavy prices for their leftist beliefs. The group even took sensitivity training together under the aegis of Barthol's psychiatrist father. Now what was everybody turning out to be, Barthol wondered, phony rock stars in long hair?

McDonald himself didn't entirely trust Rubin and Hoffman either. Coming from a genuine working-class radical background, he sensed they were playacting. As the date approached, he grew worried about the cost of the confrontational politics the Yippies were inviting. The mood of the country was shifting. A dark, ominous cloud floated on the horizon. McDonald began to think they were leading lambs to the slaughter under the batons of the Chicago police.

Representatives of the *Ed Sullivan Show* came to the Wollman Rink in Central Park the night in August that Country Joe and the Fish appeared as part of the Schaefer Beer Music Festival. Sullivan booked the band for an upcoming performance—Sunday night TV, the stronghold of middle-class America. The band had even been paid already for the show. Somehow Country Joe and the Fish couldn't lampoon the power structure enough. The rewards for the band's insolence just kept pouring forth. Drummer Gary (Chicken) Hirsh set the mischief in motion. Instead of spelling out F-I-S-H to introduce "Fixin' to Die," he suggested, let's spell out F-U-C-K.

Nothing could have prepared the musicians for what happened. The audience simply went berserk. Pandemonium. Outside, some record company representatives were trying to get in when a policeman's horse reared up and almost kicked in one person's face. McDonald surveyed the utter bedlam the band had raised with great satisfaction. Madness like this, he thought, is what you want from rock and roll.

Backstage in the dressing room, the musicians glowed. The delirious mood lasted only a short while, as manager Ed Denson entered wearing a glum look. The Schaefer people were not happy. In fact, they told Denson the band could never play the festival again. When the Sullivan representatives appeared and told the band, Keep the money, but Country Joe and the Fish won't be playing the *Ed Sullivan Show*, the bubble burst rather quickly.

The "Fuck Cheer" became notorious overnight. Hall operators across the country spread the word that the band used obscenities in its act and banned the group. Word of the deed flashed through the underground, too, where Country Joe and the Fish earned a heroic reputation as the band that said "fuck." To McDonald, it merely reaffirmed the widening dichotomy in the culture. The stupid little "Fuck Cheer" was obscene, but the war was not. It was a dumb joke, nothing more, but the audience loved it. If the establishment hated it, so much the better.

But the Democratic convention loomed. Hoffman and Rubin were reduced to battling about whether the pig they intended to nominate for president should be a good-looking pig or an ugly one. The band held a meeting to discuss options. By a 4–1 vote, it was decided to take out a full-page ad in the *New York Times* to accuse Hoffman and Rubin of irresponsible revolutionary leadership and advise everyone to stay home and not go to Chicago. Barthol was the lone dissenter.

Country Joe and the Fish went to Chicago, not to appear in the street circus, but to play the Electric Circus, the town's psychedelic ballroom, two days before the convention opened. Hoffman and Rubin turned up at the show. Someone gave McDonald a human skull as a present before he went onstage. The heat was oppressive, sweltering and muggy. The staff interrupted the show to deliver a speech for higher wages and walked out on strike.

Weary, stoned and off-guard, McDonald, Melton and pianist David Cohen waited for an elevator in the hotel lobby after the show when three Vietnam vets approached. "Don't you like America?" one asked Cohen. One of the others hauled off and knocked Melton into an open elevator. The elevator doors closed and Melton took off. The third drunken vet smashed McDonald in the face, drawing blood and breaking his nose, while his partner crashed Cohen against a wall.

Melton dashed back into the lobby, carrying a fire extinguisher, spraying it everywhere. As the Chicago police burst through the lobby doors, the three assailants beat a retreat in a yellow Corvette.

Shortly thereafter, manager Ed Denson informed bassist Barthol he was fired over the telephone. "There has been a band meeting," Denson began. He told Barthol the reason was that his bass playing wasn't good enough. But Barthol, who was an outspoken opponent of what he considered the band's Top Forty artistic direction, didn't think that was really it.

Al Kooper decided to follow up the surprise million-selling success of his impromptu collaboration with guitarist Mike Bloomfield, *Super Session*, by making a live recording at the Fillmore West over three nights in September. Kooper had never heard of the skinny Mexican guitarist who spoke broken English and huddled in the corner clutching his guitar like a security blanket, but knew him as a friend of Bloomfield, who called him Carlito.

Carlos Santana first met Bloomfield in January 1967, when the Paul Butterfield Blues Band played the Fillmore and Santana's band, in one of the group's first public performances, appeared as an opening act in an audition slot early on the Sunday afternoon show. With only a few gigs under its belt, the band didn't even have a name. Quickly, the Santana Blues Band was selected for no other reason than it simply sounded better than the Carabello Blues Band or the Rolie Blues Band.

When Butterfield wandered in later that evening, his brain decimated by a heavy load of LSD, his band's performance degenerated into a free-for-all including members of the Airplane and Dead. Santana's hustling manager asked Bloomfield if the guitarist could sit in with the Butterfield band and Bloomfield assented.

Santana's father worked as a mariachi musician and Santana still played violin in his father's band on weekends. But he was a blues fan, music he first encountered as a teenager still living in Tijuana, and Bloomfield loomed large in his view of the world, a towering figure in the ongoing blues revival spearheaded in no small part by the Butterfield band. When Bloomfield left the Butterfield band and settled in Marin County that summer, Santana often dropped by his Mill Valley home for informal lessons.

Stan Marcum was an enterprising hipster. He graduated from the barber's college on Sixth Street, but was looking for a more compelling calling. Santana was still playing with a couple of his Mexican buddies when he met Marcum. He started introducing the blues guitarist to other worlds of music—John Coltrane, Miles Davis—and other musicians. He also introduced the young musician to LSD. Slowly, Marcum began to pull together a remarkable ensemble.

He brought on board bassist David Brown, perhaps not the most skilled instrumentalist, but a black man who lent an appealing racial hue to the blend. Marcum knew conga player Michael Carabello from high school and, while Carabello was strictly a street musician, he knew Latin music from his grandmother. Although he didn't personally care for the salsa sound, he saw the Latin wrinkle as a riff the band could work.

Gregg Rolie, on the other hand, came from a white-bread suburban background on the peninsula, favored the British Invasion rock sound and actually had some professional experience as a musician. He had played keyboards with a band, William Penn and his Pals, that wore ruffled shirts and played teen dances. A guitarist friend met Santana and invited him to bring his cats down to two-car garageland in Mountain View, where Rolie joined the mess and spent the evening jamming, under the impression Santana had never played with a keyboardist before. Rolie began hitchhiking up to the City to rehearse in a smaller, more crowded garage on Potrero Hill.

Santana moved out of his parents' home and into an apartment with Marcum and his roommate Ron Estrada. He washed dishes at a drive-in called Tick-Tock and grew increasingly psychedelicized. When he tested positive for tuberculosis and spent time on his back in S.F. General, Carabello took him hits of acid to help pass the time. But Carabello was out of the band soon, replaced on congas by another street jammer, a flashy black showman named Marcus Malone.

The band eventually came to the attention of Latin music buff Bill Graham—the musicians haunted his shows often enough, if only as patrons—and he had booked the Santana Blues Band as a last-minute substitute on a bill the previous year with The Who at the Fillmore the weekend of the Monterey Pop Festival. With more raw energy than direction or polish, the group began to work occasionally at the Straight Theater. Rakow used the band at the Carousel. A slight but definite stir already surrounded the group, the name now shortened to simply Santana, when the band made its official Fillmore West debut in July.

With a live album planned, the appearance with the Kooper-Bloomfield circus would constitute the recording debut of the wraith guitarist. But Bloomfield drove himself into a hospital before the engagement ended. Between the hectic rehearsals and the performances on the weekend, insomniac Bloomfield never bothered to sleep. Crazed to the brink, Bloomfield called a doctor, who immediately admitted him to Ross General Hospital and dosed him with Seconal until he finally went to sleep. He had missed the second half of the sessions that produced the first *Super Session* album and was replaced on that record by Stephen Stills, and now he would miss the final night of the Fillmore West sessions.

Elvin Bishop showed up, as well as Santana. With Marcum and David Brown along for support, Santana handled the heady circumstance with apparent calm. He joined the three-piece band for one number, an obscure blues written by Jack Bruce of Cream and Paul Jones of Manfred Mann titled "Sonny Boy Williamson." Santana supplied a brittle but unremarkable solo, giving way to Kooper's organ, and retired. He fired off a couple of momentary volleys, sounding much like the Bloomfield disciple he was. But it was enough to draw some more attention.

That Thanksgiving Eve, as had now become his custom, Bill Graham brought together the local music community for a private celebration at the Fillmore West. After serving a generous buffet dinner, turkey and all the trimmings, Graham took the stage to introduce the evening's musical entertainment to a crowd filled with members of other bands, press, radio and other assorted functionaries of the music scene. He promised the audience the two bands that would play were going to be the next two bands to emerge from San Francisco, two bands, in fact, his new booking agency already represented—It's A Beautiful Day and Santana.

• • •

Jim Morrison of the Doors snaked his way onstage with the Airplane pounding out "Plastic Fantastic Lover," during the final concert of the joint European tour in September at the Amsterdam Concert Hall, where niches on the walls held marble busts of Mozart, Chopin, Beethoven, et al. He spent the day wandering around the smuggler's paradise, imbibing, inhaling and ingesting anything anybody on the street offered him. By day's end, Morrison had eaten a lot of hashish and chased it down with great quantities of Dutch liquor. A half-hour before he was due to take the stage with his own band, he staggered into the Airplane's performance.

In the band's typically perverse manner, the Airplane picked up the tempo, as the obviously smashed Morrison sashayed toward centerstage, holding his hands above his head like a flamenco dancer and spinning in circles. Marty Balin and Morrison circled one another like wrestlers, Balin belting the song, the microphone cord wrapping around both of them. At some particularly appropriate climactic point, Balin stepped out of the tangle and the cord dropped to the floor. Morrison gave Balin a strange, glazed look and went down like a fallen tree. Balin leaned over the inert Doors vocalist. Morrison didn't stir.

A doctor attended to Morrison backstage and he was rushed off to a hospital, leaving his hapless bandmates to perform their portion of the program without a lead vocalist. Organist Ray Manzarek sang the songs that night, while members of the Airplane watched from the wings.

The Airplane arrived for the joint European tour several weeks earlier in London, preceded by an enormous amount of speculation on the part of the hyperactive British music press on the significance of the visit of the reigning leaders of the American underground rock scene. The Doors had not yet been discovered by English audiences. "Light My Fire" spent a scant one week on the British charts and "Hello I Love You," which was serving as the group's calling card, only nudged into the Top Twenty in August. The Airplane's second and third albums, on the other hand, were both big hits in England and public interest focused on the first import from San Francisco to play swinging London.

The band came to England carrying five tons of equipment, a traveling party of fifteen, including a full light show, and toured London in a rented double-decker bus. After appearing at the Isle of Wight rock festival around three in the morning with the temperature a forbidding forty degrees, campfires scattered around the field, the Airplane returned to London to give a free concert at Parliament Hill in Hampstead Heath in a pouring rain.

But the band's two-night stand with the Doors at the Roundhouse qualified as a cultural event among the town's mod elite. Steve Winwood and Jim Capaldi from Traffic, Arthur Brown and other British rock scene notables attended, as the Airplane plowed through two-hour performances, illuminated by Head Lights, that left the capacity crowds stultified.

The Airplane was riding high everywhere. The band appeared on the cover of *Life* magazine in April, illustrating a special edition on "The New Rock." Grace Slick had become the biggest female star in the history of rock, a role she did everything she could to fold, spindle and mutilate. At one outdoor concert, she stripped to the waist when it started to rain, performing topless, she explained, because she didn't want to get her blouse wet. At a concert in Fort Wayne, Indiana, she looked out at the audience. "Which one of you has the biggest cock?" she asked.

After some sessions in March, the band finished a new album in May and June, *Crown of Creation,* a much more disciplined affair than the predecessor, *After Bathing at Baxter's.* Outside of a one-minute instrumental, all of Spencer Dryden's contributions were rejected for the finished work. Nothing so off-the-wall would be tolerated. Grace Slick dashed off a drunken monologue against an instrumental track supplied by Frank Zappa and the Mothers of Invention, "Would You Like a Snack," but the world was deemed not yet ready to hear the new queen of rock's snarling commentary about having her period.

In April, bassist Jack Casady followed Jimi Hendrix back to the Record Plant after a jam session at The Scene a couple of blocks away. With Stevie Winwood playing organ and Mitch Mitchell from Hendrix's band on drums, the impromptu quartet jammed into the morning, tapes capturing one fifteen-minute whack at a Hendrix blues called "Voodoo Chile."

Young, rich and weird, the musicians in the Airplane could afford to indulge any strange whim or act like any upstanding member of the nouveau riche. In May, the band purchased a huge house at 2400 Fulton Street, an enormous, four-story mansion across the street from Golden Gate Park. With a twenty thousand dollar down payment applied to a price of seventy thousand dollars, the monthly payments amounted to little more than three-fifty and the edifice was a showplace. It was built around the turn of the century by a lumber baron who had the elaborate banister on the grand staircase, for instance, shipped to San Francisco around Cape Horn. Opera great Enrico Caruso and his troupe spent the night of the 1906 earthquake sleeping on the floor of the house, which went unscathed. When the Airplane took over, the place was a marvel of Philippine mahogany paneling, lace curtains, crystal chandeliers and floral-patterned carpets.

Although originally envisioned as a combination office and rehearsal hall, Paul Kantner moved in immediately, settling into a large top-story bedroom which he arrayed with decanters stocked with connoisseur-grade marijuana. The group contracted with a French rolling paper company to produce king-size cigarette papers specifically for the band, who then printed custom packages for the papers with "Jefferson Airplane" calligraphed on the cover. There was also a steady supply of pharmaceutical cocaine from Merck Laboratories, still sealed in the brown bottles straight from the factory when they arrived.

In September, after returning from the European tour, the band staged a lavish feast in the Airplane Mansion, a kind of past-due housewarming. Banquet tables ran from the billiards room through the living room and out into the hall. At each place setting, alongside the silverware, was a perfectly shaped cigar-sized joint, rolled by road manager Bill Laudner. The event was catered by the Grand Ultimate Steward Service (G.U.S.S.), which employed Annie Courson, the cook who not only used to work for the Dead at 710 Ashbury, but who also ran the kitchen at the Carousel. Her pièce de résistance for the meal was a suckling pig, complete with apple in the mouth.

Somebody from the Airplane family spiked the punch bowl liberally with LSD. The wife of the city's top newspaper columnist, who helped herself innocently to several cups, sat around all night crying at how beautiful everything was. Owsley himself wired the entire building for sound and operated the system from a basement battle station. He played the new Beatles record, "Hey Jude," over and over ad infinitum, dashing around the rooms with a devilish grin on his face, the record booming out of every corner. At the end of the evening, Bill Thompson's secretary, Jacky Watts, watched a cat work its way down the decimated banquet table, eating scraps first off one plate, then another, winding up splayed on the table, unable to take another mouthful.

Although their relationship was slowly dwindling, Spencer Dryden and Grace Slick lived in the Washington Street flat above Jorma and Margaretta Kaukonen, where Slick kept an antique wooden wheelchair by the fireplace. Slick eventually also rented an apartment in Sausalito and spent nights at her other place with her estranged husband, Jerry Slick. In her absence, Dryden entertained guests of his own. Downstairs, Jorma Kaukonen frequently came out on the losing end of fights with his six-foot-tall red-headed wife, an artistic Swede with a fiery temper, and he would show up the next day at rehearsals bearing bruises.

But increasingly Slick found herself strangely attracted to Paul Kantner, despite his apparently rigid exterior and the steady procession of young women with whom he kept company. In Europe, she found herself experiencing odd feelings of warmth as she comforted Kantner briefly during an acid trip. After the Amsterdam concert, she and Dryden flew to St. Thomas in the Caribbean to an elegant resort hotel called the Lime Tree for a week's vacation and Kantner joined them after a few days, with his womanfriend of the moment. Again, Slick was surprised to discover she was not only drawn to Kantner, but even vaguely jealous of the girlfriend. Telling Dryden she found a cockroach in the bed, she split the next day, leaving Dryden behind.

On October 3, she reached new heights in her public displays at a charity performance at the Whitney Museum in New York. On a program with classical pianist Raymond Lewenthal, the Airplane appeared before a group called "Friends of the Whitney," ritzy Upper East Side types accustomed to giving money to the arts. These were the kinds of socialites Slick grew up among, attended college with and had grown to despise. She brought a bottle of Southern Comfort and proceeded to get bombed for all she was worth.

During a short press conference, Slick insulted the wife of the curator, asking her if she was sleeping with her husband or just living on his prestige. To begin the performance, she delivered a monologue, which she addressed to "all you filthy jewels out there." Since her words may have been slurred somewhat, the people in the audience who thought she said "filthy Jews" can be forgiven. She ranted on about Gucci loafers and big diamonds. She needled the ladies in the audience about wearing tight girdles and not talking to their husbands, whom they only saw at events like this, she suggested, and never at home in the bedroom.

After taping three nights at the Fillmore West later that month for a live album, the Airplane returned to New York in November to take part in the movie being filmed by French film director Jean-Luc Godard, *One American Movie.* Godard, who liked to work out of his head and avoided scripts, told the band only that they were to set up equipment on the roof of the Schuyler Hotel on West Forty-fifth Street at twelve-thirty on a Friday afternoon and start to play.

While Godard and crew filmed from across the street, actor Rip Torn and actress Paula Matter, perched precariously on a windowsill on the floor below, woke up to the sound of the Airplane slamming into "Somebody to Love." As the band moved into "We Can Be Together"—Balin screaming "Wake up, New York, wake up"—a policeman, a genuine New York City patrolman and not an actor, appeared on the roof and informed the band the disturbance was causing a traffic jam in the street below and would have to stop. The band plowed ahead. Five more policemen arrived on the scene.

When Torn and Matter made their appearance, the actor and one of the cops got in a pushing match and Torn was led away under arrest. The Airplane played on.

A week later, with tapes again capturing the performances for the live album, the band appeared three nights at the Fillmore East. On the final night of the engagement, stoned out of his skull, Spencer Dryden walked into the audience and picked up the first girl who recognized him. Sharing a limousine sandwiched between Slick and the girl, Dryden let himself and the girl into his hotel room and simply smiled at Slick in the hallway as he closed the door behind them. She flew back to San Francisco the next day with the rest of the band, but Dryden was too embarrassed to go with them and remained behind in New York a few days, feeling guilty and drinking heavily.

When he finally returned home to the Washington Street apartment he shared with Slick, who had gone directly to Los Angeles on arriving home, he found that the two hippies he left house-sitting had burned the place down. The Kaukonens downstairs were living in their front room, but his place was nothing but cinders. Dryden took his suitcases over to the Airplane mansion.

Sunlight streamed in the windows of the suite at the Chelsea that August afternoon, this time most assuredly not occupied by the road crew, but by Janis Joplin herself. Much had occurred in the intervening six months to irrevocably alter the fabric of the band.

The group's original road dog, Dave Richards, who rated the suite on the first visit to New York merely by checking in first, was no longer with the band. He quit the previous July, after coming to the unhappy realization that the job was no longer fun. He was loading equipment at two in the morning in Puerto Rico at the CBS Records convention. With mosquitos the size of his little finger nibbling at his flesh, he suddenly wondered why in the hell he was doing this. Big Brother was about to launch. Janis Joplin was being touted as the brightest new female star in rock. But Richards was no longer having a good time.

As the stakes changed, so did the personalities, especially Joplin's. She often acted like a queen bee, imperious and haughty, a distinct difference from the raucous and dowdy hippie chick who could be so disarmingly casual and friendly. She took guitarist James Gurley by surprise during the sound check at the Newport Folk Festival, where the band was to headline the prestigious Saturday night event, behaving like a full-fledged prima donna with a flunkie soundman.

The other band members were also beginning to suffer certain insecurities. Billing gradually changed from Big Brother and the Holding Company to Janis Joplin with Big Brother and the Holding Company. Those who were only recently her peers and protectors had become a mere backup band. Record producer John Simon certainly made them sensitive about their instrumental abilities and manager Albert Grossman was no better. After drawing two encores and driving the capacity crowd of seventeen thousand to the edge of frenzy at Newport, the band members were more than slightly surprised to have Grossman come backstage and, instead of offering his congratulations, issue stern criticisms. He said the band's rhythm fluctuated madly, slowed down and sped up throughout the set. Drummer David Getz felt like a glass of ice water had been dumped on his head.

The album was finally finished in June in New York, after more painful sessions in Los Angeles during the spring. Simon finally quit in frustration and asked to have his name left off the credits. With more than two hundred reels of tape recorded, Simon didn't think there was an album's worth of usable material. But Columbia had orders for more than a half-million copies in advance of the release, so the company pressed to have the record finished.

Joplin, Sam Andrew and an engineer completed the final mix in one grueling thirty-six-hour session. The label shortened the title from *Sex, Dope and Cheap Thrills* to simply *Cheap Thrills* and the Columbia Records art department prepared an elaborate photo shoot for the cover.

The band arrived to find a Madison Avenue art director's idea of a hippie pad, draped in chiffon and silly props. The musicians demolished the careful staging, doffed their clothes and jumped naked into the big brass bed together. The results were not used. Instead, the self-mocking frames drawn by underground cartoonist R. Crumb of *Zap Comix* for the back of the album moved to the front.

Joplin and roommate, Linda Gravenites, took a new flat in Noe Valley and Gravenites was not pleased to discover Joplin doing heroin almost daily. But Joplin was not the only member of the band using. Gurley and his formerly estranged wife, Nancy, who moved with their son back into Gurley's apartment while he was out on tour, continued shooting drugs. Sam Andrew also was slipping into the abyss of junkiedom. The band was becoming so nonchalant about drug use that David Getz found himself after a concert in Cincinnati with Joplin, Gurley and Andrew at a funky hippie pad passing a needle around and fixing with strangers they met that night at the show.

If Joplin was detaching from the familial bonds that once held the band together, she was still capable of honest modesty at times. Watching from the wings at the Fillmore East in August as Mavis Staples of the Staple Singers scorched, Joplin mused under her breath, "I'll never be able to sing like that." At the insistence of Pops Staples, she made an awkward attempt anyway to sing one number with the group.

Mostly, however, Joplin was assuming the mantle of a star, a distinctly nonegalitarian pose in which she was only encouraged everywhere she looked. She posed for *Vogue* with photographer Richard Avedon. She gave an interview to the *New York Times* with Nat Hentoff. She was the focal point, and she began to believe her own notices. With Sam Andrew on hand, she telephoned Jerry Miller of the now defunct Moby Grape, a band she used to enjoy informally joining for a number or two at small clubs around San Francisco, to see if he would be interested in helping her put together a new band. He wasn't.

But, by the time she called together the members of Big Brother for the August afternoon meeting in her room at the Chelsea, nobody was really surprised at what she had to say. Gurley realized the die was cast at a previous band meeting at the Landmark Hotel in Hollywood. "I have to have things the way I want and I'll have anybody killed who stands in my way," she had demanded in a fury. Gurley, pursued by demons of his own, felt helpless. She had already taken Sam Andrew into her confidence about her future plans. David Getz knew instantly what the meeting was about the minute she called.

Cheap Thrills had been released, and was on its way to selling a million copies in the first month, headed to number one on the charts, but Joplin was through. She announced her decision to the band. She would play out the remaining dates, ending with a San Francisco appearance in early December, and leave the group. Mild-mannered Peter Albin exploded. He told her angrily what a backstabbing move he thought that was. While the other band members sat around looking glum, Albin vented the anger and indignation that they all felt somewhere inside. On the elevator back down to the lobby afterward, Getz, already thinking aloud about what to do to keep the band together, got the real shock of the afternoon from Sam Andrew. "By the way," Andrew allowed, "I'll be going with Janis, too."

Joplin was learning how to cultivate her image, some of which was based on fact. Long gone were the peasant blouses and Mexican shawls; now she sported feather boas and stacks of jangly bracelets. But more than her look, she began to sculpt a character for public consumption, urging her press agent to spread the story of Joplin cold-cocking Jim Morrison with a liquor bottle at a Hollywood party. She besieged the manufacturers of Southern Comfort, her trademark drink of choice, with press clippings, until the company caved in and presented her with a lynx coat and she practiced her riposte to the press until it was as smooth as a stone on the beach: "Ooo-wee, what a hustle—can you imagine getting paid for two years of passing out."

She quickly picked up on the material rewards of her success—clothes shopping in Beverly Hills, writing boastful letters home about how much money she was going to make next year, buying a new Porsche. She had Dave Richards paint a splashy psychedelic design over the whole car, as opposed to the pin-stripes Stanley Mouse had supplied for her old Austin convertible.

With the album hitting the top of the charts in November, and the announcement of Joplin's exit from the band, the last concerts drew packed houses everywhere. At the Fillmore West in September, the place was so crowded—close to three times capacity—people forced open the closed windows and took fresh air on the fire escape. Someone even fell to the sidewalk. Tension mounted in the band. At the Houston Music Hall, after a Joplin illness caused cancellation of dates in Austin and San Antonio, her family arrived backstage following the concert in time to watch her curse out a stagehand.

At the Tyrone Guthrie Theater in Minneapolis, she discovered some Shakespearean costumes from a previous occupant and playfully brandished a sword. "Okay, varlet," she commanded, "bring me thirteen pretty boys and line 'em up against this wall. Right now!"

But onstage during the first half of the performance, Joplin paused after singing one particularly demanding number and panted into the microphone, part out of breath, part exaggerating. Peter Albin couldn't take anymore. "Now we're doing an imitation of Lassie," he cracked into his microphone and the audience guffawed. Joplin flashed. "Fuck you," she said into her microphone.

Backstage, road manager John Cooke tried to cool down the hostilities. "Man, he called me a dog," stormed Joplin. "Onstage, in front of everybody. I don't have to take that shit."

"The audience thought it was funny," offered Cooke.

"Well, I don't, goddammit," she huffed.

A reporter from a local magazine, oblivious, asked one of the band members who Joplin's favorite poet was. "Ask her," he snapped.

When the show continued after intermission, Joplin kept her back turned on Albin for the rest of the evening. The band returned to the hotel and a young lady who had followed the station wagon from the concert invited Sam Andrew to a party. The guys all left with her. Joplin went back to her hotel room alone.

Before the final New York concert at Hunter College, Joplin and Andrew stayed up for two days on speed, laying plans for the new band and working on arrangements for songs. She took Seconals the night before in a futile attempt to get some sleep prior to this intensely anticipated concert. Her bottle of Southern Comfort by her side, she grew hysterical about the condition of her voice in the afternoon prior to the concert, although by showtime, she and Andrew were pounding away at the backstage piano, working on a piece of music they had been writing together, unaware that Richard Manuel and Rick Danko of The Band were sitting around watching their drugaddled demonstration.

David Getz dropped acid that night. When the time came for the band to leave the stage while Getz played his drum solo, Joplin walked back out carrying a tiger-skin drum. Thinking she was simply pulling an upstaging stunt, Getz kicked the drum away. Joplin jumped. She thought he kicked it at her and turned back. "Fuck you, man," she shouted.

Backstage the fight continued. "I was just trying to be nice to you, man," Joplin said. "I was just bringing this drum out to you. That was really a nice thing for me to do and you, you fucker, you embarrassed me in front of three thousand people."

The show had not been very good anyway. In ten months, the band had gone from toast of New York to fiasco. The next afternoon, Joplin was in the emergency room of New York Hospital, diagnosed as suffering from acute bronchitis.

By the time the band played its final show at the December 1 benefit for the Family Dog at the Avalon—Chet Helms was having problems of his own—the only thing the musicians felt was relief.

With the band's music growing consciously, intentionally ever more complex, changes were in the wind by the time the Grateful Dead convened in September at Pacific Recording in San Mateo to begin the group's third album. Pigpen was a problem. Not only was his blues style restrictive, but his drinking was getting in the way. He missed rehearsals. He wouldn't expand his repertoire beyond the same three or four numbers he had done with the band for the past couple of years. Furthermore, his keyboard playing remained far too limited to travel the realms the rest of the band was intent on exploring.

Bobby Weir, too, lacked the command of his instrument necessary to keep up with players like Garcia and Lesh, to master the complicated time signatures and other intricacies the band was developing. He had never made a total transition from his coffeehouse folk days on acoustic guitar to electric rock guitar. He was also not contributing much material.

Garcia held a peculiar role in the band. He was the unacknowledged leader, a passive voice who never ruled by laying down the law. Not that the Grateful Dead would have ever followed such a dominant force. Secretly, each of the members believed it was their contribution that made the band special, although, if pressed, they would also all admit that it was Garcia who ultimately shaped the voice of the Dead. And Garcia was fed up with the inadequacies of Weir.

Garcia was even thinking of leaving the band. He, Mickey Hart and Jack Casady of the Airplane spent an afternoon jamming during a party at the Novato ranch, while Owsley ran tape. They took some capsules purporting to be THC, a synthesized version of the active ingredient in marijuana, that was actually a brain-blurring blend of unknown tranquilizers and other agents. Whatever it was, it worked. All three musicians were transported and the two and a half hours of tape bore witness to the cause of their elation. Garcia and Lesh were on the outs at the time and the idea of forming a power trio along the lines of Cream or the Jimi Hendrix Experience took hold for a hot moment. Hart went so far as to approach Janis Joplin about joining up as the vocalist. "Hah," laughed Joplin. "Can you imagine me turning around and seeing you guys behind me?"

Casady also made it clear he had no intention of quitting a going concern like the Jefferson Airplane, so Garcia was left with his problems with the Dead. He could come to terms with Lesh, but Weir and Pigpen posed an apparently insurmountable obstacle in recording the demanding, complex music he and Lesh had written for the next album. There was only one real solution.

At a band meeting at Pacific Recording, manager Rock Scully took up the cudgel. After some discussion of the situation, Scully told Weir and Pigpen they were fired from the band. Pigpen cried. There was little further argument, just a somber acceptance and grim mood that filled the room. Lesh wanted to move forward with business, consideration of what lay ahead. Adding other instrumentalists was discussed. Someone suggested bringing in violinist David LaFlamme, who had moved from playing with Dan Hicks and his Hot Licks to a band of his own that was making some noise at the ballrooms, It's A Beautiful Day.

The band spent most of September cloistered in Pacific Studios, the first sixteen-track studio in the area, working on three unconventional pieces—the shifting time signatures of "St. Stephen," Garcia's audio-collage "What's Become of the Baby" and the demonic discord of Lesh's "Barbed Wire Whipping Party." The madcap sessions were often fueled by a tank of nitrous oxide with several hoses.

In October, a tentative version of the revamped roster, dubbed Mickey and the Hartbeats for the occasions, made several appearances at the Matrix. However, when the Dead proper played three nights at the Avalon the same week as the first Hartbeats shows, Weir and Pigpen took the stage as if nothing had happened. If they had been fired, it had failed to take.

In November at the Fillmore West, the Dead's psychedelic assassination squad hit their ultimate target, dosing Bill Graham with some acid concealed on the lip of a soft-drink can. He spent the evening onstage, banging a cowbell with every fiber of his being. Quicksilver manager Ron Polte asked Graham how he was feeling. "The body is tired," he told Polte, "but the mind just woke up."

One answer to the band's musical quandary was to move Pigpen off keyboards, making him something like resident bluesman to deliver one or two turns per show, and bring aboard Tom Constanten, Phil Lesh's old pal who contributed some parts to *Anthem of the Sun.*

Already growing his hair in anticipation of the appointment, T.C. mustered out of the Air Force and flew directly from Las Vegas, where he had been stationed, to join the Dead in Columbus, Ohio, just before Thanksgiving. Constanten brought with him a long and serious background in experimental music. During the early sixties, he took classes with Lesh from composer Luciano Berio at Oakland's Mills College and went on to study under avant-gardist Karlheinz Stockhausen in Germany.

But if Constanten expected the position to come with the luxuries he envisioned accompanied success in the pop music field, he was disabused of that notion right at the start. With the band $40,000 in debt, the Hammond organ Constanten remembered from the *Anthem* recording sessions had long since been repossessed and he had to make do with a Tinkertoy Vox Continental.

Gary Duncan realized that all this shooting speed had to come to a stop. On and off all his adult life he had been using the drug. But now it was clear to him it was either stop or die. His frustration with Quicksilver mounted all year. He felt himself reaching a breaking point with his band, too.

Duncan had come under the spell of Dino Valente, the powerful folksinger who originally was to have been the centerpiece of the band Tom Donahue was putting together that ultimately became Quicksilver. A drug bust landed Valente—who wrote the hippie anthem, "Get Together," under his real name Chester Powers and sold the rights for peanuts to finance his legal battle—in Folsom Prison doing one-to-ten and, on his release nine months later, Quicksilver was already up and running. He stayed on the Olema dairy farm with the band when he first got out, which is where Duncan met him, but moved to a Sausalito houseboat when the Quicksilver musicians relocated to San Francisco.

Eight years older than Duncan, Valente was the big brother Duncan never had growing up in a foster family. Like Valente, Duncan served time in prison, doing a year in minimum security on drug charges. They shared their passion for motorcycles, music, women and amphetamines. He was a robust, strapping fellow with a magnetic personality, a pair of Great Danes and a string of women who waited on him hand and foot. He also liked to claim he dabbled in black magic. To Duncan, Valente was a man who did things other than lying around, like his bandmates.

Duncan was disgusted with the lack of ambition his Quicksilver colleagues had demonstrated since the release of the band's debut album in June. Just finishing the album had been difficult enough. Producer Nick Gravenites brought in his associate from Electric Flag, bassist Harvey Brooks, to serve as co-producer and the album the two made sounded more like the Flag than Quicksilver. They overdubbed brassy horn sections and thumping Chicago soul-style bass parts. The band hated the record.

But manager Ron Polte convinced Capitol Records to write off the initial fifty thousand dollars spent on recording the first album and start over from scratch. Only one track, once the horn parts were wiped off, could be salvaged. But the further investment paid off. The second time, they got it right, somehow distilling Quicksilver's ballroom sound into a compact, seamless blend of driving guitars, flowing harmonies and Cipollina's heroic, piercing guitar rides. The showpiece of *Quicksilver Messenger Service* was a twelve-minute epic titled "The Fool," written by bassist David Freiberg in an acid haze. He simply woke up the morning after a particularly spectacular eight-hour orbit and found the lyrics sitting, already written, in his typewriter.

But the band didn't stir after the release. Outside of a Fillmore East debut in June, Quicksilver did little touring. Cipollina preferred living his nocturnal life inside his Mill Valley home, tucked in away under the redwoods, every nook filled with his collections of bats, lizards and snakes. The group didn't even like to rehearse. Duncan was going stir-crazy just waiting for the band to rouse itself from this sleepy existence. After the ordeal of recording the first album, the other musicians didn't even want to return to the studio to record a second album, but decided instead to record live.

In October, Quicksilver embarked on a tour that took the band to St. Louis, Kansas City, Chicago, Milwaukee and other cities, playing free concerts as well as ballrooms along the way, before hitting the Fillmore East to begin recording the live album. Valente happened to be playing some shows at the same time at the Cafe au Go Go to promote his album, a near solo affair produced by Bob Johnston, a man of the moment from doing albums with Bob Dylan, Johnny Cash and Leonard Cohen. Polte stopped by the club, where less than a handful of people comprised the pitiful audience. Valente complained to Polte that the record label was hanging him out to dry.

The next night, Duncan went by to watch his friend and came back to the hotel determined to do something. "I'm going to help Dino," he told Polte. "I'm not going to let him hang out there by himself." Polte warned Duncan that it could conflict with Quicksilver. "Don't worry," he said. "It won't."

Duncan told the band the following night he would be leaving Quicksilver after the band returned to San Francisco. He laid out his list of grievances and Freiberg was stunned. When Duncan said the band was going nowhere, it was the first he had heard of it. The first album had been well received. The second album was about to be recorded. To Freiberg, the band's condition never looked better.

All the friends and families showed up for the final recording session November 19 at Golden State Recorders, a four-hour event where Quicksilver cut a live twelve-minute Duncan composition titled "Calvary." Freiberg chopped up and snorted a bunch of LSD. George Hunter of the Charlatans, who had started a graphic arts company and was designing the Quicksilver album cover, brought a painting he had commissioned of a cowboy riding off and his woman waving good-bye. "It looks like happy trails to me," Hunter said.

Having hit on a title, it only remained for the band to sing the Roy Rogers-Dale Evans song, but they could only remember one verse. Duncan played one final date with the band New Year's Eve at Winterland and ran off for New York to form a band with Dino Valente.

The quixotic Denver venture by Chet Helms and his Family Dog had drained the reserves. Almost overnight, the bottom fell out of the poster business. Even the home church of the Avalon wasn't doing business like before. The lease needed to be renewed and, when the police department pulled the plug on the Avalon dance permit, the building owners served an eviction notice.

Helms took his case to the public, calling a press conference and assembling some support. Helms brought to the meeting some neighborhood merchants, a representative of the local recording industry, the Chamber of Commerce, the American Federation of Musicians and his chief competitor, Bill Graham himself. "This is not a gas station," said Graham. "This is a ballroom. It has been run well and should continue."

But asked if he didn't fear the same tactics being applied to his operation, Graham turned more forceful. "I can give you a nasty answer to that," he said. "Don't get a New York boy in the gutter."

Mayor Joseph Alioto entered the act, telling City Hall reporters he supported the Avalon. He dismissed the noise complaints coming from the fleabag pensioner's hotel around the corner from the Avalon. "There are a lot of places in town that make noise," Alioto said. "I've even heard a lot of noise, late at night, from the Opera House."

Even the Beatles lent their support, sending Helms a cable and a print of *Magical Mystery Tour,* the British television special that had not been shown in the U.S., for him to screen as a fundraiser.

Helms was told he could get his permits for an under-the-table five thousand dollar payment, but opted to pursue his fate through the system. He lost two appeals hearings and when Avalon attorney Michael Stepanian collected new evidence that one old man had been offered a bribe in return for giving false testimony against the Avalon, the Board of Permit Appeals didn't even want to hear about it at the third and final hearing. Case closed.

The last weekend only four hundred customers turned up on Saturday night to hear Johnny Winter, Magic Sam and Kaleidoscope. Helms paid nine hundred dollars to rent the hall for the three nights that weekend. He'd bought out his partner, Bob Cohen, a couple of months earlier.

1969

*The blood-dimmed
tide is loosed, and
everywhere
The ceremony of
innocence is drowned.*
       —W. B. Yeats,
    The Second Coming

WINTER 1968-69

Mike Bloomfield and Nick Gravenites arrived to lead the new Janis Joplin band through rehearsals only five days before the first scheduled performance. Albert Grossman had appropriated another Canadian group that backed rock and roll singer Ronnie Hawkins—his previous Hawkins backing band was riding quite high at the time with "Music from Big Pink" as The Band—and imported the second group more or less intact to form the basis of the new Joplin outfit.

Sam Andrew took a substantial pay cut, along with an even more humbling drop from equal partner to salaried employee. But Grossman knew that Joplin couldn't possibly pull together a musical enterprise of this magnitude. After trying to secure the services of several other candidates for the role of musical director, Grossman finally turned to Bloomfield and Gravenites, fresh from the rubble of Electric Flag, another Grossman-managed act, ironically riddled with heroin problems. Bloomfield himself had been shooting junk since he was a teenager.

A horn section was assembled, including Flag alumnus Marcus

Doubleday on trumpet, which was Joplin's main objective in forming the new band, to play with keyboards and horns. No longer satisfied with her standing as the hippie rock star, Joplin set her sights on Aretha Franklin and Tina Turner.

Gravenites was a sturdy fellow, a prolific songwriter who would be a ready source of much-needed new material for the Joplin solo act. Bloomfield, aggressively eager and cheerfully sarcastic, was a less than ideal choice for dealing with this kind of high-pressure tinderbox of egos. They swept into San Francisco on December 18, Sam Andrew's birthday, for the band's first rehearsal at the Geary Temple next door to the Fillmore, with Joplin set to appear December 22 as the only outside act invited to appear at the second annual Stax/Volt Yuletide Thing at the Mid-South Coliseum in Memphis.

An audacious announcement of the second coming of Janis Joplin, this coronation of the new white soul queen was to take place at the fountainhead of the music, the cradle of deep soul, home of the late Otis Redding, Sam and Dave, Eddie Floyd and Booker T. and the M.G.'s, the very architects of the music Joplin dumped Big Brother to pursue.

Arrangements still needed to be hammered out. The bass player was substituting for a Canadian musician with immigration problems. Bloomfield and Joplin butted heads. The band didn't even have a name, although there was no shortage of suggestions—Squeeze, the Joplinaires, the Janis Joplin Revue.

After rehearsals Wednesday and Thursday in San Francisco, the group flew to Memphis. The studio receptionist wasn't entirely clear on who they were. "Here comes the Big Brothers," she sang out as they walked through the doors. The band managed a little more rehearsal Friday afternoon at Studio B of the Stax/Volt complex, watched by a clean-cut man in a suit who looked more like a banker than the brilliant guitarist of Booker T. and the M.G.'s, Steve Cropper. That evening the group attended a private party at the home of Stax president, Jim Stewart.

In a purplish red pantsuit with feather boas around the cuffs, Joplin relaxed any apprehensions floating around about inviting a hippie soul singer. She at least looked like she belonged. Tables filled with pink shrimp, bacon-wrapped chicken livers and sandwiches dyed red and green for Christmas were stationed around the living room and a giant tree covered with lights stood in one corner. Some guests arrayed themselves on the leopard-skin print couches and some simply sat on the thick red rug. Cropper wore a black velvet suit and green ruffled shirt. Stax songwriters Isaac Hayes, dressed all in black, and David Porter, all in red, were there. M.G.'s bassist Donald (Duck) Dunn drank Budweiser instead of the expensive whiskey at the bar. Joplin was a long way from the Haight-Ashbury.

The next night, she was to provide one of the concert's climaxes, followed only by Johnnie Taylor, Stax/Volt recording artist whose recent million-selling hit, "Who's Making Love," qualified him to close the show. In a corridor backstage, Bloomfield's eyes widened as he caught sight of the re-formed Bar-Kays making their way to the stage in zebra-striped flannel jumpsuits.

Four of the instrumental group's original members had died the year before in the same plane crash that killed Otis Redding, and the new Bar-Kays did the Pony, stomped, boogalooed and generally tore the place up, before giving way to Albert King, whose stately blues went over fine with the more than half black capacity crowd. The Bar-Kays returned, dressed in all red, to back up a procession of Stax soul singers—the Mad Lads, William Bell, Judy Clay—capped by the father-daughter combination of Rufus and Carla Thomas, whose raunchy act bordered on obscene even by Fillmore standards. Members of the Joplin band watched from the wings, shaking their heads.

After a brief intermission, Booker T. and the M.G.'s offered a sample of the quartet's impeccable playing, before backing the Staple Singers on a pair of richly moving numbers. Eddie Floyd worked the crowd up to a frothy frenzy with, first, "Knock on Wood" and then with "I Never Found a Girl," where he had dozens of young girls coming down the aisles to touch his hand.

After this steady stream of sleek showmanship, instead of taking the stage and picking up the momentum where Floyd left it, Joplin insisted that equipment man Mark Braunstein and his crew entirely rearrange the existing stage plot, including moving the heavy Hammond organ to the opposite side of the stage. While they spent more than a half-hour shoving equipment around and setting up microphones, the audience's ardor cooled substantially. She finally opened with a ragged "Raise Your Hand," a Stax/Volt song originally recorded by Eddie Floyd. The ill-schooled band was no match for the crisp, brassy snap and polish of the Bar-Kays and her screeching vocals didn't project the warmth and sincerity Southern soul audiences demanded. She regained her balance slightly with the second number, a cover of the Bee Gees' "To Love Somebody," but dashed offstage after a third unfamiliar number, expecting to be called back for an encore of "Piece of My Heart" and "Ball and Chain." The response was a resounding thud. Scattered applause. No encore.

Backstage, Joplin was alternately fuming and crying. Grossman and Bloomfield huddled with her, giving her a pep talk. "It's just one gig," Bloomfield told her. By the time the press wandered backstage, she could disguise her anguish with world-weary bravado. "At least they didn't throw things," she said, and retired to her room at the Lorraine Motel, the same place where Martin Luther King, Jr. had been shot to death earlier in the year.

After such a disastrous debut, Grossman was determined Joplin would not suffer any similar humiliation on her return to New York in February. He found the most obscure, remote engagement he could book in Rindge, New Hampshire ("A sound test," road manager John Cooke called it), followed by an out-of-town opening at the Boston Music Hall before the February 11–12 dates at the Fillmore East with the Grateful Dead.

Personnel continued to shuffle—bassist Brad Campbell was now in place, although his immigration status was still uncertain, along with new players on keyboards and trumpet. Joplin wasted no time in starting an affair with the new keyboard player, dark-haired and bearded Richard Kermode. The situation was anything but stable when Joplin pulled into New York. She missed a scheduled afternoon rehearsal while she played pool and drank at a Lower East Side bar.

Backstage before the show in a room painted purple especially for this gig by Graham, with Grossman snowbound at home in Woodstock, Joplin and her press aide worried about a CBS camera crew. Nobody had told them that Mike Wallace and his *60 Minutes* staff planned to film the Joplin performance for an upcoming segment on Graham and his establishment titled "Carnegie Hall for the Kids." Not only was Joplin concerned about the shaky condition of the relatively untested band, but bassist Campbell was still not exactly legal in the country, and filming him posed potential problems far more serious. While band members scurried to disguise Campbell underneath a furry hat and sunglasses, painting a mascara mustache on him, the press agent faced down a furious Graham, who did one of his trademark tirades on her. Grossman was reached by phone and a compromise was reached: *60 Minutes* would get an interview, but no live footage.

Joplin plowed into the performance with an almost desperate intensity, plunging into "Raise Your Hand" furiously, attacking the song as if she were trying to strangle it to death. In between numbers, she nervously joked around, introducing her band as "Janis and the Jack-Offs." Backstage between shows, she drank herself silly, telling newsman Wallace, in preparation for their interview, if she got out of line, he should just say "fuck." Benny Goodman and his wife came backstage to offer congratulations and Sam Andrew suggested he join Joplin for a duet on "Summertime," but the swing king begged off, saying he was only out for a social night with his wife. Frank Zappa, another backstage visitor, responded to Andrew's doubts about the band by assuring him things would straighten out in time. Grossman made it into town for the show the following night and he, too, expressed reservations about the band.

After the Fillmore dates, the group left for a series of concerts, including a sold-out show in the huge gymnasium at the University of Michigan in Ann Arbor. Joplin pulverized the campus crowd, leaving the students screaming for more when the house technicians snapped the lights on. Trailing an interviewer for *Playboy* magazine, Joplin headed off into the night to catch a young blues player at a local club. Urged to take the bandstand by the club owner, Joplin got onstage only to discover the band didn't know any of her songs. She took the writer and harp player to her hotel room, where she played tapes of her performance earlier in the evening, shot some drugs and talked into the dawn.

Worried about her weight, she went without dinner that night and, early in the morning, she prowled the hotel hallway, picking at leftovers from other people's room service trays outside their doors. She was due back in New York later that day to appear on the *Ed Sullivan Show*.

In Los Angeles, Grace Slick busied herself working on the mix of the live album. She knew her apartment in San Francisco had burned and knew her relationship with Dryden was in tatters. She saw no particular reason to hurry home. The long hours and detailed work of mixing the album offered welcome escape.

Kantner was also working on the album. At one point, standing side by side, twisting buttons and sliding knobs, their hands brushed. Slick stopped, placed her hand directly on Kantner's and looked into his eyes. An unspoken comment passed between them.

In San Francisco, Dryden was packing up belongings saved from the fire in the charred apartment. The Kaukonens upstairs called him to meet some visitors, an old girlfriend of Kantner's and her friend, Sally Mann. An attractive twenty-year-old brunette, Mann was the daughter of the mayor of Houston who ran away from home and got married at age sixteen in Mexico to a rock band manager. She mingled with the Los Angeles rock crowd and did some time on a pot bust, before hooking up with James Gurley from Big Brother and moving to San Francisco. Dryden invited the two young ladies over to the Mansion and wound up spending the night in Balin's room with Sally Mann. She started coming back, bearing gifts of cocaine, and the two found themselves embroiled in an affair by the time Slick returned from Los Angeles.

She took a cab to the Mansion and, even before seeing Dryden, Slick met Mann, introduced as the new housekeeper but whom she remembered as a former liaison of Kantner's. The two chatted amiably and, without her saying so, Slick surmised that Mann and Dryden had become lovers already. Slick asked her husband Jerry Slick to move in with her at her Sausalito apartment, but continued seeing Dryden, who was living in the Airplane Mansion.

Dryden wrote both Slick and Mann long letters, saying he loved them both. Slick spent the evening at home killing a vodka bottle. Dryden had moved his things into a room on the second floor of the Airplane house and also arranged a small room nearby for Slick. One night, Slick surprised him by knocking on his door around midnight, only to find him listening to records with Mann, whom he, once again, tried to pass off as the live-in housekeeper who stayed downstairs.

A few days later, after a couple of groupies Dryden knew from the Fillmore East dropped by the Mansion unexpectedly, Mann walked in on Dryden in bed with one of them. He found her downstairs sharing a bottle of Southern Comfort with Slick, the pair commiserating with each other about Dryden. The groupies were ushered out and the drinking went on into the night. At one point, Slick and Dryden, sitting on the grand staircase, broke down into tears. By the early morning hours, her tears evaporated and Slick, half out of her head, fell into a loud, angry monologue. She kept asking for Kantner.

Dryden finally called Jerry Slick in Sausalito, who dutifully drove in and retrieved his confused and drunken wife.

Slick underwent her second operation for throat nodes in January and spent an entire month without speaking, communicating with notes and scribbled drawings. She recovered in time for a March 8 appearance at the Honolulu International Center. The band rented a Spanish castle on the beach and took a short vacation. Ostensibly, Slick was there with Dryden but she found herself increasingly disgusted with his staying up all night, drinking on speed and sleeping it off all day in the middle of an island paradise. She wandered off to the pool one afternoon to see if anyone wanted to ride into town.

Kantner, sitting by the pool, offered her some orange sunshine. They snipped off small pieces of the tablet and went for a ride with Jorma and Margaretta Kaukonen in the hills. As the acid came on, rain clouds gathered and gently showered on them. While the effect was not especially romantic—Kantner had a girlfriend back at the house, where Dryden was waiting for Slick—away from the band like this, Slick became aware of a gentle side of Kantner's nature she had never seen before.

Back in San Francisco shortly thereafter, after a rehearsal at the Airplane house, Slick fixed Kantner a dinner of meat and potatoes. He invited her up to his bedroom to share a bottle of champagne. The next morning, manager Bill Thompson smiled to himself as he watched the couple walk downstairs together looking positively radiant.

Diane LaChambre was standing onstage watching the New Year's Eve show at Winterland featuring the Dead, Quicksilver, Santana and It's A Beautiful Day when she heard a familiar voice behind her. "I'll have to ask you to leave," Graham said.

Defiance flashed through her. "I'll have to say no," she said to Graham.

"This is the only show Bonnie's going to this year," he said.

"That's okay," replied LaChambre. "I can handle her being here."

Not only had Graham's wife insisted he end the relationship with the sensual teenager, but his big-shot attorney was aghast. The lawyer told Graham to pay her off, to get rid of her in no uncertain terms. An underage mistress could be an extraordinary liability in any divorce action, not to mention leaving Graham open to other even more drastic actions. Graham told his assistant, Paul Baratta, that he was going to give the young girl ten thousand dollars.

But Diane LaChambre had fallen in love with Graham, in love the way only a sixteen-year-old girl can—completely, unquestioningly, totally. When Graham broached the question, she was hurt and spurned any mention of money. Graham told her he wanted to send her away—was there any place she wanted to go? "I guess I could go to Tahiti to see my father," she allowed, and Graham readily agreed to take care of the arrangements.

But New Year's Eve at Winterland, she wasn't feeling so compliant. She stood her ground on the stage when Graham asked her to leave and, shortly thereafter, when she saw his wife, she calmly walked up to her and offered a greeting. In her mind, LaChambre saw no reason why Graham couldn't have his wife and his mistress, too. "Hi, Bonnie," she said. "I'm Diane."

"I know you," said Bonnie Graham. "You're going to Tahiti."

Something inside LaChambre snapped. She felt manipulated and instantly decided against going to Tahiti after all. Shaken and angry, she went backstage and found Patti Santos, vocalist with It's A Beautiful Day, who comforted the upset young girl. But before the evening was over, LaChambre and Bonnie Graham were sitting together in the Winterland office, drinking wine and talking. Bonnie Graham had given birth to her son, David, barely three months earlier and the trim, carefree hippie her husband was sleeping with made her feel wistful. She told LaChambre when she was her age she had a body like hers. LaChambre assured Graham's wife she was beautiful and asked why they couldn't be friends. Impossible, Bonnie Graham told her, such a thing was unheard of.

But the next weekend, Bonnie Graham was not in such a charitable mood. LaChambre saw her dancing, apparently drunk, on the stage of the Fillmore West while the Grateful Dead played. But the two encountered each other, standing by the top of the stairs where patrons entered the ballroom. A screaming match gave way to shoving and, in a flash, the two women were on each other, scratching, hitting and rolling on the floor. The spectacle of this catfight took place in full view of people waiting in line for hamburgers at the grill. Paul Baratta rushed up to the scene, only to discover exactly who was fighting—his boss's wife and mistress. He got a security guard to separate the two before Graham himself appeared.

The impresario drove the two women home, first dropping LaChambre off at her grandmother's home and sternly admonishing her that their relationship was now over. But within days, he had smoothed things over and installed his young lover back in the Boulder Creek summer home he kept in the Santa Cruz Mountains.

Even with all the turmoil in his personal life, Graham barely noticed. He wore a wristwatch with two faces, one set to East Coast time and one for Pacific time. He ran shows every weekend at both the Fillmore West and the Fillmore East. The Millard Agency and Shady Management operated out of offices above a liquor store on Union Street and represented, in various capacities, a list of clients including the Grateful Dead, Santana, It's A Beautiful Day and a few others.

Attorney Brian Rohan, who negotiated almost every record deal for all the San Francisco bands since cutting the Warner's pact for the Dead, kept telling Graham he ought to start a label of his own, but Graham resisted. Since the release of *Jefferson Airplane Takes Off* less than three years earlier, more than fifteen albums by San Francisco bands had hit the Billboard best-selling charts. Groups unknown as recently as the year before were selling records by the truckload.

Out of the East Bay, for instance, a bunch of longtime frat-party rockers who changed their name to Creedence Clearwater Revival recorded a tape expressly for airplay on KMPX, a psychedelicized version of the old Dale Hawkins rock and roll standard "Suzie Q," complete with extended guitar solo. Airplay on the underground radio station made the difference between the quartet's plugging away in front of a few dozen desultory dancers at a North Beach bar called Gino and Carlo's and headlining the Fillmore. An edited version of the track went on to become a nationwide hit single for the tiny Oakland-based jazz label, Fantasy Records, and the group's second album, *Bayou Country*, promised to blow through the roof courtesy of an infectious number titled "Proud Mary." No end to the San Francisco rock gold appeared in sight.

Rohan wanted Graham to start his record company by signing Santana and It's A Beautiful Day. Led by violinist David LaFlamme, Beautiful Day was a group of musicians put together and named by Matthew Katz, although they, too, had wrenched themselves loose from Katz's managerial command. Katz, in fact, was reduced to living in a bus and pressing his lawsuit against the Airplane.

With LaFlamme matching his vocals against the harmonies of Patti Santos, the quintet etched an exotic, ethereal sound that was finding great favor among ballroom patrons. Both Santana and Beautiful Day, in fact, headlined engagements at the Fillmore West before recording an album. Santana, in particular, could count on a strong local constituency.

Rohan was experiencing some difficulty interesting the record business in either group. He took Ahmet Ertegun to see Santana, but the founder of Atlantic Records and all-around savant walked away unimpressed. "Can't play," quipped Ertegun. "Furthermore, won't sell."

But Rohan found a supporter in David Rubinson, the staff producer at Columbia Records who shepherded the Moby Grape albums. Rubinson was compiling quite an impressive list of tasteful and successful projects for Columbia. He produced bluesman Taj Mahal and scored a hit record with Tim Rose on "Hey Joe." His "Time Has Come Today" made the Chambers Brothers one of the hottest acts of the day. A longtime Latin music fan, Rubinson also supervised a series of records by master conguero Mongo Santamaria. He wanted Columbia to sign both Santana and Beautiful Day. Rohan introduced Rubinson to the idea of forming a partnership with Graham to make records and Rubinson thought those two acts would be perfect to launch a new company.

Once Rubinson expressed interest, Graham became more intrigued. He knew Rubinson slightly and realized the young record producer possessed skills Graham needed to make any such enterprise go. But he was slow to commit and Rohan ended up signing the two bands for a relative pittance to Columbia. Rubinson spent much of January trying to coax a debut album out of Santana to no avail. In March, the details finally in place, he left Columbia and New York, took his wife and their young son and relocated to San Francisco.

Rubinson, Graham and Rohan formed a partnership to make records and wheeler-dealer Rohan struck two separate distribution deals with competing major labels. He placed Fillmore Records with Columbia and San Francisco Records with Atlantic, thinking he could play one off against the other to his own company's advantage. But instead of Santana and It's A Beautiful Day, Rubinson arrived in San Francisco and was presented as his first projects for the new label former Paul Butterfield guitarist and hippie hayseed Elvin Bishop and an overblown blues-rock trio called Aum, hardly an auspicious beginning.

SPRING 1969

Even before the studio opened on April 27, the Jefferson Airplane decided to record the band's next album at Wally Heider's new sixteen-track facility in San Francisco. Suspicious of Hollywood engineers and tired of recording in the bowels of the RCA building, the musicians looked forward to going home to sleep in their own beds between sessions.

Heider, who owned and operated a successful Los Angeles studio, was renowned as one of the top location recordists in the business and his foray into San Francisco represented a major investment in the city's music scene from the supposedly entrenched bastions of the recording industry in Southern California. Even before the doors opened, the Airplane booked time and shortly thereafter Crosby, Stills and Nash, a reorganized Big Brother and the Holding Company and the Steve Miller Band followed.

Both Kantner and Dryden continued to live at the Mansion. A sign reading "House of Bishops Committee Room; Bishops Only; Keep the Fuck Out" hung outside Dryden's second-floor room. Slick kept her apartment in Sausalito. The Kaukonens bought a house in the exclusive St. Francis Wood district of San Francisco and Casady and Melissa Cargill kept a home together with a pet owl in San Francisco.

The Mansion not only housed a carpeted rehearsal hall in the basement, but had become an unofficial headquarters for the local rock constabulary. David Crosby often spent time at the Fulton Street house, as did many other visiting firemen. After missing a flight out of town, Al Kooper simply took a cab to the Airplane house, knowing there would be room for him there. Between Kantner and Dryden, they saw to it that the place was always fully stocked with toys: from plastic machine guns to expensive video recorders.

Money only fueled the madness. Grace Slick walked into a fancy auto dealership on Van Ness Avenue and admired an Aston Martin. The salesman took one look at this raggedy hippie and dismissed her. Within an hour she returned carrying the eighteen thousand in cash she needed to pay for the car. She parked the car in the "No Parking" zone in front of Heider's studio because she didn't want to walk through the seedy and possibly dangerous neighborhood to recording sessions. But she still didn't bother to lock the car.

She enjoyed outrageousness—singing "White Rabbit" on the Smothers Brothers TV show wearing blackface makeup or telling an audience of fifty thousand at a free concert in Chicago's Grant Park to buy acid with the five bucks they would have spent on tickets.

On the new album, Kantner stepped forward. With the inauguration of Richard Nixon as President and the growing unrest on college campuses over the Vietnam war, Kantner called for direct political action with the album's two keystone songs, "We Should Be Together" and "Volunteers," a collaboration with Marty Balin. Another Kantner number, "Wooden Ships," flexed his fascination with science fiction, a song he wrote with Stephen Stills and David Crosby, although the ongoing lawsuit with ex-manager Katz precluded his name's appearing in the songwriting credits on the Crosby, Stills and Nash version of the song.

Jerry Garcia contributed pedal steel guitar to one number and playing piano on a number of tracks was Nicky Hopkins, a classically trained British session veteran whose licks graced records by the Beatles, Rolling Stones, Who and Kinks before he joined the Jeff Beck Group. Hopkins had recently moved to San Francisco to work on the fourth album by the Steve Miller Band. Partly because of Slick's node operation and partly because of recording in San Francisco, the new album benefited from greater attention to detail. Producer Al Schmidt was brought up from Los Angeles to once again supervise the proceedings.

With vocalist Slick spending the first couple months of the year recovering from her operation and work on the album taking place the next three months, the band maintained an even slower than usual touring schedule throughout the first part of the year. One three-city tour in May found the band balancing a college job outside Chicago with the triumphant free concert in Grant Park, followed by arrests at each of the other two stops.

In New Orleans, Casady and Thompson were among six people busted in a hotel room after a search turned up a pair of suspicious cigarettes, a particularly serious legal problem in Louisiana. Two nights later in Miami, where police played on-again, off-again with the sound system at an outdoor concert running overtime before ten thousand fans, Kantner sneered sarcastically at a cop. "Wait till we burn down your society," he said, and was promptly cited for disturbing the peace and hauled off under arrest.

While the band at large took a leisurely approach to touring that spring, Kaukonen and Casady, always itching to play, began appearing around local clubs with Kaukonen playing acoustic guitar in a return to the Reverend Gary Davis/Mississippi John Hurt style he first perfected in his Greenwich Village days. These jam-a-thons began to take on a life of their own and soon became part of a routine Jefferson Airplane performance.

The duo signed a deal to record with RCA Victor for twenty-five thousand dollars and arranged for Schmidt to produce a series of performances at Berkeley's New Orleans House for the debut album. Schmidt brought the Wally Heider remote truck and, although somebody dosed the straight-laced record producer with acid the first night, he nevertheless managed to capture an album's worth of music on tape. Kaukonen and Casady wanted to call their group Hot Shit, but were eventually persuaded to settle for Hot Tuna.

Linda Gravenites heard a whimper from the other room in the Noe Street apartment and went to investigate. She found her roommate Janis Joplin turning purple on the floor. Obviously the singer was dying from a heroin overdose. Gravenites summoned their other roommate, Sunshine, far more savvy in such matters than the seamstress. Together they dumped Joplin in a bathtub filled with cold water and slapped her until she came to. Then they walked her up and down the hills around the house until well past midnight. Gravenites was shaken and furious.

Joplin had come home for a brief interval after her initial round of East Coast and Midwestern concerts, capped by the appearance on the *Ed Sullivan Show*. She and the band would leave for an extensive European tour in April and May, but first Joplin was scheduled to make her first San Francisco appearance since leaving Big Brother, March 20–23, three nights at Winterland plus one night at Fillmore West. The night before the opening show, with the reporter from *Playboy* still in tow, Joplin and her two roommates cruised North Beach, bar-hopping, shooting pool and generally carousing.

The next day, after Sunshine copped some junk for later, they went to Winterland, where a strange mood attended the event. Sunshine and Joplin ran into Suzy Perry and some other friends they had not seen in a long time. But there was something odd about not playing with Big Brother. This was no happy homecoming. Sipping B&B backstage, Joplin chatted guardedly with friends.

James Gurley strode in, tanned and trim from living in the outdoors. After the demise of Big Brother, Gurley needed to repair mind and body. Burned out from drugs and alcohol, feeling betrayed by Joplin, Gurley took his four-wheel drive vehicle into the far reaches of Death Valley, where he lived in a cave, and he had only recently returned. Joplin brimmed over with emotion, dashed into his arms and allowed herself to feel the reassurance of his familiar embrace.

The show did not go smoothly. She left the audience waiting more than an hour before her set and, when she did hit the stage, she hardly set the place on fire. The band stumbled along behind her as Joplin screamed and shouted, almost frantically, trying out her newly adopted gospel wings and failing to fly. People began trailing out well before her hour-long set ended and those that remained got up and walked out as soon as she left the stage. Nobody called for an encore.

Stunned by the rebuke, Joplin fled to her dressing room. She proclaimed loudly that it wasn't her fault. She sang great, but the audience hated her for leaving Big Brother. John Cooke dissented. "Bad set," he said.

When Joplin and Sunshine went downstairs to retrieve the psychedelic Porsche from the garage, the car was gone, stolen. The attendant had given it to someone who said he was picking it up for her. The pair got a lift back to the Noe Street apartment, where they did up the dope Sunshine scored earlier, and went out to get some more.

On Sunday night, after the Fillmore West show ended the run, Joplin took Peggy Caserta to North Beach and picked up an early edition of the Monday *Chronicle*. Ralph J. Gleason, once her biggest champion, delivered a damning review, outspoken to the point of being blunt. "Her new band is a drag," Gleason wrote simply, suggesting she return to Big Brother and the Holding Company—"if they'll have her," he said. He didn't doubt the Joplin juggernaut was still in orbit, he only questioned the musical value of her new enterprise. "It may go over in Indiana," he mused, "after all the Iron Butterfly and Canned Heat are big there too."

Joplin fumed. She lashed out at Gleason, covering her anguish in anger. She asked Caserta to get some heroin. The two waited on a street corner in the Fillmore district after midnight to make the score and retired to Joplin's apartment to shoot up. "That motherfucker," she raged. "You wait. I'll nail that son of a bitch. I'll make him eat his fucking column. Man, I wouldn't have to sit in the fucking Fillmore all night waiting for the goddamn connection if it wasn't for Gleason."

The next week Joplin and her band flew to Frankfurt to begin the long European tour. Basking in the sunlight of adulation, freed from audience expectations colored by her departure from Big Brother, Joplin detonated blistering performances. The band finally meshed behind her. In Frankfurt, she invited the audience to join the festivities until the stage overflowed with dancing bodies. Someone stepped on Sam Andrew's guitar cord and he played away unplugged. Similar triumphs followed in Amsterdam, Copenhagen, Stockholm and Paris before hitting London the third week of April.

In London, the Royal Albert Hall performance was nothing short of a raucous lovefest, a cathartic cacophony, Joplin bursting through the customary English reserve and finally pulling together all the missing elements for incandescent, ecstatic revelry. Photographer Bob Seideman, who took the early famous nudes of Joplin, cheered and stomped alongside Eric Clapton in a box. Poster artist Stanley Mouse roared with delight. Joplin drove the capacity crowd wild, whipping through "Maybe," "The Combination of the Two," "Summertime," "Work Me Lord" and "Ball and Chain."

She beamed at the response, frequently joyfully kissing guitarist Andrew on the cheek. "I don't want to offend propriety or anything," she told the crowd, "but if you want to dance, this next one's for shakin' it up and that's what it's all about, right?"

She cracked a bottle of champagne and sipped from a glass. Saxophonist Snooky Flowers did a graphic bump and grind. "You don't need to worry about no brother or best friend taking your girl if you know how to do it," he shouted gleefully. Joplin joined in. Backstage, she was breathless, gushing.

"It was dynamite, man," she said. "I haven't been this excited in two years. Don't you know how happy we must be? We really broke through a wall that I didn't think was possible. Like ever since we've been here, the audiences we've had are the best. But everybody says 'Don't expect that of the British audience. Don't expect them to do nothing, man.' When they first got up and started dancing, it was like a big hot rush. And we just went 'Oh, yeah.'"

She adjourned to her hotel suite for a post-concert celebration that turned into a surrealistic bacchanal. Joining Clapton, Seideman, Mouse and Linda Gravenites were Andrew and Suzy Creamcheeze, a famous London groupie who had been showing Andrew the sights, introducing him to the joys of roast beef and Yorkshire pudding, and dancing onstage earlier at the Albert Hall. Also, unaccountably, there were a few teenage boys who looked like they wandered in from the streets. Someone produced some heroin and Joplin shot up, immediately announcing, "This is great—I really got off."

Sam Andrew got off, too. Almost all the way off. He overdosed and turned blue in front of everyone. Seideman cleared the suite, ushering Clapton and the riffraff out. Joplin summoned Gravenites. "Linda, come here," she shouted. "You know what an O.D. looks like."

Joplin, Gravenites and Suzy Creamcheeze struggled Andrew into the bathtub. When Seideman returned, Andrew was naked in a tub full of cold water. Suzy Creamcheeze, having dispensed with her panties, was sitting astride him, administering her own unique brand of therapy. Gravenites kept shouting "Breathe, breathe." Andrew finally told her stubbornly, "I'm going to hold my breath until you go away." Mouse ordered a room service dessert.

While Seideman and Mouse ate peach melbas, the life and death struggle took place at the other end of the suite and Joplin wandered around complaining about how everybody was shooting up all her dope. Mouse and Seideman left around dawn to walk back to their rented flat.

A couple of nights later, Joplin, Gravenites and Albert Grossman accepted an invitation for dinner from George Harrison. Andrew stayed at the hotel and slept. After sitting next to Harrison on his living room couch and listening to the so-called quiet Beatle offer a lengthy discourse on mysticism and meditation, Joplin was bored. "Hey, man," she said, "I've been wanting to make it with you for years."

But the events of the earlier evening had horrified Gravenites and when Harrison learned that she had embroidered the purse Joplin carried and asked her to make him a jacket, she decided to stay in London and not return to San Francisco with her roommate.

Chet Helms made his entrance whooshing down the giant slide on a burlap bag. He chose the Fun House for a press conference announcing his return to regular concert promotion not only because of the inherent levity of the location, but because his new hall was down the street on the other end of Playland-at-the-Beach.

On the Pacific Ocean edge of San Francisco, this decrepit amusement park was a relic of the past, good times gone by, more than the thriving, bustling center of activity it once was. The windswept midway surrounded by dingy hot dog stands and seedy arcades faced Ocean Beach with only the Great Highway standing between the park and the crashing surf. Laughing Sal, a mechanized ventriloquist's dummy in a glass case, presided over the entrance to the Fun House, her crackling laughter more eerie than inviting.

Orson Welles staged the climactic scene to his film *The Lady From Shanghai* in the Fun House hall of mirrors, which still sent a blast of air up the skirts of any female who completed the journey through the reflecting labyrinth. Helms conducted his interviews at the foot of the long wooden slide. He made a deal to occupy an abandoned slot car raceway at the northernmost tip of the amusement park. In addition to a main room, the building contained a sideroom with a fireplace, balconies, two patios and a garden. He struck a typical missionary note extolling the philosophy that would guide his latest incarnation.

"When the San Francisco sound became popular," he told the press, "the band became the focal point. But it's more than that. It's party, the whole picture. The element of party has continually diminished as rock became big business. I'll bring it back."

Indeed, the ballrooms were no longer dances, but sitdown concerts where the audience pulled up a piece of the floor or, when the performance grew especially exciting, stood in a jam-packed mob. Not only was there no longer room for dancing at the dance-concerts, but apparently the audience didn't even have the inclination. Despite the popularity of unsigned bands like Santana and It's A Beautiful Day, mostly the crowds came to see bands whose records were played on KSAN, still the dominant force on the airwaves despite the presence of two or three more stations now playing underground rock.

Helms didn't slink away into the night after the city pulled his permits the previous November following greatly exaggerated charges of sound complaints from neighbors of the Avalon. He presented a pair of concerts early in the year at Winterland. Mysterious billboards popped up around town showing a space ship descending through an atmosphere, reading "The Family Dog Is Coming Down to Earth."

Meanwhile, another group of Texas expatriates reopened the Avalon in January with the Grateful Dead, although the shows sputtered to a close within a few months. But the new Avalon promoters showed no small sense of irony in naming their enterprise Soundproof Productions.

While a new rock band called the Devil's Kitchen clattered away from a balcony in the Fun House, Helms happily explained he had already received a permit to open his new dancehall, which he would call Family Dog on the Great Highway, ready to rock, in June.

"I want that nigger to come outside," said the enraged voice of the estranged husband. Santana conga player Marcus Malone was spending the afternoon with his girlfriend at her house when her husband showed up banging on the door. Malone and the rest of the band were scheduled to go to Los Angeles the following day and begin recording the band's first album for Columbia Records. There had been run-ins with Edward Amido before—he had crashed his car into his wife's car on the street outside the previous October, the day after she reported him to the police for beating her—but no face-to-face confrontations.

Malone grew up in the Hunter's Point ghetto and had a regulation list of petty offenses for a police record. At twenty-three, he was slightly older than the other band members, who whispered rumors among themselves that Malone had made money as a pimp before joining the band. He splurged his share of the group's advance on a new Cadillac El Dorado, although he still lived with his mother on Potrero Hill.

His girlfriend's husband kicked the door down and snatched the phone away from his wife, who was calling the police. He outweighed Malone by fifty pounds and grabbed the smaller conga player around the neck. They scuffled out of the living room and through the kitchen, where Malone grabbed a knife that lay on the counter. He plunged it into Amido's side, breaking off the blade. The two tumbled out the back door and down the stairs. The fight continued on the sidewalk outside, but Malone was able to wrest himself loose. Amido was lying on the sidewalk bleeding when police pulled up. He leaned up on his elbow and pointed at Malone, who was getting into his car across the street. "He did it," Amido told the cops. "He stabbed me."

Police arrested Malone and charged him with assault with intent to kill. Three weeks later, after Amido died in S.F. General Hospital following three successive operations, the charge was changed to first degree murder.

Under the supervision of producer David Rubinson, Santana spent ten days during January in Los Angeles recording an album nobody liked. After producer Rubinson first tried recording Santana live during the band's first headline engagement in December 1968 at the Fillmore West, the sessions moved to Los Angeles, where the same union rules that so hampered Rubinson recording Moby Grape still applied. The entire album sounded wrong. Changes loomed imminently.

Rubinson had problems with an understandably distraught Malone missing sessions or showing up late. The criminal case put the band in limbo. With Marcus Malone facing a lengthy trial and probable jail time, Michael Carabello returned on congas.

Drummer Bob (Doc) Livingston wasn't the rock solid bedrock the band needed for a rhythmic foundation and his personal problems were beginning to interfere. He fell off his drum set, evidently drunk, during the New Year's Eve concert at Winterland. Gregg Rolie informed Livingston at Pacific Recorders before a scheduled session after the band returned from Los Angeles that he was fired.

Watching Livingston walk out of the studio as he walked in was Michael Shrieve, a young, fresh-faced drummer from the peninsula who made a habit of haunting the studio in search of free time for his own group. He had seen Santana perform a couple of times and met Stan Marcum when Shrieve took over the drums for a number with Al Kooper and Mike Bloomfield the same *Super Session* weekend four months earlier where guitarist Santana made his recording debut at the Fillmore West. Now seeing Shrieve again in the lobby of the recording studio, Marcum invited him to step inside and play with the band.

Shrieve jammed with the group until dawn. They all had a long talk and drove Shrieve down to his parents' home, where he still lived. He woke his folks, told them good-bye and moved up to San Francisco to join the band.

Carabello found Chepito Areas. The five-foot-tall Nicaraguan approached Carabello one afternoon while the conga player was jamming on the street out at Playland-at-the-Beach. With his hair slicked back, a gleaming pinkie ring and the air of a ghetto hustler, Areas was clearly no hippie. But once Carabello heard him play, all such cultural considerations evaporated. Areas was playing around Mission district bars in a band called the Aliens, but he quickly accepted an invitation to fall by a Santana rehearsal.

He always claimed a childhood head injury stunted his growth. Areas had already won considerable acclaim for his percussion playing in his native Nicaragua by the time he was a teenager, before he moved to New York three years earlier to find a place for himself in the Latin music scene and drifted out to the West Coast. His timbales proved to be the missing puzzle piece in the Santana sound, snapping into place just in time to begin the second attempt at recording the band's debut album. His unofficial initiation took place later in May, when the band appeared with the Jimi Hendrix Experience at the Santa Clara County Fairgrounds, and somebody in the group slipped an unsuspecting Areas a dose of acid.

He lost his mind. Crying, shaking, a deeply distraught Areas huddled in the backseat of the van on the ride home, while a solicitous Carlos Santana tended to him. Santana took the rabbit-punched acid victim home and took care of him until the LSD loosed its grip.

Bill Graham doted on the group. His booking agency represented the act. He built the band into a headline attraction at the Fillmore West long before Santana released an album. When he suggested the band work up the Willie Bobo song "Evil Ways," which was on the same album as "Fried Neck Bones," another Bobo number already in the Santana songbook, the band added the second Bobo tune largely to please this important patron.

Shrieve studied music at the College of San Mateo and Santana demonstrated a thirst for musical knowledge, although he still played mainly in one key. Rolie, too, had attended a peninsula junior college, taking business classes, before dropping out to pursue his music. Out of this cauldron of street and suburbs, black, brown and white, the musicians forged their largely instrumental music that was as serious as life.

To produce the second run at recording an album, they picked a friend of the group, Brent Dangerfield, who handled the house sound at the Straight Theater. The band liked the way he mixed live shows. Dangerfield had been a disk jockey in Salt Lake City who happened by the Straight during a visit to San Francisco on his way to Hawaii for a job. He got psychedelicized and never left, taking charge of the sound equipment at the hippie-operated Haight Street ballroom. But he had never produced any kind of recording before, which, in some twisted LSD logic prevalent at the time, actually qualified him for the job.

SUMMER 1969

Ron Polte dreamed up the Wild West Festival in a conversation with former Kingston Trio manager Frank Werber. Since Quicksilver was barely active, struggling in the absence of Gary Duncan to put together even the formalities of an album, manager Polte had time to see how far he could run with this crazy idea.

Earlier in the year, a breakfast meeting at the Airplane Mansion assembled all the power players in the San Francisco music scene. Along with managers like Polte, Rock Scully of the Dead, Bill Thompson of the Airplane, the cabal convened to consider Polte's lunacy included underground radio kingpin Tom Donahue, columnist Ralph Gleason of the *Chronicle, Rolling Stone* publisher Jann Wenner, impresario Bill Graham and Frank Werber.

Also invited was Barry Olivier, a roly-poly bearded folknik who ran the annual UC-Berkeley Folk Festival every year and gave guitar lessons in his spare time. He taught young John Fogerty to play "Midnight Special" long before Creedence Clearwater. Polte wanted Olivier to solve a ticklish political problem. If he could convince the group to put Olivier in charge, then he would have made a highly desirable end run around Graham, who would undoubtedly see himself as the logical candidate to head such a massive undertaking.

Polte laid his vision out. He described an event that would celebrate not just rock music, but the broadest possible spectrum of San Francisco artistic life, encompassing all the performing arts and every kind of music, a cornucopia of creativity splayed across the four-mile length of Golden Gate Park for the duration of a weekend, possibly an entire week.

At that moment, San Francisco rested in the middle of the pop culture universe. The music emanating from the City over the previous three years had captured the imagination of the world. The resonance of the associated phenomenology carried to every tiny hamlet in the country and virtually every country on the globe. These cultural barons meeting at the Airplane house had no reason to assume that their grandest plans could not be carried out. What had they dreamed yet in their young lives that had not come to pass?

The scene buzzed with activity. Graham resumed his custom of operating the Fillmore six nights a week during the summer months. On any given night, dozens of bands worked ballrooms and small clubs around town. The eyes of the record industry were focused on San Francisco. More than five hundred bands and more than two thousand single musicians were listed with the Musician's Switchboard, who added new musicians at the rate of ten a day.

Furthermore, rock festivals were an idea very much in the air. The Newport Pop Festival the previous summer attracted 100,000 Southern California rock fans and a similar size crowd attended the Miami Pop Festival in the middle of the Gulfstream Park racetrack in December. Other festivals were planned for the upcoming summer in Denver, Atlanta, Atlantic City and elsewhere. A couple of enterprising promoters were already planning such an event in August for Woodstock, New York.

Polte put forward Olivier as the man to head the operation, allowing that men as busy and important as themselves could not properly devote the time and energy necessary to see this Herculean task to fruition without ignoring their chief duties in life. An emboldened Olivier, looking around at the opulence of the surroundings and guessing at the decadence of his new associates, asked a fairly princely wage of five hundred dollars a week. "If you've got a great diamond," agreed Graham, "you don't skimp on the cutter."

Tom Donahue made it clear he wanted nothing to do with Werber. Some past dispute still rankled him, and Werber, over Polte's objections, was summarily excused. They decided to form a nonprofit corporation and call themselves the San Francisco Music Council. The Airplane loaned the endeavor four thousand dollars and Wenner kicked in an additional two thousand to start things rolling. No warning flag went up for Olivier when he talked to Graham's banker who, at first, made generous offers of assistance, but suddenly turned cold and remote when Olivier called back. Olivier was having too much fun.

His loud laughter echoed throughout the two-story Victorian that served as the festival's headquarters on Pine Street, booming out of his front office through the stairwell, clearly audible even on the back patio where staff members took frequent breaks to smoke joints. Olivier appointed a graduate student he knew from the Berkeley Folk Festival to serve as treasurer and slowly built a staff of more than twenty paid personnel, along with scores of volunteers worth every bit what they were paid. By May, the office was a swirl of activity, a nuthouse never too busy to consider the latest lunatic idea, a bustling beehive where every corner was crowded with another desk and phone.

Committees were formed to coordinate filmmakers, light shows, dance, classical music, photography, graphics, poetry. Plans called for eight main stages to be distributed around the park, with other smaller stages littered throughout. Three nights of paid concerts at Kezar Stadium would provide the $150,000 budget to run the craziness in the park during the days.

Olivier talked about presenting classical music ensembles like Amici della Musicia and Ali Akbar Khan doing Indian music, Chinese gong and opera. He wanted drama troupes doing Dylan Thomas and Shakespeare, Philippine dancers, strolling minstrels, jugglers, poets. The light show artists were sketching out plans for a giant jam session of their own.

One artist wanted to sculpt an eighty-foot bar of Ivory soap to float in the bay. Giant geodesic domes were envisioned. No idea was too preposterous for contemplation: from the twelve-hundred-member marching band someone wanted to assemble to the very reasonable-looking and sincere young artist who was working on plans to wire downtown office buildings to the keyboards of a Moog synthesizer perched on Twin Peaks and, quite literally, play the downtown skyline.

Even more surprising, the festival actually received some tepid encouragement and official blessing from City Hall, Mayor Alioto handing down the word to the Parks and Recreation Department that he wanted the city to cooperate. Corporate bastions like Wells Fargo Bank, Pacific Gas and Electric, United Bank of California and Greyhound Bus all made noise about getting involved. Outdoor advertising specialists Foster and Kleiser donated more than a dozen billboards to be decorated by the psychedelic poster artists.

Virtually every band in San Francisco wanted to get involved. Creedence Clearwater, probably the single hottest band in the country at the moment, had already booked a tour, but found a hole in the schedule and planned to fly across the country and play a special kickoff concert two days before the events in the park were to start. The Kezar lineup for the three paid concerts included the Dead, the Airplane, Quicksilver, Country Joe and the Fish, Santana, Steve Miller, Youngbloods, Sly and the Family Stone and the Edwin Hawkins Singers, an Oakland gospel group currently enjoying the fluke Top Forty success of "Oh Happy Day" after a KSAN deejay picked up on the track from an album released by their church. Many of the same groups would also perform for free during the daytime in the park, where performances were planned by everybody from San Francisco's first rock and roll star Bobby Freeman ("Do You Wanna Dance") to up-and-comers called Womb, who would be joined by a ninety-member choir.

Graham screamed murder to Olivier about a poster advertising one of the two benefit concerts intended to fund the operation until the Kezar concerts. Poster artists Wes Wilson and Alton Kelley created a nearly unreadable, albeit striking image, and then washed the print in garish neon colors that rendered the final result a bright, cheery mess. Graham was furious at Olivier for allowing this to happen. Airplane manager Bill Thompson, also present at the meeting in Olivier's office at Wild West headquarters, didn't agree. He told Graham that Olivier had done nothing wrong. Olivier defended the work of the poster artists by explaining they were working for an artists' festival, not a commercial concern. Graham exploded, threw a chair across the room and stormed out.

Graham was feeling the pressure. The Howard Johnson chain had announced plans in April to purchase the building where Graham ran the Fillmore West, tear it down and build a giant hotel. The chain gave Graham until the end of the year to continue his ballroom. He was going crazy. He sought out new locations and fought Howard Johnson's in the press. The *Chronicle* ran an editorial supporting Graham. He alternately threatened and cajoled. Above the stairway at the Fillmore West he draped a large banner reading "Howard Johnson Is Finger-Lickin' Good" with a picture of Graham extending his middle finger.

The offending poster notwithstanding, two simultaneous sold-out benefits raised twenty-two thousand dollars July 7 at the Fillmore West with the Jefferson Airplane, the Family Dog on the Great Highway, Joan Baez, making a rare appearance on the rock scene, and It's A Beautiful Day. A warm ovation greeted Baez, who opened with "I Shall Be Released." At the Fillmore West, a gift of red carnations and incense greeted each concertgoer and the Airplane played well past three in the morning. The festival was six weeks away.

Mickey Hart assembled the band and advisors that May in the barn of his Novato ranch. He delivered an impassioned speech about the sorry state of the Grateful Dead's finances, his narrow-focus intensity burning toward a point. The band had ignored economic realities for so long, debts had piled up and record-keeping was so poor, nobody knew who owed what to whom. We have a problem, Hart told his colleagues, and we need someone to help. "Enter Lenny Hart, my father," he announced.

Up the ramp into the barn strode this taut figure, horn-rim glasses, thick but short hair. Like an evangelical preacher, Lenny Hart regaled his select audience with a fiery sermon, pure Bible Belt theatrics. Since his son had joined the band and left the drum store, the elder Hart had remarried and become a born again Christian after a revelation in the Miami airport waiting for a plane. He lost interest in the store and let the business slide. At first, he regarded his son's new associates as nothing more than a bunch of circus freaks who played unlistenable music. But as the Dead became more and more successful, he started turning up every so often.

Manager Rock Scully and Danny Rifkin dumped slips of paper into a cardboard box for bookkeeping. At one point, Jon McIntire, a longtime member of the Dead's circle who ran the concessions at the Carousel, tried to make sense of this collection of gibberish stored at the rehearsal hall. Handsome and blond with chiseled features, McIntire was a cultured college-educated actor with no experience in business. The lack of proper books implied no question of impropriety. Scully and Rifkin were men on a mission, comrades in arms, but not any more concerned about such trivial details than the musicians themselves.

Still, after four years of steady work, the band had accumulated a debt of more than sixty thousand dollars. Spending was out of control. If Garcia wanted a new toy, he got it. Mickey Hart was building his own recording studio in the very Novato barn where this meeting had been called. Even if the band did not have the money, Scully and Rifkin could not rein in the spending. Albums had not proved profitable. In fact, the Dead was enormously in arrears on the contract with Warner Brothers, having failed to sell anywhere near enough records to offset the rather large expenses incurred in making them. Parting ways with Bill Graham's Millard Agency was bound to spell at least a temporary cash crunch, as a new booking agency would take time to start filling the band's schedule. Instead of getting ahead, the band seemed to be digging a deeper hole daily.

But reality has a way of creeping in on even the stonedest of people, and the Dead certainly qualified among those. Most band members and their associates stayed high on something virtually all the time—acid, coke, nitrous, at the very least exceptionally potent marijuana. Did they not keep the famed acid king on the team and would he not privately brew them up his most special elixirs, even though he was about to stand trial two years after the feds crashed his secret lab?

Lenny Hart whipped up support for himself, summoning no less than the spirit of God to the enterprise as he stalked the length of the barn. He hammered away at his experience as a banker, running a music store, his background as a drummer. He wanted the band to set goals. Scully sulked in the shadows. He readily admitted he could use help on the finances, but he felt betrayed by the band's bringing in an outsider, someone nobody really knew.

Only Pigpen maintained any ongoing relationship with his family. He and Veronica made a practice of going regularly to his parents' home in Palo Alto for dinner, where his younger brother and sister still lived. Garcia had watched his father drown during a family vacation when he was five years old and barely spoke to his mother, who had left the rearing of him and his brother largely to their grandmother. He hadn't even seen his own daughter since leaving his wife. The band replaced family for most of the members.

But this strange man with the fire-and-brimstone speech about the band's financial destiny was true family, Mickey Hart's biological father, and that confused the issue even more for the band members. Drummer Hart had become such a trusted piston in the group's engine that his father seemed almost already a part of the tribe, certainly not a full-fledged outsider. Both McIntire and Owsley were suspicious of the preaching, but Rifkin was nonplussed. He already had plans of his own to leave the group for Mexico and Guatemala in a couple of months and he didn't see anything wrong with Lenny Hart. When Garcia asked Rifkin what he thought, Rifkin told Garcia they might as well give him a try. And so they did. Lenny Hart was offered the position of business manager with the understanding that Scully would retain authority over negotiating a new record contract.

Concerns over finances did not interfere with the essential spirit of the group, who maintained a psychedelic hit squad inside the traveling party consisting of Hart, Owsley and trusted equipment manager, Ramrod. The assassins hit the union coffeepot on the set of "Playboy After Dark" when the band appeared that July as guests on Hugh Hefner's short-lived adventure in broadcasting, and dosed virtually the entire crew. Stagehands wandered around staring into lights. An electrician shook his head. "Ohmigawd I feel strange," he repeated over and over. Amid all the plastic party people and the inflatable dollies, the wooden Indian, clench-jawed magazine publisher held court with flaxen-faced comedian Sid Caesar, looking as dead as his career, while the grubby Grateful Dead turned the pose into a party more real than anyone dared imagine.

Janis Joplin called Sam Andrew into her room at the Landmark Hotel in Los Angeles, where she and her band were staying in June while they recorded her first post-Big Brother album at Columbia's studios in Hollywood. Andrew was feeling exhausted, helpless and disillusioned. Outside of the familial context of Big Brother, he felt alone, lost. He was also badly strung out on junk. With the exception of those few bright moments in Europe, the band had not been going especially well. Nothing had really jelled and morale had dissipated. Personnel constantly shifted. The band even changed drummers right in the middle of the ongoing album sessions. At a band meeting, when he asked Grossman if the band could share a couple small percentage points on the album, to feel like they had a stake in the proceedings, the other members looked at him with shock. Grossman simply refused and that was the end of that.

Joplin herself seemed loosed from her moorings. She was surrounding herself with the material trappings of success, growing ever more remote from her musicians, and shooting a lot of smack. Her girlfriend Peggy Caserta came down to spend some time with her, ditching her own live-in lover in San Francisco on the pretext of making a buying trip for the boutique. After spending much of one evening drinking at Barney's Beanery, the two dropped by the Sunset Strip performance by The Committee, the old San Francisco comedy improv troupe, and they ran into Joplin's ex-lover, Milan Melvin.

After the show, the three returned to Joplin's hotel room, ostensibly for a three-way sex scene. But Joplin produced a supply of heroin and proceeded to cook up a generous dose. Although Melvin protested that the amount was too large, Joplin went ahead and fixed him anyway. He immediately sank to his knees and passed out cold on the floor. With Melvin unconscious on the floor, Joplin prepared another shot for Caserta, only to have her, too, collapse on the floor next to Melvin.

"Come on, you guys," the prone Caserta heard Joplin say before passing out, "don't do this to me. Not both of you. Come on, wake up. For Chrissake. We were going to play."

It was a few nights later that Andrew was summoned to her room at the Landmark. Joplin cooked up some heroin in a spoon. She and Andrew each shot up. As the gauzy curtain descended, Joplin told Andrew he was fired. She had already hired his substitute. He was numb and didn't react. "Aren't you even going to ask why?" she said.

Andrew allowed he didn't think that made any difference. "Yeah, I guess you're right," Joplin said.

A few days later, she told Andrew his replacement couldn't join the band for several weeks and asked him if he would mind staying until then. At that point, Andrew had nothing else to do and nowhere else to go. He agreed amiably.

James Gurley loved the outdoors. Not only did he live for several weeks in a Death Valley cave after leaving Big Brother, but he also went camping in the Trinity Alps with roadie Mark Braunstein, who himself left the Joplin employ following her European tour. Gurley had told Braunstein he wanted to get away and clean up, so it surprised Braunstein when Gurley stopped and scored more heroin before he even got back to the Bay Area. Sometimes when Gurley took off on his occasional hiking trips, he didn't even bother to wait until his return, but simply brought the drugs with him.

Gurley had been planning to take a break before Joplin announced she was leaving the band. He had burrowed himself into a hole with his excesses and he needed to get hold of himself. Nancy Gurley and their son, three-year-old Hongo Ishi, had moved back in with Gurley and his roommate Richard Hundgeon. Their tumultuous relationship continued, but was currently in a euphoric upswing when they decided to make an impromptu run for the woods on the Fourth of July weekend. She was pregnant with their second child and happily left Hundgeon a note asking him to feed their pet canary called Janis.

"We have gone on a family outing until Sunday night probably," she wrote. "Have a good time and keep gettin' it on. We love you (James and Nancy got it on last night with a little seduction on the part of the latter)."

Gurley, deep in drug addiction, wanted to spend some time in the country with his wife and child to clean up. But, in classic junkie fashion, he brought along a hundred dollar bag of potent heroin. They spent a lazy Sunday rafting down the Russian River, drinking wine and getting drunk under the summer sun. By the time they pitched camp outside Cloverdale, they were both bombed and Gurley dug into his bag of junk. He was so drunk he missed his vein and jabbed the needle instead into his muscle. But he found his wife's vein.

The heroin was strong, stronger than he expected. Nancy Gurley, who had not been using regularly recently, did not have her tolerance built up. After he fixed her, she turned to read Hongo Ishi a children's story. She pitched forward, face-first, right in front of her little boy. Gurley threw her in the car, grabbed their son and raced off to find a hospital. When he looked at his wife, her face had turned black.

Nancy Gurley was pronounced dead at the Cloverdale Medical Center and her husband was admitted to the hospital, too, also suffering from an overdose. Missing the vein saved his life, as the drug spread more slowly injected intramuscularly. Sheriff's deputies interrogated him and put Hongo Ishi in the care of a foster family. The next morning, they arrested Gurley on murder charges. Richard Hundgeon hitchhiked to Garberville to identify the body and took along some of her jewelry.

In New York, when Joplin and Andrew heard the grim news, they promptly went out and scored some smack.

Opening night of the Family Dog on the Great Highway brought out an array of old-timers scarcely glimpsed on the scene anymore. Situated on the chilly, remote San Francisco oceanside, the edge of the Western world, the new Chet Helms operation drew a first-night crowd that jammed the sole beachfront road with cars and packed the relatively small hall to the bursting point and beyond before the opening act took the stage.

Wandering around the room that night were Luria Castell and Jack Towle, one-half of the original Family Dog that produced the Longshoremen's Hall dances a very long ago and far away four years earlier. The Jefferson Airplane, who played the band's first concert appearance at that show, now qualified as one of the most popular attractions in the country, well beyond playing little rooms that held fewer than a thousand people like the band did that night at the new Dog house. Another veteran of that first Longshoremen's Hall dance was also making a special appearance as supporting act, the Charlatans.

The Charlatans' founder and chief architect was no longer with the group, which hadn't appeared in the more than a year since Hunter left. Drummer Dan Hicks was also gone. He never looked back, now heading a prosperous, growing concern called Dan Hicks and his Hot Licks. But the Charlatans—or rather a simulated edition of the original band built around Richie Olsen and Mike Wilhelm—had finally released an album. The group that started it all and watched the scene burst alive around them as they stumbled backward was already a footnote, the newly minted album merely a curio, an irrelevant gesture, a quick ten thousand dollar deal.

Olsen and Wilhelm retained the services of drummer Terry Wilson, who served to spell Dan Hicks from the drum kit after Mike Ferguson was fired. Pianist Darrell De Vore, whom Hunter introduced to the other musicians, was added. The album was a mishmash of old Charlatans standbys like "Alabama Bound," "Wabash Cannonball" and "Folsom Prison Blues" along with new originals by De Vore and others. The record was an unenthusiastic coda to a misspent career, a band life that began in the summer sunshine and high hopes of the Sierra Nevadas and straggled to an end the previous year in the drizzle of Vancouver and Seattle.

Dressed in fringe and buckskin, Lynne Hughes, the Miss Kitty of the Red Dog, joined the band for a few numbers, as she had at Longshoremen's. The next week, drummer Wilson began serving a jail sentence on a pot bust and the Charlatans never performed again.

The new Helms temple of music had been anointed. He retained the credibility of poverty and, for at least one evening, he recaptured the glory of the Avalon. Ralph Gleason remembered the ramshackle building as the Edgewater, a dance hall going back to the forties. Cleanliness and Godliness Skiffle Band were supposed to play in the patio, but the electricity didn't get hooked up. Helms decorated the sideroom like a lounge, a homey respite from the hothouse atmosphere of the crowded main room, complete with sofas, paintings on the wall, rugs on the floor and fire in the fireplace. When the crowd cleared out that night, he discovered the room empty, looted of every stick of furniture, down to the bare floors.

The Wild West Festival's open meeting with the community on Monday, July 28, opened with a brief performance by a rockabilly band from Michigan, recently relocated and playing dates at a Samoan bar in the Mission district, Commander Cody and his Lost Planet Airmen. The Wild West staff arrayed themselves on the red carpeted steps leading to the altar of Glide Memorial Church.

Plans staggered toward the August 22–24 dates. Parks and Rec was showing predictable resistance, making final details impossible to fix. So many disparate ideas were under various stages of consideration, it was difficult to tell what might actually take place and what wouldn't. "If twenty percent of these plans come off, it'll still be the biggest thing ever," said one festival staffer. Disarray and disorganization ruled, but nobody doubted that out of the chaos a colossus of an event would emerge. This boundless optimism prevailed as Olivier stood up at Glide and good-naturedly started talking about the festival's plans.

Olivier introduced his treasurer, a woefully unprepared graduate student who rattled off a brief report. Questions from the floor caught him by surprise. Nobody expected any antagonism, but people were asking tough questions—or at least questions the hapless treasurer didn't know how to answer. Caught off-guard, he grew defensive. "Questions about what to do with the proceeds are irrelevant at this point," he snapped.

Leading the interrogation was an articulate, forceful black activist named Arnold Townsend, a community organizer in the Western Addition neighborhood and political firebrand involved in the recent S.F. State strike. Townsend turned up the heat under the squirming grad student. "How do you expect kids in the ghetto to relate to spending three hundred thousand dollars for three days of grooving in the park?" he demanded.

Striding in from the back of the hall came Bill Graham. The concert producer had been detained by another angry confrontation, this one with representatives of the newly formed Light Artists Guild. This union of light show groups, something that grew out of a deranged Wild West light show committee meeting, was making demands Graham deemed unacceptable and he was already pissed off when he took the microphone from the shaken festival treasurer and addressed Townsend.

"What did you say, motherfucker?" Graham said.

Townsend did not back down from Graham's intimidation tactics, but rather gave as good as he got. In a flash, any discussion that had been taking place degenerated into an obscenity-laced screaming match between Graham and Townsend, their angry denunciations bouncing off the walls and filling the air. It was more than the Hare Krishna dancers could stand. Waiting in the church lobby to perform at the close of the meeting, they decided not to wait. With Graham and Townsend still shouting at each other, a couple dozen costumed dancers in shaved heads pranced down the aisles, clinging their finger cymbals, beating their drums and chanting hare krishna, effectively ending the meeting.

The following day, a spokesman for the Haight Commune identified solely as John the Motherfucker made more specific charges at a meeting with Wild West organizers. He called for a shutdown of the Wild West and, in the same breath, demanded the S.F. Music Council expand the board to include more community representatives. He wanted a legal defense fund established to assist people busted during the festival. He wanted sleeping quarters and medical aid provided for people coming from out-of-town. And he wanted the flat-broke festival to slash one dollar off the three dollar ticket prices for the night-time concerts at Kezar.

"Stick 'em up Wild West" read a Commune leaflet. "If you don't own a radio station," read a broadside from the S.F. Mime Troupe, "a newspaper or a concert hall, then don't do nothing for free because you can't make nothing from it."

Meanwhile, the Light Artists Guild announced picket lines would be put up around the Grateful Dead show Friday at Family Dog on the Great Highway and at the Fillmore West the following Tuesday. On Friday at the Dog, a large contingent of fans milled around outside, waiting to see what would happen before paying to go to a show that might not take place, as picketers marched before both the front doors and the stage entrance. Bob Weir, Phil Lesh and Bill Kreutzman were the first members of the Dead to show up and they crossed the picket line, peering out the window every so often to check the scene outside.

Jerry Garcia and Mickey Hart arrived together. Without Garcia, there would be no show. Tension crackled around the picket line as Garcia approached Jerry Abrams, one of the ringleaders of the strike. Garcia suggested they let him pass, have the band play the show and, afterward, everybody would sit down and talk. "Well, Jerry, we kind of voted not to do that," said Abrams.

At this moment, Abrams dropped into a trance, humming his Transcendental Meditation mantra, his eyeballs fluttering underneath their lids. Garcia was torn. On one hand, he thought the light artists were being unrealistic. On the other hand, he didn't want to cross the picket line. His grandmother, who had raised him, had been a founding member of the Laundry Workers' Union of San Francisco. Garcia threw up his hands and walked away.

Garcia, Chet Helms and Dead manager Rock Scully took a couple of Guild representatives and hippie philosopher Stephen Gaskin to serve as a kind of mediator and piled into the back of the Dead's equipment truck to light up joints and start negotiations. Abrams remained on the line. Before long, the cruel ocean wind whipping off the beach through the truck chilled the talks, so they drove off to continue elsewhere. As the evening progressed, it became apparent that everyone was in similar circumstances—broke, badly in debt, unable to do anything else. Well after midnight, far too late to play that night, they agreed to call a full-scale community meeting the following day at the Family Dog. A second meet was set for Tuesday.

Helms opened the Tuesday meeting by throwing the I Ching and finding that the hexagrams spelled out the need for unity. Graham, seated with his head hunched over, looked bored. Garcia, David LaFlamme of It's A Beautiful Day and many other scenesters crowded the room. Helms pleaded poverty and allowed that he thought the time had come to create some new ways of "distributing the few potatoes available." Graham clearly didn't agree.

First off, he dismissed Helms. "Chet runs this place on a dream," Graham said, "a nice one, but he's having financial problems because, although he understands the problems of the business, he has refused to meet them."

But Graham was just warming up. "You do not tell me what to do," he said. "If you don't like the way I conduct my business, why the fuck don't you get off your asses and do it? Where the fuck does the artist come to say 'You the businessman must support us' when I personally think the light shows are not producing an income for me? The only way you can do this is kill me and step over me."

With a reporter from *Time* magazine accompanying him in preparation of a profile, the acrimonious Graham pounded away at his message, the reality of business. "I have a house in Pacific Heights and an eight thousand dollar Mercedes Benz and it's mine," he said. "I earned it."

He confronted Jerry Abrams and heatedly berated him over the ethics of the Light Artists Guild. "I will never have anyone tell me to what level I support an art, what I must pay a light show," he said. He built to a fevered climax and melodramatically announced he would close the Fillmore West after New Year's Eve rather than continue to do business in San Francisco.

"This town has never stopped rapping an honest businessman for four fucking years," he said. "I leave here very sad. I may be copping out, but your attitudes have driven me to my choice."

Stephen Gaskin recognized one of Graham's dramatic lines from a movie and identified the actor whose lines Graham was using. "Eli Wallach," he said, as Graham steamed. Gaskin continued. "When you started," he told Graham, "you had to make a choice between love and money. You've got our money, so you can't have our love. You've

236

used dramatics today to fuck over a lot of heads with your emotional trips."

Graham went berserk. He just exploded.

"I apologize, motherfucker, that I am a human being," he screamed. "I fucking apologize. Emotional? You're fucking right. Fuck you, you stupid prick. Do you know what emotions are? Stand up and have emotions. Get up and work. Get up and sing. Get up and act. You think I'm an actor? You're full of shit, man. I have more balls than you'll ever fucking see. You want to challenge me in any way about emotions? You slimy little man. You slimy . . . little . . . man."

He turned away from Gaskin and boiled over on the entire room. "Fuck you," he screamed. "Fuck you." One hippie stood up to try and calm Graham. "Don't try and get peaceful with me," he snapped. "Don't you TOUCH me." Graham turned and stomped out of the suddenly quiet room. A moment later, one of the plate-glass windows in the front shattered. Graham had already left, but, quite coincidentally, a couple of beach bums tossed a brick through the window.

With this one poisonous outburst, Graham singlehandedly destroyed any fragile remaining notions of unity or community the San Francisco music scene was struggling to nurture. The managers and bands—and, for that fact, the light shows—depended on Graham's stage to stay afloat. Only the precious few with nationwide hit records could afford to ignore the power of Graham and, in one sweeping dramatic gesture, he had made it clear where he stood. He revealed his agenda. The Wild West was under attack from external forces and the rock scene couldn't even keep peace among themselves. Any pretense Graham had maintained about belonging to a community was blown away. And there was no alternative. Helms was impotent, on the verge of ruin.

"Friday night finished the Family Dog as a business," he told the crowd after Graham left. "The dream burst Friday. I have a proposal to make at our next meeting Thursday. But if there's a picket line at the Fillmore West tonight, I won't bother to come up with a proposal and Family Dog won't operate this weekend."

One by one, the light show representatives present withdrew support for the strike. Even Abrams tossed in the towel. The strike was over.

That night, Ron Polte and Tom Donahue attended a meeting called by the Haight Commune in a last-ditch effort to salvage support for the Wild West. John the Motherfucker lashed out at the festival. He cited producers—he called them "pimp merchants of bread and circuses"—for paying a hundred and fifty thousand to rent Kezar Stadium and to "surround Golden Gate Park with four hundred pigs." The Wild West was aligned with the establishment, he told the meeting, ignoring the hip, black and Third World communities.

Donahue, who had resigned his post as KSAN general manager in May in a dispute with station owners, was deep into cocaine addiction. He rarely left his house. But he needed the Wild West. He tried vainly to rally the following day when he delivered a twenty-minute monologue at a press conference he called at the festival headquarters.

He laid everything out. He denied any collusion with police or city officials. He explained the rent for Kezar would be twelve thousand dollars, which he thought compared favorably with the twenty-two thousand dollars rent he paid for Candlestick Park in 1966, when he produced the final public performance by the Beatles. His mellifluous baritone dropped into a shade of melancholy, sounding a note of warning on the previous night's experience.

"Last night we met with a group of people who represent themselves as leaders of the hip community," Donahue said. "The meeting was run by a man named John, whose last name I don't know. I have never seen him before. Now, in the two and a half years that I was involved in the so-called underground radio scene in this town, I talked to a whole lot of street people because that's where they came when they needed something to get on the air. I want to tell you, I didn't see them there last night.

"I think there were a lot of people who are representative of a good element in the community, people who have positive ideas about how the world has to be changed and, I think, as we went along, the meeting was as fascistic as anything I have ever been to. It was as totally rigged as some of the union meetings I had seen happen.

"John stood up at the first part of the meeting, said the Black Panthers were not here tonight, but he contended they said they were with us in whatever we do and they will go along. Now if the Black Panthers are letting this white honky stand up and speak for them and say they will go along with any decision he makes and that group makes, then Eldridge better get back here in a hell of a hurry. I don't think he represents the Black Panthers or represents the other groups that were named.

"I think there were a lot of other people there last night that were afraid to stand up because of the way the meeting was being run. They would take an x-number of motions from the floor and limit discussion when some people started to talk. Then somebody would start clapping their hands beside them and raise their voices so they couldn't be heard.

"We live in a world where people are afraid, where people are paranoid. Maybe sometimes I think that the yin and yang of psychedelics, et cetera, that have opened people's heads up, that while making them sensitive, it has also brought about a kind of paranoia and suspicion of their brother that is going to stop their attempts to change this world. I find it difficult to understand the motivation of people who want to bring a halt to the getting together of their brothers in a celebration. I want to know who sent them or set them up."

Nevertheless, Donahue announced the Music Council would expand the number of seats on the board from eight to twenty-four in an effort at conciliation. But the festival ship was taking on water from more directions than just self-appointed community watchdogs. The Musicians Union was inventing the expected obstructions. With most members of the Music Council board preoccupied with their own enterprises and largely unavailable, Olivier couldn't muster the personal power to pull together the disparate forces tugging at the festival. The mayor's office was not especially helpful and the Parks and Rec Department was downright stubborn. Also, tickets to the Kezar shows were not selling.

The next Tuesday, Parks and Rec finally handed down an irrevocable decision granting the Wild West the use of only five areas in the park—the Beach Chalet, Speedway Meadow, Polo Field, Marx Meadow and Lindley Meadow. The following day, a haggard Olivier announced to a hurriedly called, sparsely attended press conference that the Wild West, ten days off, would be canceled. He cited death threats made to Ron Polte, "the certainty of violence" threatened by numerous radical organizations. And, he said, the community had shown it wouldn't cooperate.

Polte was disconsolate. "We were like a piece of bait," he said, "caught between both sides—the establishment and the anti-establishment, anti-festival people, just ready for the fuckover."

Two benefits at the Family Dog and Fillmore West the weekend the festival was scheduled made up the thirteen-thousand-dollar loss.

On Saturday, the Airplane held down the Fillmore West and the Sons of Champlin backed up blues singer Jimmy Witherspoon at the Family Dog. Quicksilver, in the band's only announced performance of the year, played Friday at the Fillmore and Saturday at the Dog, and then rushed down to the Fillmore to stand onstage and listen to the end of the Airplane set. On Sunday, as if to challenge Graham's point, thirteen light shows came together for the visual jam session planned for the Wild West at the Dog, performing to tapes. Almost eight hundred people attended.

One other event planned for the festival did occur. Artist Paul Crowley pulled off his grand scheme of parking a Moog synthesizer on Twin Peaks, hooking up skyscraper electrical systems and having classical keyboardist Margaret Fabrizzio play a fugue with the skyline.

FALL 1969

When Rock Scully jetted to England that summer to conduct some international intrigue on behalf of holding up Columbia Records for a rich recording contract, he wondered why Lenny Hart insisted he travel with a one-way ticket. On arriving at Heathrow Airport, customs officials took one look at his passport. "Mr. Scully? This way, please," they said. He was led away and searched. Finding quantities of both acid and cocaine, the authorities arrested the Grateful Dead manager.

No stranger to crossing international borders, Scully as a youth attended private schools in Switzerland, where his world-famous sociologist stepfather felt free to send his wife's two sons hither and yon, Carmel to Zurich, at will. Scully kept turning over the custom officer's calm reaction in his mind; *it was as if they were expecting him.* He couldn't shake the thought of Lenny Hart and the one-way ticket. Had he been set up?

Out on bail awaiting trial, Scully both schemed a new record deal and spent time conferring with Keith Richards over the upcoming U.S. tour by the Rolling Stones. With the steep ticket prices already drawing fire in the American press, Scully suggested that a free concert with the Airplane and the Dead in Golden Gate Park might help mitigate some of the bad publicity.

Scully knew what he was talking about. The man who staged the guerilla raid on Haight Street knew how to bamboozle Parks and Rec—draw up the permits under the guise of a hometown concert by either the Dead or the Airplane, announce the concert twenty-four hours in advance and add the Stones as a last-minute surprise guest. Richards loved the idea.

In October, the Stones holed up in a Hollywood hills mansion owned by Peter Tork of the Monkees, preparing to launch the tour. Rifkin accompanied Scully and Emmett Grogan of the Diggers to Los Angeles to meet with the band about the free concert in the park. For Rifkin, headed for parts south of the border and a leave of absence, the Stones confab would be one final detail in his Dead duties. For Scully, the event would represent an international coup of immeasurable magnitude for the San Francisco rock scene.

But Scully also had other issues to face. Back home, he discovered Lenny Hart had renegotiated the Warner Brothers record contract in his absence and re-signed the band to the label for another four albums at terms even less favorable than the previous agreement. Business manager Hart handed the band the document to sign amid some gig contracts and presented the deal as the only sure route out of debt. Scully went wild when he found out. His plans to make off with a bundle from Columbia Records boss Clive Davis had been blown up before he had a chance, undermined by someone whose mandate specifically excluded dealings of this nature. With Lenny Hart taking advantage of Scully's being conveniently preoccupied with problems of his own in an English courtroom, Scully secretly wondered how coincidental his prolonged stay abroad really was. He called Lenny Hart a thief in front of the band, but the musicians dismissed Scully's ravings as wild-eyed paranoia.

Sam Andrew left the Chelsea Hotel and went direct to San Francisco the morning after his final show with the band at Forest Hills. He hadn't even finished the set, but walked offstage and left the bandstand to his replacement.

His last few weeks with Joplin had been forlorn and depressing. He had felt distant from the other musicians, as opposed to the tightly knit fabric of Big Brother. He withdrew from contact and lost himself reading books in French and Latin to take his mind even further away. Although she had fired him, Joplin had finally spent a night with Andrew making love. After years of close friendship and Joplin's joking mewing—"Sam, why don't you love me?"—Joplin had been intrigued after a mutual friend told her what a fine lover she found Andrew.

Back in San Francisco, Andrew took a tape of the new Joplin album to David Getz's house in Fairfax and played the record for the other members of Big Brother. They were not impressed. Getz and Albin, after touring Europe the previous spring as the rhythm section for Country Joe and the Fish, had been hosting informal jam sessions at Getz's house through the summer.

They had first tried to put Big Brother back together earlier in the year, auditioning different vocalists. Grossman sent out Cambridge bluegrass singer John Herald, although nothing came of that. They worked up some songs with David Nelson, an old associate of the Grateful Dead's from Palo Alto days, and even played a show with him, Jerry Garcia and Mickey Hart at the Matrix.

Getz had worked with a couple of other Marin County bands that summer with some of the people from the Sons of Champlin, and Sons guitarist Terry Haggerty was a familiar figure at the Fairfax jam sessions. Nick Gravenites, who spent a brief moment during the summer singing with the Gary Duncan-less Quicksilver, also started hanging out.

James Gurley, his long hair freshly shorn, wouldn't touch a guitar. He was still devastated by his wife's death and only managed to dodge serious legal consequences through an aggressive defense from his lawyer, Mike Stepanian. He played bass and Albin switched to guitar, his first instrument before Big Brother. Once Andrew returned, the original Big Brother was back together and Gravenites came aboard as a kind of guest lead vocalist, although nothing was firm. Gurley and Andrew spent some time that fall living on a beach in Maui, contemplating life as coral divers, and practically commuting to and from the West Coast.

Peggy Caserta joined Joplin at Woodstock, where the San Francisco contingent included the Airplane, the Dead, Country Joe and the Fish, Creedence Clearwater, and Sly and the Family Stone, the flashy soul-rock outfit led by the former Oakland deejay and Autumn Records producer that scored a number-one record earlier in the year with "Everyday People." Bill Graham arranged for Santana, entirely unknown outside the Bay Area, to appear at the festival by having his booking agency make a package deal for the band and the Dead. Joplin, who devoted much of her energy at the festival to drinking and shooting dope, gave a performance charitably described as indifferent.

When Martha Wax ran into Joplin the next month taking some sun by the side of the pool at the Landmark in Hollywood, Wax was astonished at her sallow complexion, so white it seemed translucent. When Wax remarked on an ugly purplish bruise on Joplin's thigh, the singer laughed. She'd passed out giving herself a shot of heroin, she told Wax, and when she woke up on the floor, she still had the needle jabbed in her leg.

Grace Slick showed up onstage at the Fillmore East that November disguised as Adolf Hitler, in full uniform, hair slicked down, mustache. Rip Torn, who had developed a friendship with the band following his arrest during the Airplane's scene in the Godard movie, joined the show later in the set dressed as Richard Nixon. Torn had been trying to persuade the band to write and perform an original score for a production of *Richard III*, to be played as a satire on the Nixon administration. Somehow the group never got around to that project, although Torn eventually did mount the production.

With activities reaching a frantic, blurry pace as the touring schedule heated up that fall, the Airplane musicians struggled to keep up, often relying on copious doses of speed to help. With the band singing "up against the wall, motherfucker" on the new album, police seemed to dog the Airplane's every step. Kantner was arrested in Honolulu for possession of marijuana after cops found a scrawny little joint he would have been embarrassed to smoke. Smelling a setup, Kantner was dragged into the foyer of the group's rented house, thrown on the ground and handcuffed behind his back. The other musicians gathered around, drinking and laughing, while Kantner made fun of the cops. When he was finally taken to jail, Kantner had the band bail out the black guy sharing his cell, too, since nobody else was coming up with his bail.

In Dallas, police visited Thompson backstage and warned him that people couldn't get away with saying "fuck" onstage in their city. In Houston, Kantner grabbed a bullhorn and started exhorting the audience not to let the cops get away with cutting off the power. Confrontations with the forces of authority were becoming second nature.

When Mick Jagger announced at a New York press conference following the tour's climactic Madison Square Garden shows by the Rolling Stones that the band would be giving a free concert in San Francisco's Golden Gate Park on or around December 6, he virtually ensured it would never happen. Rock Scully's plan called for the Stones to be added to the program at the last minute, after the appropriate permits had been acquired from Parks and Rec, not before. In one deft motion, Jagger dashed that idea to pieces.

After the final concert of the tour at West Palm Beach, Florida, the Stones retreated to the remote outpost of Muscle Shoals, Alabama, to spend a few days recording. Stones road manager Sam Cutler flew to San Francisco, where Scully met him at the airport and whisked him off to the command post organized at the Dead's Alembic Sound Studios. Chip Monck, the staging wizard who presided over Woodstock and the Stones tour, began making frantic arrangements to put together a stage and facilities for a concert expected to draw 200,000 fans. The small office was a blizzard of activity. The Stones staff mingled with the Dead and their associates like Lenny Hart, who told Taj Mahal there wouldn't be time on the daylong program for him.

The Maysles brothers had been hired to make a film of the event, but five days before the concert, no site had yet been secured. The president of Sears Point Raceway, a drag strip outside Sonoma less than an hour north of San Francisco, suddenly appeared offering the free use of his land with a few minor provisions. While those details were being worked out, Monck went to work building his stage.

At the last minute, Filmways Corporation, the parent company that owned Sears Point, stepped in and demanded distribution rights to any film made at the concert. At noon the day before the concert, the Stones hired heavyweight attorney Melvin Belli to handle negotiations. Out of nowhere, Belli fielded a phone call from Dick Carter of the Altamont Raceway in the grassy hills beside the freeway across the Bay Bridge forty-five minutes east of San Francisco. Sears Point was out and Monck now had to shift into emergency overdrive to tear down his partially built stage at Sears Point and rush the pieces by helicopter to Altamont, where it had to be finished in less than twenty-four hours.

• • •

The Jefferson Airplane all boarded a helicopter leaving the freezing cold night air of Miami after the band's performance, headed straight for the flight back to San Francisco the night before the free Stones concert. Drummer Spencer Dryden slipped climbing into the copter and fell in a muddy pond, his attaché case opening in the water and his cowboy hat floating away. He scrambled back on the flight, dripping wet and angry.

Dryden didn't want to play the Stones concert. Scully kept the Airplane camp fully informed of progress on the phone, although the band was powerless to influence events from Florida. Dryden grew vocal in his opposition. He told Kantner this wasn't turning out to be the same thing as the original idea of the show in Golden Gate Park. Kantner agreed, but said he felt the band had to go through with the concert anyway and then went to sleep.

Flying through the night across the country, Dryden continued his harangue. Jorma Kaukonen battled him all the way. At three in the morning at the San Francisco Airport, the two were standing over the baggage carousel, going at it over whether to do the show or not. Thompson finally lost his patience. "Just do it," he told Dryden. "You can't be the one guy to screw it up for all these people that put it together."

A car called for Dryden and the others staying at the Airplane house at six in the morning. Marty Balin didn't even know the band intended to play until he was informed at the airport a car would be picking him up in a couple of hours. Nobody slept more than two hours before heading out to get on a pair of helicopters and fly to Tracy on the edge of the Central Valley, where the band transferred to one smaller copter for the final leg of the trip.

The copter skated over the dusty brown hills. Below, thousands of people trooped across the barren landscape in the pink morning light, abandoning their cars on the freeway and hiking into the concert site. Dryden thought he was watching a scene from a Hieronymous Bosch painting. As the copter settled down on the landing pad at the rear of the reddish-gray dustbowl where the stage and sound system had been so hastily erected, Dryden was filled with a sense of foreboding and fear. So, of course, he dropped a couple of acid tabs. Balin poured himself some drinks. The party was underway.

Santana was the first band to take the stage and before the second song started, Hell's Angels ringing the stage as security guards rained blows from sawed-off pool cues on, first, a young man trying to make his way past the phalanx of motorcycle outlaws, and, second, a photographer snapping pictures of the beating who resisted turning over his camera on demand. In the middle of the next number, some Angels dashed right across the stage, interrupting the band, to beat up someone on the other side.

Bill Laudner of the Airplane watched in amazement as one of the Angels in front of the stage followed a handful of orange sunshine with a handful of reds—sleeping pills—and chased them both with the rest of his beer. As much wild, insane doping as he had been around, Kesey, Owsley, all that, Laudner had never seen anybody swallow quantities of drugs like that before. He knew the Angels could mean trouble. In the past, the Airplane never encouraged the Angels to participate in events, but the Angels were also quite difficult to discourage. So the band adopted a tolerant attitude as the least difficult option.

Laudner stared wide-eyed as the Angels waded into the crowd, flailing pool cues in a horrifying blood frenzy. Sam Cutler tried to alleviate the crowding on the stage before introducing the Airplane, announcing over the public address system that the stage was too crowded to continue. "The musicians are playing with something like two hundred people breathing down their necks," he said to no avail. The Airplane took the stage anyway, beginning a nervous performance with a hopeful "We Can Be Together."

Marty Balin looked out into the area in front of the stage while he was singing "Other Side of this Life" and couldn't believe what he saw. The Angels were pounding some poor soul into the ground and the crowd just stepped aside to make room for them. Nobody made a move to stop it from happening. The guy, obviously tripping, was only trying to get away from the Angels and nobody lifted a finger to help. Balin rushed to the scene, snapping off his vocal midlyric while the band kept playing, Grace Slick muttering a soothing mantra. "Easy . . . easy . . . easy," she repeated.

Balin shouted at the Angels, who kept thrashing the miserable hippie. "Fuck you," Balin said, pointing at one of the attackers. He jumped off the stage, into the melee, and took a wild swing at an Angel wearing a wolf pelt over his head like a hat. He was called Animal. In a flash, the Angels circled Balin and beat him unconscious.

Thompson rounded up a couple of large stagehands, who lifted Balin's inert body to an equipment truck backed up against the stage, serving as a makeshift backstage area, and they laid him on the floor of the truck. A remorseful Animal appeared in the truck as Balin was coming to. He apologized, sort of. "You shouldn't have been messing with us doing business," he told Balin.

"Fuck you," Balin said. In a flash, Animal kicked Balin out cold again. Thompson and Laudner separated the Angel from Balin and his sudden violence ebbed as quickly as it erupted. Again, he apologized, extending a can of beer as a peace offering. He backed out of the truck.

Onstage, Kantner took his case to the public. "I'd like to mention that the Hell's Angels just smashed Marty Balin in the face and knocked him out for a little bit," he said, as the music tumbled to a halt. One of the Angels grabbed a microphone and attempted a brief incoherent dialogue with Kantner. Grace Slick, who stayed out of the way, tried to glide past the tense flashpoint.

"You've got to keep your bodies off one another unless you intend love," she said. "People get weird and you need people like the Angels to keep people in line. But the Angels, you know, you don't bust people in the head for nothing. Let's not keep fucking up."

Balin staggered back to the stage to finish the set, his bell clearly rung. He looked dazed, his eyes cloudy. The band closed with "Volunteers" and beat a hasty retreat. Kaukonen regarded Balin with disdain. "You're crazy to jump in there," he said.

"Where the fuck were you with all your knives and guns?" Balin said to the guitarist, known to fancy the hardware of violence on occasion.

Dryden, the LSD mixed with adrenaline pulsing through his brain, wanted to leave immediately and he approached Kantner, who seemed remarkably calm. "Naw, I want to watch the Stones and the Dead," he told Dryden. The drummer wandered off looking for the helicopter pad, but the landing space had been overrun by people. Already disoriented, he got lost.

He found a young man with a car who volunteered to drive him and bassist David Brown of Santana to Tracy, where they could find a helicopter back to the city. Directions proved useless, as highways were closed, choked to a standstill by parked cars, and the errant hippie couldn't even find the right direction to go. He finally broke down and admitted he was too high on mushrooms and mescaline to know what he was doing. He wasn't even seeing all that well, he told Dryden, who was in a fairly sorry state himself. Nevertheless, Dryden took over the wheel and drove everybody back to San Francisco.

Scully settled down on the floor backstage at the Fillmore West later that night, breathing deeply from a tank of nitrous oxide. His nerves were a jangled, short-circuited mess. His whole system teetered on the edge. He had spent the three previous days without sleep, snorting coke to keep going. He had arrived at Altamont before the first board was laid to build the stage, and stayed through the bitter end. Sleep, in fact, had been a precious and rare commodity for Scully the entire previous week, while he stood by the helm of this mighty undertaking. He felt like a battle-weary general after a sound defeat. The nitrous was helping him relax, sitting in a backstage haven he helped build for the Carousel Ballroom.

The Dead had been scheduled to appear at Altamont, but after the bloodbath culminating in a murder that took place during the Stones performance, the band decided against playing. The Dead were also supposed to appear that night at the Fillmore West. Although Graham canceled the show—who was going to turn up anyway?—most of the band dutifully assembled at the hall. As Scully pulled on the tube from the tank, a semblance of calm descended on him for the first time in weeks, maybe months. The door swung open and in walked Bill Graham.

Graham had been opposed to the festival from the start. He had wanted nothing to do with the Stones and the band's free concert. When the group played Oakland Coliseum for Graham early in the tour, Graham and Sam Cutler got into a fistfight onstage during the Stones set, rolling on the floor, crashing into amplifiers. There was no love lost, and Graham watched the Altamont fiasco from the sidelines, growing ever more contemptuous. His only contribution was the loan of a couple of employees needed to pull the stage together during the final twenty-four hours. Now he was breathing the fire of the truly righteous. He pointed at Scully, his finger shaking.

"Murderer," he sputtered.

Scully couldn't take it. After days of intense agony, his patience was stretched to the limit. He was sitting backstage in a dressing room he built, trying to come down, frazzled beyond description, and in front of him he saw Bill Graham, who had been no help whatsoever, glaring indignation and making wild accusations. He stood up and slugged Graham as hard as he could, hitting him in the chest. Graham stumbled backward, out of the doorway and over the top of the stairs. He fell on his ass. Scully closed the door behind him.

1970

San Francisco is a
human game preserve.
— Robin Williams

WINTER 1969-70

Life was spinning out of control for Janis Joplin. All the dope, booze, boys, money and fame were beginning to take a heavy toll. The first fissure opened November 15 at Curtis-Hixon Hall in Tampa, Florida, when police dragged her off to jail after a concert on two charges of using "vulgar and indecent language."

Language of exactly that sort had become one of her trademarks, along with the Southern Comfort and feather boa. When overstimulated fans rushed the stage, police massed in front of the stage, pushing them back and telling them to return to their seats. Joplin leaned down and tapped one of the cops on the shoulder. "Listen, mister," she announced, "I've been to more of these things than you have and no one's ever hurt nothin'. They're not hurting anything. Leave them alone."

The crowd cheered wildly. No longer was it enough for Joplin to simply leave an audience applauding madly. Nothing short of pandemonium would do. She was no longer merely a singer. She was an experience, a visiting storm that blew gusts of rock and soul into county arenas, lifting the drab populace from their humdrum little lives and granting them a glimpse of something greater. Only responses slightly short of riot conditions were acceptable.

When an intemperate, ill-advised cop walked onto the stage with a bullhorn to curb the stage stampede and get people to stop standing on chairs, Joplin lost all semblance of composure. "Don't fuck with these people," she yelled. "Hey, mister, what are you so uptight about? Did you buy a five dollar ticket?"

From the wings, someone asked her to tell the kids to sit down. "I'm not telling them shit," she snapped. But she did decide to address the situation in her own way after the next number.

"Now, listen," she told the audience, "we can't go fucking with each other because that'll give them something to chomp on. If we don't hurt nothin', they can't say shit."

As she stormed offstage at the end of the hour-long show, Joplin spied the cop with the bullhorn and royally upbraided him, suggesting she would cause him bodily harm in rather indelicate terms. She brushed past him to her dressing room, where, a few minutes later, a brace of officers presented her with a warrant and took one pissed-off Janis Joplin to jail.

Her personal life was so out-of-control at this point that even the normally unflappable Grossman took steps to introduce Joplin to a doctor about her drug problem. In early December, she visited a New York endocrinologist with a history of successfully treating drug addicts. He counseled her to stop drinking, improve her diet and prescribed dolophine, a pill form of methadone. While she started taking the heroin substitute, she careened around New York at a breakneck pace with running buddies Bobby Neuwirth and actor Michael J. Pollard.

Back home, she bought a house in a shady redwood grove on a dead end of Larkspur, the tiny Marin County town where Jerry Garcia and Mountain Girl lived across the creek in the wooded backyard. The redwood shingle, two-bedroom house, previously owned by a prosperous dentist, opened onto a deck overlooking the woods, with plenty of glass letting in sunlight and a high-beamed ceiling in the large living room built around a fireplace in the center.

Dave Richards had come back to work for her, this time as a carpenter. Longtime roommate Linda Gravenites returned to share the household and design the wardrobe for her upcoming Madison Square

Garden concert and the lavish after-party Columbia Records president Clive Davis was hosting.

After a successful warm-up concert in Nashville, where she unveiled a new song from an up-and-coming songwriter named Kris Kristofferson, "Me and Bobby McGee," she returned to New York for her own appearance at Madison Square Garden, where the previous month she had stumbled onstage, drunk and stoned, for an impromptu duet with Tina Turner, who was opening for the Rolling Stones. The night before her own Madison Square concert, she ran into New York Jets quarterback Joe Namath at his Bachelor's III bar. They adjourned privately to his apartment upstairs and Joplin was screaming at her office staff the next day to call *Rolling Stone* and tell Random Notes that Janis Joplin had balled Joe Namath. At the concert, she whimpered into the microphone, "Joe, Joe, where are you?" The performance itself was an empty ritual, her rote histrionics and grand dramatic gestures falling short in the cavernous hall, enlivened only by some spontaneous blues jamming with Johnny Winter and Paul Butterfield.

Clive Davis assembled a stunning array of glitterati at his sumptuous Central Park West apartment for the after-show party—Bob Dylan, Miles Davis and Tony Bennett, among many others. Waiters in black-tie served drinks and an enormous array of food was piled on tables in the dining area. The party had been going on for more than an hour without Joplin when she finally arrived, glassy-eyed and stuporous, apparently zonked out of her skull.

The next day she flew back to San Francisco with a twenty-two-year-old Brit she had met at a Greenwich Village bar who had also accompanied her to Nashville. She threw a belated housewarming for four hundred of her closest friends, a drunken brawl of a party where members of Big Brother rubbed shoulders with the fellows from her group, now called the Kozmic Blues Band. Even Ralph Gleason came—all was forgiven. Joplin confided to James Gurley at the party that she was going to fire her new band and start all over again, and she spent considerable time sequestered in her bedroom with Peggy Caserta and Mike Bloomfield shooting dope. So much for dolophine.

Nicky Hopkins came to San Francisco to record with Steve Miller. The sickly, skinny Englishman rated as one of the world's most regarded sidemen by virtue of his associations with groups like the

Beatles, the Rolling Stones and other British guitar groups that needed a touch of piano once in a while in the studio. He had just finished a year's servitude as an actual member of the Jeff Beck Group and had no burning desire to link up with any standing organization again in the near future.

He stayed around town, playing some sessions with the Airplane and, then, Quicksilver. Since Duncan left the band the previous January, the remaining three—Cipollina, Freiberg and Elmore—had been lazily casting about for members. The band still owed Capitol Records an album, but nobody was in any particular hurry. Nick Gravenites tried his hand at vocals. The band even made some experimental recordings with him and played a free concert in the park with Gravenites singing—Nicksilver they called it. But that was that. Without Duncan, the band played one official show the entire year.

Hopkins knocked off piano part after piano part, first take each time, a sturdy professional whose instrumental prowess matched the lacy inventions Cipollina had spun around the rhythm section. They dosed him into the band, gave him his first hit of LSD in the studio and he decided to join up. While he was still high, Cipollina took him outside and taught him how to drive on the windy road along the side of Mount Tam. He moved in with Cipollina, his pale, anemic soul brother.

Pulling material out of the band for an album had been an excruciating, slow process. Gravenites, who didn't play any part in the actual recording, co-wrote two songs and wrote another by himself, a contribution equal to Freiberg and more than Cipollina. But Hopkins contributed the nine-minute "Edward (The Mad Shirt Grinder)" and the long-suffering album was finally completed. The band was listening to mixes one night that fall at Pacific High studios, a few blocks from the Fillmore West, and decided to break and catch Joe Cocker down the street.

Gary Duncan and Dino Valente were at the Cocker show, too. Duncan had teamed up with Valente the moment he left Quicksilver. The two roared off to New York, where Duncan found himself somewhat hamstrung by the presence of his wife, Shelley, and their two-year-old daughter, Heather. Before long, she returned to Los Angeles to live with her mother, while Duncan and Valente went about the man's work of putting together a band that would be called the Outlaws.

From New York to Nashville, from Muscle Shoals to Hollywood, the two could never quite find musicians adequate to the task. Besides, they had other things to do, other highways to ride on their Triumph Bonneville motorcycles. They burned out the new bikes, bought Harley Sportsters and tore off from L.A. to Oregon, just to feel the wind in their faces.

But now Duncan was back, living in a small house in Mill Valley with his wife and daughter. When he discovered Shelley Duncan had engaged in a brief fling of her own in his absence, he came back, cleaned-up and attentive, not smoking, drinking or doing drugs that she could tell. She thought her young husband might have finally settled into the idea of being married. She knew he hadn't wanted to be married for the longest time, but he at last seemed to be accepting and even liking the idea of being with her and Heather.

When Duncan and Valente went back to Pacific High that night with the Quicksilver guys to listen to the album, they were openly arrogant and insulting, not surprising since they had been taking their arrogance powder. They bluntly described the album as a piece of shit and announced that they could easily make one better. Polte thought nothing more would come of the encounter, but was surprised to hear from Freiberg several days later that they had been singing together. Freiberg told Polte the vocal blend was superb, they could be the new Crosby, Stills and Nash. Duncan and Valente accepted an invitation to join the band for the New Year's Eve gig at Fillmore West.

The Great Experiment of Chet Helms finally came to a halt in January 1970. In the spirit of both survival and collectivism, Helms had turned over the Family Dog on the Great Highway to the community—whoever that happened to be at any given meeting—for whatever purposes they deemed worthy immediately following the light show strike the previous August.

Every Tuesday afternoon since Bill Graham stomped out of the hall after laying down an obscenity-laced verbal barrage, a hundred or so interested parties gathered at the former slot car racetrack to plan events. Expenses came off the top and then performers and producers split the proceeds equally. Thus, a rock band and a light show could receive the same fee for an evening's work, which was the beef that originally started the ball rolling.

But Helms really was quickly running out of options anyway.

Badly in debt and unable to effectively compete with Graham for name acts, his ballroom operation was withering away before his eyes at the time of the strike. Since then, he presided over meetings where anybody in the pot-filled room could suggest an enterprise, book a date and attempt to carry it off. In the last five months, some inventive endeavors took place at the hall.

A Holy Man Jam pitted acid guru Tim Leary, Buddhist thinker Alan Watts, Indian medicine man Rolling Thunder and others. Jerry Garcia's country and western sideline band, New Riders of the Purple Sage, made a habit of working the room. Garcia even regularly showed up at meetings of the Common, as the communal enterprise came to be known.

Most of the shows, however, were less inventive and lost money. A flea market attracted a total of eight interested parties. By December, Helms found himself ten thousand dollars further in debt. But it was the four thousand he owed Internal Revenue that spelled an end to the collective. When Helms brought the question of his tax bill before the group, nobody hurried to assume any responsibility. Since his name appeared on the IRS statement, Helms dismissed the group and resumed full control of the enterprise.

Spencer Dryden and Sally Mann were married in the front parlor of the Airplane house on January 26. Grace Slick, the former inamorata of the groom, served as maid of honor and Paul Kantner, her current romantic liaison, acted as best man. The ceremony was performed by the Reverend Scott Beach, director of The Committee, but also a minister of the American Humanist Institute. His stentorian tones and gilt-edged oratory earned a hearty ovation when he finished.

As the three hundred guests filled the mansion for the reception, Slick slipped the happy couple a thousand dollars as a wedding present, and quietly left for Sausalito with her husband, Jerry Slick. Kantner came back downstairs bearing a silver tray with a pile of cocaine and acid mixed together with a rolled-up hundred dollar bill to snort through. He joined the newlyweds in this unique blessing.

About fifteen minutes later, reeling from the accelerating arch of the acid blast, the Drydens retired to their room upstairs. They could hear the noise from their wedding party through the floors, but they were in no condition to join the festivities. When Kantner, equally looped, poked his head in the door, looking for Grace, they told him she had gone home to Sausalito with Jerry Slick.

He came back and joined the couple, talking about Slick until Sally Dryden phoned Slick in Sausalito and asked her to return to the Airplane house because Kantner had taken too much acid and wanted her to be with him. She came. That night, Kantner realized he had fallen in love with her.

Dryden had deteriorated dramatically since Altamont. He was drinking a fifth of Southern Comfort a day and carrying a gun. Real and imagined prowlers had been sighted around the Fulton Street mansion. Dryden himself was responsible for one psycho, fresh out of jail, showing up and parking himself in the living room. This fellow had written the drummer dozens of letters from the joint and Dryden made the mistake of responding. As soon as the guy got out, he grabbed a pal and headed for the Airplane house to see his friend, Spencer Dryden. It was only one of many things that made the other band members wonder about Dryden's judgment.

The Airplane had turned into a rich, elite group, still strange, but with enough money to indulge their most fanciful whimsies. Grace Slick spent two thousand dollars having a dining table made from a medieval torture rack with winches, screws and chains. She kept a stuffed sea lion on the rack in the parlor of the Airplane house. She also spent plenty of money on clothes. Marty Balin, on the other hand, would still wear the same pair of jeans and T-shirt for days.

Band members also dropped big money on fancy cars. Jorma Kaukonen drove a Lotus and Paul Kantner a Porsche. Jack Casady owned a Citroën and Slick rode around in the Aston Martin she bought with cash. Marty Balin preferred an everyday Volkswagen microbus.

The touring party usually numbered fifteen, including Glenn McKay's Headlights and road manager Bill Laudner, who often wore an orange jumpsuit while traveling and scooted around airports aboard roller skates.

Drugs were a constant companion to the scene. Marty Balin used to walk along the back of the amplifiers to check the individual stashes of drugs ready for personal use during the performance, just to see who was using what that particular night. Balin himself was drinking a fair amount, growing even more isolated from the other members of the group. He openly scoffed at people's cocaine use, deriding what he thought of as cocaine rhythms and cocaine music.

But it was Dryden the band cut loose. His replacement was not merely waiting in the wings, but living at the Airplane house. Joey Covington, a Los Angeles-based drummer, had auditioned the previous year for Balin and Thompson, who invited him to come to San Francisco and hang out. He added some conga drums to the previous Airplane album and joined forces with Kaukonen and Casady, who had taken Hot Tuna electric.

Dryden kept up a running stream of complaints. A small, wiry man who was seen as a troublemaker and whiner, Dryden had lost most of his intraband power when he broke up with Slick. Without Slick, his threats to quit the band no longer carried much weight. Kaukonen and Casady could gang up on him in concert driving the tempos faster and harder until he was literally huffing and puffing for breath trying to keep up.

Between the drinking, the drugs and the stress, Dryden verged on a nervous breakdown. He busied himself making tapes of strange, almost random music, and playing with the video gear the band owned. But he was taken by surprise when the band all sat down for a meeting three weeks after his gala wedding and told Dryden they thought he needed to take a rest. He hadn't complained about anything all week.

Within a few minutes, however, Dryden capitulated. Covington suggested using two drummers simultaneously on the upcoming tour, but Dryden demurred. "You've been living with this band for a year," he told Covington. "If you can't do it now, you'll never be able to."

Keeping in mind how Skip Spence helped ease his own transition into the band four years earlier, Dryden attended rehearsal the following day where Covington played and Dryden watched, helping him catch a few twists and turns. Some suggestions were made that it might be best if Dryden hung around, but he didn't want to linger. Within a couple of weeks, he had moved out of the Airplane house to an apartment in Sausalito.

Tom Constanten decided to leave the Dead. After less than two years touring with the band, the pedantic punster found himself frustrated with the sonic role assigned his keyboard work, squeezed into a crowded midsection, short-changed on the electronics and mangled in the mix.

While part of this situation could be written off as inevitable, Constanten also ascribed part to the antipathy of sound czar Owsley, who distrusted the pianist's antidrug sentiments. Constanten had become an ardent follower of the teachings of the Church of Scientology. Although he had taken, by his own estimate, a couple of hundred acid trips, Scientology made Constanten swear off psychedelics in pursuit of another channel to higher consciousness, drawing the automatic disdain of the acid king.

He also wasn't really sure there was any real musical place for him in the tangled sound of the Grateful Dead. Even a self-assured, ballsy keyboardist like jazzman Vince Guaraldi, who jammed with the band on at least one occasion at the Avalon, couldn't really sculpt out a space for himself in the clanging interplay of guitars and drums. Phil Lesh was even tactless enough to allow he preferred the playing of organist Howard Wales to what Constanten was doing after Wales sat in with the band.

But on this chilly February afternoon on the eve of the Mardi Gras season, as Constanten and Pigpen strolled the antique stores on New Orleans's Royal Street looking at vintage firearms, he felt a bittersweet camaraderie following a meeting in the Bourbon Street hotel room where plans were laid for the musical parting of the ways. He made a mental note to stop in the hotel's lobby lounge before the weekend was over and catch jazz great Earl "Fatha" Hines, who was performing there. Although members of the Airplane had been busted in the same hotel only weeks before, nobody paid any particular attention when the house detective stopped Garcia in the lobby that afternoon with a friendly admonition. "We're watching you," he said, grinning.

Constanten showed up that night at the gig and stood uncertain behind the amplifiers watching until Garcia signaled him onto the stage to take his seat behind the keyboards. The band was playing before a jam-packed audience of six thousand sweaty fans at the opening of a new Tchoupitoulas Street ballroom, a former warehouse with vast brick walls and a low ceiling imaginatively called The Warehouse. The band started off the postmidnight performance playing two new songs with a surprising melodic, lyrical bent, "Uncle John's Band" and "Cumberland Blues." Almost two hours later, the Dead brought the show to a close with a rocking "Cosmic Charlie" and, despite the crowd's insistent cheers, did not return for an encore.

Constanten and Pigpen had already hit the sack by three in the morning when the police burst into their room and rousted them out of bed to search the premises. The rest of the band returned to the hotel to find a squadron of state and New Orleans police waiting, their rooms already turned inside-out. Police arrested nineteen people—everybody but Constanten and Pigpen—handcuffed them all together, took them downtown and paraded them in front of press photographers.

Operating over the phone from the Bay Area, Lenny Hart quickly arranged bail, although the band and crew spent eight hours in jail before being released. The first thing they did was change hotels. Constanten didn't even go to the show that night. The following night, a steady downpour kept the crowds away, but support act Fleetwood Mac joined the Dead in a benefit for the band's legal defense fund. Nobody remembered to catch Earl Hines before leaving town.

The next week, the Dead entered Pacific High Recording in San Francisco to begin recording a new album, songs with a sound and style far removed from anything the Dead previously attempted, a departure greatly influenced by two factors: lyricist Robert Hunter's growing fascination with the songwriting of Robbie Robertson of The Band and David Crosby and Stephen Stills's spending time at Mickey Hart's ranch.

Stills, an accomplished horseman, liked to ride the hills of Marin and also did some recording in Hart's barn. The whole quartet— Crosby, Stills, Nash and Young—had spent the previous fall in San Francisco cutting their second album and Crosby held some solo sessions with Garcia, Lesh and Kreutzman serving as backup band. Their choir-boy harmonies began to infect the Dead, and Stills and Crosby specifically spent time singing with Garcia, Lesh and Weir, showing them some of the nuances of harmony vocals in a potting shed behind Garcia's Larkspur house. Where vocals for the Dead had always been a loathsome chore, an awkward deed, now the band's three vocalists started to face singing with a new confidence and a fresh blend.

The Band struck Hunter as a revelation, a warm and homey sound that felt like old wood and paint rather than polished metal. *Music from Big Pink*, the group's first album, introduced the concept of harmony vocals that didn't have to be sweet and airy. To his ears, these guys just howled. And it worked. But the second album, with "The Night They Drove Old Dixie Down," incited Hunter's sense of history and pointed the way. The Dead looked back to their bluegrass and country beginnings.

Hunter and his lady lived with Garcia, Mountain Girl and Sunshine at the big house in Larkspur. He would sit upstairs, knocking out lyrics on a typewriter, every so often picking up his guitar and strumming away. Through the floor, Garcia, downstairs, would hear Hunter and, by the time the lyricist came down with a sheet of paper to present his collaborator, Garcia would already have the tune pretty much worked out. The songs came together so fast, it was almost as if they just appeared.

With the band's fourth album, a double-record set recorded live, the band's accumulated debt on the Warner Brothers contract amounted to close to $200,000. So recording the new album was approached somewhat differently. The songs were all rehearsed for a full month before entering the studio, with an eye toward reducing studio expenses. In nine days, *Workingman's Dead* was done.

Sam Cutler, the Rolling Stones road manager who ran the Altamont operation, returned from England, his duties with the Stones ended, and bunked up with Garcia in Larkspur. With nothing else to do, Cutler joined some other friends of Garcia's, experienced in bookkeeping, in unraveling the mysteries of the Dead finances, something Lenny Hart had failed to do in his nine months on the job as manager. Discrepancies began to turn up almost immediately.

With jail sentences hanging over their heads in Louisiana, where mere possession of marijuana could easily earn five years, and a deepening disaster on the business front, the music became an oasis of joy—simple, sunny, as comfortable as well-worn furniture. The musicians threw themselves into the recording, finishing the album in a nine-day whirlwind, while dark clouds hovered outside the studio.

Tension between the band and Lenny Hart had been growing for some time. People the band trusted with work were beginning to leave. There were flare-ups but no direct confrontations with him. Even equipment manager Ramrod, who went all the way back to riding on the bus with Kesey and the Pranksters, threatened to quit if the band didn't do something about Lenny Hart.

But when a finance company appeared one night following a concert to repossess Pigpen's organ, the matter of Lenny Hart could be ignored no longer. Phil Lesh and Mickey Hart met Lenny Hart the next day at a Formica-topped hot dog stand. Lesh demanded the books. Lenny Hart refused. In an instant, Mickey Hart knew his father had been stealing money from the band. His world turned black. He knew his father had been involved in shady dealings before, but he had never suspected he would rob the band. And he felt responsible for putting his father in a position to take the money.

While the band pondered what to do, filing criminal charges among the options, Lenny Hart hired an attorney and offered to pay back the stolen funds. But the band's financial records were such a mess, bookkeepers couldn't even approximate the amount of money missing. They finally arrived at a figure of seventy thousand dollars that without doubt had disappeared mysteriously. Hart left ten thousand down and went to Los Angeles with Garcia to negotiate rights for some music on the soundtrack of *Zabriskie Point*. He took the check, cleaned out the band's other bank accounts and disappeared into the night.

Musicians dutifully trooped into the rehearsal hall in back of the courtyard behind the Paisley Penguin, a Fillmore Street boutique operated by the sister of Hillel Resner. Resner, under the persona Dr. Stars, served as personal astrologer to the members of Santana. He and his brother, having gone broke running the Straight Theater, had rented the building for a printing company they were operating, and agreed to rent a workshop area to Santana for rehearsal space, provided the group soundproofed the room. An army of carpenters from the Grateful Dead camp, wood butchers with saws in one hand and burning joints in the other, added layers and layers to the existing walls, even going so far as to insert an eighth-inch-thick sheet of lead as one layer. The interior of the room shrank, as walls covered walls, without effectively accomplishing more than muffling the sound.

Santana had been the unqualified surprise hit of the Woodstock festival the previous fall. Guitarist Carlos Santana appeared before the crowd of a near half-million peaking on a potent dose of mescaline. But he frequently tripped. The other members were given to slightly different, perhaps less ethereal vices. But they had money to burn.

A year before, the members of Santana had been practically indigent, scuffling to pay the rent. But the first album charged up the charts and the band took to the road with Country Joe and the Fish and soft-rockers Bread as support acts. Santana also flew over to London to perform at the Royal Albert Hall. The single of "Evil Ways," the Willie Bobo song the band learned to placate Bill Graham, had been released in January and almost immediately crashed Top Forty radio. Although their means changed, their ways didn't.

Gregg Rolie, the business student from the suburbs, bought a house in Mill Valley. Conga player Michael Carabello put down money for a house for his parents. A lot of fast, expensive cars were purchased. Michael Carabello started riding around on his new Harley with his cousin, the Hell's Angel.

Proceeds were shared equally among the band members, with manager Marcum and his partner, Ron Estrada, splitting another equal share. Decisions were made by majority vote, although the musicians tended to look toward Rolie as the solid citizen of the band.

As the group began to contemplate a second album, Rolie found a song he wanted to sing from a recent album by the British blues band Fleetwood Mac, "Black Magic Woman." The group rehearsed daily, sometimes in ten- to twelve-hour stretches. In order to broaden the tones and expand the palette, the band brought in a grand piano and invited an old friend, Alberto Gianquinto, to play.

Gianquinto knew many of the musicians from high school. A one-time major league baseball prospect, he went to Chicago to play blues and landed a spot in the James Cotton Blues Band. He recorded and toured with the former Muddy Waters sideman for a couple of years before returning to San Francisco to teach and play. He was a brilliant musician, capable of intense, ringing flurries or graceful, light grooves. He brought a restless creativity and a troubled spirit to the band. He contributed a key composition to the new album, "Incident at Neshubur."

But Gianquinto had one major drawback. He was a hardcore junkie. He had been shooting heroin for years. And he moved in with bassist Brown and the band's management team, Marcum and Estrada.

Three weeks after Bill Graham's former right-hand man, Paul Baratta, left his employ, he announced he would be producing concerts of his own, right under Graham's nose, at Winterland, two blocks from the original Fillmore. Graham, still facing imminent eviction at Fillmore West, thought he had the inside track on landing the rights to mount shows at the 5400-seat ice rink. He had used the larger arena on occasion over the years to accommodate larger attractions and held a right of first refusal on all concerts in the building.

But building owners asked Graham to sign a lease guaranteeing sixty thousand dollars in rentals a year and he refused to sign, thinking nobody would dare compete with him anyway. The owners decided to hire Baratta and promote shows on their own. He immediately lined up an appearance by The Doors for the first weekend in February. With Howard Johnson's expecting to put Fillmore West under the wrecker's ball the next month, the pressure on Graham mounted.

The Fillmore Records and San Francisco Records labels made their bows in October, with Elvin Bishop and Aum releasing albums on Fillmore (distributed by Columbia Records) and Cold Blood on the San Francisco label (distributed by Atlantic Records). Boasting a petite lead vocalist with a big voice named Lydia Pense, Cold Blood experimented with the white soul band sound that Joplin was trying with her Kozmic Blues Band. The band had already signed with Atlantic, but came to Graham's label as part of the distribution deal. Producer David Rubinson found the musicians problematic, but coaxed a credible performance out of the group. A single of the old Stax/Volt tune "You Got Me Hummin' " even dented the charts when it was released in January.

Rubinson also produced a folky album with a green-eyed Judy Collins clone named Victoria and signed a bad-ass East Bay white soul band called Tower of Power. He looked hard for talent. A rock band from New Jersey passed through town and earned a glowing notice from a reviewer for the afternoon daily. Rubinson grabbed the group before the band left town and cut an unimpressive demo with Steel Mill featuring a young vocalist named Bruce Springsteen. But Graham's entrance into the record field was anything but impressive.

His wife moved into her own apartment with their son in February, obviously preparing to file for divorce. LaChambre, his teenage mistress, was still very much in the picture, two suicide attempts, one abortion and many thousand dollars later. After one fight, she demanded he deliver a large amount of cash or she would go public with their secrets. The money was delivered. She took a cab to Sausalito, bought a bunch of clothes and threw the rest of the money in the water. He sent her home from New York once after discovering her in her hotel room with a rock singer. He assured his young love he and his wife had broken up. But she would check up on him and find evidence to the contrary, invariably leading to a screaming match. Graham could not shake himself loose of this destructive relationship.

But he moved decisively on the Winterland affair. Graham went to Baratta with his most ingratiating face. He told Baratta he thought parting company had been a mistake, that he had undervalued his closest associate. He dangled his new Los Angeles operation in front of Baratta. Graham had recently taken a lease on an old wrestling arena in Los Angeles called the Shrine Auditorium and thrown a New Year's Eve show under the name Shady Productions, but had not committed to a regular operation. "I need a quarterback," he told Baratta.

Baratta accepted the position. Then Graham mentioned the upcoming Doors concert at Winterland, almost as an afterthought. Suddenly Baratta understood the whole Los Angeles gambit had been another Graham subterfuge to get rid of competition, in this case, himself. But he agreed to allow the Doors show to go under the banner of "Bill Graham Presents." By March, Baratta had relocated to Los Angeles to run the Shrine.

SPRING 1970

Going to Rio for Carnival in February was a last-ditch effort by Janis Joplin to kick heroin once and for all. She confided in her New York endocrinologist that she had had six overdoses since she started shooting smack. He prescribed another round of dolophine and recommended a psychiatrist in San Francisco. She went.

On the Brazil trip, she took roommate Linda Gravenites, who hated Joplin's using drugs. At the airport, Joplin handed a substantial stash to Peggy Caserta and flew off empty-handed. In Rio, she and Gravenites prowled the streets and the balls, even gaining entrance to the coveted Municipal Ball. She and Gravenites took an oceanside suite and joined the samba line that coursed through the heat of Rio night and day during the annual revelry.

On the beach, Joplin was wearing a whimsical white bikini with strategically placed blue handprints when she met David Niehaus. A large, burly dropout and former Peace Corps volunteer who was vagabonding around the world, Niehaus and his traveling companion moved into Joplin's lavish digs. She kicked drugs and fell in love. The romantic idyll was interrupted only by a motorcycle crash in which she sustained a slight concussion that landed her in the hospital for a couple of days.

Although they were supposed to travel back to San Francisco together, Niehaus had problems with his papers that resulted in a two-day delay in his leaving Brazil. By the time he arrived in Larkspur, he barely recognized his traveling companion, her skin gray, her mood skittish. Plopped back into her rock queen life, shooting dope and making plans to put together a new band in time for a summer tour, she had little space left for Niehaus. He wanted to whisk her away on his world travels. She wanted him to go to work as her road manager. It wasn't working.

But when Niehaus, returning from a solo two-day ski trip, stumbled across Joplin and Peggy Caserta, entangled naked and stoned atop the fur rug on the bedroom floor, he knew the time to leave had come. He headed off to Asia.

Linda Gravenites also moved out, tired of the drugs, after a fight. In a sense, Gravenites was Joplin's final tie with her early days in San Francisco, a last link with a reality that was quickly ebbing from view. In Gravenites's place, Lyndall Erb, a more conventionally deferential rock star housekeeper, moved into the Larkspur house. Erb was not likely to challenge Joplin about her personal habits.

When Big Brother played the Family Dog in March, Joplin dropped by. Nobody really remembered her songs, so the onstage reunion turned into a loose jam. But when Bill Graham heard about the impromptu event, he wanted to restage the spontaneity the following weekend at the Fillmore West. With some rehearsal under their belts, Joplin and Big Brother were able to reprise the old repertoire, along with a new song, "Ego Rock," she sang as a duet with the current Big Brother vocalist, Nick Gravenites.

Joplin threw herself into work. She went to Los Angeles in March and cut a quick piece with the Paul Butterfield Blues Band, with another young Grossman protégé named Todd Rundgren producing. With the polished horn sound of the enlarged Butterfield unit and Paul's own piping harmonica, Joplin romped through "One Night Stand," a role reversal take on the old love 'em and leave 'em theme, but nothing further came of the session and the tape just sat on a shelf somewhere.

She went about assembling her own new backup group, which

she called the Full Tilt Boogie Band, with Grossman at her side. She kept guitarist John Till and bassist Brad Campbell from the Kozmic Blues Band and drafted another Ronnie Hawkins alumnus, pianist Richard Bell. She found organist Ken Pearson on a Jesse Winchester record and drummer Clark Pierson playing with saxophonist Snooky Flowers from the Kozmic Blues Band at a topless club on Broadway.

When Bobby Neuwirth showed up in town with songwriter Kris Kristofferson in tow, on a crazed impulse born at a cocktail party in Manhattan, Joplin and the two went on a wild three-week tequila run. Joplin woke her house guests with piña coladas and kept the booze flowing until they crashed, exhausted, late every evening, only to start the whole routine again the next morning. She developed a mad crush on the handsome Rhodes scholar with the soft drawl and didn't want to let Kristofferson out of her sight. They careened through the night, sampling the wares of every bar in Marin County, culminating this insane tequila-drenched escapade with a mad bash in honor of Michael J. Pollard at her Larkspur place.

With preparations beginning early in the day, hours before the party started everyone at her house was already bombed. By eight in the evening, the place was packed with people. Lyle Tuttle, whose well-publicized tattooed torso served as the chief advertisement for his North Beach tattoo parlor, stitched tattoos on anyone who wanted them, getting progressively drunker and a little less steady as the evening wore on. Lyndall Erb opened her bedroom door to discover strangers making love on her bed. Guitarist John Till hid out in the woods, sick from a combination of liquor and codeine pills. Kristofferson passed out in a car parked outside. By dawn, the party finally dissipated.

For a shakedown performance by her new band, Joplin topped a benefit for the Hell's Angels at a Marin County ballroom called Pepperland. Grossman flew out for the show. Opening the evening was Loose Gravel, the new band fronted by Mike Wilhelm of the Charlatans. Wilhelm was surprised when he saw Joplin, sloppy drunk, talking loud and looking disheveled and disorderly. Her complexion was blotchy, her face doughy. The atmosphere crackled with strange vibes. Grossman sat in the dressing room, silent, nervously knitting his fingers together, obviously wishing he were somewhere else. Drunken Angels had the run of the place, even hovering over the musicians onstage as they played.

During the Big Brother performance, Gravenites tried to ignore the couple that climbed up onstage, stripped off their clothes and went at each other like dogs in heat. But he had to step over them to get to the microphone. A crowd from backstage gathered to watch the sex act from the wings, including Michael Pollard and Joplin, who was swigging from a bottle she kept in her purse. Terrified of getting dosed, she always made a habit of keeping her own bottle and not sharing. So when a Hell's Angel standing beside her asked for a drink, she curtly refused. When he insisted, she simply snapped. "Fuck you," she said.

He grabbed her bottle and began beating her over the head. One of his fellow bikers stopped him before he could do any permanant damage to the star of the show, but he had already knocked her cold. Later, when she asked Michael Pollard in his motel room how the show was, admitting she couldn't remember anything, she broke down and cried, even though he assured her she had been fine.

Meanwhile, at the Trident in Sausalito, Neuwirth, Kristofferson and John Cooke ran across Peggy Caserta and her live-in love, who also happened to be an old friend of Cooke's. Many drinks later and lines of cocaine were spread across the table. Caserta took off with Kristofferson for the Stinson Beach summer home she and her girlfriend owned. The others followed, stopping at a liquor store on the way. By the time the second car negotiated the treacherous twisting road over Mount Tamalpais, Caserta had Kristofferson in bed and, no sooner did she finish, than her girlfriend climbed in the loft. "My turn now," she said.

After she finished with him, she got up to go to the bathroom, but in a drunken haze, took a wrong turn and walked off the back deck, falling into a tree and breaking a couple of ribs. The party ended with a trip to the hospital and Cooke never made it to Pepperland that night.

David Freiberg looked down in the front row at Fillmore East and there was Girl Freiberg. He hadn't laid eyes on his errant wife for about six months, ever since she split town with a roadie from an English rock group. From time to time, being a wife and mother just no longer appealed to the young ex-runaway and off she would go. Of course, Freiberg himself didn't act all that married, but when he saw her fresh face staring back at him from the audience that night in April, he knew how much he had missed her.

The idea of going to Hawaii without the so-called old ladies didn't particularly appeal to Freiberg at the moment. With Girl back in town for the first time in months, he voted against the idea of going to the islands to make the next record. Of course, he was the only one in the band to vote against the plan.

Quicksilver had spent virtually the entire previous year coming up with a mediocre album. But with Duncan and Valente on board, the band lacked neither motivation nor material. Valente thought up the Hawaii trip. With Duncan as his constant ally, the domineering Valente found himself in a position to command the group. Valente ordered Freiberg, for instance, to stop playing softball as a member of the Dead's team. He was the songwriter and the singer. He was the man with the plan. Now he was in charge.

Opaelua Lodge sat high on a remote mountaintop on the north end of Oahu, overlooking Pearl Harbor. Built entirely from Eureka redwood, the former sugarcane plantation looked like something out of the antebellum south, complete with gas lights and seven miles of dirt road leading to the place.

During the Second World War, the military had built multileveled subterranean bunkers under the lodge to house radio equipment, some as far as a hundred feet down, rooms as big as a small house connected by steel ladders. Dan Healy, the band's old neighbor, had been prospering as an engineer for Mercury Records, working with acts like the Sir Douglas Quintet, Blue Cheer and Mother Earth. Healy built a portable recording studio for the band, which he set up and thoroughly tested before crating it up and putting the works aboard a freighter headed for Hawaii.

He reconstructed the studio that May in the enormous living room of Opaelua Lodge. Local carpenters partitioned off the dining room and built a drum booth. The bunkers served as echo chambers. Generators were installed because the lodge did not have any electricity. Three weeks were spent just supplying power to the enclave. And the power plant had to be moved into the bunkers because the noise was too loud. An exhaust pipe ran out of a gun slit. When a piston broke and spewed burning oil out of the exhaust pipe, the sugarcane field caught fire and a natural disaster was barely averted as they managed to beat out the fire. Since there was also no telephone, a two-way radio system was rigged to connect with a friendly local, who patched through outgoing calls. Expenses mounted rapidly.

Teepees were erected on the front lawn. Band members collected women like scalps, sometimes installing one girlfriend of the moment in the house and another in a teepee. Regular forays were made into town to jam at a nightclub called the Red Noodle and replenish the supply. Before long, the musicians began competing among themselves over women and bickering.

Back in Marin, three wives waited to be summoned. When the band left, the wives were told they would be joining their husbands in a couple of weeks. Finally tired of waiting for an invitation that never came, the three women elected Shelley Duncan to go to Hawaii and check up. She took a flight with Big Brother and the Holding Company, who were headed over to play the Diamond Head Crater in June with the Grateful Dead and Quicksilver. Her husband was furious. He stuck her in a hotel and sent her back on a plane the next day.

The tension proved unbearable for Nicky Hopkins, a church mouse of a fellow who couldn't deal with all the heavy-handed machinations emanating from Valente. He told the group he would stay and finish the album, but he would be leaving Quicksilver as soon as the band returned stateside. Valente didn't mind. He wanted to get rid of Cipollina and Freiberg, too.

Although Healy trapped a lot of material on tape, practically enough for two albums, the sessions did not run all that smoothly. Valente grew more overbearing, more demanding. If he couldn't make his point arguing, he would simply grab the person he was talking to and shake. Plenty of drugs helped fuel aggressive behavior. Ugly scenes were commonplace. He started brandishing guns. He could easily intimidate easygoing characters like Freiberg or Cipollina. Healy exploded at one of Valente's gun-waving incidents.

Duncan also liked to shoot pistols. Much time was spent recording the sound of a gun fired over the canyon. Polte took offense at all the gunplay in the middle of this paradise. Gunplay, after all, was where he came in. He was tired of the lack of sleep, worn down by the constant friction and tension. But the guns were the end. When the band finished recording after two months in the islands and returned home, Polte quit.

SUMMER 1970

Grace Slick discovered she was pregnant while the Airplane was in England that June appearing at the Bath Festival. In her deliberate way, Slick had decided to have a baby with Paul Kantner. She thought it over a good deal. The combination of two such opposite personalities intrigued her and, once she decided, Slick didn't ask, but simply informed Kantner of her plan.

She left her apartment in Sausalito that spring and moved into the big house. She maintained a room separate from Kantner's, on a different floor even, but they had become very much a couple, more or less monogamous.

Slick had caused a stir that April when she showed up for an afternoon tea at the White House for alumni of Finch College hosted by Tricia Nixon with freak-o radical Abbie Hoffman as her escort. She had met Hoffman at an Airplane concert several months earlier. He and his wife, Slick and Kantner had spent a hilarious afternoon together touring the battlefield at Gettysburg. When the invitation to the White House tea arrived, Slick knew immediately who to invite to go with her.

She dressed for the event in leather boots and jacket, purple midi-skirt and see-through black crochet top with pockets over the breasts. Hoffman, his hair cut short from a recent stint in Cook County jail for the trial of the Chicago Seven, wore a suit and tie, his hair greased down. Slick filled her right-hand pocket with powdered LSD. She wanted to dose President Nixon.

They were met at the gate by security police and one of the Finch alumni organizers. She introduced Hoffman as her bodyguard. "I never go anywhere without my bodyguard," she explained.

"This is the White House," the Finch organizer told Slick, "and I assure you they have very good security."

"I wouldn't let Miss Slick go in there alone," interjected Hoffman. "They lose a President every three years. It's a dangerous place." Nevertheless, they were not admitted.

Slick wasn't the only member of the Airplane family to intentionally get pregnant that spring. When Melissa Cargill, Jack Casady's live-in lover for the past few years, asked Casady to father a child with her, he declined. The responsibility of fatherhood just didn't appeal to him. But when he returned from tour, Cargill informed him she had gone ahead and become pregnant anyway. He just wasn't the father. Cargill told him she had gone to her previous paramour, Owsley Stanley, who did not share Casady's reluctance. After some initial resistance, Casady came to accept the bizarre scheme and agreed to act in every way, except biologically, as the father.

The Airplane continued to only tour intermittently. With both *Volunteers* and a greatest-hits collection titled *The Worst of the Jefferson Airplane* released the previous winter and still selling strongly, nobody was rushing into the studio to record another Airplane album. Kantner even took the time to start recording a solo album, using half the Airplane, half the Grateful Dead, Freiberg from Quicksilver, Graham Nash and David Crosby. He called the group working on his science-fiction song cycle Jefferson Starship.

The relaxed schedule only drove Casady and Jorma Kaukonen stir-crazy. By March, when the live album recorded the year before with the two musicians and harmonica player Will Scarlett relaxing in a folk vein was finally released, the Kaukonen-Casady ensemble, Hot Tuna, had undergone substantial changes.

To begin with, the group was now an electric rock band. The new Airplane drummer, Joey Covington, had been playing with Tuna for many months. Different second guitarists passed through the ranks, including Kaukonen's younger brother, Peter Kaukonen, who returned from living in Los Angeles in time to join the electric Tuna. With the promise of an additional twenty thousand dollars by RCA Victor Records, Tuna also convinced Marty Balin to sign up.

Hot Tuna worked local clubs around the Bay Area when the Airplane wasn't touring and opened for the Airplane when the band did go on the road. Under the stimulating influence of whopping doses of pharmacopoeia, the musicians would play until the joints in their fingers stiffened. Snorting the contents of a couple of amphetamine capsules familiarly known as Black Beauties could keep anyone awake for days, with energy to spare. Sometimes Balin would just drop by, sing a few songs and leave, knowing that Kaukonen and Casady could go on forever, braiding together instrumental lines in endless extemporaneous inventions. It was a drive to play, an almost compulsive need for self-expression unfulfilled by the relatively restrictive confines of the Airplane.

Plans called for the next Hot Tuna album to be recorded in Jamaica. Swimming in crystal-clear waters, enjoying the tropical sun in a small village outside Kingston, the musicians couldn't quite work up enough harmony to make a record. Kaukonen and Balin barely spoke. Kaukonen complained to RCA over the phone that Balin was the problem because he wouldn't work. Balin wanted to rehearse, but could only convince the rest of the band to hold one rehearsal. He was also angry when he found out about the extra twenty thousand paid for his participation. He thought that might be his money or, at least, that he could have been told about the bonus.

He retreated into a haze of 151 rum and ganga smoke. He was having a great time hanging out with the villagers. The other band members scoffed at his efforts to befriend the locals, but they changed their tune when Balin copped some outrageous Jamaican grass through his newfound associations.

The band did play a couple of nights at an Ochos Rios nightclub and heard about an amazing Rastafarian drummer who lived in the hills. Before they could locate the Jamaican percussionist, however, police arrested one of the traveling party, a drug dealer friend of Kaukonen's who came along to hold the stash. Suddenly, Jamaica turned a little too hot for the Tuna and the band split the scene without having spun an inch of tape.

Somewhere during the spring Janis Joplin invented "Pearl," her slatternly, drunken alter ego, a party girl awash in beads and jangly bracelets with a ready line of jive, a fuck-anything, drink-it-all, rock and roll babe. She dubbed Peggy Caserta "Ruby." As Joplin sank deeper and deeper into a morass of alcohol, the image appealed to her. Adrift in a golden tequila haze, Joplin grew increasingly needy. Public spectacles, indiscriminate sex, unbridled tirades, her behavior betrayed a nagging insecurity and her growing reliance on the trappings of her stardom surprised and put off a lot of her older friends.

Pearl took over the Joplin stage persona that summer once she started touring with the Full Tilt Boogie Band, as she named her new aggregation. After a round of warm-up dates in Florida that June, she pulled into Louisville, where she drew a modest crowd of four thousand in the cavernous confines of Freedom Hall. She felt the chilly air of repression just glancing out in the audience from behind the stage curtains. "Shit, man," she said, "why do those country club chicks with the panty girdles always have to be sitting in the front rows? They are probably so tight, they couldn't move if they wanted to."

Once onstage, however, she instantly dug into her inciting-to-riot act. "Some dance hall you got here," she said, hand on hip. "You know, sometimes we go into a place and take a quick look around at the hall, a quick look at the dressing rooms, and a quick look at the audience, and we say, well, if we're going to have a party here, we're going to have to do it ourselves."

Someone in the audience shouted a request for "Try Just a Little Bit Harder" and Joplin blanched. "I beg your pardon," she said. "I'm doing my part, honey."

She turned up the heat under the audience with "Try," letting the Pearl character give the song a slightly tawdry context. "Honey, if you've had your eye on a piece of talent and that chick down the road has been getting all the action, then you know what you gotta do." Wham. The drum kicked the song to life and Joplin sang "Try-y-y-y-y, just a little bit harder."

She jumped off the stage into the front row, grabbed one pretty young boy, and pulled him to his feet to dance. He knew what to do. He reached out and grabbed her breasts. She loved it.

Before the performance ended, however, Joplin got what she wanted, kids rushing the stage, clogging the aisles, as rent-a-cops tried driving them back with their clubs and flashlights. "I permit them to dance," she yelled to one officer. "In fact, I demand it." The cop stalked away, shaking a fist at her as he went.

She took *Zelda*, the best-selling biography by Nancy Mitford, on the road with her that summer. The Fitzgeralds were a lasting passion for Joplin, whose life often assumed the proportions of a tragic heroine from a Fitzgerald novel. One passage of a letter from Fitzgerald to his wife during one of her stays in the hospital struck Joplin particularly and she frequently recited it: "They keep saying we destroyed each other, I don't think that's true. I think we destroyed ourselves."

Another key role model in Joplin's life was twenties blues queen Bessie Smith, who sang "gimme a pigfoot and a bottle of beer." She was a black flapper who died in a lonely highway accident and, when the *Philadelphia Inquirer* launched a campaign to put a headstone on the grave of Bessie Smith that July, Joplin pledged to pay half the cost (which turned out to be two hundred and fifty dollars).

At the end of June, Joplin joined a traveling troupe of more than one hundred and thirty rockers for a five-day train trip across Canada called the Festival Express. Along with the Grateful Dead and the New Riders of the Purple Sage, Joplin found herself ensconced with Delaney and Bonnie, Buddy Guy, Mountain, Eric Andersen, Tom Rush, Ian and Sylvia, Rick Danko of The Band and others. Rattling down the tracks through the desolate but beautiful north country, this band of merry men and women practiced nonstop drinking and song-swapping.

They drank the bar car dry and took up a collection to replenish the stock in Saskatoon. John Cooke plunked down some four hundred dollars at the liquor store and returned with a selection that included the biggest bottle of Canadian Club whiskey anybody ever saw. The frolic continued. For Delaney Bramlett's birthday, the Dead dosed the birthday cake.

Joplin participated more in the drinking than in the singing, but at one point she pulled out her Gibson Hummingbird and strummed a chord. "I only know one song, honey," she cackled, "but I'm going to sing it anyway." With Garcia laying some sweet licks behind her on his pedal steel guitar, Joplin belted out Kristofferson's "Me and Bobby McGee." The entire company joined voices on the chorus and the song instantly became the unofficial anthem of the Festival Express, sung at every conceivable juncture, as if the wistful ballad somehow summoned up the essence of this great experience.

The train ran from Toronto through some mighty remote outposts on its way to the final destination of Calgary. To these bejeweled hippies from San Francisco and Los Angeles, Saskatoon was as exotic as Outer Mongolia. The entire excursion proved to be such robust revelry, various alternatives to the trip ending were considered, from hijacking the train to San Francisco to a sit-down strike. Joplin and Eric Andersen simply sang the trip to a close with a duet of Hank Williams's "I'm So Lonesome I Could Cry."

"I promise never to drink again, Your Honor," mumbled Jerry Garcia in the morning light of the Calgary depot, as he made his exit. "How's my head? I need a lobotomy."

"I got the Dead drunk," announced Joplin proudly.

She paused in Seattle on her way home long enough to set off firecrackers at the Edgewater Inn on the Fourth of July. She canceled the third night of concerts in Hawaii to fly back to Austin and participate in an evening honoring Ken Threadgill, a nightclub owner who had fostered her career in its infancy. Around eight hundred people bought tickets for the occasion, but when word spread that Janis Joplin would attend, more than five thousand showed up at the Party Barn, a rambling building outside town on the way to Lake Travis.

A respectful Joplin, in her brief turn onstage, offered a version of "Me and Bobby McGee," telling the crowd the song's author was going to be famous, a comment she underscored by following that song with her rendition of another Kristofferson composition, "Sunday Morning Coming Down." When an old friend asked if she was happy with her position in life, she laughed. "I wrote the part," she said.

From Texas, she went straight to San Diego, where she played a concert with Big Brother and the Holding Company as opening act. Also attending the concert that night was Paul Rothchild, the record producer who had gone on to great success supervising records by The Doors since trying to convince Joplin to leave Big Brother four years before. Rothchild would be producing her next album, scheduled to start the following month in Los Angeles.

Joplin couldn't resist walking out into the audience, fluffed out in all her finery, during Big Brother's set, ostensibly to check out the band's show, but with the actual result of sending a murmur of recognition rippling through the crowd and upstaging her old pals. On the plane ride back to San Francisco, she sat next to James Gurley, who thought she seemed desperate for attention. She bought a round of drinks for the entire cabin, anxious, he thought, for everyone to know that Janis Joplin was aboard. She tried talking Gurley into leaving Big Brother, going to New York and joining her band. He declined. To Gurley, she seemed miserable, grasping at straws of happiness.

Bill Graham stormed past Herbie Herbert, Santana equipment manager, in his workshop into the rehearsal room where the band was diligently playing. Herbert heard the music stop, heard the shouting, but paid little heed. He was fixing some equipment and tending to business of his own when Gregg Rolie appeared over his shoulder. "Herbie, we've got a problem with Bill," he told Herbert. "There's been a band meeting and we've decided to go with Stan and Ron. Can you come and talk with Bill?"

In the rehearsal room, Graham was screaming, fit to be tied. "And I heard this from my secretary," he shouted. "MY SECRE-TARY." Herbert, a small mountain of a man, physically insinuated himself between Graham and the musicians. He stared into Graham's face and calmly began to explain the situation.

He told the raging promoter that the group had come to a decision. Stan Marcum and his partner, Ron Estrada, were old friends. They had been with the group from the beginning. The band would stay loyal to their friends. Graham could still be the promoter of the Santana concerts, but he shouldn't be greedy, Herbert told him. The band had no intention of paying out commissions to two managers.

Graham slunk away. Herbert and the musicians went back to their respective tasks. But the end had not been heard.

Since Graham started his talent management and booking agencies, he had operated under the delusion that he both booked and managed Santana. Under that assumption, he had begged the band onto the *Ed Sullivan Show,* bartered the group into Woodstock, hounded Columbia Records president Clive Davis until he allowed Santana to be included on the Atlantic Records movie soundtrack album, and generally promoted the cause in any way he could. His FM Productions acted as producers of the band's concerts throughout the country, not just San Francisco. Although no contract existed, he clearly thought he was the manager, his deal based on a handshake.

Nobody in the band took great pains to dissuade him, but also nobody for a minute thought of him as anything other than the band's booking agent and biggest booster.

Since the release of the Woodstock movie in April, Santana stock soared into the stratosphere. The sales of the debut album approached two million and the *Woodstock* soundtrack album streaked to the top of the charts when it was released in June. The band made a grand European tour during the summer, playing sold-out concerts in England, Denmark and Germany and culminating with a triumphant appearance at the Montreux Jazz Festival in Switzerland, where Chepito Areas made an impressive guest appearance with the Clark Terry big band and blues great Champion Jack Dupree cooked barbecue for the band. The outgoing Areas also shocked the band's astrologer, Dr. Stars, by standing at his hotel room window and waving his male member at female passersby. "Hey, baby," he shouted. "Come suck on this."

In London, the band attended a private screening of the rough cut of the Rolling Stones movie shot the previous December at Altamont. The musicians viewed the cinematic replay of the horrific events with all the fascination of watching a car crash in slow motion, an orchestrated version of the day leading to the inevitable, awful crescendo, but decided against allowing the Santana performance to be included.

Santana was an uneasy alliance of street and suburbs, an unsophisticated mix of young men who played hard music, used hard drugs and took eager advantage of the many available women. They were a pack of wolves. Cocaine blew through the band like a sandstorm. Conga player Michael Carabello never left for tour without at least an ounce in his luggage and the FM Productions representative who traveled with the group always carried a spare ounce or two in case somebody in the group ran out.

Heroin also invaded the band like a cancer, spreading from Alberto Gianquinto to managers Stan Marcum and Ron Estrada and bassist David Brown. Gianquinto, who lived with his black wife, Marcum, Estrada and Brown, associated himself with the militant Black Panther Party. He stockpiled guns at their house and convinced the band to perform at a Panther benefit at Berkeley Community Theater. Gianquinto toured with the band earlier in the year, his grand piano putting a high polish in the sound, but Rolie grew uncomfortable around the seedy piano player with all his dope and his low-life friends. He was just a little too authentic for Rolie.

As his own drug habit increased, Marcum became less available, not showing up at jobs or rehearsals. Before long, the band nicknamed him "Casper the Friendly Ghost" because he was seen so scarcely. With an accountant/business manager handling the actual income, dispensing cash virtually on a daily basis, and Graham's office sorting through the job offers that rained down on any act as hot as Santana, Marcum could keep the ball rolling with very little effort.

In August, Graham produced a concert with Santana, Miles Davis and the Voices of East Harlem at Tanglewood, the massive open-air facility in the Berkshires best known for classical performances. Graham stood on the side of the stage clanging a cowbell. The next day, Marcum phoned Graham in New York from San Francisco to tell him the band was quitting his agency. Graham went nuts. As soon as he returned to San Francisco, he made his way to the Paisley Penguin and confronted the band, only to be shown the door by Herbie Herbert.

Marcum opened his own office on the fourth floor of a poultry warehouse near the San Francisco waterfront. A sign mimicking the Coca-Cola symbol but reading "Cocaine" hung prominently on the office wall. Marcum rarely showed up for work until after dinner. Herbert arrived at the office once to find the receptionist dissolved in tears. He asked her what was wrong. "I'm too high," she said. "I've taken too much coke."

Don't take any more, Herbert suggested, stop doing it. "I can't," she sobbed. "The whole safe is full of it."

Marcum also changed lawyers, hiring Herb Resner, a respected older attorney who happened to be the father of the band's astrologer. Resner renegotiated the contract with Columbia Records and brought the band back a check for one million dollars in royalties. He went to meet with Graham at the request of attorney Bill Coblentz, a big wheel who served on civic commissions. An agitated Graham accused Resner of stealing Santana away from him and demanded some $650,000 in fees. Resner scoffed at the arrogant and uncouth promoter. "Are you calling me an animal?" Graham asked.

"I didn't use the word," replied Resner, "but if it fits . . ."

Before Resner could even finish his sentence, Graham leaped out of his chair and throttled Resner around the neck, emitting inarticulate grunts from his throat. A stunned Coblentz pulled Graham off. "Gentlemen, gentlemen," he said.

Chet Helms ran out of money. Almost five years to the day since he started throwing dances in the basement ballroom of 1090 Page Street, he decided to quit. He kept a roof over his head only through informal extracurricular activities, trading in the odd antique or harmless contraband. Grossly undercapitalized from the start, Helms could not afford to book any of the big names at the Family Dog that would draw large crowds and was forced to rely on the intermittent generosity of local bands capable of filling the room. He no longer represented any competition to Graham. Family Dog on the Great Highway clearly had run its course.

He canceled the insurance. He swept up the place and returned the keys. He owed considerable back rent, so he applied the security deposit to his bill. He closed the dancehall without regret or sadness, just a sense of relief.

But Ron Polte, whose brother continued to manage Quicksilver, and the manager of It's A Beautiful Day came to convince Helms not to quit. They saw his operation as the only remaining alternative to working for Graham and feared the leverage Graham would have once the Fillmore was truly the only game in town. They also knew that Helms offered an important stage for up-and-coming bands the scene could ill afford to lose. They appealed to Helms to try one more time, offering their bands as attractions. Flattered, Helms agreed.

The night of the It's A Beautiful Day show, Helms found himself trapped in Mill Valley with no phone. He felt fully confident that his staff would handle the show without any difficulty in his absence. But when the sound company hired for the evening called up and canceled a couple of hours before showtime, It's A Beautiful Day's manager showed up at the site to encounter a panic to find a last-minute sound system for the show.

He exploded and took control of the show. He dismissed the opening act, sent his crew across town to retrieve his band's sound system and set it up. He ordered Helms's staff to stand aside while his people ran the show. Without Helms on hand, his staff complied.

By the time Helms showed up at the ballroom, expecting to find a show in full swing, the room was dark and empty, the show long over. It's A Beautiful Day played one set early in the evening and the concert ended about two hours early. He walked into his office to speak sharply with the band's manager and saw lines of cocaine spread across the top of his desk. Helms hated coke. Since his youthful bout with methedrine, he had looked on all hard drugs as a scourge. He fell into a heated shouting match with the band's manager over the events of the evening, wiped the tiny piles of blow on the floor with one swipe of his hand and ordered the man out of his office.

Mortified, angry and betrayed, Helms immediately scrubbed the show scheduled for the following weekend by Quicksilver and closed Family Dog On the Great Highway forever.

FALL 1970

Little Richard stood up on the top of the grand piano, as the stage around him filled with dancers. He surveyed the insanity he had insti gated. Three numbers into his show and the Olympic Auditorium in Los Angeles was coming apart at the seams. He wanted more. He kept telling the crowd to come up. As many as two hundred people crowded up on the stage, alongside the band. Too many.

With a sudden crack, the stage split open in the center. All the instruments and people fell into the yawning hole. Richard was flung to the floor, catapulted like a toy from his perch atop the piano, as the band, the dancers, the equipment, all slid into one gigantic pile as if nothing less than the earth itself opened up and swallowed them whole.

The newspapers splashed the incident across their pages with gory, inflammatory headlines. Little Richard claimed serious injuries, broken bones, the works. But the truth was he was a little sore and nothing more. Only four people were hurt and nobody sustained any drastic damage.

But Paul Baratta knew this would signal the end of the Bill Graham incursion into Los Angeles. He already felt like he had been exiled to an outpost so far away, the mail didn't even arrive regularly. Police harassment troubled the shows from day one. The Los Angeles operation received, at best, cursory attention from headquarters. Baratta had been hung out on his own, flapping in the breeze.

Graham had suckered him; he should have known. He had seen Graham seethe over the slightest imagined threat, the flimsiest perceived competition. He had watched first-hand as Graham pitched turf wars with a ferocious intensity. He had heard Graham rant madly over the Carousel, the Avalon, even Helms's hapless Family Dog on the Great Highway. Of course, Graham had bought him off to keep him out of Winterland and shipped him down to Los Angeles to make sure he stayed out of the way. Graham had no real desire to battle existing local promoters in Southern California. He just wanted to get rid of Baratta.

When Graham hired Baratta back earlier in the year, after Baratta booked The Doors into Winterland, Graham checked the incipient threat by agreeing to guarantee the Winterland proprietors sixty thousand dollars annual rent. So certain was Graham that he had stopped any chance of real competition, he never paid.

Meanwhile, Graham started tying up the Berkeley Community Theater, a 3300-capacity reserved-seat high school auditorium across the bay. With ticket prices scaled from $3.50 to $5, he stood to take in almost as much money in two nights at Berkeley as he could in four nights at Fillmore West, with lower overhead. He had already run several successful shows at the hall and began trying to lock up all available dates through the middle of the next year. He reserved forty-six prime dates for the first half of the year. If he could control all the dates, whether he threw shows or not, no other promoter could use the facility unless Graham would be willing to relinquish his hold. For such a position of power, Graham was more than willing to pay whatever the modest cost in deposits and penalties.

From his emotionally charged pledge to close down his concert business in San Francisco and leave town less than a year before, Graham had moved into this aggressive position in the market. With Howard Johnson still unable to put together the deal to build on the site, the Fillmore West continued to operate under a stay of execution.

Graham even engaged in some discussion over purchasing the Orpheum Theater down the block from the Fillmore.

But the Winterland owners wanted their money. When Graham made it clear he did not intend to pay, they approached Baratta again. Graham closed down his operation in Los Angeles so fast, he failed to pay both Little Richard and support act Country Joe and the Fish for the final concert. Both acts took him to the union over the matter. He also refused to reimburse Baratta for expenses on his own credit card. The war was on. This time Baratta was out for blood.

Baratta found willing support immediately. With major booking agencies contending with Graham as a talent buyer in both San Francisco and New York, Baratta was frustrated at those echelons of the business. He booked the red-hot Elton John, only to have the agency back out at the last minute and give the act to Graham. Fierce bidding wars between the two drove up prices for touring attractions. Graham paid $12,500 for three nights of The Kinks at Fillmore West to take the band away from Winterland's $10,000 offer. But the local bands, the same ones who started the Carousel so they wouldn't have to work for Graham, were not susceptible to his tactics.

Baratta announced his first show would feature the Jefferson Airplane, Grateful Dead, Quicksilver Messenger Service and Hot Tuna on October 4 and 5 at Winterland.

Ruth Garcia ran her car off the road and, ironically, was taken to the emergency ward of S.F. General Hospital, where she had worked as a nurse for the past twenty years. She had only recently linked back up with her son, Jerry. His grandmother had essentially raised him, after his father died and his mother took over running the bar they owned. By the time she remarried, young Jerry Garcia was already a remote and diffident son. When he left high school to join the Army, he never looked back on his family. He didn't speak to his mother or older brother the Marine for years.

He brought Mountain Girl to the hospital to meet his battered and bruised mother, fighting for her life against the massive internal injuries she had sustained in the car crash. Older brother Clifford Garcia, who had also recently started a renewed relationship with his long-lost younger brother, sat vigil at the bedside, while Jerry Garcia ferried back and forth between his mother's hospital room and the recording studio.

The Dead began recording the follow-up to *Workingman's Dead* in September at Wally Heider Studios. FM stations across the country had jumped on "Uncle John's Band" and "Casey Jones" from *Workingman's* when it was released the previous May, and the band actually began to experience some popularity outside the LSD grapevine, an acceptance that threatened modest prosperity with the business end of the operation firmly in the hands of Jon McIntire after Lenny Hart disappeared. That summer the band experimented with a repertory program at the Fillmores on both coasts that presented acoustic and electric sets by the Dead proper sandwiched around a middle set by the New Riders of the Purple Sage.

The New Riders had evolved the previous summer, when Garcia bought a pedal steel guitar from a music store in Denver and started backing up John (Marmaduke) Dawson, another old associate from Palo Alto days. After an LSD revelation that spring, Dawson had decided to take a more serious whack at singing and songwriting and looked to Buck Owens and Merle Haggard for inspiration. Dawson played Wednesdays at a Menlo Park coffeehouse in their old neck of the woods and, with Garcia picking pedal steel behind him, they began to draw overflow crowds.

With another old Palo Alto running buddy, David Nelson, on guitar, Dawson and Garcia put together a band in the hayloft at Mickey Hart's ranch. Hart played drums and, at first, Dead lyricist Robert Hunter tried his hand at playing bass. Soundman Bob Matthews replaced Hunter, but Phil Lesh finally stepped in and filled the bass chair. That August, the band tested the waters with some shows at the Family Dog on the Great Highway, with a hippie honky-tonk repertoire that ranged from truck driving "Six Days on the Road" to a countrified "Honky-Tonk Woman."

Garcia's proficiency on the difficult instrument grew so rapidly that in October he recorded the brilliant steel part on "Teach Your Children" by Crosby, Stills, Nash and Young. But he was waking up early in the morning and playing for several hours each day before even leaving his bedroom.

Lesh stepped out of the New Riders and Dave Torbert, who played with guitarist Nelson in the New Delhi River Band, picked up the bass. This cozy ensemble joined the summer caravan, mixing musically with the Dead onstage and off. Dawson put his hand into writing "Friend of the Devil," a number the band slated for recording on the new album. Nelson picked mandolin with the band during the folksy, acoustic sets on the road that summer. After three months, the New Riders country mood rubbed off on the Dead, who had turned a corner with *Workingman's* and proceeded further down the same road with the next album.

Phil Lesh took the acoustic guitar David Crosby gave him to the hospital and played his father the music he wrote for the song that became "Box of Rain," the first lead vocal Lesh ever sang on a Grateful Dead record. As the band prepared to enter the studio and record, his father died.

Ruth Garcia was placed on a respirator. For Jerry Garcia and Mountain Girl, the ordeal was a period of intense suffering. They felt helpless and guilty. Mountain Girl, the mother of Ruth Garcia's baby granddaughter, felt horrible that they had never met before the accident. After lingering a couple of weeks, Ruth Garcia died and the Grateful Dead guitarist and his mate joined dozens of nurses for the funeral of the mother he barely knew. Then he went home and dove into work.

The pink cocaine was a little slushy and more difficult to sell than Seth Morgan liked. With more than a half-pound of the tainted load and seven thousand dollars of his money tied up, Morgan was anxious to move the goods. A trust-fund baby, descendant of banker J. Pierpont Morgan, taking courses at Cal Berkeley and trading drugs between New York and Berkeley, Morgan grew up in a Park Avenue apartment where the likes of T. S. Eliot and Robert Lowell used to visit his poet father. Sexual escapades got him thrown out of prep schools up and down the East Coast, before he finally wormed his way into Berkeley.

Morgan had a biker buddy who knew Lyndall Erb, the girl working as housekeeper for Janis Joplin. The two rode their Harleys over to the Larkspur house one afternoon late July, Morgan thinking that the rock queen might like to buy a little blow.

Although Joplin expressed no interest in the coke—"I don't use that shit," she told him, "makes me nervous"—the four of them headed out for a few rounds of drinks and dinner in a Mexican restaurant. Morgan, a cunning buccaneer with a kind of evil, sleazy charm, ended up flipping a bowl of guacamole in Joplin's lap and walking out on the meal. She followed him and an intense affair began. He moved into her Larkspur pad, his '41 Ford pickup truck parked outside, shortly after Joplin returned from her high school reunion in Port Arthur, Texas.

She flew from a blazing performance August 12 before forty thousand fans at Harvard Stadium to the tiny Texas coastal town where she grew up, taking a twin-engine commuter plane for the final leg into the Golden Triangle Airport that served the Port Arthur-Beaumont-Orange area. She hated the town, rarely visited and never performed there. Her recollections of her high school years as an ugly duckling beatnik amid the football and cheerleader crowd were far from nostalgic. She went to the Thomas Jefferson High School Class of '60 reunion to thumb her nose, to flaunt her celebrity at people she thought had spurned her and shunned her, a pain that time and fame would apparently not erase.

She took her trusty roustabouts, John Cooke, Bobby Neuwirth and the limousine driver they customarily used in New York, although no limousines were available for hire in Port Arthur. Her parents planned to leave town that weekend and evidently didn't feel their oldest daughter's first visit home in almost two years event enough to change their plans.

With blue and pink plumes in her hair, dressed in purple and white satin and velvet with gold embroidery, sandals and painted toenails, weighted down with bracelets and rings, she strolled, drink in hand, into the Petroleum Room of the Goodhue Hotel, a room set aside for Joplin to hold a pre-reunion press conference. In an almost mean-spirited way, she had managed to make the provincial high school reunion about her.

Asked what she had been doing since she left Port Arthur, Joplin set an immediate tone. "Ooooh, hangin' out," she said. "You know, just hangin' out. Tryin' to get laid, stay stoned—no, don't say that. That doesn't work in Port Arthur."

She milled around the cocktail party, shot a little pool downstairs and had a few more drinks. By the time the dinner portion of the evening was underway, Joplin was crocked. When it came time to hand out the joke awards, they gave her a tire, the mileage award for having come the furthest distance to attend the event. "What am I going to do with a fucking tire?" she said at the podium.

Before the dancing started, Joplin and her party made their exit, stopping at the hotel bar for further fortification before heading across town to catch Jerry Lee Lewis at a local nightspot. Joplin and entourage went backstage and she introduced her younger sister, Laura Joplin, to the ferret-eyed rock and roll immortal. In an even tone of voice, he remarked that the young woman might be good looking if she didn't try so hard to look like her sister. Janis Joplin hauled off and clipped Lewis on the side of his head. He didn't miss a beat. He fired right back, catching Joplin full in the face. The men with her closed ranks around Joplin and led her away. She wept uncontrollably. "Why did he have to do that?" she repeated.

By September, when she settled into the Landmark Hotel in Hollywood to record the new album, she and Seth Morgan had begun to talk seriously about marriage. Bright and literate, he could match wits with Joplin at her best. Depraved and decadent, he could keep pace with her on those counts, too. He had money of his own and, unlike David Niehaus, who shrank from her public persona, Morgan actually reveled in her fame. She was his cocksman's trophy. He was also an arrogant, willful man she could not bend to her bidding. Her chief complaint about their relationship was that she could not get him to spend as much time with her as she wanted.

He flew down to Los Angeles on weekends during the recording sessions. But during the week, Joplin renewed her acquaintance with Peggy Caserta, where matters were predictably dicey. Caserta, staying at a nearby Hollywood hotel with a new girlfriend, also still maintained her relationship with her live-in lover in San Francisco. Not coincidentally, Joplin also renewed her acquaintance with heroin.

Paul Rothchild, who was producing the album as an independent producer hired by Columbia Records, won the unprecedented concession of cutting the new Joplin album outside of Columbia's studios. At Sunset Sound, James Taylor was recording in the next room. The sessions were typically grueling, but Joplin found she could cope with the pressure and workload better on dope than booze. Rothchild was getting results.

With the Full Tilt Boogie Band functioning crisply and smartly behind her, Joplin stamped herself on a variety of hand-picked material. When she finally committed her version of "Me and Bobby McGee" to tape, she had transformed the wistful, melancholy song into a full-fledged personal statement, a gospely chant with a ringing chorus light-years removed from the standard issue Nashville reading Roger Miller gave the song. Rothchild also captured an impromptu performance by Joplin on guitar, singing a quavery piece of ephemera she and Bobby Neuwirth comped off a line from playwright Michael McClure: "Lord, won't you buy me a Mercedes Benz." All signs pointed toward the album's reigniting Joplin's sagging fortunes.

On Thursday, October 1, Joplin met with her attorney and executed a new will, splitting her estate equally between her parents and her brother and sister. Her previous will endowed only her younger brother. She left Lyndall Erb control of all her personal effects and home furnishings. She also looked over a prenuptial agreement she had asked her attorney to draw up for Seth Morgan to sign. Her current fantasy was to marry Morgan aboard a cruise ship bound for Mexico. She called San Francisco City Hall and inquired about marriage licenses.

On Saturday, the band laid down the instrumental track for the last song of the album, "Buried Alive in the Blues," a Nick Gravenites song custom-ordered for the album. Gravenites flew to Los Angeles to finish the composition during the sessions and Joplin approved the band take, planning to add her lead vocal the following day. She called Morgan in Larkspur, who was spending the evening snorting the pink with a few buddies around a spitting fire in Joplin's living room. Joplin wanted him to change his travel plans and fly down that night, rather than the next day. Morgan demurred. When she called back later, he had one of his friends tell her he had gone to the store. Joplin and the band adjourned, as was their custom, to Barney's Beanery for some postsession drinks, before returning to the Landmark.

Around one in the morning, she emerged from her room to ask the desk clerk for change from a five-dollar bill. She spent a few minutes chatting, got her Marlboros from the vending machine and went back to her room. The next evening, Morgan phoned John Cooke at the Landmark just before the road manager was to leave for the studio. Morgan couldn't locate Joplin at the hotel or the studio and, when Cooke saw her decorated Porsche still sitting in the parking lot, he went to the front desk for a passkey and investigated. They found her lying on the floor, in blouse and panties, her nose broken in the fall, the change from the five dollars clutched tightly in her fist.

The entire evening was bound to be weird from the start. Baratta's maiden promotion at the Winterland was set to be broadcast live in quadraphonic sound simultaneously on two different radio stations and televised in color on the San Francisco public television station. That did nothing to keep people away from the hall. Before showtime, Winterland was packed to capacity and some three thousand late-comers were sent away.

Although no mention was made of it, John Cipollina would be making his final appearances with Quicksilver. He, too, was through with the Dino Valente show. With his shoulder-length hair and signature piercing guitar sound that worked like a surgeon's scalpel inside the brain, Cipollina was the most obvious symbol of the band he had helped found. Too gentle to fight, too slow to scheme, he turned the band over to the Valente Duncan axis simply because they wanted it more than he did. He tagged along until the final work on the album was finished and then announced he was following Polte and Hopkins. He advised Freiberg to leave, too, and Freiberg said he probably would in a year or so.

For the Winterland concerts, Quicksilver brought along the five-piece horn section the band had been using in the studio to overdub some parts on the next album, the second of the two records recorded in Hawaii. The musicians huddled backstage to throw together some last-minute head arrangements for existing Quicksilver material and the resulting performance was something of an uptight mess.

Hot Tuna opened the show with a few numbers and introduced a tall, skinny, arthritic fifty-three-year-old black gentleman, looking even older than his years, who called himself Papa John Creach. Bent and stiff, he produced a violin and filled the air with screeching blues runs, simple melodic figures, meshing easily with the improvisations of the Kaukonen-Casady-Covington blues-rock trio. Covington had tripped across the veteran lounge musician playing on a cruise boat running between Los Angeles and Catalina and invited him to San Francisco to jam with Tuna.

The Dead was up and rolling when the word began to circulate backstage that Joplin was dead. The underground radio disk jockeys scurrying around backstage, providing intermission coverage of the event between acts, made idiotic comments. The television reporters were even worse. But this was how the news stumbled and tumbled out in San Francisco.

The members of Big Brother all gathered at Dave Getz's house. Photographer Bob Seideman, an old friend who took the notorious bare-breasted poster photo of Joplin, was also there. Nobody knew what to say.

No announcement was made from the stage at Winterland. The Airplane closed the evening, but when the band returned to perform again the following night, Marty Balin didn't come. He thought the band played horribly the night before. He was ashamed of the coked-up music and frazzled performances. Deeply depressed about Joplin's death, he didn't want to go to Winterland.

He sent a friend to tell manager Thompson that he would not be making it to the gig. Thompson drove over to his Mill Valley home, distraught, to convince Balin that the show must go on. Adamant, pissed off and tired, he brandished a knife at his onetime roommate. "Leave me alone," he snapped.

Thompson was convinced. Balin didn't think he had quit the band. But when nobody called to ask him about missing the show, he began to suspect the other musicians didn't care whether he ever sang with the band he built from his own imagination again. He never did.

Joplin left twenty-five hundred dollars in her will specifically for the purpose of throwing a party for her friends after her death. "The drinks are on Pearl" read the invitation, even though many of her friends had never before heard the recently adopted private nickname. Musicians from the Airplane, Dead and Quicksilver all joined Big Brother and the Holding Company at the Lion's Share in San Rafael. Hongo Ishi, the three-year-old son of James and Nancy Gurley, played drums with the band briefly. Gurley was living with Cheryl Littledeer and she had recently given him a baby son, Django, named after the Belgian gypsy guitarist.

Bill Graham used Joplin's wake as a ruse to get his secretary, Vicki Cunningham, to finally go out with him. The voluptuous blonde had gone to work for Graham almost two years earlier and, in all that time, she had deflected Graham's advances, suggestions and invitations. Cunningham was smitten with attorney Brian Rohan, who made her laugh like nobody ever had. But Rohan, deep in his cups, was in no condition to engage in any kind of involved personal relations. When Graham asked her to accompany him to the Joplin party, she couldn't resist. Of course, when he picked her up, he pleaded confusion. "It must have been last week," he said.

Since his wife, Bonnie, filed for divorce the previous May, Graham stopped all attempts to reconcile with her. He saw a therapist who recommended he end his relationship with young Diane

LaChambre, but he couldn't bring himself to cut it off with her. She was a beguiling temptation to Graham, who would ignore her phone calls one week and then spend the next weekend with her in the Santa Cruz Mountains, snorting cocaine, proclaiming his love.

LaChambre thought that once his wife moved out, she would have Graham to herself. But, instead, she found herself embroiled in an up/down, yes/no relationship even more than before. When she became pregnant, Graham told her firmly he didn't want the baby. Depressed and hurt, she underwent an abortion. But when she called him at home one night and Vicki Cunningham answered the phone, calmly informing the young woman that she and Graham had been seeing each other for some time, LaChambre flew into a jealous rage.

She stormed into Graham's office the next day, pushed her way past Cunningham, screaming at Graham. She clawed at his face and kicked at his legs, as he pushed her down on the floor, sitting on top of her, slapping her and pulling off his belt to restrain her flailing hands. He yelled at Cunningham to stay out of his office and she closed the door. In a few minutes, the door burst open and a crying LaChambre dashed out of the office.

His personal problems rarely gave him pause. Work suffused his life so totally, very little room remained for any other considerations. His battle with Baratta, the former aide-de-camp turned warring general, consumed him. When Baratta announced a show starring the Dave Mason/Mama Cass band, Graham went on the warpath. With Mason hot off a smash debut solo album following his on-again, off-again stint with Traffic, his collaboration with the former star of the Mamas and Papas was expected to be one of the big attractions of the coming months. Graham used his not inconsiderable charm, power and intimidation tactics to win the act away from Baratta to no avail. The larger capacity of Winterland carried the day.

At the last moment, however, Mason and Mama Cass decided they weren't ready to go public with their act and postponed, leaving Baratta to frantically fill with a decidedly less attractive bill: Four Tops, Bread, Merry Clayton and Joy of Cooking. But shows featuring Ike and Tina Turner and Steve Miller both came off. His large rear projection screen gave the light shows the broadest canvas yet to be found in Bay Area concerts. He met in New York with the powerful agent Frank Barsalona, who represented many of the top English rockers, and left under the impression Barsalona would work with the

San Francisco promoter who would pay his acts the largest fee. Somehow Baratta never managed to land any of his acts regardless of his bids. In December, he drew a full house to see Sly and the Family Stone. But behind his back, the Winterland owners had already decided to do business with Graham.

The beleaguered Graham flew to the Winterland corporate headquarters in Minneapolis to negotiate Baratta out of business. He agreed to pay a stiff annual rent of $100,000 against ten percent of his gross proceeds. The hall owners, leery of bankrolling Baratta against Graham any further, opted to take Graham's money. While Baratta had failed to garner any big scores following his opening weekend, he had dates on the books upcoming with the Grateful Dead, Steppenwolf and Mason-Cass. His shows definitely cut into Graham's business at Fillmore West and the bidding wars made it more expensive for Graham to operate, since he was going up against a promoter with a hall more than twice the size of his ballroom. He was pouring money into the battle and paying the large annual rent to the Winterland landlords began to look like the cheap way out.

Graham couldn't seem to succeed on any of the other fronts he tried. His management company lost Santana, the one potential paydirt strike the operation was mining. He chiseled money out of other clients like bluesman Taj Mahal, who complained that Graham collected double commissions, a percentage as manager and a separate percentage for his booking agency.

His record labels failed to launch. The three partners—Graham, Rubinson and Rohan—couldn't get along. Rohan delighted in egging on the other two in fights. Although Cold Blood and Tower of Power both qualified as exciting new acts, the labels couldn't seem to find interesting talent with which to make records.

Rubinson's assistants, Jeffrey Cohen and Bruce Good, caught Rod Stewart and the Small Faces at the Fillmore West one night that May and brought the Cockney vocalist across the street to the Fillmore headquarters to play him songs. The singer had only a short time remaining on his solo recording contract with Mercury Records and after several hours, he allowed that if the company could put up forty thousand dollars in advance, he would sign with the Fillmore family. Cohen and Good were beside themselves at the prospect. They woke Rubinson up on the phone at two in the morning with the news, but he responded with surprising coolness. In the morning, he told them he didn't think Stewart would be worth the money.

After putting out new, undistinguished releases by a street singer named David Lannan and a nondescript hard-rock band called Hammer, Graham scaled back the operation, cutting studio hours and trying to slow the hemorrhaging cash flow.

When the door opened to Wally Heider Studio that November and in walked Eric Clapton, along with the other members of his current group, Derek and the Dominoes, fifteen-year-old Neal Schon practically went into shock. Only a few weeks before, he was playing with some nowhere band in a small peninsula club and now he was in a room with his idol, arguably the top guitar in the rock world.

But his life had changed rapidly after the night that summer that Gregg Rolie and Michael Shrieve wandered into the Poppycock in Palo Alto and caught the hot-rodding teenage guitar player. They closed the club down that night and jammed until dawn. Rolie picked him up at his parents' house a day later and drove him to the studio, where Santana was putting finishing touches on a second album. He missed school that day. Before long, he forgot about high school altogether.

He spent hours in an adjacent studio, wailing away, while Santana recorded. He played with the band in after-hours sessions, lights low, joints glowing, with the musicians just blowing out the circuitry after long, nerve-racking hours of the scrupulous work of recording. Word began to get around town about the teen guitar phenom.

He jammed with the Elvin Bishop Group at Keystone Korner in North Beach, where the guys from Aum caught him and invited Schon to play with them. Bishop took him to the Fillmore West, where they both swapped licks with B.B. King during his set—all heady stuff for a shy, gawky adolescent.

Clapton brought his band to Heider's to check out Santana. Before long, an epic jam session was underway. With a guitar in his hands, Schon was anything but shy. His molten blues licks oozed, trickled and sputtered. All through the night, Derek and the Dominoes and Santana played the blues and Schon was in the thick of the action every step of the way. The following night, Clapton invited Schon to the Dominoes concert at the Berkeley Community Theater and brought him out onstage to play the encore. After the show, Clapton asked Schon to join the band.

He didn't want to move to London. He had never even left San Mateo for longer than overnight. He told his friends in Santana about Clapton's offer. While some members of the band had already been pressing for Schon to be included in the lineup, Carlos Santana had made it clear he didn't want a second guitarist in the band. But with Clapton trying to whisk young Schon off to England, his reservations were swept aside in the consideration. The musicians voted Schon into Santana the next day.

Now thoroughly in command of Quicksilver, Dino Valente decreed a Hawaiian vacation for the entire group. This time, the women would come along. With Cipollina, Hopkins and Polte out of the picture, he pretty much could have his way with the group. Valente told equipment manager George Bonney to stow the handguns—two snub nose .38s, a .45 automatic and .357 magnum—and ammunition with the equipment.

He packed up everything just right, except for the bullets to the last gun. Those he forgot about and left in his pocket. At the San Francisco Airport, while the rest of the group boarded the flight, Bonney, who always claimed to be a distant relative of Billy the Kid, remembered the bullets and excused himself to the bathroom, planning to empty his pockets. But when he saw the gate closing, he changed his mind and rushed to get onboard, setting off the metal detector.

Instead of remaining calm, backtracking and losing the evidence, Bonney panicked. He reached into his pocket to grab an ounce of grass. While bystanders and airport personnel watching hit the deck, assuming he was pulling out a gun, he took off running. As he dashed through the terminal, he unwrapped the Baggie and waved it over his head, letting the pot spill out behind him.

Inside the cabin, the band and their ladies settled into their seats, entirely unaware of the commotion Bonney had set off outside the gate, until security officers boarded the flight and escorted the whole traveling party off the plane. Bonney was under arrest. Marshals found eight .38 bullets in his pocket and an additional fifty rifle bullets in his handbag.

The band members and their families were lined up beside their luggage and each told to stand next to his bag while police opened and searched every one. When the search turned up more grass in David Freiberg's bag, the cops placed him, too, in custody. Freiberg faced his third conviction on pot charges. "Don't bust my daddy," said three-year-old Jessica Freiberg.

The band did manage to get to Hawaii a couple of weeks later, after Freiberg and Bonney were arraigned, settling on the relatively unspoiled island of Kauai. Valente and Girl Freiberg tangled. He was openly critical of her bold and independent ways and she thought he was a domineering pig. When Valente threw a fit of temper over some small matter and insisted the band pack up and leave immediately, nobody budged, less out of open resistance than fatigue and sheer shock. He drove off in a huff. But when he returned several hours later, still ranting and demanding everybody split, the party was over. Everybody packed up and went home.

1971

*Please don't take it
the wrong way, but in
the year 1971, that's
a very stupid question.*
— Bill Graham, at the
press conference
announcing the closing
of the Fillmores, asked
if he thought the
"drug scene" influenced
today's teens

WINTER 1970-71

Dr. Stars, the astrologer, accompanied Santana to Hawaii for the New Year's Day show at the Crater Festival. The band had played the first festival in the bowl of the Diamond Head crater the year before. But this year, Santana and company stayed at a sumptuous beachfront compound called the Otani mansion, a huge main house surrounded by bungalows, tropical gardens, swimming pool, tennis court and a rock wall at the edge of the beach.

The Crater Festival would be the first full concert with Neal Schon as a member of Santana. Spirits were upbeat in the band. Some members conspired to kidnap Jose Feliciano from his hotel—his wife, perhaps wisely, wouldn't allow him to leave—and they jammed into the night.

The trip was as much a party as it was a concert appearance. Dr. Stars found the bathroom stocked with a bowl full of cocaine. In fact, the band attended a luau thrown in the group's honor and practically nobody ate because of copious doses of the powerful appetite suppressant.

When one of the sidemen hired to augment the band on this trip turned up at the luau with a local lovely and slipped into one of the cabanas with her, Dr. Stars joined the gathering throng that followed the couple and watched the conga player pump himself into the young lady. As the mood shifted to something more threatening than whimsical, the astrologer, who didn't fancy participating in gang rape, quietly withdrew.

But such scenes were not without precedent among this gang of street kids turned rock stars. Road manager Herbie Herbert procured a willing victim the year before, right out from under the nose of Pigpen of the Dead, at the Miami Pop Festival. Because she had won an award as outstanding employee at the Burger King outlet where she worked in her native Buffalo, the band gave her the nickname of the Burger Queen. She continued to show up from time to time and entertain the band, at one point taking on all comers, while Herbert manned a home movie camera, filming guitarist Carlos Santana finishing his turn at the young woman's favors and making way for the next.

Bassist David Brown was notorious among even this group of raunchy young males. Women found him especially attractive, a sweet and gentle black man, anatomically gifted. Almost the entire band snuck into his bedroom at the Hawaiian mansion one night to surreptitiously watch him work out with an especially beautiful, young Polynesian girl.

In February, Santana was holding rehearsals prior to a special trip to Africa and another series of European dates, and Chepito Areas didn't show up at the rehearsal hall or answer his phone. David Brown and Neal Schon were dispatched to his house to check out the situation. They found the percussionist lying in a pool of blood on his bedroom floor, unconscious but alive. He had apparently suffered an aneurysm the night before, his brain just bursting inside his head, which may or may not have had anything to do with all the cocaine.

He lay near death in Franklin Hospital. Last rites were performed. But with the crush of the impending dates, having a key member of the group lying in a coma put the band in a quandary. As was often the case in band decisions, Carabello and Santana butted heads over the issue. These two did not get along well, brusque, boisterous Carabello with his biker buddies and the secretive, psychedelic Mexican who kept to himself.

Santana and Rolie fought, too. Bad blood boiled through the

band. When the musicians stopped talking and started playing, Santana was a big, bad machine. Music came out as if somebody turned a crank. A few pops on the conga drum, a stuttering bass line and, crash, off they went. But other forms of communication between band members were more chancey.

Guitarist Santana was a guarded personality who tried to exert control through more devious ways. Shrieve and he walked to rehearsal at the Penguin one day and Santana told Shrieve some things he wanted the band to do. "You can't make them do that," Shrieve reminded him. "It's not your group."

"Not yet," said Santana.

A chill rippled through drummer Shrieve as he realized the guitarist had private plans. The drummer had naively believed the band was an equal partnership. Any such idealistic notions were crushed the instant he realized the band's namesake sported some hidden agenda.

But the group was finally convinced to go ahead and tour without Areas, the tiny timbales ace. Willie Bobo, the famous Latin percussionist and author of "Evil Ways," was contacted and he agreed to join the band for the tour, while Areas lay in a hospital, possibly a vegetable for the rest of his life. Doctors did not hazard a prognosis. He faced steep odds against his recovery. Meanwhile, someone broke into his apartment and stole his drums.

Santana joined Eddie Harris and Les McCann, Roberta Flack, the Voices of East Harlem, the Staple Singers, Ike and Tina Turner and Wilson Pickett on a bill mixed with local African performers March 6 before a crowd of 100,000 in Black Star Square, Accra, Ghana, celebrating the fourteenth anniversary of the country's independence. The concert, titled "Soul to Soul," was filmed for a theatrical feature and recorded for an album.

Bobo, veteran of Latin jazz groups led by Cal Tjader, hardly could have been prepared for the fast company of Santana. He fell painfully ill in Ghana with intestinal problems and, when medicine failed to help, Eddie Harris and Les McCann arranged for treatment from a tribal witch doctor. Bobo was able to perform at the gala concert, although musically he could never quite handle the big, sweeping groove of Santana. He entered a hospital as soon as the group arrived in London.

At the suggestion of Carlos Santana, San Francisco-based percussionist Coke Escovedo flew to London as an emergency replacement for Bobo. He was working with Tjader himself at the time, but the Santana band pushed a ten thousand dollar pile of cash in his lap and off he went. The concert at London's Hammersmith Odeon drew the cream of England's rock royalty, from Paul McCartney to Jimmy Page. Security, not recognizing him, sent Eric Clapton packing when he came backstage to pay respects.

At the Olympia Theater in Paris, Mick Jagger came backstage and found Michael Carabello. "Great set, Carlos," he said mistakenly, as the guitarist glowered in a corner. Jagger did love the band, though, and wanted Santana to stay around France long enough to play for his wedding. But the group wanted to go home.

Escovedo wasted no time in ingratiating himself with Carlos Santana. The guitarist always held himself slightly remote from the rest of the group. More than a matter of taste in drugs, language barriers or reluctance to join the rowdy street-corner banter people like Carabello kept up, Santana seemed to the other musicians naturally reserved, an insecure young man interested in little outside of music and women. Escovedo became his confidant. He insisted to Marcum that he and Santana share a room on the road, sat next to the guitarist at meals, always seemed to be at Santana's elbow.

With the baby due around the end of the year, Grace Slick and Paul Kantner moved out of 2400 Fulton Street around Thanksgiving into a place of their own in Bolinas, a remote spit of land on the ocean, about forty minutes north of San Francisco. From Kantner's top floor, octagonal bedroom in the Airplane house, they could see the tiny coastal enclave where they eventually found a rambling $100,000 ranch-style home with a swimming pool in the front yard, the Pacific Ocean in the backyard and a geodesic dome in the garden. Surrounded by redwood walls with video security cameras watching the front door, nursery and garage, Kantner and Slick retreated into this domestic sanctum, Slick decorating her new home, Kantner installing a sixteen-track studio in the basement. He even stopped using coke.

Balin had bailed out of the Airplane, but the others went through the motions of keeping up at least the pretense of the group. A great deal of money was at stake, although the musicians could barely stand one another. Kaukonen and Casady concentrated their efforts on Hot Tuna, with spry violinist Papa John Creach—called Uncle Tom Screech behind his back—now an official member and Texan drummer Sammy Piazza replacing Joey Covington, now that he served full-time with the Airplane. Casady, immersed in alcohol and cocaine, weighed an emaciated one hundred twenty-three pounds. Kaukonen was increasingly hostile and stubborn over group matters.

While manager Thompson entered into protracted negotiations over a new recording contract, potentially worth millions of dollars, the remaining Airplane members tried to pull a new album out of themselves. Sessions started before Balin left and he wrote three songs in the hopper to be recorded, now junked.

Essentially the band started over from the beginning in December, when a Hot Tuna/Santana jam produced a thirty-minute tape edited down to a three-minute ballad written and sung by drummer Covington, "Pretty As You Feel." Little Richard came in to add piano to another Covington number, "Bludgeon of a Bluecoat." He changed the key and tempo until it sounded like—what else?—a Little Richard number. Often the easiest way to get the group to record was for the musicians to come to the studio separately and overdub each individual part.

Meanwhile, Thompson passed on the offer by Ahmet Ertegun of Atlantic Records to buy the band Green Gulch Ranch, a sylvan glade on the slopes of Mount Tam, in favor of reworking an all-encompassing agreement with RCA Victor that would give the Airplane and the group's various spinoffs a record label all their own. After months of wrangling, RCA agreed to underwrite the operation in exchange for a solo album by Grace Slick, three solo albums by Paul Kantner, three albums by Hot Tuna and five albums by the Airplane, who were experiencing great difficulty simply finishing one more record together.

And, with his wife about to give birth to another man's child, Jerry Slick finally filed for divorce. On January 25, 1971, his ex-wife gave birth to a seven-pound daughter. Although there was some joking about naming the child god—the small *g* for humility—the birth certificate read China Wing Kantner.

SPRING 1971

Mickey Hart couldn't stand the shame any longer. Nine months after his father hightailed into parts unknown with who knows how much money belonging to the Dead, the drummer quit the band. He left during a series of shows in New York and went home. These had been dark days for Hart. Nobody in the band openly blamed him for Lenny Hart. They didn't have to. Mickey Hart blamed himself enough for everybody.

Increasingly depressed, occasionally suicidal, the drummer holed up at his ranch, frequently medicating himself for the pain. He spent time expanding his recording studio in the barn and running around with his portable Nagra recorder taping Indian classical musicians and other exotic music from the far corners of the world. The Dead hired private detective Hal Lipset to track Lenny Hart. He located the Sunshine account, a Nevada bank account Lenny Hart had opened where he transferred Dead funds without authorization. Lipset could never come up with an exact figure of how much money Lenny Hart embezzled, but more than $150,000 was found to be missing for sure.

Under the stewardship of manager Jon McIntire, the band prospered, relatively speaking. McIntire never managed to impose effective spending controls, but the band was developing a considerable following on the East Coast and concert fees had begun to escalate. Nevertheless, when Mountain Girl found a house to buy in Stinson Beach, Jerry Garcia did not have the ten thousand dollars he needed for down payment. He borrowed the money from Warner Brothers as an advance against a solo album, the only way he could devise to raise the necessary funds.

The Dead guitarist devoted his life to playing music. He could be a caring father to Mountain Girl's daughter, Sunshine, but when Mountain Girl wanted to have a second child, Garcia was not enthusiastic. Regardless, she went ahead and had Annabelle the previous year and, with two young children to raise, she bowed out of the Dead social scene. Moving to isolated Stinson Beach meant removing herself from any kind of casual contact with the crowd.

In April, during the band's third New York engagement already that year, the Dead recorded all five sold-out nights, Sunday through Thursday, at the Fillmore East. The second night Duane Allman played guitar for the first few songs of the second set, drawing blood with his cascading bottleneck solo on the blues, "It Hurts Me Too," trading solos with Garcia.

The next night, Bob Dylan came to hear the band and sat in the light show booth, where McIntire joined the illustrious guest. Midway through the band's second set, the Beach Boys climbed onstage and provided background vocals while Pigpen sang the Coasters oldie, "Searchin'." The two groups also collaborated on "Riot in Cell Block No. Nine," before the Dead handed over the stage and instruments to the other group from California.

McIntire ran into the entire band, rushing up the stairs to the light show booth to meet Dylan. He stopped Phil Lesh. "Why aren't you out there playing with them?" he asked.

"I want to watch the Beach Boys," said Lesh.

The Boys held forth for forty-five minutes—with and without the Dead, who returned to the stage and joined forces for an epic "Help Me Rhonda." Dylan was impressed. "Fuck, they're good," he said, before splitting after the light show flashed the word "Dylan" on the screen, imperiling his privacy.

The following night, Tom Constanten reunited briefly with his old comrades, pulling up the piano bench for "Dark Star." The final night of the engagement, the band kept playing into the night. When the exit doors opened to the Fillmore East after the final "We Bid You Goodnight," sunlight streamed in from the dawning skies.

Bill Graham called a press conference at the Fillmore East the next day with the surprising announcement he would close both the Fillmores. He set the final date for the Fillmore East at June 26 and said the Fillmore West might continue as long as August or September.

Graham was frustrated, stressed and bleeding money. Although the Fillmore East could still net as much as fifteen thousand dollars profit on a good week, the Fillmore West had been struggling to break even. His management firm and booking agency were not making the money he expected and the record labels represented a major loss for the rock impresario millionaire. But money, he said, wasn't the issue.

"The final simple fact is that I am tired," he told the press conference. "The only reason to keep the Fillmore in operation at this point would be to make money, and, though few have ever chosen to believe me on this point, money has never been my prime motivation. And now that it would become the only possible motivation to continue, I pass."

The last straw came about because Sol Hurok, the grand old man of the arts, called Graham and asked him to book a month of dates at the Metropolitan Opera House with him. Graham idolized Hurok, a Russian immigrant who had made it in America getting the dirt under his fingernails. He was dazzled by the opportunity to take his rock shows out of the Lower East Side and began by making a list of the groups he wanted to present with Hurok. At the top of his list was The Band.

He contacted the group's manager and explained about the heavy expenses, the unions, the security, pitched him on the prestige, the cultural breakthrough that playing the Met would represent. He knew the fee he offered was far less than the twenty-five thousand dollars a night The Band earned as a minimum. "Do you mean to tell me you expect my band to play for fifty thousand a week?" asked the manager.

Graham hung up the phone furious, his grand plan thwarted by a matter as menial as mere money. He started another list. At the top of one side of a sheet of paper he wrote "Negatives" and on the other side he wrote "Positives." He accumulated a long list of "Negatives," but on the other side of the page he could only think of money. He flew back to San Francisco, stewing in his vivid emotions. On Tuesday, he confided to friends in San Francisco his plans. On Thursday, he held his press conference in New York.

He rambled on emotionally for more than ninety minutes, venting paranoia and rage at all the unseen factors, as he saw it, that forced his hand. Five years earlier, the power belonged to the man who rented the hall and threw the show. He could pay his top band a thousand dollars per weekend and take home many times that, in cash stuffed in his knapsack. Times had changed. Making a few million dollars a year had grown tougher. Power shifted to the acts that attracted the ticket-buyers and, by proxy, to their agents.

"I continue to deplore the exploitation of the gigantic-hall concerts," he told the press, "many of them with high-priced tickets. The sole incentive of too many has become money. The conditions for such performances, besides lacking intimacy, are professionally impossible, according to my standards."

Graham lashed out at agents who could dictate entire bills, make Graham buy acts he didn't think musically valid, raising their prices in what he called "the unreasonable and totally destructive inflation of the live concert scene." He even lambasted his audiences for no longer demonstrating "musical sophistication."

But he saved his choicest remonstrations for the press. "For six years, I have endured the abuse of many members of the public and the press," he said. "The role of 'Anti-Christ of the underground' never appealed to me."

Less than a month after coming back from Europe, Santana turned around and headed back to the continent again with dates in England, France, Sweden, Denmark, Germany, Belgium, Holland and Italy and a return appearance at the Montreux Jazz Festival. Chepito Areas made a miraculous recovery from the near-fatal brain hemorrhage and rejoined the band, although his replacement Coke Escovedo remained in the lineup as well.

Also on the tour was Doug Rauch, bass player from Voices of East Harlem. Shrieve met him standing onstage in Ghana and invited Rauch to come stay with him in Mill Valley. Drug problems made regular bassist David Brown a question mark. During one recent concert, he nodded out while playing, passed out on his feet and fell over backward. Brown played the rest of the set on a chair. The band carried Rauch on the European tour like spare parts.

By the time Santana arrived in Milan, there was no sign of the equipment truck. Road manager Herbert driving the trailer from Paris, got lost in the Alps and was forced to turn around and double back. Italian customs officials at the border stalled the trip even further, until a bribe of an entire case of flashlights smoothed the way.

The band waited nervously at the rickety, gargantuan arena until the time came to cancel the sold-out matinee performance. The audience took the announcement, made by the band standing on the stage, poorly. "We can't do what you want us to do," pleaded a distraught Gregg Rolie.

Before a riot erupted in their very faces, Michael Carabello grabbed the microphone and told the seething crowd that the band would play the concert the following afternoon and that the show would be free. Thus mollified, the audience departed in relative peace and civility. By the time for the evening concert, Herbert and crew had made it to Milan and set up all the equipment, ready to play. But the show terrified the band. With sharply elevated balconies towering above the arena floor, the musicians felt like they were playing in the bottom of a very large teacup. Herbert watched in horror as a hard roll thrown from high in the balconies crashed on Rolie's keyboard and broke off a couple of keys. Before he had time to think more than a flash of relief that the roll didn't break anything more serious, like Rolie's fingers, Herbert himself was knocked out cold, as a heavy glass Coke bottle from similar reaches bashed his skull. At the end of the show, the stage looked like a bomb site, covered with litter and debris.

The next morning, at a hastily called band meeting, the musicians elected to get out of town. No free concert. No makeup date. Just leave. Herbert was told to pack up the equipment and move out. But the Italian promoters were suspicious. He concocted a story about how he and his crew would put the equipment in the truck, while the promoters attended to cleaning the stage area.

But before Herbert could make good his getaway, the promoters pulled out pistols and took prisoner one of the crew. With his associate held at gunpoint, Herbert would not have been inclined to leave anyway, even if he could. But with the fence surrounding the amphitheater securely locked, the truck couldn't leave regardless. An unsuspecting Mike Shrieve, having missed the morning band meeting, arrived and tried to climb the fence to get inside, when Herbert found him. They managed to persuade the promoters to release their crew member.

They snuck out through a tunnel, hailed a passing van and, dumping wads of lire on his seat, convinced the young driver to drive them away. At this point, the promoters gave chase through the narrow streets of the ancient city, although Herbert, Shrieve, et al. finally made it safely to Montreux. The band's London-based booking agent, who had originally arranged the Milan concerts, negotiated the return of the group's equipment and back Herbert went, uncertain what fate awaited him, to deliver the agreed-upon pile of cash and reclaim the lights, sound and musical equipment for the band to finish the tour. The scheduled appearance in Rome was canceled.

Rock bands did not yet routinely travel the globe. International touring was in its infancy, but Santana was one of the few bands for which there was considerable demand outside the English-speaking world. Still nobody in the business had enough experience to plot tours geographically. The next month the band left a concert in Seattle, headed for two benefit concerts in Rio de Janeiro and a four-song appearance at the International Song Festival, which would be telecast globally, but primarily in Europe. A grateful Brazilian government supplied the musicians, at their request, with some outstanding marijuana. After the three quick shows, the band turned around and flew back to the States to appear in Denver.

David Brown did not make the trip. Drugs were exacting a heavy toll. He was arrested after smashing up his Porsche in an early morning rain and the cops found some reds. His time-keeping abilities disintegrated. He could no longer hold up his end. When his arm became infected, he was sent on a leave of absence, replaced temporarily by Tom Rutley, a suburban jazz musician from the College of San Mateo big band.

Sessions for the new Jefferson Airplane album dragged on. Relations between band members were strained to the breaking point and tension filled their every hour in the studio together. With Slick and Kantner enjoying their newfound domesticity too much to leave town, tour money rolled to a halt. Still, Slick felt the unspoken demands.

She drank. Her humor no longer loosened up Casady and

Kaukonen, who were practically in a band by themselves at this point. Between the disintegration of the group, the pressures she felt, and the demands of new motherhood, Slick was torn. Kantner, emotionally remote, offered little help. So she got bombed.

Sometime around dawn May 13, while she drunkenly drag-raced Kaukonen home from the studio, she lost control of her Mercedes on the curving approach to the Golden Gate Bridge and slammed into a retaining wall. Blood covered the pavement when the ambulance arrived. The attendant thought she was dead.

When manager Bill Thompson arrived at S.F. General, Slick was mumbling incoherently, her head wrapped in a blood-soaked towel. Kaukonen was already there. Amazingly, she had only suffered serious concussions and moved to Mount Zion Hospital as soon as she could. She stayed in the hospital for more than a week, but asked for no visitors. She argued with the nurses, who kept her under sedation because she kept getting up and moving around instead of lying quietly and resting.

Her face was cut, but she had narrowly escaped death. The impact of the crash threw her across the car into the passenger's side. The driver's seat was crushed to a pulp. The Airplane canceled concerts and recording sessions while she recuperated.

The Grateful Dead continued the live recording Memorial Day weekend at Winterland, where a jug of apple juice spiked with acid made the rounds. An announcement was even made from the stage about passing around "liquid refreshment." By midnight, nearby Mount Zion Hospital was treating some thirty unsuspecting young fans who guzzled more of that apple juice than proved circumspect. Police arrested seven people outside Winterland, after nabbing one gentleman, naked and bleeding, running down the street. "The water is polluted," he told the cops. "There's LSD in the water."

Graham was furious. He told a *Chronicle* reporter the next night he didn't know anything about the incident. "At the end of the evening," he said, "I saw five or six people who didn't seem to be in control of themselves and my opinion was that someone must have passed something around. The heavy use of drugs and need to escape by young people is one of the reasons I'm backing away from this business."

●　　●　　●

The Dead knew for a fact that the best possible name for the upcoming double-record live album would be "Skullfuck." No question. With the band's contract guaranteeing artistic control, the decision did theoretically belong to the band. McIntire phoned Warner Brothers president Joe Smith to tell him the happy news. Smith came unglued. "You can't do this to me," he pleaded.

McIntire only laughed. "It's not me, Joe," he said. "It's all of us. We're all doing this to you."

The band convened a meeting with Warner Brothers leadership at a conference room in the Hyatt Continental on Sunset Boulevard in Hollywood, the most convenient location large enough to contain the band's sprawling entourage. Around three dozen members of the band and extended family, roadies, girlfriends, some of the New Riders, the entire tribe, sat around a large table, plopped on the floor, stood against the wall and discussed the question of the album title with the Warner's executives for almost two hours.

There was no anger, no recriminations. The Dead representatives spoke rationally, plainly and without condescension, explaining to the record industry professionals exactly why it made perfect sense for the record to be called "Skullfuck." People offered long, detailed explanations, delving into the meaning of the term on many levels. The Warner's people sat and smiled. None of the chain stores like Korvette's, they said, would carry the record with a title like that. Then we don't want to be in those stores, replied the Dead.

The album was eventually released without any title.

But, to the Grateful Dead at this stage, all things seemed possible. Reality rarely intruded. The world often bent to their peculiar viewpoint. And things fell out of the sky, like the trip to France.

"Gotta passport?" McIntire asked Rosie McGee, Phil Lesh's girlfriend who worked in the Dead office. "Want to go to France? We need you to speak French." He told McGee, who was born in Paris and spoke fluent French, they would leave that day and go ahead of the band, who would follow two days later. A French fashion designer with political aspirations named Jean Bouquin had decided to produce an outdoor rock festival to be called "Free Freedom Three Days"—in English because it sounded better that way—at a Western-style dude ranch outside Paris. He needed the Grateful Dead as the event's centerpiece and offered McIntire the lordly sum of $100,000 to make it happen.

Bouquin had arranged a deal with French film composer Michel Magne to record the event and house the groups. Magne owned and operated Strawberry Studio, a recording facility he built in a renovated seventeenth-century chateau where Chopin once stayed, Chateau d'Herouville. Magne hoped the festival might produce some publicity for his combination recording studio/spa resort, where the band was quartered on arriving that Friday in June.

The Dead were greeted by a thundering, howling rainstorm, an improbable occurrence in France at that time of year. With the festival suddenly canceled and the weather worsening by the minute, the band was left with little to do. Jerry Garcia went to sleep for twenty-four hours. Pigpen was felled by a mysterious, virulent bug. McIntire fielded inquiries about playing for another promoter, as long as the group was already in the country, only to discover the gentleman in question beaten up by thugs and hospitalized. McIntire suspected Bouquin. He was certain an ominous car tailed him through the streets of Paris when he went to the hospital to visit the poor man.

On Sunday, a rented Mercedes-Benz ferried three shifts of the Dead troupe into Paris for a whirlwind round of tourist sites: Champs Élysées, L'Arc de Triomphe, Tour Eiffel, Notre Dame. At the Eiffel Tower, some bewildered American hippie recognized Garcia. "Wow, Jerry Garcia," he muttered. "What are you doing here?" Garcia himself wondered.

On Monday, the skies cleared and Garcia and Lesh, itchy to play music, decided over a buffet lunch of cold cuts, fresh fruit, breads and cheese to play outdoors that night. The crew spent the afternoon setting up the three tons of equipment, tie-dyed speaker cloths arrayed on the grounds in front of the chateau like some kind of psychedelic California banner. Word spread enough for some Parisian press and locals to make a crowd around two hundred strong, as the band started to play shortly after dark. Pigpen recovered enough to get into his duty-free Wild Turkey and sing. The band performed for three hours, illuminated by bright lights from French television, who shot the performance and broadcast the results the following week. The villagers lit hundreds of candles and placed them around the pool, lending the outdoor concert the unearthly air of a religious shrine. Eventually, however, as the evening progressed, the candles were extinguished as people either fell or were pushed into the water.

Bill Ham and his Light Sound Dimension Band took over after

the Dead. With the television lights gone, the LSD Band performed under the swirling, pulsing colors of a light show using the facade of the chateau as a backdrop. The next day, Rosie McGee made strenuous use of her language skills, as airport and customs officials delayed the group's departure. But the following day, one week after McIntire first appeared at her desk, she was back at work wondering if the whole thing had actually happened.

SUMMER 1971

Carlos Santana installed himself in the Tower House, a landmark home high on the ridgetop above Mill Valley. A former museum that had belonged to one of the town's pioneer families, the new Santana home only underlined his growing alienation from the group. Living on a mountaintop in a three-story castle-like edifice, the guitarist could pursue his life with a maximum of solitude, remote from the world as he was from the other band members.

The other musicians suspected Coke Escovedo of pouring poison into Santana's ear, plumping up his ego and causing divisive trouble. He certainly ran down the band's hapless management, but Escovedo held no loyalty for Marcum and Estrada. About the same time that Escovedo was suggesting the group dump the managers, some apparent financial problems surfaced with regard to the group's finances. Although Marcum himself was not implicated directly, he did fire attorney Herb Resner over a seventy-five thousand dollar investment Marcum had never approved, even though the deal turned out to make money. But Escovedo was able to gain some support within the group for dropping Marcum and Estrada at an acrimonious band meeting.

The band also held another meeting at Rolie's house in Mill Valley to discuss problems of a more personal nature. The musicians all agreed drinking and drugs were out of control and steps to curb their use should be taken. Santana himself disagreed that using psychedelics represented any kind of problem, although he concurred that the excessive cocaine use in the band had to stop. He had quit using blow, for the most part, the year before. Everyone agreed. Nothing changed.

The mood in the band was very grim. The in-fighting and backstage dramas reached their peak. Hot-blooded Chepito Areas would get into screaming matches with guitarist Santana in Spanish, lapsing into English for choice invectives like "pussy" or "faggot."

Work on the third album had been underway almost a year. Not only was production slowed by the band's constant touring, but the group insisted on recording finished tracks over after returning from the road. The band would play the songs live and decide the recordings back home could be improved.

Schon and Santana conducted guitar duels. On "Toussaint L'Overture," a number written by the politicized Alberto Gianquinto and named after the historic Haitian revolutionary, Schon and Santana re-recorded solo after solo. Santana would come to the studio, listen to Schon's most recent overdubbed part and do his over again. Schon would do the same thing, each trying to top the other. Schon kept going until he cut one brain-blurring, gut-wrenching solo engineer Glen Kolotkin thought Schon could never surpass. But he came back to the studio one more time, made Kolotkin erase the magical part and recorded in its place something considerably less exciting, losing a performance he could never recapture.

On "No One to Depend On," a song written by Carabello and Coke Escovedo, guitarist Santana objected to a line in the song about junkies. He wanted nothing to do with drugs. At least, he vehemently objected to having any such reference on the record. He and Carabello went at it, although Santana ultimately prevailed on this point.

With the band's record deal structured to include generous amounts of free studio time, the group would use the studio for days at a time. The crew would bring in a refrigerator, stock it with ice cream, fruits and candy and put cartons of cigarettes on top. The musicians would jam for hours, rolling tape as they free-associated with their instruments. The next day, the band would listen to the previous day's recordings and select, perhaps, eight bars around which a song would begin to be shaped. Perhaps not the most efficient route to production, this approach employed the machine-like qualities of the extraordinary collaborative musical prowess of Santana. And, their ranking as one of the best-selling rock groups of the day did allow them a certain latitude in the creative process.

Young, rich rock stars could also indulge extravagances in ways more boring wealthy people might not think to, like Rolie's Mangusta. He sauntered into the snitzy dealership in his street clothes and the salesman gave him short shrift. The following day, Rolie returned with a paper bag stuffed full of cash. He walked up to the salesman sitting next to the man who had waited on him the previous day and dumped the purchase price on top of his desk. Rolie drove the sleek, expensive sports car home right off the showroom floor.

By summer, the album neared completion. The shimmering, savage sound of Santana, augmented by the Tower of Power horns and trumpeter Luis Gasca on one track, roared through the disk beginning to end. For all the antagonism and conflict, the band could still count on the music. But quietly, Carlos Santana was growing deeply dissatisfied.

David Rubinson finally admitted the record company partnership didn't work. He arranged to sell his shares back to Bill Graham and start his own firm. He kept the meager publishing catalog the operation had built and took one act with him, a trio of sisters from Oakland called the Pointer Sisters, who sang background vocals with Elvin Bishop.

His relationship with Graham began disintegrating almost the day he landed in San Francisco to start work. Graham did not take to partners comfortably. The two battled constantly and the third partner, attorney Brian Rohan, was no help. A wild-eyed Irish alcoholic who liked to back door Graham's current romantic interest, secretary Vicki Cunningham, Rohan was a smart-mouth dealmaker who only found the ongoing Rubinson-Graham battles amusing. Fillmore Records staffers Jeffrey Cohen and Bruce Good once left pies for the partners to throw at each other in a room where a meeting was about to take place.

But the end came when Rubinson was accused of embezzling money from the company by Keeva Kristal, Graham's new right-hand man whom Graham knew from poker games at the Concord when Graham had worked as a bus boy in the Catskills. At a vicious meeting in attorney Bill Coblentz's office, Rubinson brought his lawyer from Los Angeles and listened to Graham and Kristal claim Rubinson funneled money out of the company by giving it to acts the label represented. Rubinson blew up. He stood up and walked out. "Fuck you," he said.

By June, Rubinson and Graham no longer spoke. But, before that, as soon as he heard about Graham's plans to close the Fillmores, he began campaigning to record the final concerts live. Graham paid him, as usual, no attention. He steamrolled ahead with plans for a gala final night at the Fillmore East. After the audience got dosed with acid at the Winterland show in May, police scrutiny increased and Graham hurried up his closing date at Fillmore West. In the second week of June, he surprised a company meeting, set to plan a Fourth of July party, with the announcement.

"The execution is here," he said somberly. "The end of the month we're gonna close this place. What it would take to continue, I don't have. And if I did, I wouldn't want to give it."

He told his staff he wanted to use the final week to present a series of concerts with all the old-time San Francisco bands, a last hurrah. For his Fillmore. For San Francisco.

Bert Decker ran a documentary film company that had already won an Oscar for a film on Robert Kennedy. When he read that Graham planned to close the Fillmores, he phoned Graham to suggest filming the closing. "Fuck you," said Graham, who was caught up in closing the New York operation. He passed the call to Keeva Kristal, who told Decker he would approve the film if Decker raised fifty thousand dollars by noon four days later. Decker scrambled for money with friends, relatives, anyone he knew, landing the final fifteen thousand dollar investment a few hours ahead of the Friday deadline. On Monday, he and his crew started filming.

Graham finally came into his own as an actor. It was a role he had been rehearsing for six years and nobody could play Bill Graham like he could. Decker recognized an instinctive actor in his prime subject, someone who sprang to life when the camera rolled, waving Vicki Cunningham away with a call from CBS News while he cajoled

Santana co-manager Ron Estrada on another line, getting stern with Boz Scaggs, leaning back in his chair, his arms folded behind his head, beaming a Cinemascope smile.

Cameras caught Graham in a heated exchange with Mike Wilhelm of the Charlatans, who came to the office to plead a place on the bill for the final week for his new band, Loose Gravel. Graham bantered casually with him, but told him firmly that he was only booking bands he knew and liked and, having never heard Wilhelm's current aggregation, he would not add the band to the bill. "Well, I'd just like to say," Wilhelm said, toeing the floor like a recalcitrant schoolkid, "fuck you and thanks for the memories."

Graham started pushing Wilhelm out the door, screaming at him. "The next time you say 'Fuck you' to me, I hope it's out there somewhere with no cameras around. I'll take your teeth out of your mouth and shove 'em through your nose. Fuckin' animal."

"I don't hate you at all," offered Wilhelm.

"If you give me, I love you," Graham said. "But if I don't give you, I'm a 'Fuck you,' right? Get out of here. GET OUT OF HERE. Go down the stairs. Go out the building. Go out of this building."

Graham chased Wilhelm to the top of the stairs, yelling all the way, then turned and gave a little smile and shrug for the camera to catch.

He closed the Fillmore East on June 27 before an invitation-only audience that arrived to find a rose pinned to every seat. The refreshment stands were giving away ice cream sandwiches, Hershey bars, salted peanuts, soft drinks. And when supplies ran low, they were replenished. Kegs of beer ran all night. Rock illuminati from John Lennon and Yoko Ono to Ahmet Ertegun and Clive Davis roamed the lobby. "It must be very weird for you," said songwriter Jerry Leiber to Graham.

"It is very weird," said Graham.

Graham received a standing ovation when he first appeared onstage to introduce the opening act, bluesman Albert King, who had also appeared on the opening night bill with Big Brother and the Holding Company thirty-nine months before. Country Joe McDonald sang a few songs. Unscheduled performances by Mountain, Edgar Winter and White Trash and the Beach Boys paved the way for the announced headliners of the evening, the J. Geils Band and the

Allman Brothers Band, who were still playing when the sun rose over New York the next morning. Radio covered the entire event live.

The next day, Graham flew back to San Francisco, where he held forth that night for several hours on the underground rock station KSAN. The final Fillmore shows were set to start forty-eight hours later, but first there was the last basketball game.

Ever since opening the Fillmore West, Graham obsessively relived his brief childhood in postwar Bronx through basketball games on the dance floor of the ballroom. He had royal purple uniforms made up and named his house team the Fillmore Fingers, after Graham's trademark one-finger salute. The team's symbol was proudly emblazoned on the chest of the jerseys. Graham was a rough, often dirty do-or-die competitor on the court, fully capable of cheating, lying, overruling infractions on his own part, whatever it took to win. When confronted by someone who suggested that basketball was just a game, Graham thought he was crazy.

"Are you out of your fucking mind?" he said. "Why play if you're gonna lose?"

On the last Tuesday, the Fingers took on the FM Productions team, a kind of in-house World Series, a serious contest with much at stake. Tempers flared in the close game during the final five minutes. The referee was threatened. Punches were thrown and a player was knocked down. The player's father charged the court and Graham restrained the man from offering retribution. A tall, young, black man, watching from the sidelines, made a comment Graham didn't appreciate. "Get out of the fucking building," Graham thundered.

"You play dirty, you motherfucker," said the kid, carefully walking backward as Graham advanced.

Graham backed the offending spectator off the floor and down the stairs, under the watchful eyes of his security guards, but by himself. He walked him out the front door and onto the Market Street sidewalk. He turned, trotted back to the court, clapped his hands together, signaled time in. "Keep it moving," he shouted. "Keep it moving."

The Fingers won 60–58.

The glass-encased bulletin board where he customarily posted a list of coming attractions contained a sort of bizarre assemblage. Under the

May press release announcing his intention to close his ballrooms, Graham pinned a small upside-down American flag and two flowers. At the bottom was a drawing of a thick wooden cross. On each of the four arms of the cross was nailed a hand—the nail right through the palm—each one flipping the finger.

Boz Scaggs headlined the first show of the final week on Wednesday. A onetime schoolmate of Steve Miller who moved to San Francisco to play in his pal's band, he recorded on the first two Miller albums and, after some acrimonious disagreements, left to pursue his own muse. His band had been making a lot of noise on the local scene and qualified as the town's favorite new band of the year. Also appearing was soulish Cold Blood, old-time rock and rollers the Flamin' Groovies and newcomers Grootna, a band coached by Marty Balin, who directed the band to Columbia Records, as far away from the Airplane's new label as he could get.

On Thursday, It's A Beautiful Day and the Elvin Bishop Group joined Lamb, an intriguing folk-rock group that recorded for Fillmore Records, and Stoneground, a communal hippie troupe formed by Tom Donahue as the house band for his cross-country caravan filmed for the movie *Medicine Ball Caravan*. But the proceedings did not begin in earnest until Friday.

Jerry Garcia played steel guitar with opening act the Rowan Brothers, two young, freshly scrubbed youths who were managed by Garcia's mandolinist friend, David Grisman. He also picked his steel during the New Riders set before joining the Grateful Dead proper and rambling on until around three in the morning.

Yogi Phlegm, who opened the Saturday show, used to be called the Sons of Champlin before opting for the unappealing name change in a typical bit of Marin County hippie perversity. Hot Tuna stood in for the Airplane. Kaukonen and Casady and company played for three hours, but that was as close to an Airplane performance as was going to take place at the final weekend of the Fillmore.

Marty Balin would have nothing to do with the band. Grace Slick was still recuperating from her car crash injuries, but, probably more crucial, was Paul Kantner's distinctly unsentimental bent. He never liked funerals. When his mother died when he was a young boy, his father sent him to the circus instead of to her service.

Quicksilver went through the motions to close the penultimate evening, Dino Valente fronting a Cipollina-less band with an unwieldy horn section. Bassist David Freiberg, a court date and probable jail sentence hanging over his head two weeks hence, knew this could easily be his final appearance with the band.

"This is going to be the greatest motherfucking evening of our lives," announced Graham at the start of the final night on Sunday, introducing Tower of Power, the funky, raw soul band from the East Bay. Backstage a ripple went through the crowd as John Fogerty of Creedence Clearwater walked through the throng in a bright turquoise outfit with an Elvis Presley haircut.

At this point, Creedence was arguably the most popular rock and roll band in the world, riding a crest of eight consecutive Top Ten singles, each one written, produced and sung by Fogerty. His creative dominance had become such a tangled issue in the band that the other members had successfully won the right to write and sing on the next Creedence album. But before those sessions could take place, his older brother, Tom Fogerty, quit in a huff after more than eleven years in the band. Tonight would be the group's first appearance as a trio since the three musicians played together in high school as the Blue Velvets.

Separated at the time from his wife and two small children, following a long-distance love affair with a European woman he met on tour, Fogerty was a troubled man whose life, celebrated and rewarded as he could be, was in deep turmoil. The band only skirted the San Francisco scene and accomplished all this enormous international success without much involvement with the provincial music community, save for a Grateful Dead psychedelic assassination that miraculously spared the almost totally straight creative leader of the band. Nevertheless, the surprise announcement of the band's appearance that last night of the Fillmore was greeted by a leonine roar.

Fogerty's stunning new look gave the crowd the same flash that occurred backstage. No more Dutch Boy haircut and flannel shirts, now he looked like a rock and roll star ascending into the pantheon before the crowd's very eyes as he blasted into "Born on the Bayou" to kick start the band's set.

For the previous two weeks, the Santana band had given Graham grief over playing the final night. Some of the band members genuinely did not want to do the show. Others were concerned that the live broadcast would lead to bootleg versions circulating of material from the third album, finished at long last that very week. Graham acquiesced to the group's every demand, but the debate about whether to play continued virtually right up to showtime.

Charging out of the box with "Incident at Neshubar," Santana made it clear that the band had come to play, and with a vengeance. Ever vigilant road manager Herbie Herbert, who spoke directly to KSAN general manager Tom Donahue about the broadcast ban on the Santana set, quickly noticed that the show was going on the airwaves regardless. He picked up a small hatchet the band carried in the toolbox and went to work on the phone lines feeding the broadcast. As he hacked the cable apart, he felt someone jump on his back and try to wrestle him to the floor. He turned around and delivered a roundhouse blow before realizing he had just knocked out the station's top female disk jockey. He finished chopping off the broadcast.

Storming through a towering, epic performance, Santana brought the freight train of shrieking guitars and polyrhythmic drive to rest on a beatific plateau, floating out on an ethereal version of the introspective Miles Davis modalities of "In a Silent Way," a song the band never performed before or since, a benediction, as it turned out, not just on the Fillmore, but on Santana itself.

Santana gave way to a sprawling jam session, a rumbling, cacophonic din that massed musicians on the stage, as many as could fit, and grew more unwieldy with every passing moment: Van Morrison, Mike Bloomfield, Vince Guaraldi, Lydia Pense of Cold Blood, Carlos Santana, Jack Casady, Sweet Linda Divine, Sam Andrew, John Cipollina, George Hunter. Sometime around five in the morning, Graham put on the scratchy recording of "Greensleeves," his regular exit music, one last time.

That Sunday night at the Fillmore turned out to be the final public performance by the original Woodstock roster of Santana. These same six musicians would never take a concert stage together as a band again. Shortly thereafter, Carlos Santana started skipping rehearsals for the tour. He dodged the other band members, more secretive than ever. Finally, he issued his ultimatum—either fire Michael Carabello or tour without him. After great discussion, the band made the decision and left town without him.

The first concert in Boston went splendidly. Neal Schon covered Santana's guitar parts with ease. But the next night in Washington,

D.C., while managers Marcum and Estrada slept at the hotel, some shouts from the crowd unnerved the already anxious Schon. With the next performance scheduled for the Felt Forum at Madison Square Garden, Carabello bowed out. The group caved in and summoned guitarist Santana from San Francisco. Manager Marcum took Carabello and Chepito Areas, leaving the band without a percussion section of any kind. One of the road crew stationed himself behind a set of congas and waved his hands over the drums for the first show. A musician in the audience approached Herbie Herbert backstage and said he knew all the parts and could play the second show. They grabbed a cab to Queens, picked up his conga drums and Mingo Lewis joined the band.

Gregg Rolie, furious and disgusted, waited in the hotel lobby for the arrival of Carlos Santana. When he saw the smirking guitarist stride into the hotel, Rolie buttonholed him. In no uncertain terms, Rolie laid out his intentions. He would finish the tour, he told the guitarist, but, after that, he was through. He was quitting the band. He would not stand for the kind of high-handed back-stabbing that Santana had used to rid the band of Carabello. But neither would he abandon his commitment to play the remainder of the dates already booked. "I'll play," he said evenly. "Don't look at me. Don't talk to me."

With the end of the band apparently at hand, Herbert decided to take drastic, but ultimately futile, action. At Cobo Hall in Detroit, he dosed everybody's stage drinks with a liberal amount of LSD. Rolie, who had never taken anything stronger than a couple of hits of some Jamaican grass while sitting on the side of the Woodstock stage watching Sly and the Family Stone, watched his fingers turn into tiny baseball bats and the keys transform into rubbery, moving targets. He knew what was happening and looked at guitarist Santana, who looked vaguely apprehensive. "What's going on?" said the confused guitarist.

"You don't know?" Rolie muttered. "You mean you're like this all the time?"

The tour came to a close with a soccer stadium concert in Puerto Rico, while the band vacationed at a remote villa in the Virgin Islands, landing their chartered plane on an Air Force runway, a privilege arranged by Rolie, who traded a show at the base in exchange.

Rolie knew the end was in sight. Signs of the fall of the empire were everywhere. The band flew in women from Miami, who arrayed themselves around the pool without bathing suit tops, a policy handed down by the group. One of the women was raped during the band's performance at the Puerto Rico concert. Maine lobsters were air-freighted in daily. One soldier went A.W.O.L. and spent the night at the compound, drunk and disorderly. Rolie went horseback riding, attended a cockfight. He brooded and he drank.

Carlos Santana pretended nothing was wrong. He wanted all the problems to go away. One afternoon, in the swimming pool, he playfully splashed water at Rolie. Rolie warned him to stay away. But the guitarist didn't realize the pent-up fury roiling inside the keyboard player and kept on splashing him. Rolie lost control. He grabbed the scrawny Mexican around the throat and all the repressed hostility rushed out in a blur.

He dunked Santana like a washing machine, holding him under the water until he gasped for breath, letting him up for a moment and then putting him back under. He played rough, more rough than he knew. Herbert jumped in the pool in a panic and pulled them apart. He dragged Santana, spitting water out of his lungs, up on the side of the pool. An unrepentant Rolie went over and asked the shaken Santana if he was okay. "I told you not to fuck with me," he said, and walked off.

The film company that shot the final week at the Fillmore brought a sixteen-track remote recording van to capture the soundtrack. The tapes found their way into the hands of Fillmore Records staffers Jeffrey Cohen and Bruce Good with the mandate to turn the mess into a live album. Coming into the project late in the game didn't help and Cohen and Good worked long and hard to pull together an acceptable record from the event.

Mixes were difficult, with tracks mysteriously assigned to peculiar instrument combinations. The recording was not done with any special eye toward post-production and the pair sweated out some dicey passages, only to find the musicians not appreciative. They tucked, for instance, a particularly bad guitar chord by Dino Valente of Quicksilver into the track, where it lay, barely audible. On playing back their mixes for Valente, Cohen pointed out the cosmetic touch on the wrong chord. "Did I play it?" asked Valente. "Then it wasn't a mistake."

Not immune from show business thinking was Bill Graham himself, who visited the studio to hear some of their work one afternoon.

He heard himself introduce the Elvin Bishop Group. "You know, that introduction sounds a little unexciting," Graham commented.

Helpful Jeffrey Cohen volunteered that Graham could overdub a new, more exciting introduction and the producers would be able to add the ambience and make it indistinguishable from the genuine article. "Really?" said Graham.

A microphone was set up inside the studio. Graham paced back and forth, envisioning the crowd, feeling the atmosphere, working himself up into a proper method-actor mood. He pumped his fist into his palm and nodded at the control booth. The tape rolled. "Ladies and gentlemen, the Elvin Bishop Group," Graham intoned. Cohen could not tell the difference between the new introduction and the original.

But Graham wasn't done. He signaled for a retake, worked himself up and, once again, delivered his *sotto voce* announcement: "Ladies and gentlemen, the Elvin Bishop Group." He made another half-dozen passes at the introduction before finally expressing contentment with his performance. Cohen still could not tell the difference. But he added some applause from the Santana portion of the program, mixed it all together and eventually cut the number from the album entirely.

Pigpen collapsed in August at his home. His kidneys failed and he was rushed to the hospital where the doctors duly informed him his options were limited. Drink and die, they told him. His alcoholism had advanced to the stage where he barely ate. Once a burly, corpulent figure, Pigpen had become a sallow wraith. He and Veronica would go to a restaurant and she would order him a steak. To satisfy her, he would saw off a small bite, chew and swallow, glare at her and go back to his drinking.

But he entered rehabilitation at Sequoia Hospital on the peninsula, one of the few alcohol treatment centers in the area at the time. He had lost an alarming amount of weight and he had damaged his internal organs. But he stopped drinking.

A month after Pigpen was hospitalized, the band broke in a new keyboard player, Keith Godchaux. Pigpen moved to emeritus status in the band when he finally recovered enough to return to the fold. He traveled with the band when he felt like it and sang when he felt like it—which wasn't all that often. Mostly, he stayed home in the small suburban house he and Veronica shared, watched TV and became friendly with his Corte Madera neighbors.

One night, he and Vee sat in their living room and Pigpen spoke up over a commercial break. "I don't want you here when I die," he said. He didn't even look at her.

She laughed. It was the first she had heard about him dying. His health problems seemed to be in the past. She made light of his comment, but obedient to his wishes as always, she moved out shortly thereafter. Less than two months later, March 8, 1973, his neighbor found him dead on his living room floor, the quiet, lonely death of an old bluesman at age twenty-seven.

A few days before he died, Pigpen sat at a piano, banging away with more confidence than grace, rolling a tape. He ran through an assortment of very sad blues songs, his voice sounding like an old black man who remembered the cotton patches and roadhouses of long ago and far away.

"We had a good thing goin' seemed like a long time," he sang, "seemed like a long time. I didn't realize . . ." And the tape cut him off.

His family laid him out in an open casket, in his leather jacket with the skull patch and his dirty brown cowboy hat, in a traditional Roman Catholic service at Daphne Funerals of Marin. His death came as a shock to his friends and bandmates, who thought he had weathered the worst more than a year before. The religious service did not appeal to his closest associates, but they had already gathered over the weekend and drunk themselves stupid on his behalf at Bob Weir's house.

He was buried at Alta Mesa Memorial Park in Palo Alto and the headstone featured the familiar emblem of a skull with a lightning bolt across the top. The inscription read "Ronald C. McKernan—1945–1973—Pigpen was and is now forever one of the Grateful Dead."

THE MUSIC

A collection of disparate personalities with several musical strains often running in different directions at the same time, the Jefferson Airplane caromed over far-flung stylistic ground. In the process, the band littered a body of work with a remarkable number of extraordinary peaks, some better known than others, all fraught with a kind of character unique to this unusual group of musicians.

Overshadowed by the landmark second album, *Surrealistic Pillow,* and all but entirely unknown outside San Francisco, the group's auspicious 1966 debut, *Jefferson Airplane Takes Off,* nonetheless represents something of a modest masterpiece, a minor gem easily overlooked in the wake of things to come. But the recording faithfully executes Marty Balin's vision of a rock band playing folk music and, if RCA Victor had been any kind of a record company, "It's No Secret" from the LP would have taken its place on AM radio stations across the country alongside similar folk-rock confections of the moment by other exponents of the burgeoning movement like the Byrds, the Turtles and even lesser lights like the Leaves or the Left Banke.

But *Jefferson Airplane Takes Off* boasts a maturity and singleness of purpose missing from any of the band's apparent peers. The band proves equally adept at pop-rock melodics ("It's No Secret"), fleshed-out folksiness ("Come Up the Years"), bohemian angst ("Bringing Me Down") and down-the-alley blues ("Tobacco Road"). Balin serves notice as both a promising songwriter and a passionate vocalist, biting into the album's opening track, "Blues From an Airplane," with an almost eerie melancholy, weaving his quavery tenor through a fabric of rich harmony vocals.

The rumbling, rolling bass of Jack Casady bolsters the rhythms in intriguing and surprising ways and, with guitarist Jorma Kaukonen, gives the band some serious horsepower in the engine compartment. Vocalist Signe Anderson takes a fine solo turn on the Memphis Minnie classic, "Chauffeur Blues," but her tones are too warm, too soft, her vibrato too practiced, to give Balin the challenging, dangerous high-dive platform he found with Grace Slick. The band stamps its own imprint on the Dino Valente song "Let's Get Together," more than a year before the more saccharine treatment by the Youngbloods turned the song into a hippie anthem.

Even the outtakes from these sessions released on later compilations sound confident and poised, not merely promising but fully realized on their own terms. "Go to Her," included on the 1992 CD boxed set *Jefferson Airplane Loves You*, was a song the band tried to record for both the first and second album, without ever matching the live performances to the musicians' satisfaction. The rip-snorting "High Flyin' Bird" also survived in the Airplane's concert repertoire enough to show up in the film of the band's performance at the 1967 Monterey Pop Festival (also included on the 1992 Monterey Pop CD boxed set).

Of course, "Runnin' 'Round the World"—like the studio version of "High Flyin' Bird," to be found on the 1974 release, *Early Flight*—is probably best known for setting the tone of the band's relationship with RCA Victor. Originally released on the B-side of the single of "It's No Secret," the label pulled the song off the album because of objections to certain implications of the word *trips* in the lyrics.

While *Surrealistic Pillow* was very much an album of its time, selling shoulder-to-shoulder with certified icons of the era—Beatles,

Stones, Cream, Hendrix—the album's reputation has not lasted through the years with the durability, say, of the first Doors album, also released that summer. But the Airplane's second album is every bit an assured, towering achievement, one of the cornerstones of sixties rock, a deeply personal synthesis of the varied musical agendas in the group, forged into a supple, streamlined unity.

From the modified Bo Diddley drumbeat from Spencer Dryden that opens the record to the elegantly soulful Jorma Kaukonen solo guitar piece, "Embryonic Journey," the band confidently maps out its own territory. Balin can cut harshly sarcastic into "Plastic Fantastic Lover" or croon the elegiac "Today," a stately ballad given Spectorian overtones with little more than an echo on the drums and Grateful Dead guitarist Jerry Garcia's rhapsodic figures twisting through the heart of the melody.

Of course, Grace Slick brought more to the band than "Somebody to Love" and "White Rabbit," two songs she performed with her previous unit, the Great Society. But *Surrealistic Pillow* is not even remotely her album, even if her force of personality clearly revitalized the group and those two songs were responsible for the album's vaulting the Airplane into the front ranks of contemporary rock.

Again, the outtakes are illustrative. Three can be found on *Early Flight*. "J.P.P. McStep B. Blues" is a song by Skip Spence, who was putting together the Moby Grape at the time, but who recorded this offbeat tune with his erstwhile colleagues from the Airplane, a harmonica bobbing and dodging around the tight-knit harmony vocal line. "Go to Her" was even more powerful this time, Balin and Slick bouncing off each other with fervor and feeling, the band driving the track into the realm of desperation. And "In the Morning," a powerful six-and-a-half-minute late-night jam featuring Garcia and John Hammond on harmonica with the regulation Airplane rhythm section, showcases the convincing facility with the blues Kaukonen did not fully explore until Hot Tuna, the kind of offhand musicianship bred by the San Francisco ballrooms.

A sterling sample of what the Airplane actually sounded like in that native environment was unearthed for the three-disk *Jefferson Airplane Loves You* box. Nine songs recorded live at the Fillmore Auditorium in spring 1967 capture the band at a fiery peak. Five songs from the band's Monterey Pop Festival set, apparently a more stilted performance, have also been preserved on the four-disk Rhino Records boxed set of live recordings from the historic June 1967 rock festival.

Any expectations that the Airplane would somehow capitalize on the success of the second album with the next were totally confounded by *After Bathing at Baxter's*, a sprawling, loose-jointed pastiche that is almost entirely Paul Kantner's album. Extravagantly experimental in that summer of *Sergeant Pepper*, the unfairly maligned album consists of five pseudo-suites, songs and song-fragments stitched together by imaginative instrumental montages.

Deliberately strange, delightfully deranged, *After Bathing at Baxter's* throws a gauntlet in the face of the mainstream millions who bought *Surrealistic Pillow*. Kaukonen, Casady and Dryden improvise madly for nearly ten minutes in the middle of the record. Grace Slick rewrites James Joyce. Kantner romanticizes teenage runaway Martha Wax and celebrates psychedelia in word and deed. Balin is all but entirely absent from the proceedings.

With *Crown of Creation*, the band's 1968 fourth album, the Airplane tried a return to conventionality. Despite a noteworthy contribution by Balin ("If You Feel") and Slick's interpretation of David Crosby's "Triad," the album remains an incidental aside, especially when compared with the epic live album the band laid down later the same year.

Recorded at both Fillmore East and Fillmore West, *Bless Its Pointed Little Head*, a title supplied by Slick after seeing the cover photo of Casady clutching a bottle of wine, finds the Airplane very much at home, ripping off intense transformations of the *Surrealistic Pillow* songs, treating Donovan's tribute to the band, "Fat Angel," to a relaxed and atmospheric outing, letting Kaukonen dig into the blues and finishing off with a snaking, swooping eleven-minute improvisation.

Catching the turbulent mood of the country's youth uprising, *Volunteers* was largely viewed as a return to form at the time. Revolving on two key tracks, Kantner's "We Can Be Together" and the Kantner-Balin number, "Volunteers," the album was really an erratic collection of songs from the group's various wings without much cohesion. Kantner's collaboration with David Crosby and Stephen Stills, "Wooden Ships," did presage his science-fiction explorations.

Kantner, in fact, used most of the Airplane, some of the Grateful Dead, Quicksilver and other associates like Crosby and Graham Nash to record his 1970 solo album, *Blows Against the Empire*, an often exhilarating and imaginative piece that follows a sci-fi plotline through one side. He continued this theme with the 1971 Airplane single, "Have You Seen the Saucers," a gleeful celebration of UFOs backed with Slick's denunciation of President Nixon's Operation Intercept, "Mexico." Neither track was released on an album until the *Early Flight* collection.

By the time the group recorded *Bark*, the Airplane was splitting apart in fractious pieces and the album sounds like the record was made by several different groups—Kantner dreaming sci-fi visions of "Rock and Roll Island," Slick singing in phonetic German, new drummer Joey Covington crooning a ballad backed by a combination of Hot Tuna and Santana. On "Third Week in the Chelsea," Kaukonen came as close as he could to actually saying the group had come to an end.

Grateful Dead

The elusive essence of the Grateful Dead defied recording. Until *Workingman's Dead* in 1970, the band fumbled at the process, not that every effort wasn't epic in its own way. But the delicate chemistry of the Dead never made a comfortable translation to the recorded medium.

The 1967 debut, *Grateful Dead,* leans heavily on the musicians' folk-blues moorings and imposes a rigid structure on the most concise numbers from the group's early ballroom repertoire. The leering Pigpen blues specialty, "Good Morning Little Schoolgirl," gave San Francisco underground radio an airplay staple.

A grand experiment, *Anthem of the Sun* (1968) never satisfied anybody, although the compositions stayed in the band's repertoire for years, cornerstones of the Grateful Dead canon. With Mickey Hart bringing the second set of drums and shaking up the time signatures, the Dead unveiled the singular bubbling, simmering rhythms, over which Garcia, Weir and Lesh would stitch a kaleidoscopic tapestry.

In the band's efforts to edit together sessions from three different studios and live recordings from more than a dozen shows, the hundreds, if not thousands, of splices robbed the final album of the very consistency the musicians sought. Instead of two seamless album sides, *Anthem* is a herky-jerky hodge-podge, although hardly hurting for imagination and creativity.

The following year, *Aoxomoxoa*, at least, returned the semblance of songs to the recording concept, although the dense recording style, the jungle of ideas crisscrossing every which way, makes the third album the Dead's least accessible, most difficult work. In 1971, Dead engineers Bob Matthews and Betty Cantor remixed both *Anthem of the Sun* and *Aoxomoxoa*, although any improvements were debatable and earlier pressings with the original mixes are now high-priced collectors' items.

The Dead's own first attempt at capturing the trademark concert experience on record, *Live Dead*, foundered under tinny, thin sound and the limits of the LP format. By the time the double-record set was released in late 1969, the band was already headed into the studio to cut the acoustic-flavored *Workingman's* album, which would herald a whole new approach to the studio for the band.

Workingman's and its successor, *American Beauty*, may have reflected the obvious influences of The Band and Crosby, Stills and Nash on the Dead, but the musicians also drew on their own not insubstantial backgrounds in folk and blues, making for a smooth, natural transition. FM airplay of numbers like "Casey Jones" from *Workingman's* or "Truckin'" from *American Beauty* gave the group a first taste of widespread popularity.

Recorded after drummer Hart left the band, the Dead's 1971 live double-record set, untitled but popularly known as the "Skull and Roses" album or "Skullfuck," as the band wanted to call the record, paints an uneven portrait of the group circa 1971, when the Dead had been touring in a repertory fashion with the New Riders of the Purple Sage and opening the shows in an acoustic configuration. While the production quality improves substantially on *Live Dead*, the repertoire includes some entirely inconsequential numbers like "Mama Tried," "Me and Bobby McGee" and "Johnny B. Goode."

A couple of early sound board tapes from the Avalon Ballroom found their way onto disks in the wake of the band's popular breakthrough. *Vintage Dead* presents a side-long version of "In the Midnight Hour" and four other typical covers from the band's 1966 bar band songbook. *Historic Dead*, one side Avalon performances and the other recorded at the Matrix, features similar Pigpen-led workouts on old blues. Although neither contain much interest beyond the purely documentary, since the Dead sued these records out of existence, both qualify as rare records now.

Another scarce curio from the Dead's early days is *The Acid Test*, a bizarre album edited from fourteen hours of Ken Kesey, Ken Babbs and assorted other Pranksters fooling around in the studio in early 1966 with the Dead noodling in the background at Sound City Studios. Phil Lesh and Owsley Stanley stayed in the lobby, wrapped in conversation, but who could tell?

Owsley Stanley also recorded and edited *History of the Grateful Dead, Vol. 1 (Bear's Choice)*, a fine live album from February 13–14, 1970, at Fillmore East, mixing pieces from the acoustic portion of the program with Pigpen and company doing extended justice to "Smokestack Lightnin' " for more than eighteen minutes.

But, finally, out of the vapors of time, the band itself resurrected a set of 1968 tapes recorded live at the Shrine Auditorium in Los Angeles. Longtime Dead sound wizard Dan Healy, using some expensive advanced technology, worked nothing short of miracles on these recordings, released as twin compact disks, *Two From the Vault*, by the band's own merchandising department on Grateful Dead Records.

Like Ellington at the Cotton Club or Presley on the "Louisiana Hayride," these performances capture a time and place on which American music turned. With Pigpen at the forefront, the band twisted the blues around behind his own extrapolations, pushing the music into surprising corners and around unseen curves. And when the group leaves the blues for higher ground, the instrumental inventions curl into places rock music never before went.

Breaking barriers, inventing the road they travel, these musicians can be heard on *Two From the Vault* taking this excursion when it was still fresh, still challenging and still a little scary. Grateful Dead 101.

Big Brother and the Holding Company/Janis Joplin

As long as Janis Joplin remained harbored in the bosom of Big Brother and the Holding Company, she made music with true character. Not pristine, pretty music, but a raw, sloppy brew potent on its own terms, Big Brother's gift was a special amalgamation of which Joplin was only a part. Outside of the bonds of Big Brother, she became little more than a commodity.

Like the other San Francisco bands, Big Brother developed along fairly intuitive, sometimes random lines. Certainly there was no great plan to launch a star from the band's ranks, but the idea of trying out a "chick singer" struck a resonant chord with the members. Others were tested before Chet Helms provided them Janis Joplin.

The framework was already in place. James Gurley singed the corners of the sound with unruly, ecstatic guitar that was his approximation of John Coltrane through Lightnin' Hopkins. Bassist Peter Albin, a folk and bluegrass guitarist, and drummer David Getz, an artist whose most recent musical position before joining the band was playing Dixieland jazz, gave Big Brother a loping, buttery bottom, a feel-good rhythm section with more heart than precision.

Add the unfettered squalls of Joplin's rusty-nail voice and Big Brother could transcend even the repressive production of the first album. Recorded under prohibitive conditions, the 1967 Mainstream Records debut, *Big Brother and the Holding Company*, nevertheless contained some priceless pearls among the oysters. Joplin's mumbling, bleating vocal on "Women Is Losers" contains not a hint of the self-deprecation the lyrics imply, but rather a haughty, insolent riposte. The tension between the song's intended message and Joplin's attitude lifts the piece into another realm, a personal statement on sexual politics that Joplin clearly felt more than understood. In "Down on Me," she delivers a simple plea for love and understanding, all the while making the song really about her own terrified, desperate perspective.

The earth-shattering performance Big Brother gave at the 1967 Monterey Pop Festival, now available as part of the Rhino Records boxed set, led to the band's Columbia Records 1968 debut, *Cheap Thrills*, being among the most highly anticipated releases of the era. Virtually on the strength of reputation alone, since the Mainstream album barely circulated, Big Brother and the Holding Company had been predetermined stars even before the new record was recorded.

Janis Joplin never made another record to rank anywhere near this. *Cheap Thrills* encapsulated the Big Brother experience, from the raucous, exuberant opening of "Combination of the Two" to the cataclysmic "Ball and Chain." Joplin's raw-nerve vocals are matched every step of the way by Gurley's frantic, manic guitaristics. Without a soft bed of keyboards to bounce off, Joplin grates against the screechy guitars. Nothing is rounded off, sweetened or scented. Given the prominent role Joplin's swagger plays in all this pathos and exaggerated emotional drama, the essential collaborative essence of the work can be easily missed.

Outtakes from the project that surfaced on the posthumous 1982

Janis Joplin collection, *Farewell Song*, not only show a greater depth of material, but raise serious questions about the original track selection for the album. "Harry" is not even one minute long, nothing more than an anarchistic crescendo, a touch of offbeat whimsy all but entirely missing from the band's big hit album. "Catch Me Daddy" would have easily been one of the most popular tracks on the album, if it had been included, all gospel raunch and erotic breathing.

Big Brother made two undistinguished albums without Joplin, *Be a Brother* (1970) and *How Hard It Is* (1971), with Nick Gravenites and Kathi McDonald sharing lead vocal duties. Joplin made an inconspicuous guest appearance singing background vocals on *Be a Brother*, an album that also featured Gravenites's rejoinder to Merle Haggard's "Okie from Muskogee," "I'll Fix Your Flat Tire, Merle."

Drummer Getz polished off some 1966 tapes of Big Brother for the 1984 release, *Cheaper Thrills*, on his Made to Last Records, a souvenir of more innocent times. The band sounds supremely loose and unaffected. Even through the low-fi production values, the sprawling spirit, the bursting energy, just barrels through the years, ragged and untamed.

Joplin went on to record two solo albums. The first, *I Got Dem Ol' Kozmic Blues Again Mama!*, finds Joplin mining an ersatz Memphis soul vein without much success. Her overwrought vocals pumped some blood into "Try," but otherwise the album suffered from indifferent material, including some songs she just never should have tried, like the Bee Gees' "To Love Somebody" or Rodgers and Hart's "Little Girl Blue." The ham-fisted rock musicians played without the crisp efficiency and attention to detail commonplace on records by true soul queens like Aretha Franklin and Tina Turner, Joplin's most obvious aspirations on this lame effort.

With this valuable property suddenly in jeopardy, the forces guiding her career—notably manager Albert Grossman and Columbia Records president Clive Davis—took responsibility for making sure the next album would be a commercial winner. Her dying while making the record certainly helped ensure the album's acceptance, but *Pearl* was already a surefire piece of recording industry manipulation, a Hollywood handjob.

Widely hailed at the time, this is an album built on a reputation, not one to build a reputation. The one genuine moment on the record comes when producer Paul Rothchild trapped an a cappella

"Mercedes Benz," Joplin caught in a rare moment of self-parody. Otherwise, the album is a routine, thoroughly professional treatment of Joplin as pop-soul vocalist, modeled after the Memphis pop sound of producer Chips Moman, whose American Group productions had been making fatback Top Forty hits with everybody from Dusty Springfield ("Son of a Preacher Man") to Elvis Presley ("In the Ghetto"). Joplin even used a song by A.G.P. songwriters Dan Penn and Spooner Oldham, "A Woman Left Lonely," on *Pearl*. But no matter how she scrunches up her feet, those glass slippers never fit.

The inevitable releases after her death began with a double-record set, *Joplin in Concert*, which unintentionally exposes the Joplin myth. With one record devoted to Big Brother and the Holding Company, both live recordings made during the *Cheap Thrills* period and a 1970 Fillmore West reunion, and the other disk composed of performances with the Full Tilt Boogie Band on the Festival Express in Canada during summer 1970, comparisons are inevitable.

Big Brother wraps Joplin in a cloak of music, a unique, personal sound that she wears like garlands around her neck. The Full Tilt Boogie Band plays the role of sidemen, competent but shapeless. Leaving Joplin alone to sculpt the music, she oversings, overemotes and spews all over the accompaniment. But the clincher is the "Ball and Chain," recorded with the Boogie Band. She sounds tired, indifferent, as the band struggles to lend the piece any excitement. Three years after she shocked the Monterey Pop Festival and, with a single performance, established herself as the reigning female vocalist in rock, she had disintegrated into a lifeless caricature going through an empty exercise. And this is the version Columbia Records chose to include on *Janis Joplin's Greatest Hits*.

The double-record soundtrack to the 1975 documentary, *Janis*, includes an entire album of early recordings from her folk music days, along with an assortment of live recordings with Full Tilt Boogie Band, Kozmic Blues Band, three tracks from *Pearl*, and one cut from *Cheap Thrills*. *Farewell Song* (1982) collected up the remaining odds and ends: early live Big Brother, an awful Kozmic Blues Band concert number, an equally poor piece with the Full Tilt Boogie Band, the *Cheap Thrills* outtakes and one fascinating and exquisite piece, "One Night Stand."

Joplin recorded "One Night Stand" with the Paul Butterfield Blues Band in 1970 fresh from her Rio de Janeiro sojourn. She was between bands—Kozmic Blues Band was history and she had yet to put together the Full Tilt Boogie Band. On this track, Joplin can be glimpsed performing with shimmering accompaniment she cannot overpower, splendidly produced by Todd Rundgren. It raises more questions than it answers, but on "One Night Stand," for once, Joplin can be heard to full advantage outside the confines of Big Brother and the Holding Company.

The 1993 three-CD boxed set, *Janis Joplin,* confirms the epiphany of *Cheap Thrills,* including not only the entire seven-song repertoire of the original album, but three outtakes from the same sessions. This definitive retrospective of her career spans from acoustic blues stylings on a 1962 home recording and the 1965 "Typewriter Tapes" with Jorma Kaukonen on guitar through virtually the entire *Pearl* album from 1970.

The set charts the parabola of a young singer seeking a style, settling into her unique and powerful expressions with Big Brother, and the disintegration that ensued once she left the collaborative nest of the original band, a slide only partially arrested by the manipulative productions of Rundgren on "One Night Stand" and Rothchild on her final album.

QUICKSILVER MESSENGER SERVICE

After recording their first album in the studio two times before finding the results acceptable, Quicksilver decided to cut the band's second album live. *Happy Trails,* better than any other record of the period, captures the sound of the San Francisco ballrooms.

The 1968 debut album, *Quicksilver Messenger Service,* contains stale renditions of the band's concert staples, as close to the real thing as canned tomatoes are to vine-ripened. But *Happy Trails* (1969) let the pieces breathe. "Who Do You Love" was edited *down* to twenty-five minutes. Between these two albums and the two tracks of the 1968 movie soundtrack album, *Revolution,* some idea of the true accomplishment of Quicksilver may be gleaned, although the reality of the persuasive power of the band vanished long ago into the smoke of the Fillmore.

Gary Duncan left the group following the final recording session for the second album. Consequently, the third album, *Shady Grove,* (1970) finds a meandering Quicksilver in search of a focus, which arrives in the tandem form of Dino Valente and the return of Gary Duncan. The Hawaiian sessions that simultaneously produced the next two albums—and the band's only two hit singles, "Fresh Air" and "What About Me"—spelled an end to one of the great groups of the San Francisco ballrooms, essentially reducing Quicksilver to backup band for singer-songwriter Valente. Not that Valente wasn't talented—his 1968 solo album on Epic Records was a stunning one-man tour-de-force, produced by Bob Johnston, who was handling records by Bob Dylan, Johnny Cash and Leonard Cohen at the time.

But with Valente as an overpowering force in Quicksilver, the group immediately became less interesting, less invigorating and, soon enough, less two or three of the main players. The titles of the two Hawaiian albums tell the story in neat bookends—*Just for Love* (1970) and *What About Me* (1971). A two-CD set, *The Best of Quicksilver Messenger Service: Sons of Mercury* (1968–1975), released in 1991 by Rhino Records, chronicles the rise and fall.

COUNTRY JOE AND THE FISH

With the versions of "Section 43" and "Bass Strings" that appeared on the 1966 *Country Joe and the Fish* three-song EP on the Rag Baby label run by Country Joe McDonald and his manager Ed Denson, the group probably etched the definitive recorded example of genuine acid rock. Like so much indigenous folk music, this evanescent music seemed to subtly but significantly alter shape whenever confronted by the recording studio.

When the band returned to the studio to re-record the songs, along with the other selections that appear on the band's 1967 Vanguard Records debut, *Electric Music for the Mind and Body,* this spontaneous group of musicians could not duplicate the sinuous, mysterious atmosphere of the original recording.

Still, the first Vanguard album remains one of the most vital, original works of the time, a delicious basket of strangeness and sentiment. From the political satire of "Super Bird" to the garage rock of "Love," from the weirdly wonderful "Not So Sweet Martha Lorraine" to the ethereal experimentalism of "Grace," Country Joe and the Fish felt free to indulge their creativity in whatever shape the expression might take. In doing so, the band articulated another ethos of the times.

The second album, *I Feel Like I'm Fixin' to Die,* continued the same philosophy, with fewer highpoints, although the title song became probably the single most important antiwar song of the sixties. By the third album in 1968, *Together,* the band had succumbed to the court jester role, complete with a brilliantly realized parody of James Brown, "Rock and Soul Music."

In 1980, Rag Baby Records assembled all three Country Joe EPs, *Collectors Items: The First Three EPs,* including the Vietnam Day 1965 release, *Songs of Opposition,* making available on an album for the first time the original versions of "Feel Like I'm Fixin' to Die Rag," "Bass Strings" and Section 43." The latter two were also used in the comprehensive CD history of the group, *The Collected Country Joe and the Fish 1965 to 1970,* released in 1987 by Vanguard Records.

THE CHARLATANS

The unreleased album by the Charlatans on Kama Sutra Records must rank among the greatest lost albums of the sixties. Produced by Erik Jacobsen, hot off a string of hits by the Lovin' Spoonful, the tapes in circulation portray a band practiced in the same kind of old-timey moods as the Spoonful, but with a fierce attitude, a nervous edge, a grizzled posse with guitars. "Alabama Bound" sounds like certain Top Forty radio fodder, all twelve-string guitar and chugging drive. The only pieces of the sessions to see the light of day have been a 1966 Kapp Records single, "The Shadow Knows," speeded up in mastering, and a burly, jangling "Codine," included on the 1991 CD *San Francisco Nights,* by Rhino Records (although some of the tracks turned up on a French bootleg, *Alabama Bound,* in the late '80s on Eva Records).

The only official album released by the band, *The Charlatans,* offers a pale reflection of the original band, released in the band's final moments in 1969. Founder George Hunter designed the cover, but otherwise had nothing to do with the record. Drummer Dan Hicks had moved on to other pursuits and the remaining Charlatans, who had not performed together for a year before making the recording, mixed pieces of the band's old repertoire with originals composed specifically for the album.

Hicks, of course, drew considerable style, influence and experience from the Charlatans in creating Dan Hicks and his Hot Licks, whose 1968 Epic Records debut, *Original Recordings,* is a priceless gem. His parched wit and laconic manner light up the acoustic ensemble on durable Hicks ditties like "How Can I Miss You When You Won't Go Away" (a Charlatans favorite), "Canned Music," "I Scare Myself" and "Milk Shakin' Mama." The back cover photograph was taken in George Hunter's apartment.

MOBY GRAPE

With a debut album so good the record company was convinced to put out five singles simultaneously, Moby Grape should have been one of the big new groups of 1967. Victims of overhype, inept management and self-destructive vices of their own choosing, instead the musicians of Moby Grape splintered before really even finishing the second album.

The taut, compact rock songs that packed *Moby Grape* all rode on the charging, three-guitar attack and stacks of three-part harmonies that later influenced the Doobie Brothers so specifically. Between the finger-picking style of Peter Lewis, the stinging sound of Jerry Miller and the piston-like rhythms of Skip Spence, the guitars opened up the melodic songs like surgeons. Maybe all five singles could have been hits without the hysteria.

The gimmick-laden second album, *Wow*, included a bonus record of *Grape Jam*, some informal sessions featuring guests like Mike Bloomfield and Al Kooper that directly inspired their million-selling *Super Session* album. The Grape album proper also sported a track recorded with a society dance band and Arthur Godfrey on ukulele that could only be played at 78 RPM.

The album's best song, "Murder in My Heart for the Judge," had been lingering in the band's songbook since the beginning of the group and some of the other individual efforts were noteworthy. But, largely, the album seemed a distinct letdown from the launch, definitely not the second-stage booster the band needed. Of course, the group broke up during the sessions anyway, and, despite several reunions over the years, were never able to live up to the initial promise. A two-disk CD set was released in 1993 by Columbia Records that featured several unreleased tracks from those sessions.

The Music

SOPWITH CAMEL

Naturally, the first San Francisco band to crash the Top Forty charts came from the outer edges of the scene, the bottoms of the dancehall bills, and brandished a frothy, lightweight sound all but entirely out of keeping with the general demeanor of the San Francisco rock groups.

But "Hello Hello" was an undeniably irresistible ditty, a tuneful, catchy sing-along with a cheery lilt. Songwriter Peter Kraemer could supply a certain kind of charm to his vocals and "Postcard from Jamaica" showed some of the same kind of songwriting instincts that made "Hello Hello" so attractive. Producer Erik Jacobsen gave the band his best Lovin' Spoonful polish on the 1967 Kama Sutra Records album. But the Camel was ultimately nothing more than a footnote in the San Francisco story.

GREAT SOCIETY

Outside of the unreleased Autumn Records single producer Sly Stone painfully extracted from the group of "Somebody to Love" and "Free Advice," the only representation of this early San Francisco rock group has been some 1966 live tapes released, at first, on two albums, *Conspicuous Only in Its Absence* and *How It Was,* but now compiled on compact disk, *Collector's Item,* by Columbia Records.

Guitarist Darby Slick enjoys some intriguing extemporaneous outings on these live recordings, although his sister-in-law, Grace Slick, is the drawing card. Her appeal comes through loud and clear, even on these modest recordings. On the band's hypnotic version of "Sally Go Round the Roses," she brings a haunting quality to the number, a richly evocative piece of the San Francisco ballroom sound. These Great Society versions of "Somebody to Love" and "White Rabbit" are not fairly compared with the hit singles the Jefferson Airplane made of the two songs, but there is no problem understanding why the Airplane raided the Great Society for Grace Slick.

STEVE MILLER BAND

Ballroom patrons barely recognized the Steve Miller Blues Band when the group's first album came out in 1968. "Blues" had been dropped from the band's name and the music on the album was a sleek, shining

345

pop-rock amalgam with more in common with the Beatles than the kick-ass band that used to wail endless choruses of rocking blues numbers like "Mercury Blues" or "Your Old Lady," the two numbers the band recorded on the soundtrack to the movie *Revolution.* The Miller band previously made a recording debut backing Chuck Berry on his album *Live at the Fillmore,* and bandleader Miller could be heard honking away on his harmonica on the "Rockin' at the Fillmore/ Everyday I Have the Blues" medley.

But nothing really could have prepared local followers for the glossy touch of *Children of the Future,* a confident opus recorded in England that mixed bluesy shades with studio psychedelia. Bandmate Boz Scaggs contributed a couple of key numbers. Drummer Tim Davis, a fixture of the ballroom shows, was strangely limited in his vocal performances on the record.

"Living in the U.S.A.," from the second album, *Sailor,* restored some of the band's blues sound and Miller introduced his character, "Gangster of Love." His "Quicksilver Girl" on the 1968 album was said to have been inspired by Girl Freiberg. By the third album, *Brave New World* (1969), Scaggs was gone, the membership stripped down to a trio, although keyboards on the album were played by another old college classmate of Miller's, Ben Sidran. Together they wrote "Space Cowboy" after cutting a track that was a dead ringer for the Beatles' "Lady Madonna" and Sidran reintroduced the Gangster of Love character.

After the fourth album, *Your Saving Grace* (1969), Miller went to Nashville in 1970 for Sidran to produce *Number Five,* a strange departure with Nashville session players augmenting the basic band. A cunning careerist who used the San Francisco ballrooms as a woodshed, Miller parlayed his experience into a seasoned craftsmanship that turned out some of the most lasting classics of seventies rock.

CREEDENCE CLEARWATER REVIVAL

After years on the fraternity party/pizza parlor circuit of the East Bay, John Fogerty of the Golliwogs cast his eye at the psychedelic scene across the bridge. With a head full of fifties rock and roll, Fogerty had listened to enough KMPX to devise a tape specifically for the underground radio station. He took the Dale Hawkins rockabilly classic "Suzie Q," with a guitar hook originally played by teenaged James

Burton, and extended the three-minute rock and roll song into an eight-and-a-half-minute guitar workout. He changed his group's name to Creedence Clearwater Revival and presented the tape to the radio station.

The tape did the trick. The station played the song. The band started drawing crowds and signed to record with Oakland's Fantasy Records, a small label specializing in jazz where Fogerty worked in the shipping department. The 1968 single of "Suzie Q" off the album, *Creedence Clearwater Revival,* almost made the Top Ten. With the next album, *Bayou Country,* where Fogerty's psychedelic touches were now more refined, stylish bits like the feedback intro to "Born on the Bayou," the 1969 single "Proud Mary" broke everything wide open for the El Cerrito boys who had been playing together for ten years.

Fogerty produced a string of hit records with Creedence that not only made the group the most successful American rock band of the day, but endured to become some of the best-loved records ever.

It's A Beautiful Day

Bursting on the scene in 1968 with a fresh sound, It's A Beautiful Day belonged to violinist David LaFlamme. Although Matthew Katz helped build the band around the talented musician and even named the group, the considerable appeal of the band revolved around LaFlamme.

With harmony vocals by Patti Santos lending the band an Airplanesque touch, LaFlamme fashioned an exotic, often Mediterranean sound that made the 1969 Columbia Records debut, *It's A Beautiful Day,* an enchanting album. Adorned by a striking George Hunter-designed album cover, the record featured the billowy "White Bird," the evocative instrumental "Bombay Calling" and the mini-epic, "Time Is." None of the band's subsequent four albums improved on the original outing.

Sons of Champlin

Not well known outside the Bay Area, the Sons of Champlin nonetheless may have recorded the best album to come out of the San Francisco ballroom scene. The group's 1969 double-record debut,

Loosen Up Naturally, contained neither photographs or even the names of the musicians, but there was no mistaking the persuasive sweep of the soulful music.

With the Lou Rawls-inspired vocals by Bill Champlin leading the charge, the Sons tore into spiritual hymns of LSD evangelism with the intensity of the James Brown band. The horn section punched the songs. Geoff Palmer spread vibes across the midsections. Terry Haggerty rifled off jagged, jazzy guitar parts. The repertoire ranged from the side-long "Freedom" and the near eight-minute "Get High" to "Jesus Is Coming," a single not included on the album, only available by sending away to Capitol Records, that made the band a favorite of Oral Roberts (until he met the group).

The Sons made two more albums for Capitol and, after briefly changing the name to Yogi Phlegm, continued to record through the seventies, until the band broke up and Champlin himself pursued a career as a session musician that led to his joining the multi-platinum popsters Chicago. Capitol released a CD collection of the first three albums, leaning heavily on the exceptional debut, in 1993.

SANTANA

Guitarist Carlos Santana spent the next twenty years trying to duplicate the sound and fire of the first three albums by the original band. These three albums burned a swath through the international music scene with a searing, pulsing sound, fueled by Latin percussion, hard rock drive and Santana's own piercing guitar.

No better argument for the collaborative essence of rock music need be made than these three albums. A delicate balance of personalities, the original Santana band was a combustible combination, a sum definitely greater than its parts.

The 1969 debut album, *Santana,* showed the influence of departed conga drummer Marcus Malone on numbers like "Soul Sacrifice" and "Jingo"—taken from one of the classic albums of African percussion, *Drums of Passion* (1965), by Nigerian drummer Olatunji. But with the 1970 second album, *Abraxas,* the band had clearly shifted into a realm all its own.

Vocalist Gregg Rolie transformed Fleetwood Mac's "Black Magic Woman" into a haunting classic. The group absorbed the New York big band salsa of Tito Puente's "Oye Como Va," guitarist Santana voicing an entire section's worth of horn parts. Alberto Gianquinto provided a seamless fusion of rock and Latin on "Incident at Neshubar."

Rolie flooded the sound with Hammond B-3 organ. Santana drove home the melodies. Conga drummer Michael Carabello and timbales ace Chepito Areas peppered the mix with spicy percussion. Drummer Michael Shrieve anchored this mean music machine. Nothing else on earth sounded like Santana.

With Neal Schon added to the lineup, the band tackled the third album with an expanded lineup that included Gianquinto, percussionists Rico Reyes and Coke Escovedo, trumpeter Luis Gasca, the Tower of Power horn section and others. The powerful sound of the 1971 album, *Santana*, takes off from the platform its predecessor provided, blasting into the next level.

While Schon brought the band a decided rock element, the Santana group just kept evolving on its own terms. "Guajira" refined the Latin-rock synthesis beyond anything the band had previously accomplished. "Toussaint L'Overture" smokes out of the gate and never lets up. Big and brassy, "Everybody's Everything" lets the Tower of Power horns fatten up the basic sound. Schon delivers a straight-ahead rock solo with the Latin battery racing through the rhythm. The entire album reeks of an almost arrogant self-assurance, the swagger of a street gang, the scientific skill of a team of surgeons, turning out a gleaming, steely album that makes up what it lacks in warmth with big, rolling grooves and razor-edged playing.

HOT TUNA

Born out of the incessant desire to play, the boredom of hotel rooms and the slack touring schedule of the Airplane proper, Hot Tuna was started by guitarist Jorma Kaukonen and bassist Jack Casady, friends and musical associates since childhood, as an extra outlet for their creative energies. The 1970 debut album, *Hot Tuna*, drew directly from Kaukonen's Greenwich Village folk days, where he met Reverend Gary Davis and came under the spell of the delicate style of Mississippi John Hurt.

The album, recorded live at Berkeley's small New Orleans House, caught Kaukonen finger-picking acoustic guitar, Casady braiding bass lines into the blend, and chromatic harmonica player Will Scarlett adding some texture to a set of traditional coffee house selections. At home with the material, Kaukonen excels at this intricate folk-blues playing. As strong a player as Casady is, Kaukonen so totally suffuses this record with his exquisite guitar and vocals, it practically becomes his solo record.

But the lure of electricity beckoned and, by the time the second Tuna album was recorded, not only had Kaukonen plugged in his guitar, but the band had gained two members in drummer Sammy Piazza and violinist John Creach. The volume changed, but the style didn't. On the 1971 release, *First Pull Up Then Pull Down,* Kaukonen simply fit the country blues standards to the electric rock quartet format and played on. And on and on. Instrumental improvisation lies at the heart of Hot Tuna and, with minor alterations, Kaukonen and Casady continued to follow this format throughout the history of Hot Tuna.

PAUL KANTNER/JEFFERSON STARSHIP

With Kantner, Grace Slick, most of the rest of the Airplane, some of the Dead, Crosby and Nash, Freiberg of Quicksilver making a record together, the sprawling, indulgent result could hardly be surprising. But Kantner's mini-epic on side two, a song cycle about the hijacking of an interstellar spacecraft, is an ambitious and imaginative experiment, a sweeping ride on piano and acoustic guitar. Kantner built up a backlog of creativity unexpressed in the context of the Airplane and on this 1970 album, whoosh, out it comes, including the charming, if somewhat incongruous Rosalie Sorrels folksong, "The Baby Tree," sung to the accompaniment of banjo.

NEW RIDERS OF THE PURPLE SAGE

The first Grateful Dead cottage industry, the New Riders at first featured as many as three members of the Dead in the band, although when the band's 1971 debut album, *New Riders of the Purple Sage,* was released, only Jerry Garcia on pedal steel guitar remained a full-time member. By the next album, he, too, had been replaced.

Still, Phil Lesh helped supervise the first album and Mickey Hart drummed on some tracks, before Spencer Dryden, late of the Jefferson Airplane, signed up. While the band really revolved around singer-songwriter John (Marmaduke) Dawson, perhaps not surprisingly, much of the album sounds like *Workingman's Dead* or *American Beauty.*

Garcia makes the pedal steel sing in unexpected ways, but only brings small nuances to the whole record in his role as sideman. When Dawson's songs rise to the occasion—"Glendale Train," "Last Lonely Eagle"—the record shines. Mostly, however, the material suffers from a drab sameness that the luster of the Dead cannot transform.

Relix Records, a label specializing in music from this era, released two CDs of early New Riders material in 1986, *Vintage*, a live recording from 1970, and *Before Time Began*, a set of early studio tracks including six 1969 demos featuring Lesh, Hart and Garcia of the Dead in the band.

Cold Blood

Featuring pint-size, blond-haired soul shouter Lydia Pense, Cold Blood offered one of the bright moments in the brief history of Bill Graham's ill-fated foray into the record business. The debut presentation on the Atlantic Records-distributed San Francisco Records in 1970, *Cold Blood* showcased Pense's throaty quavery vocals amid a big, brassy sound, a band that played extended arrangements rather than just blowing. But Pense put enough grit into an obscure Sam and Dave number, "You Got Me Hummin'," to crack the charts.

Tower of Power

The other bright spot on the Bill Graham roster, the 1970 Tower of Power debut album on San Francisco Records, *East Bay Grease*, is something of a forgotten classic. With the band's certified soul sound opened up, instrumentalists holding free sway throughout the album's six long tracks, each breaking the five-minute barrier, the ten-man band stomps through uptempo funk like "Back on the Streets Again" and makes achingly poignant the shimmering "Sparklin' in the Sand."

SUMMER OF LOVE

MISCELLANY

AUTUMN RECORDS

After Tom Donahue sold the Autumn Records masters in 1966 to his Los Angeles-based distributors, the tracks have turned up on a variety of collections over the years. With Sly Stone as house producer, the label boasted finely recorded, balanced tracks, from Bobby Freeman's dance-craze rocker, "C'mon and Swim," to the British Invasion sound of the Beau Brummels' "Laugh Laugh." If Donahue never exactly achieved his goal of establishing a regional company with a national presence, he came close, paving the way for San Francisco to be taken seriously as a talent pool by the record industry.

Autumn missed out on the ballroom bands. The Charlatans and the Warlocks—just prior to changing their name to the Grateful Dead—both made auditions for the label, but the only ballroom band to actually record for Autumn was the Great Society and that was in the company's final, waning days.

San Francisco Roots (1976) on JAS Records collects some of the best of the Autumn catalog, including singles by the Beau Brummels, Freeman, Great Society, Mojo Men, Knight Riders and the Tikis, a group that featured future multi-platinum record producer Ted Templeman (Doobie Brothers, Van Halen). *Nuggets—Volume Seven: San Francisco,* a 1985 Rhino Records package, plumbs the Autumn masters, including the Brummels, the Mojo Men, Great Society, the Vejtables and a solo outing by Vejtables vocalist Jan Ashton, along with a couple of singles from the early folk-pop group We Five, the Charlatans' single, "Codine," and "Bass Strings" from the original Country Joe and the Fish EP.

The 1991 Rhino set, *San Francisco Nights,* uses some of the same cuts mixed with an eccentric selection of assorted tracks by other San Francisco bands, hardly definitive. Juxtaposing big hits by Sly and the Family Stone and the Youngbloods (New York transplants) against obscure numbers by such little-known bands as Mystery Trend or Sons of Champlin, the album cannot make up its mind what it is.

The Music

MONTEREY POP

With the San Francisco bands and English acts carrying the day at the historic Monterey International Pop Festival in June 1967, the deluxe four-CD boxed set released to coincide with the festival's twenty-fifth anniversary by Rhino might have concentrated more heavily on the underground bands from the Fillmore and Avalon.

Of course, the shattering performance by Big Brother and the Holding Company is represented, as is the Saturday night headline performance by the Jefferson Airplane. The Steve Miller Blues Band is featured doing "Mercury Blues" and Country Joe and the Fish perform "Sweet Martha Lorraine." Missing in action: Grateful Dead, Quicksilver Messenger Service, Moby Grape.

WOODSTOCK

The original triple-record set, *Woodstock*, captured such highpoints for the San Francisco bands as Country Joe McDonald leading the crowd of half-million in the infamous "Fish" cheer, the unknown Santana pulverizing the crowd with "Soul Sacrifice," and Sly and the Family Stone whipping the audience into a frenzy with "I Want to Take You Higher." The Airplane also contributed "Volunteers" to the first set and an additional couple of songs to the sequel album, *Woodstock Two*. Omitted from the audio documentaries were disastrous performances by the Grateful Dead and Janis Joplin and a routine appearance by Creedence Clearwater.

FILLMORE

Over the years, dozens of artists recorded live at the two Fillmores, from well-known sessions like Cream and the Allman Brothers to obscure pieces like jazz flautist Charles Lloyd or *Live at Bill Graham's Fillmore West*, a 1970 Mike Bloomfield-Nick Gravenites-Taj Mahal jam session attempting to re-create the aura of *Super Session* with little or no success.

Although Bill Graham had never planned to record the final nights at the Fillmore West, the movie company shooting that week rolled in a sixteen-track recording van to capture the soundtrack for the film. When the movie people were done, reels of tape were passed along to Fillmore Records staffers Jeffrey Cohen and Bruce Good, who proceeded to make a most listenable record out of the mess the movie engineers left behind, *Fillmore: The Last Days*, a documentary that, for better and worse, enshrined a wake for an entire scene.

Santana's version of Miles Davis's "In a Silent Way," a once-in-a-lifetime performance, captures an extraordinary moment in the remarkable career of a band that would never perform together again and didn't know that at the time. Quicksilver was already a carcass, propped up for the moment with a horn section and Dino Valente. The Dead without Hart sounded like the band could only manage to go through a cursory run-through, and Hot Tuna stands in for the disabled Airplane. The bulk of the jam sessions included on the record were taken from earlier in the week, when the stage was a little less crowded and chaotic than closing night, when all the luminaries and semiluminaries came to play. But Taj Mahal, Boz Scaggs and Elvin Bishop represent the good humor and camaraderie of the scene with ease.

The original three-record boxed set also included a facsimile poster and ticket and a seven-inch disk with seventeen minutes of Bill Graham railing against the music industry, describing his plans and recollecting his Fillmore years. "It was a combination of some luck," he said, "being in the right place at the right time for all of us, and there was skill and a lot of devotion and dedication. By them and by me."

THE PLAYERS

PETER ALBIN—Along with his brother, Rodney, who ran the rooming house at 1090 Page Street, Peter was a former bluegrass musician from the peninsula. When the jam sessions started in the downstairs ballroom, he picked up the electric bass to become part of the nucleus of Big Brother and the Holding Company.

SIGNE TOLE ANDERSON—Marty Balin heard her sing at the Drinking Gourd and asked her to join his new, unnamed band. She became the first female vocalist in Jefferson Airplane and recorded the band's first album, before quitting after having a baby.

SAM ANDREW—Army brat and guitarist, Sam started jamming with Peter Albin in the basement at 1090 Page Street, forming the core of what would become Big Brother and the Holding Company.

CHEPITO AREAS—The tiny Nicaraguan timbales *wunderkind* was playing on the street at Playland-at-the-Beach when Santana conga player

Michael Carabello spotted him, just in time for Areas to join the band recording the first album.

MARTY BALIN—Folk singer, poet, artist, dancer and one-time teen pop recording artist, Balin saw the vision that would become the Jefferson Airplane, personally put the band together and even drove the nails into the walls of the Matrix, the nightclub built specifically to debut this new sound in folk and rock.

PAUL BARATTA—Another failed New York actor who knew nothing about rock music when he joined the concert production business, Paul Baratta went to work as Bill Graham's right-hand man in the summer of 1967. Within two years, he learned enough to challenge Graham toe-to-toe throwing shows at Winterland.

BRUCE BARTHOL—Living in the apartment above Berkeley's folk club, Jabberwocky, with Joe McDonald and Barry Melton, when the former folkies started their electric rock band, Country Joe and the Fish, Barthol rented an electric bass and joined the band.

DAVID BROWN—The original bass player with Santana, Brown was a black man who contributed greatly to the band's physical image, but whose musical skills suffered at the hands of his personal habits.

MICHAEL CARABELLO—A street savvy conga player, Michael Carabello quit the Santana band in its earliest stages, only to return in time to record the first album following the arrest for first-degree murder by his replacement, Marcus Malone.

JACK CASADY—Washington D.C.-area childhood friend of Kaukonen, Casady was invited to join the Jefferson Airplane after the original stand-up bassist was jettisoned.

PEGGY CASERTA—Owner of a Haight Street hip boutique, Caserta became involved in a long, complicated affair with Janis Joplin during the recording of *Cheap Thrills* in New York.

The Players

JOHN CIPOLLINA—The black-haired lead guitarist wanted to join the Charlatans, but ended up forming Quicksilver Messenger Service with Jimmy Murray, Gary Duncan, Greg Elmore and David Freiberg.

BOB COHEN—A Pine Street communard who helped build the light show in a box for the Red Dog Saloon in Nevada City, he ran the light shows at the Avalon and wound up as Chet Helms's partner in the enterprise.

TOM "BIG DADDY" DONAHUE—A kingpin Top 40 deejay at KYA, Donahue and partner Bobby Mitchell ran a record label (Autumn Records), a nightclub, owned racehorses and produced concerts, including the final public performance by the Beatles at Candlestick Park in 1966. He fathered "underground radio" at KMPX, before leading his staff on strike and taking over KSAN in 1967.

SPENCER DRYDEN—A Los Angeles-based jazz and strip club drummer, Dryden was invited by manager Matthew Katz to join the Jefferson Airplane in time to record the band's second album, *Surrealistic Pillow*.

GARY DUNCAN—The one-time Nevada lounge band guitarist was sleeping on a North Beach basement floor when he met John Cipollina at the Longshoremen's Hall. He quit Quicksilver in 1969 to start a band with Dino Valente, but after a year, he and Valente decided to team back up with his old bandmates in Quicksilver.

GREG ELMORE—The quiet drummer belonged to the Brogues, a Central Valley Top 40 band, with guitarist Gary Duncan, and was a founding member of Quicksilver Messenger Service.

MIKE FERGUSON—An antique dealer and honky-tonk piano player, Ferguson's sense of Victoriana helped sculpt the image of the Charlatans. He was fired by bandleader George Hunter after he left a Winterland gig because he spilled barbecue sauce on his pants.

JOHN FOGERTY—Growing up in the East Bay in a rock band with two junior high school friends and his older brother, Fogerty felt somewhat remote from the Fillmore and Avalon scenes, trapped in a circuit of fraternity parties and pizza parlors as leader of the Golliwogs. He fashioned a tape of the old Dale Hawkins hit, "Suzie Q," with the local underground radio station in mind, complete with extended guitar solo, and vaulted right into the ranks of Fillmore attractions with the renamed Creedence Clearwater Revival.

DAVID FREIBERG—Half the folksinging team David and Michaella, one-third of a group called Folksingers for Peace that was deported from Mexico, Freiberg turned to rock during a jail sentence when he kept hearing his old friend David Crosby singing to him from the radio with his new rock band, the Byrds. He linked up with the nascent Quicksilver Messenger Service on his release and learned to play bass.

JERRY GARCIA—Former bluegrass banjo player and beatnik Army dropout, Garcia became a deft, inventive improviser of rock guitar in the lead guitar chair of the Grateful Dead.

DAVID GETZ—"Baby Dave," jazz drummer and artist, gave the rhythm section of Big Brother and the Holding Company a much-needed solid foundation.

RALPH J. GLEASON—Distinguished jazz critic for the *San Francisco Chronicle,* Ralph Gleason caught on early to the burgeoning new rock scene, and his coverage of the bands not only spread the word, but made Gleason one of the few universally respected figures of the scene.

PATRICK GOGERTY—Gogerty, a ragtime pianist from Los Angeles, replaced Mike Ferguson in the Charlatans and became an object of derision among the other musicians in the band's waning days.

BILL GRAHAM—A failed actor who discovered rock shows by throwing a benefit for the perennially financially beleaguered theatrical troupe he managed, Graham opened the Fillmore Auditorium to the new sounds and became the most important concert producer in the business.

NICK GRAVENITES—The original San Francisco connection for the Chicago crowd, Gravenites was a musical handyman who wrote songs for the Paul Butterfield Blues Band ("Born in Chicago") and finally located permanently in San Francisco with Butterfield guitarist Mike Bloomfield to form the Electric Flag. He produced the first, unreleased Quicksilver album and served as muscial director for the first Janis Joplin solo group.

ALBERT GROSSMAN—This Machiavellian manager of Bob Dylan, The Band and many others signed Big Brother and the Holding Company with an eye toward making a star out of the group's female vocalist, Janis Joplin.

MICKEY HART—Son of a pair of rudimentary drummers, Mickey Hart served in the President's drum and bugle corps, before moving to the Bay Area to reunite with his father, Lenny Hart. He jammed with the Grateful Dead one night at the Straight Theater and stayed.

CHET HELMS—He brought the missionary zeal he learned from his Baptist minister grandfather to his work as the impresario of the Avalon Ballroom.

DAN HICKS—A jazz and dance band drummer from Santa Rosa, Hicks replaced George Hunter's upstairs neighbor in the Charlatans and broke off from the band to lead Dan Hicks and his Hot Licks.

GEORGE HUNTER—Founder of the Charlatans, non-musician bandleader Hunter's wacky vision and determination first got the San Francisco music scene rolling in the silver lode hills of Nevada.

ROBERT HUNTER—An old Palo Alto colleague from when he and Jerry Garcia lived in adjacent parked cars, Hunter became the Grateful Dead's lyricist *in absentia* while in New Mexico, but soon returned to the Bay Area and began collaborating with Garcia in earnest.

JANIS JOPLIN—The bohemian blues and folk singer from Texas ran home from San Francisco after first moving to town and picking up a mean amphetamine habit. She returned at the behest of her old Austin friend Chet Helms to join the rock group he managed, Big Brother and the Holding Company.

PAUL KANTNER—A folk singer who became the first willing accomplice Marty Balin could find in forming his new band, Jefferson Airplane. He grew up in boarding schools after his mother died at an early age and remained largely remote from the ongoing battles of the band.

MATTHEW KATZ—Jesuit-trained intellectual, he moved from Los Angeles to manage the Jefferson Airplane, who fired him before the first album was released. He played Svengali to Moby Grape, before that band also fired him. Also put together and was the original manager of It's A Beautiful Day.

JORMA KAUKONEN—Gifted folk-blues guitarist whom Paul Kantner remembered backing a Texas blues singer named Janis Joplin at a San Jose nightclub and invited to join the new group he and Marty Balin were forming. Kaukonen named the band "Jefferson Airplane."

KEN KESEY—The best selling author of *One Flew Over the Cuckoo's Nest* fell into the yawning maw of the burgeoning LSD movement and, as head of the Merry Pranksters stationed at his rustic La Honda retreat, led guerilla warfare on the culture.

PETER KRAEMER—A songwriter and vocalist for Sopwith Camel, the first San Francisco group to actually crash the Top 40 with "Hello Hello."

BILL KREUTZMAN—Playing under the name Bill Sommers, Kruetzman left a wife and family living on the peninsula when he moved to San Francisco to pursue full-time his position as drummer for the Grateful Dead.

DIANE LACHAMBRE—Sixteen-year-old sexpot LaChambre was spotted by Bill Graham one night at the Fillmore West, and became his mistress.

PHIL LESH—Classical music devotee and student of the avant-garde, Lesh became the electric bassist in the Grateful Dead after years of playing trumpet in school orchestras.

PETER LEWIS—Son of actress Loretta Young, songwriter-guitarist Peter Lewis was invited by Matthew Katz to move to San Francisco to join a group the manager was forming that eventually was called Moby Grape.

MARCUS MALONE—Older than the other members of the group, streetwise Malone brought a showman's flair and percussion show-pieces to the Santana band when he replaced Michael Carabello in the band's early days. Arrested for murdering his girlfriend's estranged husband the day before the band was slated to start recording its first album, Malone himself was quickly replaced by Carabello.

STAN MARCUM—A hipster working as a barber, Marcum introduced young Carlos Santana to LSD and jazz and, acting as manager, began pulling together a band around the teenaged Mike Bloomfield disciple.

COUNTRY JOE MCDONALD—His father a victim of McCarthyism, Joe McDonald mustered out of the Navy and moved to the Bay Area to become a beatnik. Country Joe and the Fish was the electric, LSD version of his agit-prop jug band he formed with guitarist Barry Melton.

RON "PIGPEN" MCKERNAN—The central figure of the early Grateful Dead performances, organist McKernan, whose father was a rhythm and blues disk jockey, gave the band a front man who could convincingly growl out blues and soul standards.

BARRY MELTON—He grew up next door to Woody Guthrie in New York, but McCarthyism chased his family to the San Fernando Valley. After spending his teen years running into Hollywood to drink up the folk scene around the Ash Grove, Barry Melton moved to San Francisco to attend college. The future lead guitarist of Country Joe and the Fish met Joe McDonald at a jam session and struck an immediate rapport.

JERRY MILLER—The guitarist relocated from the Pacific Northwest with his Top 40 band to San Francisco and auditioned for the new band former Jefferson Airplane manager Matthew Katz was putting together that became Moby Grape.

Steve Miller—His father was an amateur tape recordist who captured performances by Les Paul, T-Bone Walker and Charles Mingus in their living room. Miller knocked around the Madison, Wisc., Chicago and Dallas music scenes before moving to San Francisco and putting together the Steve Miller Blues Band.

Bob Mosley—Peter Lewis brought bassist Mosley and a drummer up north when Katz invited him to start a band with former Jefferson Airplane member Skip Spence. The drummer didn't work out, but Mosley stayed to help form Moby Grape.

Mountain Girl—Born Carolyn Adams, she earned her nickname living in a cabin above Ken Kesey's La Honda compound. Kesey was the father of her daughter, Sunshine, but they drifted apart and she moved in with Grateful Dead guitarist Jerry Garcia.

Jimmy Murray—John Cipollina brought Jimmy Murray with him when Quicksilver Messenger Service first came together, and the lanky blond served as the band's original lead vocalist until the work load got too serious for the unambitious Murray.

Richie Olsen—Olsen was the first musician recruited by bandleader Hunter to form the core of the Charlatans. Trained as a clarinetist, he played bass with the rock group.

Ron Polte—He left a life a crime in Chicago to live differently in California. Introduced to LSD, he became an evangelist of the new community and manager of Quicksilver Messenger Service.

Ron Rakow—Part con man, part visionary, Rakow was a sometime-Grateful Dead associate who promoted the idea of the bands running their own dancehall at the Carousel Ballroom and supervised that hapless operation during the brief tenure.

Brian Rohan—Caustic Irish lawyer who represented Ken Kesey at one point, leading to his negotiating record deals for virtually every San Francisco rock band of the sixties. He was a partner in the two Bill Graham record labels.

The Players

GREGG ROLIE—An experienced musician who played suburban teen dances with William Penn and his Pals, Rolie brought a mainstream rock sensibility to the forming of Santana and served as organist and the vocalist for the original group.

DANNY RIFKIN—He ran the rooming house at 710 Ashbury that became the original headquarters of the Grateful Dead. A brainy schemer, Rifkin and Rock Scully handled what could laughingly be called the business affairs of the Grateful Dead during the band's early years.

DAVID RUBINSON—The hip young staff producer at Columbia Records who signed Moby Grape and took a crack at producing the first Santana album was inveigled to move from New York to assume command of Fillmore Records in partnership with Bill Graham, with predictable, disastrous results.

CARLOS SANTANA—A Mexican immigrant who arrived in San Francisco as a teenager who barely spoke English, the young guitarist was a faithful follower of the blues and modeled himself after Mike Bloomfield of the Butterfield Blues Band.

NEAL SCHON—The teenage guitar phenom was discovered by Gregg Rolie and Michael Shrieve of Santana in a Palo Alto nightclub and brought onboard in time to record on the band's third album.

ROCK SCULLY—He was attending graduate school at S.F. State when he met Danny Rifkin, who managed a rooming house in the Haight/Ashbury. The two promoted a couple of dances with the Charlatans, whose leader they knew from campus, before falling in with the Grateful Dead and managing that unmanageable group.

MICHAEL SHRIEVE—Romanced briefly by the Jefferson Airplane, Shrieve walked into Pacific Recording one afternoon and left a member of Santana, stopping by his parents' house to pick up a few possessions on the way out. He added a rock solid sock the band much needed to start work on the debut album.

GRACE SLICK—Raised in an enclave of the rich and privileged in Palo Alto, Slick married the boy next door, Jerry Slick, and moved to San Francisco to pursue life as a bohemian. She, her film student husband and his brother formed a rock group, the Great Society, that played several early Fillmore and Avalon engagements and brought her to the attention of the members of Jefferson Airplane.

SKIP SPENCE—Marty Balin thought he looked good and told him to learn drums and join the Jefferson Airplane. When he left the Airplane, manager Matthew Katz built Moby Grape around Spence's songwriting and singing skills.

AUGUSTUS OWSLEY STANLEY III—The celebrated acid king spent a small fortune developing the sound system for the Grateful Dead, chief beneficiaries of his largess during the band's formative stages. He stayed close to the group as a sound technician and associate, and was universally known as Bear.

DON STEVENSON—The drummer for the Frantics joined his bandmate Jerry Miller in the original lineup of Moby Grape after their old pal, Bob Mosley, arranged an audition.

MICHAEL STEPANIAN—Burly Armenian attorney who played rugby in another part of the park the day the Human Be-In took place, Stepanian was the criminal defense attorney most favored by San Francisco rock bands in trouble with the law.

SLY STONE—Born Sylvester Stewart in Vallejo, he recorded gospel songs as a child with his family, scored a minor regional doo-wop hit on his own as a teenager and was working as the Bay Area's top R&B disk jockey when Tom Donahue tabbed him to serve as house producer for Autumn Records. He recorded hits with Bobby Freeman and the Beau Brummels and cut the first version of "Somebody to Love" by the Great Society, before forming his own group, Sly and the Family Stone.

BILL THOMPSON—Marty Balin's roommate and *Chronicle* copy boy, Thompson went on to become manager of the Jefferson Airplane after the group fired Bill Graham.

The Players

DINO VALENTE—Originally slated to be the centerpiece of a folk-rock band that became Quicksilver Messenger Service, his arrest and subsequent jail sentence forestalled that proposition. On his release, he spent time with the band, but didn't actually join the lineup until he spent a fruitless year's odyssey with Quicksilver guitarist Gary Duncan trying to form a band.

BOB WEIR—Growing up among the ranks of the socially privileged, Weir was dispatched to a San Francisco private school specializing in troubled youth. He was still a teenager when he joined the Grateful Dead on guitar.

MIKE WILHELM—High school friend of George Hunter who became the third member of the Charlatans, Wilhelm was a skilled blues and folk guitarist who was the first real musician in the group.

ACKNOWLEDGMENTS

A Dickensian account of the lives and works of several dozen major characters depends on the generosity of many people. In many ways, these people entrusted me to tell their stories. But, also, in a real sense, this is the tale of a community and proof that the spirit of goodwill and sharing central to the precepts of that community still exists is the extraordinary cooperation this project received. Thanks are due to many.

Nicholas G. Meriwether, more than a research assistant, but a colleague in every sense of the word, attended virtually every interview session, slogged through countless thousands of documents and library pages and spent his own wonder and intellectual curiosity. He intends to produce a Ph.D. thesis for Cambridge University that draws on the same material, an academic companion to the popular account.

As with all research enterprises, libraries proved invaluable. Thanks go to the periodical room at the main branch of the San Francisco Public Library; the Doe Library and Bancroft Library of the University of California, Berkeley; the J. Paul Leonard Library at S.F.

Acknowledgments

State University; the newspaper libraries at the *Denver Post* and *Rocky Mountain News;* and, especially, the library at the *San Francisco Chronicle,* whose librarians tackled seemingly picayune tasks with unfailing good humor and persistence (honorable mention to Richard Geiger, Kathleen Rhodes and Johnny Miller). I am also deeply indebted to work in the *Chronicle* files done by the inestimable Ralph J. Gleason and John L. Wasserman.

Also thanks to my long-time employers the *San Francisco Chronicle* for all the opportunities over the years and the support in completing this project.

A number of law firms opened their old files to our investigations. Michael Stepanian of 819 Eddy Street was a never-ending source of documents, anecdotes and recollections. Peter Harvey of Horning, Janin and Harvey dusted off some *Katz v. Buchwald* depositions. Chuck Breyer of Coblentz, Cahen, McCabe and Breyer dug up another pile of depositions from the same case. Lynne M. Staley, Industrial Relations Representative, Division of Labor Standards, Department of Industrial Relations, found some long-lost Labor Commission hearing transcripts on Moby Grape.

Other authors and journalists, fellow toilers in this vineyard, were munificent in their assistance. Many colleagues who have written important books in the same field graciously supplied raw interview tapes, transcripts, collected research from their files: Paul Grushkin (*The Art of Rock*); Ben Fong-Torres, ex-Senior Editor, *Rolling Stone;* Gene Sculatti (*San Francisco Nights*); Blair Jackson (*Grateful Dead, Goin' Down the Road*); Mike Dolgushkin (*Deadbase*); Jerilyn Lee Brandelius (*Grateful Dead Family Album*); David Gans (*Playing with the Band, Conversations with the Dead*); Grateful Dead publicist and biographer Dennis McNally. Jerry Pompili and James Olness of the Bill Graham Archives also provided key documents and ready research.

Not only did the people whose story this really is freely provide their time for interviews, but also many endured follow-up phone calls taxing twenty-five-year-old memories. Many thanks to all: Peter Abram, Jerry Abrams, Peter Albin, Sam Andrew, Marty Balin, Paul Baratta, Bruce Barthol, Bill Belmont, Mark Braunstein, Julia Brigden, Kyle Brown, Michael Carabello, Jack Casady, William Cashman, Bob Cavallo, Mario Cipollina, Allen Cohen, Jeffrey Cohen, Robert Cohen, Bill Collins, Tom Constanten, David Crosby, Vicki Cunningham, Mike

367

and Trish Daly, Ronny Davis, Bert Decker, Spencer Dryden, Gary Duncan, Shelley Duncan, Bonnie Fabert, David Freiberg, Carolyn Garcia, Jerry Garcia, Art Gerrans, David Getz, Patrick Gogerty, Veronica Barnard Grant, Nick Gravenites, James Gurley, Terry Haggerty, John Handy, Leslie Haseman, Mike Wilhelm, Mickey Hart, Dan Healy, Chet Helms, Herbie Herbert, Dan Hicks, Richard Hundgeon, George Hunter, Robert Hunter, Erik Jacobsen, Gary L. Jackson, Paul Kantner, Julius Karpen, Fritz Kasten, Jorma Kaukonen, Alton Kelley, Glen Kolotkin, Al Kooper, Peter Kraemer, Lucy Lewis, Peter Lewis, Bill Laudner, Bill Loughborough, Stan Marcum, Joe McDonald, Jon McIntire, Barry Melton, Jerry Miller, Steve Miller, Ron Nagle, Mark Naftalin, Marushka Nelson, Barry Olivier, Richard Olsen, Ron Polte, Ron Rakow, Diane Ravenscraft, Herb Resner, Hillel Resner, David Richards, Mark Richardson, Danny Rifkin, Brian Rohan, Gregg Rolie, David Rubinson, Jacky Sarti, Boz Scaggs, Neal Schon, Ginger Schuster, Rock Scully, Michael Shrieve, Darby Slick, Grace Slick, Sue Swanson, Bill Thompson, Lonnie Turner, Mark Unobski, John Villanueva, Martha Wax, Steve Winwood.

None of this would be possible without the skill and dedication of *agent extraordinaire* Frank Weimann of the Literary Group. Thanks, also, to Kevin Mulroy, who thought enough of the idea to sign it up, and thanks to editors Christopher Schelling and Ed Stackler of Dutton/Signet for shepherding it through.

Inspirational support and spiritual guidance provided by Thelonious Monk, Mose Allison, and Erik Satie.

Regards to the Rock Bottom Remainders.

Special thanks to Keta and Carla for all the love, understanding and support.

INDEX

Index

Index